COMPETITION LAW IN CRISIS

A common criticism of the competition rules posed by EU authorities is that they are too inflexible, thereby prohibiting adequate responses to economic and industrial shocks. *Competition Law in Crisis* challenges this suggestion through an examination of competition responses to crises past and present. With an analysis spanning the response of UK and EU competition authorities to the economic and commercial outfall of the 2008 financial crisis, the COVID-19 pandemic, and potential responses to the climate crisis in the context of post-Brexit British industrial policy, the book argues that relaxing the competition regime is precisely the wrong response. The rigidity of competition rules in the UK and EU has both normative and positive implications for not just the methodology used in competition analysis, but also the role of competition law within the legal order of both jurisdictions. The book concludes with a discussion of the place of the competition in the UK's and EU's legal order.

BRUCE WARDHAUGH is Professor of Competition Law at Durham University (UK). He has also practiced law in Canada. He writes extensively on the competition issues surrounding collusion and cooperation in markets.

Competition Law in Crisis

THE ANTITRUST RESPONSE TO ECONOMIC SHOCKS

BRUCE WARDHAUGH

Durham University

CAMBRIDGE
UNIVERSITY PRESS

CAMBRIDGE
UNIVERSITY PRESS

University Printing House, Cambridge CB2 8BS, United Kingdom

One Liberty Plaza, 20th Floor, New York, NY 10006, USA

477 Williamstown Road, Port Melbourne, VIC 3207, Australia

314–321, 3rd Floor, Plot 3, Splendor Forum, Jasola District Centre, New Delhi – 110025, India

103 Penang Road, #05–06/07, Visioncrest Commercial, Singapore 238467

Cambridge University Press is part of the University of Cambridge.

It furthers the University's mission by disseminating knowledge in the pursuit of education, learning, and research at the highest international levels of excellence.

www.cambridge.org

Information on this title: www.cambridge.org/9781108833967

DOI: 10.1017/9781108987707

© Bruce Wardhaugh 2022

First published 2022

A catalogue record for this publication is available from the British Library.

ISBN 978-1-108-83396-7 Hardback
ISBN 978-1-108-98399-0 Paperback

To Jennifer

Contents

Preface

For the sake of variety, except when referring to the American regime, we use 'competition' and 'antitrust' interchangeably. We also use the present numbering of the European Treaties' Articles; however, when not possible, the relevant referent should be obvious.

This work was first conceived as a work on competition, sustainability and the environment. Indeed, that was the idea which I had when I first approached one of my editors at Cambridge University Press in very early March 2020. Within a few weeks, the focus of my project had changed, to consider the role of competition law in crises more generally. This work was written during the Covid-19 pandemic and the initial phase of Brexit, and as such these crises were ongoing when the book went to the publisher (November 2021). Much of the early economic impact of Brexit has been camouflaged by the effects of the Covid-19 crisis, and any response by the UK government has been slow. The full economic effects of this episode in the history of the UK (and Europe as a whole) will not be felt for a while; nevertheless, I have been able to examine the government's actions to date.

This work reflects my recent thinking on competition law and its relation to other legal and social norms, particularly those encompassed by Art. 101(3) TFEU. My thinking on this has changed slightly over the past decade, and I am now somewhat more sceptical about a wide role for non-economic considerations in competition law.

The law is stated as of 15 September 2021, and all websites were last visited on that day. Of course, there are no guarantees that these sites will provide ongoing content.

Acknowledgements

Although containing discussions of two recent crises, Covid-19 and Brexit, this work has its origins in several years of thinking about the role of competition law in the economy more generally. I thank those whom I have spoken with in the past for their comments. Some of my earlier thoughts found in Chapter 6 were published in the *Manchester Journal of International Economic Law* (2021) vol. 18, pp. 70–100.

I have also received financial assistance from the British Academy/Leverhulme Trust Small Grants Programme (SRG20/201069). This underwrote some research away from my home (when the country was not in lockdown). The final stages of the writing of this book coincided with my move to Durham University. Durham Law School supported and encouraged its staff to continue with research in spite of the pandemic and gave me the flexibility I needed to complete this book. It deserves thanks for this.

However, the greatest support for this project was from family: Jennifer and Jason. Not only did they put up with me writing (and gave me the literal and figurative space to write — a no small matter during a Pandemic lockdown), but they also assisted with the copy-editing. My wife, Jennifer, also assisted with proofreading and deserves special thanks for 'coming out of retirement' (after my last project) to do all of this. (Of course, any errors are mine alone.)

Table of Authorities

GENERAL COURT/COURT OF FIRST INSTANCE CASES

EU REGULATIONS

EU DIRECTIVES

EU SOFT LAW

UK CASES

UK DECISIONS

UK LEGISLATION

US CASES

US LEGISLATION

INTERNATIONAL CASES

INTERNATIONAL DECISIONS

INTERNATIONAL LEGISLATION

Introduction

0.1 THE PURPOSE OF THIS WORK

As its title suggests, this work is concerned with the role played by competition law in the face of economic shocks. At the outset, we must clarify two points. First, in the context of this work, we take 'competition law' to include its usual (and somewhat circular) meaning of laws which promote healthy competition and market behaviour among business entities to ultimately benefit consumers, but we also include state aid and the reaction of competition authorities as encompassed by our working definition of 'competition law'. The reasons for our possibly wider than usual definition should be apparent to those working with competition law and policy. State aid provided to firms, industries or regions could provide a competitive advantage, to the detriment of other, unsubsidised, firms, industries or regions. Further, as we will see throughout the course of this work, competition authorities' reactions (or inactions) towards the behaviour of firms operating in the economy, in spite of the literal wording or spirit of the relevant law, can influence or be determinative of how (or if) aided firms continue to operate.

However, as we will also explore, competition law does not work in a vacuum. A jurisdiction's competition regime is a significant part of the legal regime which regulates that jurisdiction's market, and hence commercial activity within that market. How markets are regulated will have social consequences in that jurisdiction, insofar as the conduct of buyers and sellers is affected. But competition law is not the only means of regulating markets; other regulatory programmes perform this function – the legal regimes governing labour and employment, banking, utilities, insolvency and companies also have similar regulatory effects within a market. As a consequence, the competition regime on its own is not likely to be ideal for shaping economic behaviour, encouraging investment or mitigating social problems.

The second term in need of clarification is 'shock'. There is no consensus on a precise definition of 'economic shock'. A shock may be an 'I know it when I see it'[1] event, and such events share a number of common characteristics. They are sudden events (and as a result may be unexpected or unpredictable), which have a significant macroeconomic impact on one or more firms or industries and within a geographic area or sectors of the economy.[2] We – like almost everyone else – are concerned with negative shocks, as these produce (or are caused by) declines in consumption, yielding (depending on the specifics) unemployment, reduced spending and inflation, all of which results in the degradation of the metrics (e.g. gross domestic product (GDP), unemployment rate, inflation rate) used to measure a healthy economy.

History is replete with such shocks. The Tulip Bubble of 1634–1637 and the South Sea Bubble of 1720 are merely two early instances of speculative bubbles exploding to shock the greater economy.[3] The twentieth and twenty-first centuries witnessed economic shocks including the Great Depression, periods of inflation and hyperinflation, oil supply shocks, collapses in the financial and banking industries, and the wholesale closure of industries which were often concentrated in particular regions. Regulatory responses to these were varied, with differing efficacy. Cynically, one could take the view that as we've seen so many of these, we merely await the next 'unprecedented crisis'.

This book examines the response of European competition law to a number of economic shocks which have occurred since the latter half of the twentieth century. By 'European' we mean the competition law of the European Union (including its predecessors) and its Member States. The latter is important. Member States have an obligation to apply the provisions of EU competition law 'where they apply national competition law to agreements and practices which may affect trade between Member States'.[4] Where the agreements or practices in question only have domestic effect, they are regulated by Member State law, which is modelled on and aligned with EU law. Indeed, the need for congruence between Member State law and EU law is such that the European Court of Justice (ECJ) is frequently called upon to answer questions of EU law which are in turn applied in national competition proceedings under Member State law.[5]

Some of the crises we consider are local, in the sense that their consequences manifested themselves in a region or area within one Member State – hence the initiatives proposed in mitigation are local, or are arrangements proposed within a Member State. As such, national authorities will examine these initiatives and

[1]   Stewart J in *Jacobellis v. Ohio*, 378 US 184, 197 (1964), albeit in a different context.
[2]   See Constable, 'What Is "Economic Shock"?' and Black et al., 'Shock'.
[3]   See e.g. Garber, 'Famous First Bubbles'.
[4]   Article 104 TFEU and Regulation 1/2003, Recital 8 and Article 3.
[5]   Article 267 TFEU.

arraignments, albeit under Member State law which should be isomorphic to, and not merely imperfectly reflect, EU law.

We will also examine UK law, policy and practice. Until 31 January 2020, the UK was a Member State of the EU, and as such it was required to ensure that its national competition regime was consistent with EU law, and its authorities (and Courts) applied EU law when required. We consider some of the legal implications of the UK's departure from the EU ('Brexit') later in this work. One touted advantage of Brexit was that it granted the UK flexibility to modify its competition regime in a manner which would permit it to avoid the perceived excesses of the EU's regime. In the minds of those seeking Brexit, this divergence from 'Brussels' rules' was a benefit. Freed from these 'shackles' the UK could pursue an industrial and trade policy fit for 'Global Britain'. Yet divergence is contingent on any subsequent trade or association agreement negotiated between the UK and EU. Further, the EU's regime is one of the two major competition regimes which serve as models for antitrust regimes worldwide (the other is the US's), and other regimes may not be perfectly isomorphic to EU's regime; considering a regime based on – yet slightly different from – the EU's will have instructive value for those using (or considering) it as a model.

One significant aspect of EU law that had an apparent influence on its application in times of crisis rests in its adoption of a More Economic Approach (MEA) in the early 2000s. The MEA is a methodological approach to antitrust analysis, which contains a normative and positive element. The normative element is that only the effects of a given practice should matter for antitrust analysis, and not the (legal) form that the practice takes. In particular, by 'effects' of a given practice, the proponent of the MEA means the welfare effects (usually consumer welfare) of the practice. The positive element is the use of orthodox price theory to measure these welfare effects.

Additionally (and hand in hand with the MEA), the 2000s were shaped by a change in or 'modernisation' of EU competition law.[6] This modernisation programme shifted the Commission's oversight of potentially anticompetitive agreements from a notification regime[7] to a self-assessment regime.[8] Among other touted advantages of the modernisation programme's requirement for self-assessment was that by no longer having to consider notified arrangements, Commission resources would be freed up, which would allow it to have both a more proactive role in the development of competition policy and to set its own agenda in the enforcement of competition rules.

---

[6] Wesseling, *The Modernisation of EC Antitrust Law.*

[7] Governed by Regulation 17 First Regulation implementing Articles 85 and 86 of the Treaty [1962] OJ 13/204 (English special edition: Series I, Volume 1959–1962 at 87–93).

[8] Governed by Regulation 1/2003 supra, n. 4.

While this present work's focus is on EU (and its Member States' law) we will make one fruitful comparison with the American regime. During the Great Depression of the 1930s, in an effort to promote economic recovery, the National Industrial Recovery Act of 1933[9] suspended the application of the antitrust laws. It allowed for the formation of cartels and monopolies. It was declared unconstitutional in 1935.[10] In retrospect, that Act was a policy disaster and likely prolonged the Depression. But it nevertheless provides an instructive warning regarding the consequences of loosening competition regimes.

In this work, we examine crises which have arisen from downturns in particular industries, and how they were treated by the competition authorities before and after the MEA/modernisation programme. Our analysis shows a significant difference in approach that the Commission (and other authorities) have taken. This difference was almost certainly a result of the shift in analytic methodology and enforcement priorities of the mid-2000s.

In examining recent crises, we first consider the financial crisis of 2008. The mitigation of this crisis involved considerable state aid and the relaxation of the merger control regime, to reduce the risk of further bank failures. We also consider the antitrust response to the economic shock arising from the Covid-19 crisis. After which we examine Brexit, which was presented as an opportunity for the UK to derive a home-grown industrial policy. We argue that subsequent actions by the government have squandered that opportunity (if there ever was one).

The final crisis we consider is the environment/sustainability crisis. We regard the environment crisis as an economic crisis. Changes in the earth's temperature have affected industries and the livelihoods of those working in them across the globe. Mitigation strategies will require wholesale industrial closure – eliminating carbon-based fuels is the obvious example. Additionally, and most significantly from our perspective, privative initiatives put in place in an attempt to contribute to reducing the problem may resemble practices condemned by the competition authorities, and themselves be viewed as running afoul of the competition laws.

There is a common strand which runs through our analysis of the crises we discuss. This is to address the claim that competition law and policy stand in the way of effectively resolving a crisis, by prohibiting measures which could purportedly mitigate the crisis. If this is true, then competition laws are part of the problem. We aim to cast doubt on this claim to show why this criticism – at least in its more extreme versions – is misplaced.

Our analysis of these crises and the antitrust response to them will make three points. First, as we will see, every crisis is different, necessitating that every response will also differ. Second, central to any response to a crisis is to recognise the interplay among the elements of the competition regime and the interplay that this regime

---

[9] Pub. L. 73-67, 48 Stat. 195.
[10] *ALA Schechter Poultry Corp. v. United States*, 295 US 495 (1935).

has with the legal order as a whole. Getting this balance right is essential to any mitigation strategy. Third, the competition regime generally works well in guiding a response to mitigate economic shocks.

An all too frequent response to a business or industrial downturn is for the firm or firms involved to 'crisis-wash' their situation, i.e. to feign that their situation is not of their own making, but a result of another overarching problem. The suggested resolution is to permit the suspension of competition rules to 'solve' the problem (and capture additional rents, but this – of course – is not mentioned). Similarly, in environmental matters, we can see 'greenwashing' of claims extoling the benefits of (otherwise) anticompetitive behaviour. We argue that critically evaluating such claims and proscribing the anticompetitive practices which rest on these justifications are important functions for competition authorities in this crisis-filled era. Indeed, much of our argument is centred around the position that the place of the competition regime in a market economy is to address market failure caused by the monopoly problem. In economic crises the suspension of competition law to introduce monopolies as a (or part of the) solution is the wrong approach, and it often aggravates the situation. The anticompetitive effects of the monopolies will often persist once the crisis has passed.

In recent crises, the Commission and Member State competition authorities have performed this task very well. In fact, as we will see, their contributions tended to mitigate some of the worst effects of the crises, and possibly their vigilance preventing additional harm from arising.

However, this does not necessarily imply that the existing regimes are perfect. These regimes may need some readjustment to make them more effective in addressing some of the problems which we may face in the future. Such recalibration, though, is more procedural. Competition authorities must recognise the value of clear *ex ante* guidance and the necessity of working with stakeholders to aid in the implementation of crisis mitigation strategies, which do not further harm consumers or the economy generally.

0.2 AN OUTLINE OF WHAT FOLLOWS

As this work will consider the use of competition law in responding to economic crises, it is essential to describe the EU competition regime in a manner which outlines the regime in a way which can be used to illustrate how competition law can assist or hinder responses to economic shocks. This is the purpose of Chapter 1. This chapter is fairly descriptive. It focuses primarily on EU law, as EU Member States have used EU law as a foundation for their domestic competition regimes and have a duty to apply EU law when applying their own law.

The framework of the present EU competition regime rests in the competition provisions of the EU Treaties (particularly Treaty on the Functioning of the European Union (TFEU) 101 and 102) and the European merger regime (established by Regulation). These provisions, designed for 'normal times', *inter alia*, place strict limits on the extent to which competitors can coordinate their activity with each other, and limit the circumstances under which firms can merge.

Coordination among competitors is generally prohibited where the agreement has by its 'object or effect the prevention, restriction or distortion of competition within the internal market' (TFEU Art. 101(1)), unless they are exempted (e.g. through a block exemption) or can be shown to be beneficial (TFEU 101(3)). Yet not all cooperative behaviour among competitors necessarily has this effect. Some forms of cooperation (e.g. agreement on standards) can generate social and economic benefits without restricting competition among products. Indeed, standardisation may promote product competition. In Chapter 3 we see how standardisation successfully promoted animal welfare, promoting it to a better extent than a proposed collusive solution would have. This is further explored in Chapter 7 on the environmental crisis, where environmental (or 'green') standards may be part of the solution.

Mergers in the EU are scrutinised to determine if they 'significantly impede effective competition in the common market or in a substantial part of it, in particular as a result of the creation or strengthening of a dominant position' (Regulation 139/2004, Art. 2(3)). Competition authorities prohibit mergers which substantially lessen competition. However, a merger that otherwise substantially lessens competition could be approved if one party would inevitably exit the market ('a failing/exiting firm' defence); but there is a high burden to establish this defence.

Mergers can be used in crises to 'prop up' or otherwise support a firm which may be exiting the market. In normal times, this can occur as part of an insolvency regime. In crisis times, a merger may be encouraged by a government (which in turn relaxes the competition regime to facilitate this). This crisis-drive solution is – as we will see – problematic. A relaxation of a merger regime, in times of crisis, is done precisely to permit an anticompetitive merger to take place. Had the merger not been anticompetitive, no relaxation would have been needed. But once the crisis is over, the anticompetitive consequences of the merger remain – as do its economically detrimental consequences.

We also consider the state aid provisions of the Treaties. These provisions attempt to ensure a level playing field in competition between firms in all Member States, by prohibiting subsidy wars among Member States, thus supporting inefficient firms and industries. However, state aid can be – and has been – used in crisis circumstances. The attempts to mitigate the consequences of the 2008 financial crisis and the 2019 Covid-19 pandemic relied significantly on the use of state aid mechanisms.

However, the competition provisions of the Treaties are not ring-fenced from other Treaty provisions. There are numerous policy clauses that establish the general goals of the EU, and link treaty provisions to achieve these goals. Employment, sustainability and the environment are among these goals. Unfortunately, some elements of the competition community, including perhaps the Commission, tend to view the TFEU's competition provisions in isolation from the rest of the Treaties. This has particular consequences for the application of competition law and is explored throughout this work.

Chapter 2 focuses on the past practice of the EU (including Member States) and the UK's authorities, when they considered firms' responses to industrial downturns. Given that these crises occurred both before the advent of the MEA to competition, this allows for a contrast with that approach. The MEA is considered in Chapter 3. However, before considering the MEA, we make a brief detour to consider the American New Deal experience to mitigate the problems of the Great Depression. This programme included, *inter alia*, the wholesale suspension of antitrust laws, in order to incentivise industry to cooperate to mitigate the economic crisis. With the benefit of hindsight, this was a disastrous experiment, and likely prolonged the Depression. This historical lesson is significant for our purposes.

Past practice (in both the EU and UK) took into account non-economic consider-ations in assessing agreements among competitors and mergers – particularly in times of economic crisis. This permitted wide scope for collaboration among competitors. In Chapter 2, we consider three forms of response to previous crises: allowing 'crisis cartels'; relaxing conditions under which a failing firm defence (FFD) is available (perhaps along with greater use of public interest criteria in merger control); and enhanced use of state aid to support failing firms.

Crisis cartels are industry-wide cooperative agreements ostensibly designed to mitigate the greater economic consequences of a downturn (e.g. via orderly down-sizing or other agreed forms of reducing output). In the pre-MEA era (at least some) industry-led restructuring programmes designed to alleviate the socio-economic consequences of a downturn in the industry could escape some of the prohibitions on coordinated activity. This chapter examines the use of crisis cartels in the 1980s and 1990s (*Dutch Brick*,[11] *Synthetic Fibres*[12] and other responses to industrial down-turn, including the use of public policy considerations in merger control as exempli-fied by Ford/Volkswagen[13]).

Other merger-based crisis responses include relaxing the conditions under which the FFD is available, and redrafting merger law to allow otherwise anticompetitive mergers to proceed on account of the 'public interest'. The failing firm 'defence' requires competition authorities to approve an otherwise anticompetitive merger, if several strict conditions are met. In times of crisis, calls to weaken the FFD's conditions are frequently heard, and a public interest consideration was explicitly invoked during the 2008 financial crisis (Lloyds/HBOS[14]).

---

[11] Commission Decision of 29 April 1994 (IV/34.456) [1994] OJ L131/15 (*Stichting Baksteen*).
[12] Commission Decision of 4 July 1984 (IV/30.810) [1984] OJ L207/17 (*Synthetic Fibres*).
[13] Commission Decision of 23 December 1992 (IV/33.814) [1993] OJ L 20/14 (*Ford/Volkswagen*).
[14] CMA, Anticipated Acquisition by Lloyds TSB plc of HBOS plc.

Chapter 3 discusses the shift to the MEA, and how it was applied in two crises: *Irish Beef*[15] and *UK Dairy*[16] and a sustainability/animal welfare initiative (the Dutch Chicken of Tomorrow (CoT) initiative[17]). These illustrate the use of the MEA to analyse and ultimately condemn such practices. Of these, the Dutch CoT initiative is the most controversial (the UK Dairy industry was an obvious cartel and the Irish Beef industry may have been one – but, *prima facia*, it looks very similar to *Dutch Brick* and *Synthetic Fibres*). However, in spite of the initial controversy surrounding the rejection of the CoT initiative, stakeholders devised an alternative programme based on standards (rather than collusion on production) which more effectively promoted the desired goal of animal welfare. Competition law was no barrier to this latter programme.

Nevertheless, the first two cases provide evidence that competition authorities have ended their tolerance for restructuring schemes which take a wide perspective on the requirements of TFEU 101(3). But with the MEA, all such schemes are strictly analysed using the lens of consumer welfare. This, of course, has an advantage. It is not as easy for undertakings to 'crisis-wash' their behaviour – to 'dress up' otherwise anticompetitive practices as 'industrial crises' to disguise a pernicious cartel. But the downside of this new approach is that broader social concerns cannot be taken into consideration to the degree that they were in the past, and the new approach may not be consistent with other goals of the EU (linked to competition via 'linking clauses' such as TFEU 11 and Treaty on European Union (TEU) 3(3)).

With the results of the authorities' post-MEA approach in mind, Chapter 4 turns to the competition policy responses to the financial crisis of 2008 and the Covid-19 pandemic of 2020. In mitigating the consequences of the financial crisis, Member State governments increased state aid to the sector, and expanded public policy considerations in merger to permit otherwise uncompetitive mergers of financial institutions (e.g. in the UK the Lloyds/HBOS merger[18]). As we will see, state aid, on the whole, was an effective means of mitigation. Merger was not.

Chapter 5 considers the economic response to the Covid-19 crisis from a competition law perspective. In mitigating the economic impact of Covid-19, governments have again resorted to the use of state aid, but more interestingly, they have also apparently increased room for cooperation among competitors, at least in the UK. Furthermore, some industries have called for relaxing merger control rules so that they can survive. We argue that governments had little choice but to use state aid as a means of preserving their economies. The difficulty was in distinguishing which

---

[15] Case C-209/07, *Competition Authority v. Beef Industry Development Society Ltd and Barry Brothers (Carrigmore) Meats Ltd.* ECLI:EU:C:2008:643.

[16] *Tesco et al. v. OFT* [2012] CAT 31.

[17] See the ACM's (Dutch Competition Authority) website: www.acm.nl/en/publications/publica tion/13789/ACMs-analysis-of-the-sustainability-arrangements-concerning-the-Chicken-of-Tomorrow.

[18] Supra, n. 14.

business and industries would survive post-pandemic (and thus merited saving) from those that would not. To a large degree, vast resources have been shifted to preserving zombie firms.

The economic disruption resulting from the pandemic has resulted in suggestions from the business community that these rules should be relaxed. As examples, the grocery industry pressed for competition rules to be relaxed so that major grocery chains could ensure that stores remained open and stocked in the face of staff shortages and supply chain/logistics disruptions.[19] Relaxing the rules, the industry argued, would allow the public to be better served. The chairman of JD Sports criticised the decision to block that firm's proposed takeover of a rival as being 'absurd' given retail conditions,[20] suggesting that merger rules be relaxed to allow the retail sector to survive. The grocery industry's pleas were successful: the government relaxed the competition regime applicable to that industry;[21] and in another recent merger case (Amazon/Deliveroo), the adverse consequences of the pandemic on Deliveroo's business was viewed as a significant reason for the merger to be approved. At the time, Deliveroo met the criteria for a failing firm; yet, in the next stage of the pandemic, its financial position had changed for the better. This chapter shows our scepticism of the need to heed any such calls for a relaxation of the competition regime.

Chapter 6 examines the competition responses to Brexit. The rhetoric surrounding the UK's post-Brexit relationship with Europe was informed by three shibboleths – sovereignty, fisheries and the ability for the UK to pursue its own industrial policy in its new form as 'Global Britain'. Brexit had its economic costs, but those in favour felt they were worth paying to obtain greater freedom in these areas. However, as we see in that chapter, any opportunity that the government may have had to reshape the UK's competition regime – in particular its subsidies/state aid regime – to pursue a 'made in UK' industrial policy was squandered. Rather, the government has introduced a subsidies regime that makes granting subsidies a much easier process, without the need for *ex ante* approval. This, we argue, is a retrograde step. Brexit will have an economic cost and this new regime is only one of its costs. The immediate costs of this decision have been hidden – under the cloud of the costs of Covid-19.

Chapter 7 considers the relationship of competition law to environmental and sustainability initiatives. There is an emerging academic position that the competition rules, as currently understood, may hinder collective responses to the environmental crisis. Given the strict focus that the regime has on consumer welfare, its scepticism towards horizontal cooperation, and the tendency of some scholars (and

---

[19] Sawer, 'Supermarkets Could Join Forces'.

[20] Butler, 'JD Sports Says Blocking Footasylum Merger Is "Absurd" amid Covid 19 Crisis'.

[21] The Competition Act 1998 (Groceries) (Coronavirus) (Public Policy Exclusion) Order 2020 (SI 2020 No. 369, 27 March 2020) and CMA, Approach to Business Cooperation in Response to COVID-19 (25 March 2020).

policymakers) to view competition problems in isolation from other problems, this regime is viewed as prohibiting cooperative arrangements which could otherwise underlie sustainability and environmental initiatives.[22] Competition policy is seen as part of the problem and not part of the solution to a problem.

This chapter considers the criticisms of the current understanding (and application) of competition policy by those who feel it presents an obstacle to environmental and sustainability initiatives. Here we examine the competition authorities' responses to the Dutch Chicken case and recent environmental initiatives.

Our view is that in these cases, the rules are properly interpreted and applied. While the rules at times require the monetisation of apparently non-economic benefits (which is an imprecise exercise), they nevertheless prevent the 'greenwashing' of collusive arrangements. Further, as we note, the competition regime itself does not preclude the development of environmental measures – *CECED* and Dutch Chicken are proof in point. Standardisation – the solution in Dutch Chicken – provides a way forward. It may well be the case, however, that the authorities might wish to give greater attention to Treaty-linking clauses and recognise the difficulty inherent in their present methodology in its treatment of long-term effects and benefits of a given arrangement. Further clarity (in the form of enhanced guidance) and perhaps an eye towards alternative methodologies (with these linking clauses in mind) may improve the competition regime's response.

The general argument and conclusion of this work is that the competition regime works reasonably well, even when challenged by crisis situations. But it is not perfect. These imperfections are no reason to demand a wholesale rewrite of the regime, or to condemn it as being part of the problem.

Much of this latter criticism rests on unrealistic expectations of what competition law can do in a crisis context. It, alone, cannot cure all problems. Its role in the economy is to promote greater wealth and the efficient use of resources. It does this by addressing the market failure associated with the monopoly problem.

However, not all crises are caused by monopoly problems. Other forms of market failure, such as externalities in environmental matters, or sudden decreases in demand, may give rise to economic problems. Suspension of the competition regime in these times, with an introduction of monopolistic market failure into the situation, is unlikely to solve the problem. This is the main lesson of this work.

---

[22] See e.g. Kingston, *Greening EU Competition Law and Policy*; Gerbrandy, 'Solving a Sustainability-Deficit'; Holmes, 'Climate Change, Sustainability, and Competition Law'.

1

The Legal Framework

1.1 INTRODUCTION

The central focus of this monograph is to assess the efficacy of the EU's competition regime in responding to crises, and in particular economic shocks. It is thus necessary for us to outline precisely what is meant when we refer generically to the 'EU's competition regime', and to identify the features which may aid or hinder industry and government activities in mitigating economic crises. However, prior to doing so, it is useful to briefly discuss our view of the role of a competition regime in a market economy. This social goal of competition is contrasted with the legal regime which a particular jurisdiction (the EU, in our case) may implement. A particular legal instantiation may imperfectly reflect that normative position because of flawed implementation, or the incorporation of additional values that hinder the realisation of its idealised goal.

The purpose of the present chapter is to outline this goal, and then identify the legal provisions that the EU uses to realise it. Our suggestion is that the social goal of the competition regime is to facilitate the growth of an economy's wealth, by identifying and addressing market failures associated with the monopoly problem. The latter part of this chapter outlines the EU's legal provisions. Its discussion inevitably is descriptive. Nevertheless, description is needed, as it establishes the basis for the further analysis conducted in later chapters. This analysis is conducted in Chapters 2 and 3, which show how a change in the interpretation of the EU's competition regime (through the so-called MEA) have brought this regime closer to our ideal paradigm.

1.2 THE GOALS OF COMPETITION POLICY

Market societies can be viewed as possessing two different elements: a system by which wealth is created, and another system by which wealth is redistributed. The former is created through the market, and the latter is through a tax and transfer regime. The principles of orthodox price theory show that in a competitive market, the actions of all involved will led to an optimal, and wealth maximising, outcome for all involved.[1] However, the conditions of perfect competition are very rarely – if ever – realised, and resulting market failure will prevent the 'invisible hand' directing market forces to achieve this outcome. In such a regime, the purpose of competition law is to eliminate (some of) these market failures, metaphorically releasing the invisible hand from its handcuffs. Hence the social goal of competition law is to increase surplus and reduce deadweight losses; in other words, to allow the market to 'grow' wealth via the elimination of market failures associated with monopoly.

As an example, the economic harms associated with cartel activity include the shifting of wealth from consumers to producers and the creation of deadweight losses.[2] Deadweight losses are, in effect, 'frustrated non-consumption': that is, the social loss arising from a consumer who is unable (or unwilling) to buy a product at an elevated price but would have been able and willing to buy the product at the (lower) competitive price, where the price elevation resulted from cartel activity. In effect, this view suggests that a proper role of competition law is to prevent social losses caused by an abuse of market power.[3]

We note that this view of the social goal of competition law is not neutral between the goal of maximising total welfare or consumer welfare.[4] Our view suggests that the goal of competition policy should be to maximise total welfare.[5] This is consistent with the suggestion that the purpose of the market is to produce wealth. However, this contrasts with the contemporary view of this goal: that competition law is to favour consumer surplus. With a few exceptions,[6] consumer welfare protection is the global standard.[7] The justification for preferring consumer surplus seems to be premised on distributive concerns: the assumption that it is better to spread out gains over a larger set of market participants, i.e. consumers.

---

[1]   See e.g. Kerber, 'Should Competition Law Promote Efficiency?' at 96.

[2]   On these harms, see e.g. our *Cartels Markets and Crime* at 37–48.

[3]   See Kerber, n. 1 at 101.

[4]   'Consumer welfare' is the aggregate of consumer surplus (the savings to a consumer by purchasing a good at a price below their reservation price, i.e. the price above which they would not buy the product). 'Producer welfare' is the aggregate of producer surplus (the price producers are paid, less the costs of producing the goods – such costs include return on investment). 'Total welfare' is the sum of consumer and producer welfare.

[5]   See Kaplow, 'On the Choice of Welfare Standards' at 8–17.

[6]   The most notable is the Canadian merger control regime, which uses a total welfare criterion (as a matter of statutory interpretation of the Competition Act (RSC, 1985, c. C-34) s 96(1): *Commissioner of Competition v. Superior Propane Inc* (2003) 23 CPR (4th) 316 (FCA) and Duhamel, 'On the Social Welfare Objectives of Canada's Antitrust Statute'.

[7]   On the EU position see e.g. Commission, Guidelines on the Application of Article 81(3) of the Treaty [2004] OJ C-101/97; in US law, see *Reiter v. Sonotone Corp.*, 442 US 330, 343 (1979), quoting Bork, *Antitrust Paradox*.

We suggest that these concerns are misplaced, as they conflate the wealth-generating function of the market with redistributive concerns. The latter, we suggest, is a second stage, which is consequent on the prior, wealth-generating stage. One can clearly envisage situations (most likely in merger cases) where, although consumer welfare may be reduced, total welfare is significantly increased.[8] Preferring consumer welfare to greater total welfare in this situation results in a deadweight loss to society.

However, it is evident that wealth generation is only one social concern: save under the most libertarian view, a society needs a tax and transfer system to provide public goods and address inequalities. Elements of the state aid regime, as we will show, contain this sort of redistributive feature.

Our suggestion is that this any redistributive system should follow upon, and be separate from, the wealth creation system of the market as reinforced by the competition regime. A direct tax and transfer scheme will likely be a more efficient and responsive means to effect redistribution than indirectly performing a similar function through the competition regime.[9] Hence, we argue that introducing redistributive concerns into the competition regime, or disapplying or modifying its provisions for redistributive reasons, merely reduces that which is available in the second stage,[10] where it can be used in a more targeted manner. In the latter part of this work we examine several economic crises where the competition rules have been not been strictly applied, thereby introducing additional market failure into a market where market and competitive conditions are suboptimal.

This optimal vision of the social goals of competition policy is often in contrast with how legal regimes pursue this policy. Competition law is not just reflective of the social goals and norms behind it; but as *law* the actions of those administrating and enforcing the regime must be consistent with the legal regime, including, but not limited to, the wording of the relevant legal provision.

The dichotomy between the social goal of competition policy (as a means of enhancing wealth production) and its positive implementation (via the jurisdiction's legal regime) leads to a host of issues, several of which are significant to our task. In particular, there are concerns which attempt to identify the goals which are found in the positivistic expression of competition law, and the significant concern which arises when competition authorities attempt to 'force' an interpretation of the law to capture such a social goal which may be divergent from the expressed (or written) goal(s) of the relevant legal provisions. This may give rise to a rule of law problem. As we will see in Chapters 2 and 3, a reasonable interpretation of the history of EU

---

[8] See e.g. Kaplow, n. 5 at 13–14.
[9] See ibid. at 13–18.
[10] Or redistributes to those who are not intended beneficiaries, see Schinkel, 'On Distributive Justice by Antitrust'.

competition law has been a shift towards reinterpreting the written legal provisions, with a wealth-maximising social goal in mind.

1.3 THE RELEVANT EUROPEAN LEGAL PROVISIONS

As an international organisation, the EU is a creation of Treaty, governing the relationship of its twenty-seven Member States who have agreed to work in their common interest. The most recent incarnation of its foundational treaties was agreed on as the Treaty of Lisbon,[11] which amended the previous treaties governing the competences, operations and institutions of that organisation. As a result of the Treaty of Lisbon, the EU's two constituent Treaties are the TEU[12] and the TFEU.[13] These treaties establish an autonomous legal order which governs the EU, its citizens and its Member States.[14]

With the exception of merger control, the legal basis of the EU's competition regime is set out in Articles 101–109 of the TFEU. Competition regulation and control of state aid have been elements of the EU's predecessors' legal orders since the Treaty of Paris (1952), which established the European Steel and Coal Community,[15] and the Treaty of Rome (1957), which established the European Economic Community.[16] Reflecting its recent origins, the EU merger control regime is governed by Regulation.[17]

To ensure consistency among Member States, and thereby guaranteeing a level playing field within the internal market, Article 104 TFEU obliges Member States to apply EU law (in particular its anti-cartel and anti-abuse of dominance provisions) when applying national law. As a means of giving effect to this provision, national competition law reflects EU law. This reflection typically takes the form of transposing the Treaty provisions into national law, making necessary changes (e.g. reference to a national rather than European market). To ensure that national law

---

[11] Treaty of Lisbon Amending the Treaty on European Union and the Treaty Establishing the European Community, signed in Lisbon, 13 December 2007 [2007] OJ C-306/1.

[12] Consolidated Version of the Treaty on European Union (TEU) [2012] OJ C-326/13.

[13] Consolidated Version of the Treaty the Functioning of the European Union (TFEU) [2012] OJ C-326/47.

[14] The autonomy of the EU's (and its predecessors') legal order has been recognised since at least the ECJ's 1964 judgment in Case 6-64, *Costa v. ENEL*, ECLI:EU:C:1964:66, e.g. at 593; and more recently Case C-459/03, *Commission of the European Communities v. Ireland* ('MOX Plant'), ECLI:EU:C:2006:345, para. 123.

[15] Treaty of Paris Establishing the European Coal and Steel Community (ECSC) 18 April 1951, 261 UNTS 140, Articles 4(c) (state aid) and 65–66 (competition).

[16] Treaty Establishing the European Economic Community (Consolidated Version) [2002] OJ C-325/33, Articles 85–90 (competition) and 92–94 (state aid).

[17] Now Council Regulation (EC) No. 139/2004 of 20 January 2004 on the Control of Concentrations between Undertakings (the EC Merger Regulation) OJ L-24/1; formerly Council Regulation (EEC) No. 4064/89 of 21 December 1989 on the Control of Concentrations between Undertakings as Corrected [1990] OJ L-257/13.

perfectly reflects EU law (and guaranteeing consistency throughout the Union), Member State courts can use the Preliminary Reference procedure under Article 267 TFEU.

The competition and state aid regimes do not sit in isolation from other elements of the Treaties. There are other provisions which not only establish the Union's goals (in perhaps an exhortative manner), but also interlink the more stipulative Articles to the goals. These are explored later in this chapter.

The substantive provisions of EU competition law are set out in TFEU Articles 101 (joint conduct) and 102 (unilateral conduct); procedural matters are found in Articles 103–105; and Article 106 provides that Member State may not immunise undertakings (whether public or otherwise, and including those providing services of general interest) from the competition or state aid provision.

1.3.1 *Undertakings as the Subjects of EU Competition Law*

The concept of an 'undertaking' is a jurisdictional element of EU competition law.[18] Articles 101 and 102 apply only to the activities of undertaking, the Merger Regulation applies to 'concentrations' among undertakings[19] and the state aid provisions prohibits, *inter alia*, competition-distorting favouritism to 'certain under-takings'.[20] 'Undertaking' has the same meaning in all these provisions.

'Undertaking' is not defined in either the Treaties or secondary legislation. The case law definition is that 'the concept of an undertaking encompasses every entity engaged in an economic activity, regardless of the legal status of the entity and the way in which it is financed'.[21] What is key is that it engages in economic activity; its legal status or means of financing is irrelevant.

Summarising the case law on what constitutes an economic activity, Jones, Sufrin and Dunne remark:

> The case law indicates that the characteristic features of 'economic activity' are (a) the offering of goods or services on the market (b) where that activity could, at least in principle, be carried on by a private undertaking in order to make profits'. It is economic, therefore, if it could be carried out in a market by a private undertaking or if it offered in competition with other operators which do seek to make a profit, even if the entity does not, or does not seek to, make a profit, or is not set up for an economic purpose.[22]

---

[18] This outline is not intended to be a comprehensive discussion of the nature and function of 'undertaking' as a jurisdictional limit to EU competition law. See e.g. Jones, Sufrin and Dunne at 141–150; Odudu, *The Boundaries of EC Competition Law* at 23–56.

[19] Merger Regulation, n. 17 Articles 1–3 .

[20] TFEU Article 107(1).

[21] Case C-41/90, *Höfner and Elser v. Macrotron GmbH*, ECLI:EU:C:1991:161, para. 21.

[22] Jones, Sufrin and Dunne, n. 18 at 142, footnotes with reference omitted.

Where an entity is responsible for exercising what otherwise would be a sovereign function of the state, a public interest function or functions which provide a social benefit or public good, the ECJ has held that the entity may not be an undertaking for the purposes of competition law.[23]

This is significant. An obvious beneficiary from such an exemption would be environmental schemes that provide a public good or use the state's police power; however, other uses cannot be *a priori* excluded. Yet, the law at the margin is confusing. As Odudu notes:

> The function that is subject to Article 81 EC is economic activity. The Court suggests three cumulative elements of economic activity: the offer of goods or services; the bearing of economic or financial risk; and the potential to make profit. By identifying the three positive elements of economic activity, it is possible to see a number of situations when the Court considers that the elements are not satisfied. The offer of goods or services is required: work, consumption, and regulation do not satisfy this requirement. The potential to make profit must exist: it is impossible to profit from redistribution or the provision of public goods.[24]

To the extent that crisis resolution involves the creation of entities which stand outside of economic activity so characterised, they may be able to fulfil their mandate unrestrained by the limits of competition law. To this extent, the competition regime in no way foils crisis resolution.

1.3.2 *Article 101: Control of Joint Action*

Article 101 TFEU is the EU's provision regulating cooperation between undertakings. It recognises that some forms of cooperation between competitors may be socially useful, yet other forms are harmful. The Article's provisions (which are replicated in Member State – and UK – legislation) thus separate beneficial from harmful collusion.

The structure of that Article establishes the conditions under which cooperative arrangements are permitted and prohibited. Paragraph 1 establishes a general prohibition against decisions, agreements or concerted practices, entered into by undertakings (or associations of undertakings) that affect trade between Member States and which have as their 'object or effect the prevention, restriction or distortion of competition within the internal market'. It then enumerates five

---

[23] See e.g. Case C-364/92, SAT *Fluggesellschaft mbH v. Eurocontrol*, ECLI:EU:C:1994:7; Case C-343/95, *Diego Calì e Figli Srl v. SEPG*, EU:C:1997:160; Case T-319/99, *Federación Nacional de Empresas de Instrumentación Científica, Médica, Técnica y Dental (FENIN) v. Commission*, ECLI:EU:T:2003:50; and Cases C-159/91 and C-160/91, *Christian Poucet v. Assurances Generales de France (AGF) and Caisse Mutuelle Regionale du Languedoc-Roussillon (Camulrac) and Daniel Pistre v. Caisse Autonome Nationale de Compensation de l' Assurance Vieillesse des Artisans (Cancava)*, ECLI:EU:C:1993:63.

[24] Odudu, n. 18 at 54–55.

specific sets of prohibited agreements. These sets of agreements are of the sort that typically underlie hardcore cartels, in other words those sorts of industry practices which have a pernicious effect for consumers – as they raise the price of a good or service without providing any other countervailing benefit.[25]

The alternative[26] conditions that the agreement must by its 'object or effect' have adverse consequences for competition on the internal market is significant to the application of EU competition law, and hence the justification of agreements under that regime. Agreements that (only) have the effect of restricting or distorting competition are easier to justify than those whose object has the aforesaid consequences. As explored later, there has been a subtle shift in interpretation of this condition that can have a bearing on the use of competition law in the resolution of economic crises.

Paragraph 2 provides that agreements contrary to the provisions of Article 101 are void. Contractual voidness (and resulting severability of void provisions) is determined under national law.

Paragraph 3 is the 'saving' or legal exception provision of the Article. It provides that the provisions of Paragraph 1 do not apply agreements which meet the four cumulative[27] criteria of Paragraph 3. Under the pre-2004 regime, governed by Regulation 17, undertakings were obliged to notify the Commission regarding any arrangements that could infringe 101(1) prior to entering into them. The Commission, after assessment, would either approve or prohibit the intended arrangement.

There are two interpretive points of significance, which follow from the wording of Article 101 and its implementing legislation. First, the concept of 'the prevention, restriction or distortion of competition within the internal market' is undefined, requiring further interpretation.

One theme of this book is how Article 101 has been interpreted since the late 1960s, and how an alteration of this interpretation has shaped the 'European' response to crisis resolution over the past four or so decades. Since the late 1990s, the Commission's approach to this assessment has developed into an MEA. This approach has normative and methodological elements. Its normative principles are that competitive harm is equated with reduction in consumer welfare, and the protection of consumer surplus is all that matters for competition law. The methodological element is that consumer surplus is measured via the tools of orthodox price theory, and – when needed – supplemented by other techniques such as game theory.

---

[25] See e.g. Case C-67/13 P, *Groupement des cartes bancaires (CB) v. Commission*, ECLI:EU:C:2014:2204, para. 49.
[26] Case 56/65, *Société Technique Minière v. Maschinenbau Ulm GmbH* (STM), EU:C:1966:38, para. 249.
[27] Case T-185/00, *Métropole télévision SA (M6) et al. v. Commission*, ECLI:EU:T:2002:242, para. 86.

The new approach marked a change from the Commission's previous approach. The previous approach could be characterised as being less reliant on the tools of economics, and possibly more accommodating to the incorporation of non-economic goals within the assessment of commercial arrangements.

This has implications for assessment under Article 101(3). As we shall see in what follows, the provisions of 101(3) have historically been used to justify so-called crisis cartels. These are arrangements (typically of a 'hardcore' cartel nature, usually involving agreed output restrictions) which purport to have offsetting benefits. In the past, the 101(3) justification for these benefits has taken a wide view of what is meant by 'benefit'. But since the advent of the MEA, and its strict focus on consumer welfare as measured by orthodox price theory, the understanding of 'benefit' has consequently narrowed.

Our second point is that, under the present regime, governed by Regulation 1/2003, undertakings are to self-assess the compatibility of their proposed agreement or arrangement with the competition laws. To aid in this process the Commission has promulgated a number of Block Exemptions; agreements which fall within these are automatically viewed as compatible with Article 101. The Block Exemptions recognise the beneficial consequences that such agreements have and deem them to be compatible with 101. Additionally, the Commission has published guidelines (which – unlike Block Exemptions – do not act as safe harbours) to aid in the self-assessment process. Although in principle any agreement may obtain the benefit of 101(3),[28] in the absence of a safe harbour of an exemption or falling squarely within the relevant guideline, it is almost unheard of for an agreement to be so exempted.[29]

The implications of this for crisis management are profound. It possible that competitors could develop an arrangement that actually alleviates a crisis. To this end, this arrangement may provide social and economic benefits. Yet such cooperation is almost unprecedented and would be manifested in a regulatory environment in which competition authorities are (understandably) concerned about undertakings 'crisis-washing' (or otherwise disguising) their cartel activity. Further, in the face of the significant sanctions that the EU has meted out for anticompetitive arrangements, undertakings may be reluctant to enter into novel cooperative activities, out of a concern that the authorities may sanction this cooperation after making a type

---

[28] Case C-209/07, *Competition Authority v. Beef Industry Development Society Ltd and Barry Brothers (Carrigmore) Meats Ltd.* (BIDS), ECLI:EU:C:2008:643, para. 21; Case T-17/93, *Matra Hachette SA v. Commission*, ECLI:EU:T:1994:89, para. 85; Cases C-501/06P etc., *GlaxoSmithKline Services Unlimited v. Commission* ('GSK'), ECLI:EU:C:2009:610, paras. 89–96 (affirming Case T-168/01, *GlaxoSmithKline Services Unlimited v. Commission*, ECLI:EU:T:2006:265, para. 233.

[29] The Decision of the Luxembourgish Competition Authority in *WebTaxi* seems the be the only such case: 2018-FO-01 – *Webtaxi*, Decision of 7 June 2018.

I error (false positive). In the absence of guidance from the competition authorities, this (legitimate) concern may put a stop to beneficial cooperative arrangements.

1.3.3 *Article 102: Control of Unilateral Action*

The behaviour of dominant undertakings is controlled by Article 102 TFEU. An abuse under 102 can only be committed by a dominant undertaking. Textbook analysis tells us that a dominant undertaking is one which has sufficient economic strength to behave independently of its customers, suppliers and competitors. In *Hoffmann-La Roche* the ECJ defined dominance in the following terms:

> [A] situation where one or more undertakings wield economic power which would enable them to prevent effective competition from being maintained in the relevant market by giving them the opportunity to act to a considerable extent independently of their competitors, their customers, and, ultimately, of consumers.[30]

Market shares can be evidence of dominance but are not necessarily determinative of dominance.[31] The list of behaviours enumerated by (a)–(e) is not exhaustive; rather, it might be best to consider the prohibited behaviour as the dominant firm's using its market position 'as to reap trading benefits which it would not have reaped if there had been normal and sufficiently effective competition'.[32]

In some crises, the price of goods may rise, but charging a high price is not necessarily an abuse. Although an excessive price is an 'unfair' price, not all high prices are unfair. In this context 'unfair' is 'whether the difference between the cost actually incurred and the price actually charged is excessive, and, if the answer to that question is in the affirmative, whether a price has been imposed which is either unfair in itself or unfair when compared with competing products'.[33] In *United Brands*, the ECJ noted that an excessive price is one which 'has no reasonable relation to the economic value of the product supplied'.[34] This analytic methodology requires competition authorities to play the role of price regulators in all but exceptional circumstances.[35] This is a different role than that usually assumed by competition authorities.

The purpose of competition law is not to protect every undertaking. It is of the essence of competition in a market economy that some firms will exit the market, and it is the efficient firms which should survive. Hence, the focus on exclusion is

---

[30] Case 85/76, *Hoffmann-La Roche v. Commission*, ECLI:EU:C:1979:36, para. 38.
[31] Ibid. paras. 40 and Case C-62/86, *AKZO Chemie v. Commission*, ECLI:EU:C:1991:286, para. 60.
[32] Case 27/76, *United Brands v. Commission* ('UBC'), ECLI:EU:C:1978:22, para. 249.
[33] Case C-177/16, *Autortiesību un komunicēšanās konsultāciju aģentūra/Latvijas Autoru apvienība v. Konkurences padome* (AKK/LAA), ECLI:EU:C:2017:689, para. 36; Case 27/76, *UBC*, ibid. paras. 249–266 and *CMA v. Flynn Pharma Ltd et al.* [2020] EWCA Civ 339 paras. [59]–[98].
[34] *UBC*, ibid. para. 250.
[35] Case C-117/16, *AKKA/LAA*, n. 33, is one of these exceptions.

the consequence that the practice in question may have for an 'as efficient competitor'.[36]

A dominant undertaking can take 'reasonable steps' to protect its own commercial interests.[37] But it is not a reasonable step to engage in a practice for the sole purpose of strengthening a dominant position. A dominant undertaking can engage in practices which strengthen that position, so long as these practices also generate efficiencies which benefit consumers. This is the defence of objective or commercial necessity.[38]

While 101 and merger concerns tend to dominate the discussion of the role of the place of competition law in crises, questions of the application of competition to dominant undertakings in these situations also remain. The Commission's ABG Decision, in the context of the Dutch Market during the 1973 Oil Crisis, is a case in point.[39] The crisis was caused by the Organization of the Petroleum Exporting Countries' limitation of oil production and embargo of exports to the Netherlands (due to the latter's support for Israel in the October 1973 war). The product market in question was premium (high-octane) and regular motor petrol. At the time, the maximum prices for motor fuel were fixed by the Dutch government and were fixed below the spot price for oil.[40] ABG was a purchasing cooperative, which acquired its supply from seven major oil importers and refiners (BP, Shell, Esso, Mobil, Chevron, Texaco, Gulf Oil).

As a result of the decreased flow of oil to the Netherlands, governmental authorities recommended a 15–20 per cent reduction in consumption. Nevertheless, the major importers and refiners substantially reduced their supply to ABG, beginning on 1 November 1973, in comparison to the previous year's deliveries. This was particularly the case with BP, ABG's largest supplier:

> BP delivered 4 721 m³ in November 1973, 3 646 m³ in December 1973, 2 179 m³ in January 1974, 2 040 m³ in February 1974, 3 224 m³ in March 1974 in comparison with a monthly average [from the preceding year] of 12 083 m³, reduced to 9 666 m³ after the reduction of 20% recommended by the Dutch authorities.[41]

Rather than providing petrol to ABG, BP and the other major producers provided it to their regular customers.[42] Given the market barriers it faced,[43] and the loss-

---

[36] Case C-413/14 P, *Intel v. Commission*, ECLI:EU:C:2017:632, paras. 135–136, the Court quotes Case C-209/10, *Post Danmark v. Konkurrencerådet* ('Post Danmark I'), EU:C:2012:172, para. 25.

[37] Case 27/76, *UBC*, n. 33, para. 189.

[38] Case C-209/10, *Post Danmark I*, n. 36, paras. 40–42.

[39] Commission Decision 77/327/EEC of 19 April (IV/28.841) (*ABG/Oil Companies Operating in the Netherlands*) [1977] OJ L-117/1.

[40] A consequence of this was that the domestic price ceiling was below spot price, ibid. at 5.

[41] Ibid. at 6.

[42] Ibid. at 9.

[43] Ibid.

making nature of purchasing oil on the spot market and selling it for the (regulated) price, ABG could not function.

Given the crisis, the Commission held, '[i]n the prevailing circumstances each of these companies found itself in a dominant position relative to its customers'.[44] In not allocating the oil to its customers on an 'equitable basis', the major oil companies committed an abuse of their dominant position.[45] Assuming the Commission's analytic method remains consistent, ABG provides guidance for resource allocation in times of scarcity.

From the perspective of other crises, such as that involving environmental or sustainability concerns, 102 considerations enter when an undertaking may be established – either via industry action or governmental fiat to remedy a particular problem (e.g. waste disposal, hazardous material recycling), when that undertaking is in a position of dominance. Similarly, any claim based on public necessity that such an undertaking invokes to justify its practices will be scrutinised in this way.[46]

1.3.4 *Merger Control*

The EU's merger control regime is governed by Regulation. Prior to the first Merger Regulation (1990),[47] the Commission was required to use the provisions of Article 102 (then 85 or 81) and would do so to prevent the creation or strengthening of a dominant position on the relevant market in question. This dominant position-focused test was transposed into the first Regulation.[48] The present Regulation, Regulation 139/2005,[49] has replaced that standard with a 'significantly impeding effective competition' (SIEC) test.[50]

The regime governed by the EU Merger Regulation (and its implementing Regulations) requires that the merging parties notify the Commission prior to implementing a proposed merger[51] with a Community dimension.[52] The Commission will vet the proposed merger within a strict time frame. The standard for approving a merger is whether or not the merger 'would significantly impede effective competition, in the common market or in a substantial part of it, in particular as a result of the creation or strengthening of a dominant position'.[53]

---

[44] Ibid.

[45] Ibid.

[46] See generally, Kingston, *Greening EU Competition Law and Policy* at 307–326.

[47] Council Regulation 4064/89/EEC on the Control of Concentrations between Undertakings, corrected version, n. 17.

[48] Ibid. Article 2(2)–(3).

[49] Supra, n. 17.

[50] Ibid. Article 2(2)–(3).

[51] The EU Merger Regulation uses 'concentration' to describe mergers.

[52] EU Merger Regulation n. 17, Article 1(2)–(3).

[53] Ibid. Article 2(2)–(3).

The burden of proving that the merger fails this test is on the Commission.[54] It is contrary to Article 7 of the EU Merger Regulation to implement a merger prior to Commission approval.

A merger has a community dimension when specified turnover tests are met (including requiring that the turnover takes place in more than one Member State). As the EU merger regime is a 'one-stop shop', should the Commission have jurisdiction, this – in most cases – pre-empts a Member State authority's review of the proposed merger. Nevertheless, under Article 9 of the EU Merger Regulation, the Commission has the power to refer the proposed merger to Member State authorities when that Member State has a distinct market and the proposed merger threatens that market.

Save in the circumstances defined by Article 9 of the EU Merger Regulation, Member States cannot apply national law to mergers which have a community dimension.[55] Nevertheless, under Article 21(4) a Member State 'may take appropriate measures to protect legitimate interests other than those taken into consideration by this Regulation and compatible with the general principles and other provisions of Community law'. Such measures involve interests like public security (defence policy),[56] media plurality,[57] financial stability[58] and (sometimes) plurality of competitors in a regulated industry.[59]

After its analysis the Commission can either approve the merger as proposed or with commitments (either proposed by the parties or imposed by the Commission) or prohibit the merger. The parties can, of course, abandon their plans. If the merger does not have a community dimension (or is otherwise remitted to a national competition authority), it is considered under national law. Although there may be a difference in Member States' merger control laws' jurisdictional thresholds, and jurisdictions differ in their notification requirements, it is the SIEC standard is that used in merger assessment under national laws, albeit with reference to a non-community market.

Notwithstanding that there are numerous reasons why firms merge,[60] the sorts of mergers of concern to us, i.e. in the context of an economic crisis, are motivated by corporate restructuring and a desire to exit the market – either as part or in lieu of an

---

[54] Ibid. Article 2.
[55] Ibid. Article 21(3).
[56] Case COMP/M.1858 – *Thomson-CSF/Racal (II)* (20/07/2005).
[57] Case COMP/M.5932 – *News Corp/BskyB* (21/12/2010) [2011] OJ C 37/02.
[58] Case COMP/M.759 – *Sun Alliance/Royal Insurance* (18/06/1996).
[59] Compare Case COMP/M.567 – *Lyonnaise des Eaux/Northumbrian Water* (21/12/1995) with Case COMP/M.1346 – *EDF/London Electricity* (27/01/1999). National interest cannot be invoked contrary to Treaty principles, see Case C-196/07, *Commission v. Kingdom of Spain*, EU:C:2008:146.
[60] See the discussion in Whish and Bailey at 833–836.

insolvency process. There is an economic argument that ease of market exit has a bearing on competitive conditions in that market.[61]

The premise here is based on ease of entry to a market. Ease of entry improves competitive conditions in a market. Where there are supra-competitive returns in a market, easy entry allows for these supra-competitive returns to be 'competed down' to a competitive return. This will occur unless there are barriers to entry. A significant amount of EU competition policy, particularly that surrounding the enforcement of Article 102, is devoted to the eradication of entry barriers to promote competitive markets. In particularly the Commission notes:

> An undertaking can be deterred from increasing prices if expansion or entry is likely, timely and sufficient. For the Commission to consider expansion or entry likely it must be sufficiently profitable for the competitor or entrant, taking into account factors such as the barriers to expansion or entry, the likely reactions of the allegedly dominant undertaking and other competitors, and the risks and costs of failure.[62]

To the extent that there are sunk costs involved in attempting to compete, a potential competitor will be deterred from market entry. Hence, the extent to which market exit is 'cheap' or 'easy' (thereby mitigating sunk costs) will influence the willingness of potential competitors to enter the market.[63]

Market exit through merger is therefore a viable way of mitigating the sunk costs of entry. An advantage to 'exit by merger' over 'exit by bankruptcy' is that the former may have better potential to recognise and mitigate the consequences that 'market exit' has on other corporate constituents (such as shareholders, employees, suppliers and those indirectly dependent on the undertaking in question).[64] 'Exit by merger' can occur within the context of an FFD in a merger.

The FFD allows competition authorities to approve mergers in circumstances where the merger would otherwise be prohibited, given that the merger constitutes a SIEC. The defence predates the first merger regulation. Notably in 1989, the Commission approved the creation of a joint venture between Krupp Stahl AG and Mannesman Rohrenwerke AG, on the following basis:

> The measures as a whole will allow Krupp's production to be restructured and consolidated and to optimize the efficiency of the Huckingen plant as regards the production of cast iron and crude steel. In a Community context, the measures

---

[61] Bailey and Baumol, 'Deregulation and the Theory of Contestable Markets', and Baumol, Panzar and Willig, *Contestable Markets*.

[62] Guidance on the Commission's Enforcement Priorities in Applying Article 82 of the EC Treaty to Abusive Exclusionary Conduct by Dominant Undertakings, OJ [2009] C-45/7 (Guidance Paper), para. 16.

[63] See e.g. Shepherd, '"Contestability" vs. Competition' at 573–576.

[64] This has been recognised in the USA, see e.g. *United States v. General Dynamics*, 415 US 486 (1974) and *International Shoe Co. v. Federal Trade Commission*, 280 US 29 (1930).

contribute considerably to restructuring, since they will lead to a considerable reduction in production capacity for crude steel and sections.[65]

However, it was not until 1993 that the Commission was to precisely define the conditions under which that defence would be available.

Kali und Salz[66] concerned the industrial consequences of German reunification on the European rock salt and potash market. The case involved a proposed merger that would consolidate the production of these two commodities in a joint venture between Kali und Salz, a subsidiary of BASF (a West German company) and Mitteldeutsche Kali AG (MdK), a former East German, state-owned company. At the time of the decision, MdK's sole shareholder was Treuhand, 'an institution incorporated under public law whose task is to restructure the former GDR's [German Democratic Republic] State-owned enterprises so as to make them competitive and then to privatize them'.[67]

At the time, MdK's economic situation was 'extremely critical'.[68] The cause, as identified by the Commission, was a collapse of markets in Germany and eastern Europe.[69] MdK was loss-making and was surviving due subsidisation by Treuhand. Further support would necessitate state aid, in contravention of the Treaty.[70] Accordingly, the Commission concluded that unless acquired, MdK would exit the market: 'Even if this does not happen immediately, for social, regional and general political reasons, a closure of MdK is to be expected in the near future with a sufficient degree of probability'.[71]

The proposed concentration would create a near monopoly in potash on the German market (98 per cent), and a strong, if not dominant, position on the Community market excluding Germany (60 per cent). Other competitive constraints were weak.[72] Other than Kali und Salz, there were no other, alternative purchasers for MdK.[73] MdK would therefore inevitably exit the market, and its market share would inevitably be obtained by Kali und Salz.

As such, any concentration involving Kali und Salz and MdK would not be the cause of the deterioration of competitive conditions in the market. But on appeal, the French government challenged the Commission's second criterion, i.e. the need for the acquiring undertaking to inevitably absorb the market share of the failing firm. The Court held that this was necessary, as:

---

[65] Commission, *XIXth Report on Competition Policy*, para. 76.

[66] Commission Decision of 14 December 1993 (Case No. IV/M.308) (*Kali-Salz/MdK/Treuhand*) [1994] OJ L-186/38-56.

[67] Ibid. Recital 3.

[68] Ibid. point 73.

[69] Ibid. point 75.

[70] Ibid. point 76.

[71] Ibid. point 77.

[72] Ibid. points 46–62.

[73] Ibid. points 80–85.

[A]bsorption of market shares, although not considered by the Commission as sufficient in itself to preclude any adverse effect of the concentration on competition, therefore helps to ensure the neutral effects of the concentration as regards the deterioration of the competitive structure of the market. This is consistent with the concept of causal connection set out in Article 2(2) of the Regulation.[74]

As Commentators have noted, the consequences of the Commission's rejection of France's argument are that the FFD will justify merger to a monopoly, but not merger to a less concentrated outcome (resulting from the failing firm's partner not acquiring the entire share failing firm's market share).[75] The *Kali und Salz* criteria still underlie the European FFD.

The second criterion was eventually relaxed, albeit by the Commission, in *BASF/ Eurodiol/Pantochim*.[76] This case was viewed a 'rescue merger'.[77] Eurodiol and Pantochim (both chemical manufactures) had entered bankruptcy proceedings; they would exit the market at the end of this process unless a buyer was found. BASF (a larger manufacturer of, *inter alia*, chemicals) had proposed to buy the other two firms during the bankruptcy process, and neither those administering the bankruptcy nor the Commission could find an alternative purchaser.[78] The first and third criteria were met.

In contrast to the situation *Kali und Salz*, where the acquirer would take over all of the market share of the failing firm, in BASF, the failing firms' assets would exit the market. The exit of the assets of Eurodiol and Pantochim from the market would be detrimental to consumers of the relevant chemicals. Although the merger would result in the deterioration of competitive conditions in the market, this deterioration would be less significant than the deterioration that would occur should the firms' assets exit the market.[79] BASF relaxes the *Kali und Salz* criteria, now in bankruptcy cases, it is merely the failing firm's assets which would need to exit the market – not the more onerous condition of the acquiring firm capturing the entire market share of the exiting firm.

The FFD has been applied to failing divisions. The *Kali und Salz/BASF* criteria are applied strictly in these situations. The Commission is rightly sceptical regarding the motivation surrounding claims of 'failing divisions' of an otherwise profitable undertaking. It remarks in *Rewe/Meinl*:

> In such a case of a 'failing-division defence' and not of a 'failing-company defence', the burden of proving that the defence of lack of causality is valid must be especially heavy. Otherwise, every merger involving the sale of an allegedly unprofitable

---

[74] Ibid. para. 116.

[75] Kokkoris and Olivares-Caminal, *Antitrust Law amidst Financial Crises* at 118–119.

[76] Commission Decision of 11 July 2001 (Case COMP/M.2314) (*BASF/Eurodiol/Pantochim*) [2002] OJ L-132/45.

[77] Ibid. points 135–163.

[78] Ibid. points 144–148.

[79] Ibid. points 151 and 163.

division could be justified under merger control law by the seller's declaring that, without the merger, the division would cease trading.[80]

The failing-division defence has been infrequently invoked,[81] and has been less frequently successful.[82]

The Commission is quite right to take a careful approach to the failing firm/ division defence, as one does not need to be very cynical to see the potential for its misuse. However, the defence is part of a market exit process. To make market exit difficult or costly is to impose a sunk cost on firms, deterring market entry – with consequent costs to the competitive structure of that market.

1.4 THE EU STATE AID REGIME

Treaty provisions regulating state aid have been part of the European project since its origin. Article 67 of the European Coal and Steel Treaty (ECSC Treaty)[83] prohibited Member State activity with harmful effects on the coal and steel industry. The provisions of Article 92 of the Treaty of Rome are virtually identical to the present provisions of Article 107 TFEU. The need for a prohibition on state aid can be traced from the ECSC Treaty, via the Spaak Report, to the Treaty of Rome. The Report, which was key to the framework in establishing the European Economic Community (EEC), *inter alia* stressed the need to control such subsidisation to ensure that conditions of competition are not distorted within the Community.[84] The original rationale for state aid was based on internal market considerations, primarily the idea of establishing a level playing field to eliminate competitive distortions.

Subsidies granted by Member States to support inefficient industries or undertakings may start a subsidies race, where a Member State's subsidies are matched by others, beginning a 'race to the bottom' – and thus away from efficient, market-based competition.[85] In addition (and as a more recent justification for the regime), the Commission notes, 'state aid does not come for free'.[86] The taxpayer ultimately pays for state aid. Hence, a Member State that might otherwise wastefully expend state aid has to draw those funds from supporting other national policy goals.

---

[80] Commission Decision of 3 February 1999 (Case No. IV/M.1221) (*Rewe/Meinl*) [1999] OJ L 274/1.

[81] Commission Decision of 27 May 1998 (Case No. IV/M.993) (*Bertelsmann/Kirch/Premiere*) [1999] OJ L-53/1; *Rewe/Meinl*, ibid.; Commission Decision of 2 April 2003 (Case COMP/ M.2876) (*Newscorp/Telepiù*) [2003] OJ L-110/73; and Commission Decision of 2 September 2013 (Case No. COMP/M.6360) (*Nynas/Shell/Harburg Refinery*).

[82] E.g. Commission Decision of 9 October 2013 (Case No. COMP/M.6796) (*Aegean/Olympic II*), and *Nynas/Shell/Harburg Refinery*, ibid.

[83] Treaty Establishing the European Coal and Steel Community. Paris, 18 April 1951 UNTS 3729 (ECSC Treaty).

[84] Comite Intergouvernemental, Rapport des Chefs at 57ff.

[85] State Aid Action Plan, paras. 6–7.

[86] Ibid. para. 7.

Notwithstanding this, there are situations where state aid is necessary, particularly when, as a result of market failure, market incentives are not sufficient to encourage appropriate investment. It can also be used as a means of redistribution. In these circumstances, judicious use of state aid may provide appropriate the appropriate incentive. The Commission remarks:

> State aid measures can sometimes be effective tools for achieving objectives of common interest. They can correct market failures, thereby improving the functioning of markets and enhancing European competitiveness. They can also help promote e.g. social and regional cohesion, sustainable development and cultural diversity, irrespective of the correction of market failures.
>
> However, state aid should only be used when it is an appropriate instrument for meeting a well defined objective, when it creates the right incentives, is proportionate and when it distorts competition to the least possible extent. For that reason, appreciating the compatibility of state aid is fundamentally about balancing the negative effects of aid on competition with its positive effects in terms of common interest.[87]

In effect the EU's state aid regime is designed to allow Member States to walk a fine line between permitted interventions to remedy market failure (or wealth redistribution), and prohibited, competition-distorting subsidisation.

The existing substantive provisions regulating state aid can be found in Article 107 TFEU. The Article establishes a general negative presumption regarding state aid, prohibiting such aid unless it fits within the Treaty exceptions. The procedural provisions of Article 108 allow for a regime whereby the Commission is prenotified of any Member State plan so that it may vet the plan for consistency with the regime, prior to its implementation.

Where market failure exists, a reasonably prudent market player may not be willing to enter the market. In circumstances like this, the Treaty recognises that state aid is appropriate, and provides exceptions so that Member States may intervene to mitigate market failure in order to promote Treaty-specified policy objectives. These are found in Article 107 (2) and (3). Historically these exceptions have been narrowly construed.

Crisis response can be addressed in the contest of Article 107(2)(b), 'aid to make good the damage caused by natural disasters or exceptional occurrences'; 107(3)(b), 'aid to ... remedy a serious disturbance in the economy of a Member State'; and 107 (3)(e), 'such other categories of aid as may be specified by decision of the Council on a proposal from the Commission'.

Article 107(2)(b) usually serves as the legal basis for disaster relief aid.[88] This provision has served to justify relief for 'natural occurrences such as floods [and] earthquakes as well as major fires, nuclear accidents and the closure of airspace

---

[87] Ibid. paras. 10–11.

[88] This aid is also covered by Article 50 of Commission Regulation (EU) No. 651/2014 of 17 June 2014 Declaring Certain Categories of Aid Compatible with the Internal Market in Application of Articles 107 and 108 of the Treaty (Consolidated Text) [2014] OJ L-187/1 (GBER).

following acts of terrorism'.[89] This provision is interpreted narrowly and allows for the granting of aid only to mitigate the consequences of these disasters or circumstances, and not to general market conditions which any undertaking faces.[90]

Article 107(2)(b) was used in the context of the Covid-19 outbreak as a legal basis to support undertakings whose commercial interests were harmed as a consequence of the pandemic.[91] This provision was not the only provision invoked to mitigate against the economic consequences of the pandemic.

Article 107(3)(b) is also narrowly construed, and any disturbance which a Member State wishes to mitigate must affect the economy of the Member State and not merely a region or part of that state.[92] Again, as will be discussed, measures used to mitigate the 2008 financial crisis[93] and the Covid-19 crisis[94] rested on this provision for their legality.

Article 107(3)(e) (which allows the Council to specify other forms of aid) does not appear to allow for the grant of aid to individual undertakings; '[r]ather it enables the Council to specify categories of aid, in addition to those already specified in Article 107(3)(a)–(d), in respect of which the Commission has a discretion'.[95] Additionally, under Article 109, the Council can make appropriate Regulations for 'the application of Articles 107 and 108'.

It is on this latter basis that the Council enacts legislation[96] to enable the Commission to promulgate Regulations regarding the applicability of these two Articles, and in particular Block Exemption Regulations. Of particular importance is the General Block Exemption Regulation (GBER).[97] That Regulation is designed to simplify the process of granting aid, to permit Member States to grant 'good aid'

[89] Bailey and John, *Bellamy and Child: European Union Law of Competition*, para. 17.044.
[90] Joined cases C-346/03 and C-529/03, *Atzeni and Others v. Regione autonoma della Sardegna*, ECLI:EU:C:2006:130, paras. 79–80.
[91] Communication from the Commission to the European Parliament etc., Coordinated Economic Response to the COVID-19 Outbreak Brussels, 13.3.2020 COM(2020) 112 final; see also Communication from the Commission, Temporary Framework for State Aid Measures to Support the Economy in the Current COVID-19 Outbreak [2020] OJ C-91I/1, point 15; Nicolaides, 'Application of Article 107(2)(b)'.
[92] Case C-103/96, *Germany v. Commission*, ECLI:EU:C:2003:509, para. 106.
[93] Communication from the Commission on the Application of State Aid Rules to Measures Taken in Relation to Financial Institutions in the Context of the Current Global Crisis [2008] OJ C-270/8; later revised: Communication from the Commission on the Application, from 1 August 2013, of State Aid Rules to Support Measures in Favour of Banks in the Context of the Financial Crisis [2013] OJ C-216/1.
[94] See Communication, 'Coordinated Economic Response', n. 91 at 10; Communication, 'Temporary Framework', n. 91 points 14, 16–20.
[95] Bailey and John n. 89, para. 17.068, the authors identify shipbuilding and the coal industry as recipients of such aid.
[96] E.g. Council Regulation (EU) 2015/1588 of 13 July 2015 on the Application of Articles 107 and 108 of the Treaty on the Functioning of the European Union to Certain Categories of Horizontal State Aid (Codification) [2015] OJ 248/1.
[97] See n. 88.

without prior scrutiny.[98] The GBER includes provisions for aid for environmental protection and aid to remedy the effects of natural disasters.[99] Although the Block Exemption was set to expire on 31 December 2020, in July 2020 its validity was prolonged until 31 December 2023.[100]

The resolution of the 2008 financial crisis occurred within the regulatory context of this regime, as are the ongoing attempts to mitigate the economic impact of Covid-19. It was also within this regulatory context that other attempts at industrial reorganisation took place in the face of industry decline – and we examine later in this work the extent to which the regime may have magnified industrial crises.

1.5 THE TREATIES' POLICY-LINKING CLAUSES

The EU's competition (and state aid) provisions do not sit in isolation. Rather, these provisions are part of a set of Treaties (with related instruments) that establish the European project and serve as a foundation for its legal order. This is unlike other jurisdictions, for example the USA, where the competition regime is governed by a statute (or more precisely a set of statutes) which was enacted to remedy a particular problem, and possibly amended (or supported by complementary statutes) in light of subsequent developments.

Additionally, and unlike the statute-driven regime characteristic of non-EU juris-dictions, the Treaties that incorporate the EU's competition provisions contain policy-linking clauses. These clauses set out the EU's goals, and stipulate that (but not how) the Union is to act to achieve this set of goals. This recognition of the linking clauses, and how they relate to the competition regime, is necessary. To ignore these links, we suggest, is to misread the Treaties, thereby undermining the accuracy of the proposed interpretation of EU law.

Some of the most important of these linking clauses are covered in Sections 1.5.1 and 1.5.2.

1.5.1 *Treaty on European Union*

Article 3 (ex Article 2 TEU) is the most aspirational of these clauses. It notes that the Union shall (*inter alia*) establish an internal market, working for sustainable devel-opment and price stability, and aiming at full employment and a 'social market economy'.

---

[98] European Commission, General Block Exemption Regulation (GBER) Frequently Asked Questions (March 2016) at 1.

[99] GBER, n. 88, Articles 36–50.

[100] Commission Regulation (EU) 2020/972 of 2 July 2020 Amending Regulation (EU) No. 1407/2013 as Regards Its Prolongation and Amending Regulation (EU) No. 651/2014 as Regards Its Prolongation and Relevant Adjustments [2020] OJ L-215/3.

1.5.2 *Treaty on the Functioning of the European Union*

Article 7 (new to the Treaty) TFEU mandates consistency among Union policies and activities, which is expanded on by *Article 9 (new)* that requires the Union to 'take into account requirements linked to the promotion of a high level of employment, the guarantee of adequate social protection, the fight against social exclusion, and a high level of education, training and protection of human health'. *Article 11 (ex Article 6 TEC)* TFEU is a further mandate for the requirement of environmental protection to be integrated into Union policies; and *Article 12 (ex Article 153(2) TEC)* imposes a similar requirement for consumer protection. *Article 13 (new)* recognises the sentience of animals and a resulting need to take their welfare into account, subject to 'respecting the legislative or administrative provisions and customs of the Member States relating in particular to religious rites, cultural traditions and regional heritage'. Finally, *Article 37 of the EU Charter on Fundamental Rights* requires the integration of a high level of environmental protection in Union policies.

These clauses stipulate that at a constitutional level the Union is, and hence its institutions (including the Commission) are, to take into account policy goals such as employment, sustainability, the environment and consumer protection in all its activities.

However, resolving how these general policy goals are to be incorporated into all courses of Union action is a difficult problem, and one about which there is no consensus. The problem is particularly acute within the competition regime, established under TFEU Articles 101 and 102; and the Commission's embrace of the MEA has aggravated this problem.

It is a matter of historical fact, as we will see in Chapter 2, that until the Commission's adoption of the MEA at around the turn of the century, the Commission took into account non-economic goals and considerations in its activities including its enforcement Decisions. With adoption of the MEA, the Commission is disinclined to take other, non-economic policy goals into account. This is a result of the view that the MEA is not just a positive methodology for market assessment; it is a normative approach to the goal of competition law. Under the MEA, consumer welfare is the sole focus of competition policy; all else is irrelevant.

There are of course advantages to excluding non-economic goals from competition analysis.[101] The foremost is legal certainty.[102] With only one goal to consider, and a methodology which should produce a unique answer, this adds clarity to legal decision making, providing certainty for commercial strategies and corresponding

---

[101] See Townley, *Article 81* at 30–41 for a discussion of the relative merits of incorporating (or excluding) other policy goals in competition analysis.

[102] See Odudu n. 18 at 170–172.

investment. Where a number of possibly incommensurable factors need to be taken into account, any 'balancing' test is open to error and allows for claims that judges (or competition authorities) are entering into policy fields outside their remit.[103]

Finally, there is a strong efficiency-based argument for such exclusion. Townley put this as follows:

> Distorting or restricting competition to realise specific non-economic objectives is normally an inefficient way of achieving the end in question. It can be costly and ineffective. Economists advocate the use of optimal policy instruments; the best one to use depends on the non-economic factor being pursued. . . . [T]his does and not imply that objectives or public policy considerations other than economic efficiency are not important, but simply that if a government wanted to achieve them, it should not use competition policy but resort to policy instruments that distort competition as little as possible.[104]

Addressing non-competition public policy concerns within the context of the competition provisions may be an inefficient, expensive and thus suboptimal means of achieving the non-competition goal. Rather, such goals should be addressed, independently, through their own policy instruments.

Yet these considerations of certainty, predictability and efficiency in advancing policy goals are not the sole underlying goals in the EU's legal regime. There are rule of law considerations which require Union institutions to act in accordance with what is stipulated in the Treaties. In this regard, the ECJ, in *Les Vertes*, held:

> It must first be emphasized in this regard that the European Economic Community is a Community based on the rule of law, inasmuch as neither its Member States nor its institutions can avoid a review of the question whether the measures adopted by them are in conformity with the basic constitutional charter, the Treaty.[105]

This requirement has not gone unnoticed in the academic community.[106]

There almost no case law on this point; one exception is *Test-Achats*.[107] This case concerns a claim by a consumer association regarding its right to be heard during the procedure leading to a merger clearance. The Commission took the position that such an association had no standing during a Phase I procedure.[108] The General Court disagreed, holding:

---

[103] See Townley n. 101 at 39.
[104] Ibid. at 30, Townley's footnotes omitted.
[105] Case 294/83, *Parti écologiste 'Les Verts' v. European Parliament*, ECLI:EU:C:1986:166, para. 23.
[106] See e.g. Townley n. 101, passim; Kingston n. 46, passim; Nowag, *Environmental Integration*, passim; Holmes, 'Climate Change, Sustainability, and Competition Law'; Gerbrandy, 'Rethinking Competition Law'; Kingston, 'Integrating Environmental Protection'; Cseres and Reyna, 'EU State Aid Law and Consumer Protection'.
[107] Case T-224/10, *Association Belge des Consommateurs Test-Achats ASBL v. Commission*, ECLI: EU:T:2011:588.
[108] Ibid. paras. 25, 38–39.

[F]irst, point (b) of the second subparagraph of Article 2(1) of Regulation No 139/ 2004 provides that, as regards appraisal of concentrations, the Commission must take into account, inter alia, the interests of the intermediate and ultimate consumers. *Second, under Article 153(2) EC, which essentially has the same wording as Article 12 TFEU, consumer-protection requirements must be taken into account in defining and implementing other EU policies and activities.* Furthermore, Article 38 of the Charter of Fundamental Rights of the European Union … provides that EU policies must ensure a high level of consumer protection.[109]

Consumer protection is therefore explicitly linked to merger control. This argument would similarly apply to linking other social policy concerns (e.g. environment, employment) with economic policy concerns (including other aspects of competition law and state aid).[110]

There are therefore constitutional reasons not to view the EU's competition (and state aid) regime as somehow ring-fenced from the rest of the Treaties' other goals and provisions. Yet, there is a lesson to be taken from the efficiency-based arguments mentioned earlier. It is often a more efficient solution to design a particular policy instrument to achieve a desired goal. The task is therefore to design one which is consistent with other aspects of the legal order, and to ensure that all instruments are correctly interpreted in accord with this constitutional mandate.

Throughout the remainder of this book, we examine how the EU (and Member State) authorities have taken non-competition policy goals into account in their assessment of a competition problem. This will allow us to assess whether or not competition law is the source of, or otherwise aggravates the situation requiring, a non-competition policy response. Key to our assessment is the very real concern that crises (or crisis-washing of a situation) are often seen as opportunities for undertakings to engage in opportunistic activity. This opportunism manifests itself in suggestions that under the circumstances, a suspension of the competition regime is appropriate, or that other values (possibly incorporated in a Treaty) become paramount.

1.6 CONCLUSION

With this in mind, we can now turn to see how these competition tools have been applied to mitigate economic crises of one sort or another. A significant feature that influences how the competition regime can be 'relaxed' to 'mitigate' crises is the extent to which a strictly economic (or consumer welfare driven) outcome is seen as the goal of competition policy. Prior to the advent of the MEA, other considerations were taken into account, and as a result the authorities permitted the formation of industry-wide crisis cartels. Indeed, perhaps the American Depression-era

---

[109] Ibid. para. 43, emphasis supplied.
[110] See Cseres and Reyna, n. 106 at 13–14.

experiment of wholesale suspension of antitrust laws exemplifies that approach. As we will see, this American experiment was a failure. The EU's pre-MEA approach was never invoked in a situation that was as grave as the circumstances of the 1930s. While wholesale suspension of the competition regime would have clearly been more than a few steps too far, an examination of this approach is insightful. We turn to these two tasks in Chapter 2.

2

The Pre–More Economic Approach to Competition's Role in Crisis Management

2.1 INTRODUCTION

The competition policy of the EU (and its predecessor organisations) can be conveniently divided into two phases: before and after the MEA. This approach, which originated roughly at the turn of the twenty-first century, has two prongs. It is first the normative claim that in competition matters (and analysis of these problems) only economic effects (and, in particular, consumer welfare effects) matter. The second is the positive claim that orthodox price theory is the appropriate methodological instrument to measure these competitive effects. In many respects, the development of the MEA had a profound impact on how competition law would be used within the EU, and particularly its relationship with other EU policies. Indeed, it would be fair to say that the MEA has made collective responses to economic and other (including environmental) crises more difficult, as the methodology of that approach may fail to include other considerations that may not fit into an economic calculus.

Additionally, EU competition law did not arise out of a vacuum. The Treaties, which gave us the institutions that would later evolve into the European Union, arose out of a post–World War II settlement that was designed both to assist in the rebuilding of Europe and to build economic linkages within Europe's economies so that the conditions that gave rise to World War II would never again occur.[1] Part of this settlement was the creation of restrictions on cartels and state aid. The latter was to ensure a level playing field for undertakings of all participants in the European project; and part of the motivation for the cartel prohibition was to control their use, given how they had been misused pre-war (particularly in Germany) in mobilising the war effort.

---

[1] We have discussed these purposes of the European Treaties in *Cartels Markets and Crime* at 168–180; see also Harding and Joshua, *Regulating Cartels* at 69–73, and Gerber, *Law and Competition* at 69–91.

In this regard a third stage, a prehistory of EU competition law, should be added to any consideration of EU competition law, particularly those studies which concern the response of competition law to economic crises. It is trite to note that the Great Depression had a significant impact on North American and European economies, and likely gave rise to the conditions which resulted in the formation of those communities which now take the shape of the EU. It is also worth mentioning that a common, pre–World War II response to an economic crisis was through cartelisation: either suspending the effect of competition law or otherwise encouraging collusive economic organisations.[2] The Depression era's relaxation (or wholesale repeal) of competition law provides an apt point of comparison by which such demands can be assessed. We show that this reflexive response was incorrect and only exacerbated the problem.

This chapter examines the pre-MEA approach to the relationship between competition policy and economic crises. We do this by considering the role of competition (or, in some cases, cartel and cartel-like behaviour) both prior to the Treaties of Paris and Rome and in the pre-MEA era of the European project.

Section 2.2 examines the role of competition in crises during the pre–World War II era. Our focus is on the mitigation of the Depression. In examining the role of competition law in the Depression era, we take a brief detour to both the USA and the UK. The American experience is fruitful. Roosevelt's New Deal programme included enacting the National Industrial Recovery Act (1933).[3] This Act repealed the effect of the Sherman Act[4] and permitted the formation of industry-wide cartels. In retrospect, this suspension of competition law was a disaster and likely prolonged the Depression in the USA.

In the UK, a similar industry-wide cartelisation programme was implemented in the coal industry. The Coal Mines Act of 1930[5] mandated an industry-wide cartel to manage production of British coal. This programme was also a failure and did little more than prolong the crisis in that industry, at the expense of the British public. Yet, at the same time, the coal industries in Germany and France appeared to weather the storm of the Depression (or at least fared better than their American and British counterparts).

In Section 2.3 we examine the post-Treaty (but pre-MEA) interpretation of the EU's competition regime and how this interpretation was applied in efforts to mitigate economic crises. These crises tended to be industry wide but less 'profound' than the economy-wide crises of the Depression, which – of course – does not mean these more modern crises are of less significance for those affected by them. Here the provisions of the predecessors to TFEU Article 101 were interpreted in a manner

---

[2]   This has occurred recently with the Covid-19 crisis, see e.g. Sawer, 'Supermarkets Could Join Forces', and Butler, 'JD Sports Says Blocking Footasylum Merger Is "Absurd"'.

[3]   Pub. L. 73–67.

[4]   15 USC §1.

[5]   (20 & 21 Geo. 5) ch. 34.

which allowed for the formation of crisis cartels and permitted industry-wide arrangements to address environmental problems and create employment.

Notwithstanding this approach to Article 101, the Commission took an apparently harder line with state aid, which is considered in Section 2.4. The Commission's approach to failing firms in mergers was developed in the period immediately prior to the advent of the MEA. Its strict criteria permitted for limited application to cases where mitigating employment losses may have been a concern. And in considering Member States' use of state aid, the Commission was true to Treaty intent – bailing out inefficient undertakings was a non-starter. Section 2.5 follows, in which we examine the Commission's pre-MEA treatment of environmental concerns. This sets a baseline for the examination of subsequent developments.

The chapter ends with an evaluation of the approaches that have been examined. The clear result of our analysis is that the wholesale disapplication of competition law should not be a crisis response. The experience of the 1930s is more than sufficient evidence of this. The more tempered response of the pre-MEA experience may be an illustration of addressing a problem by simultaneously applying competition law while keeping an eye on other Treaty provisions.

2.2 THE PREHISTORY: COMPETITION AND CRISES BEFORE 1945

2.2.1 *American Antitrust and the Great Depression*

It is not the purpose of this section to discuss the legislative prehistory of the Sherman Act.[6] Although it was not the world's first antitrust regime,[7] by the mid-1920s it was certainly the world's most effective. By the start of that decade, the Department of Justice had initiated 195 prosecutions;[8] and the US Supreme Court had added clarity to the somewhat open-ended provisions of the Sherman Act. The key clarification was, of course, the Supreme Court's 1911 judgment in *Standard Oil*[9] that Section 1 of the Sherman Act only prohibited practices that were 'unreasonable' restraints of trade, thus giving birth to the 'rule of reason'.

That rule required a court, in all but the most pernicious cases of anticompetitive conduct, to take into account all relevant factors in order to determine whether the practice in question advances or harms competition as classically stated by the Supreme Court in its *Chicago Board of Trade* (*CBOT*) decision.[10]

---

[6] See Wardhaugh, n. 1 at 108–125 and the works cited therein.

[7] Canada's Combines Act of 1889 (52 Victoria Ch. 41) predated the Sherman Act by one year. That Act was ineffectual. See Ball, *Canadian Anti-trust Legislation* at 21–34.

[8] Posner, 'A Statistical Study' at 366; in addition, according to Posner's figures, during 1915–1919 the FTC brought 206 restraint of trade cases involving competition matters (ibid. at 369) and 74 private matters were brought prior to 1920 (ibid. at 371).

[9] *Standard Oil Co. of New Jersey v. United States*, 221 US 1 (1911).

[10] *Board of Trade of the City of Chicago v. United States*, 246 US 231, 238 (1918).

Nevertheless, what is relevant to this section is the set of 'facts peculiar to the business' which the Court was willing to take into consideration. *CBOT* involved the Board restriction on after-hours sales, requiring them to be made at the closing price, which had the effect of fixing the overnight price at the closing price. The Board justified this rule on the basis that it restricted working hours and hence improved employment conditions for those in the trade. The Court accepted this justification.[11] Social considerations, at least in 1918, could be taken into account and pursued via a private agenda, in a manner consistent with the competition regime.

But by 1927, it was clear that the rule of reason could not be used to justify pernicious anticompetitive activity, particularly price fixing. This was made clear in *Trenton Potteries*.[12] That case involved an appeal of criminal convictions for price fixing. The defendants argued that the trial judge erred in charging the jury that if they found the defendants had fixed prices, the jurors could return a guilty verdict, whether or not the prices as fixed were reasonable.[13] The Supreme Court held that no error was made, as earlier case law shows that fixing prices, irrespective of the reason, was illegal.[14]

Similarly condemned were information-sharing agreements, usually mediated by trade associations. Such agreements, known as 'open competition plans' or 'open price', were designed to insulate industry members from 'cutthroat competition', by substituting 'cooperative competition'.

These were common in the first three decades of the twentieth century. A leading statement of this view of competition can be found in Arthur Jerome Eddy's *The New Competition*.[15] Chapter 10 of this work, *inter alia*, provides guidance on how to form and run a trade association[16] and suggests the following result for such organisations:

> The business will be placed upon a more scientific and rational footing. Instead of competing under conditions of jealous distrust and suspicion, wasting time and money in doing things they either should not do at all, or should do with a fraction of the expenditure, members will cooperate to accomplish as a unit the things they

---

[11] Ibid. at 241; however, Sullivan and Grimes, *Law of Antitrust* at 221 suggest that the Board's real motivation may have been to obstruct after-hours trading (at reduced commissions), thus enforcing a cartel on commissions.

[12] *United States v. Trenton Potteries Co.*, 273 US 392 (1927).

[13] Ibid. at 395.

[14] *United States v. Joint Traffic Association*, 171 US 505 (1898); *Addyston Pipe & Steel Co. v. United States*, 175 US 211 (1899); *Swift and Co. v. United States*, 196 US 375 (1905); *Dr Miles Medical Co. v. Park and Sons Co.*, 220 US 373 (1911); *Maple Flooring Association v. United States*, 268 US 563 (1925); *Cement Manufacturers' Protective Association v. United States*, 268 US 588 (1925).

[15] *The New Competition*.

[16] Ibid., 7th ed. at 123–156.

rightfully may do. Finally, the open price policy – the new competition, with the friendly association it involves, tends to make business life a little better worth living.[17]

Echoing Eddy's words, one such trade association, representing the linseed oil industry, stated that their association's purpose was to 'promote better and more safe, sane, and stable conditions in the linseed oil, cake, and meal industry and increase its service to the commonwealth'.[18]

Another association, the American Hardwood Manufactures' Association, described the purpose of their plan in the following terms:

> The purpose of the plan is to disseminate among members accurate knowledge of production and market conditions so that each member may gauge the market intelligently instead of guessing at it; to make competition open and above board instead of secret and concealed; to substitute, in estimating market conditions, frank and full statements of our competitors for the frequently misleading and colored statements of the buyer.[19]

This purpose would be accomplished through an 'open competition plan', which the association described as:

> [A] central clearing house for information on prices, trade statistics and practices. By keeping all members fully and quickly informed of what the others have done, the work of the Plan results in a certain uniformity of trade practice. There is no agreement to follow the practice of others, although members do follow their most intelligent competitors, if they know what these competitors have been actually doing.[20]

To be effective, the plan required members to submit a significant amount of detailed cost, price and sales data to the association's secretary, who in turn would compile the data and circulate the data among the association's members.[21] However, after litigation, a majority of the Supreme Court held that this arrangement, like that of the Linseed Oil Association, violated the Sherman Act, and did so in no uncertain terms.[22] These associations' activities were no more than, in American terms, 'facilitating practices', or in European competition language, 'concerted practices'. It is in this legal context that antitrust met the Depression.

---

[17] Ibid. at 150.
[18] *United States v. American Linseed Oil Co.*, 262 US 371 (1923); another such association was considered in *Cement Manufacturers' Protective Association et al. v. United States*, 268 US 588 (1925).
[19] *American Column and Lumber Co. v. United States*, 257 US 377 (1921).
[20] Ibid. at 393.
[21] Ibid. at 394–398.
[22] Ibid. at 409–412.

2.2.2 *American Antitrust Responses to the Great Depression*

A convenient, but simplistic, date to mark the start of the Great Depression (at least in the USA) is 29 October 1929. That date is often considered the height of the stock market crash, with the Dow Jones dropping roughly 23.5 per cent in four days of trading.[23] The date is simplistic, as the crash was a symptom of the Depression, not its cause, given that the macroeconomic conditions that gave rise to the Depression had existed for some years.

While there is little consensus among economists as to the exact macroeconomic causality of the Depression,[24] the usual suspects include banking runs and panics,[25] costly credit intermediation (which denied or made loans costly to individuals and smaller enterprises, thus accelerating a drop in demand – the late 1920s had seen a significant increase in the availability and use of consumer credit)[26] and monetary policy (with an overvalued dollar linked to a gold standard).[27] Other policies adopted in the 1930s may have exacerbated these conditions. While the economic causes are not clear, the effects were obvious. There was a profound drop in demand across all sectors of the economy. This in turn led to a self-reinforcing deflationary cycle. Given the adherence to the gold standard, there was little room for monetary expansion to break the cycle, as retrospective analysis shows.[28]

Faced with this economic crisis, the Hoover and Roosevelt administrations attempted a number of policy responses to mitigate the crisis, each with varying efficacy. The Hoover administration was uncertain as to whether too much or too little competition was (part of) the cause.[29] Hoover, an engineer by profession, was vaguely sympathetic to some 'scientific' controls over the economy particularly in resource industries.[30]

Similar concerns were exhibited by the Roosevelt administration. In his 1933 inaugural address, drawing upon a war analogy, Roosevelt recognised the need to address the Depression's effects, and sought wide powers 'to wage a war against the emergency'.[31] His first set of proposals designed to relieve the economic situation, the so-called 'First New Deal', involved a host of measures to deal with

---

[23] The Dow Jones Industrial Average closed at 301.2 on 25 October 1929; it closed at 230.1 on the 29th. Historical stock data available at: https://stooq.com/q/d/?s=^dji.

[24] An excellent and accessible discussion of these causes can be found in Temin, 'The Great Depression' at 301–328; see also Eichengreen, 'Viewpoint: Understanding the Great Depression'.

[25] This is the preferred candidate of Friedman and Schwartz, *Monetary History of the United States 1867–1960*.

[26] Bernanke, 'Nonmonetary Effects of the Financial Crisis in the Propagation of the Great Depression'.

[27] See Temin, n. 24 at 310–313.

[28] Ibid. at 313.

[29] Meese, 'Competition Policy and the Great Depression' at 283–286.

[30] Ibid. at 286.

[31] First Inaugural Address of Franklin D. Roosevelt.

banking, securities regulation, investment in public works, rural regions and industrial recovery. An integral part of this package was the National Industrial Recovery Act[32] (NIRA), which was designed to 'rehabilitate industry and conserve natural resources' (s. 1).

The NIRA allowed industries to develop codes of 'fair completion' (s 3(a)). Upon approval by the president (or his delegate), 'such code shall be the standards of fair competition for such trade or industry or subdivision thereof' (s 3(b)), and any violation of the code would be deemed to be unfair competition contrary to the Federal Trade Commission Act[33] with criminal consequences (s 3(f)). An aim of the NIRA was to attempt to ensure that the benefits of 'fair competition' would also flow to employees. As such, Section 6 of the NIRA required that codes include provisions for unionisation and minimum wages and maximum hours of work.

The effect of the NIRA was to suspend the full force of the Sherman Act, and permit the formation of Eddyesque Trade Associations. Within two years, 550 codes were approved,[34] and as Meese notes, these codes were 'were a full-scale assault on free competition'.[35] Cole and Ohanian observe:

> Most industry codes included trade practice arrangements that limited competition, including minimum prices; restrictions on production, investment in plant and equipment, and the workweek; resale price maintenance; basing point pricing; and open-price systems. Minimum price was the most widely adopted provision, and the code authority often determined the minimum price in many industries.[36]

However, not all industries were able to agree on such codes.

The Supreme Court's 1935 decision in *Schechter Poultry*[37] held that Title I of the NIRA was unconstitutionally vague. Section 3 of the NIRA permitted the president to approve industrial codes (which had criminal sanctions for their violation) to promote 'fair competition', yet nowhere defined the term or further specified standards by which such competition is to be measured. The Act-wide grant of approval power to the president was an unconstitutional delegation of legislative power.[38] The result of this judgment was to eliminate the legal basis for the grant of industry-wide antitrust exemptions.

Although the Court had struck down legislation by which such industry-wide arrangements could be exempted from the antitrust laws, this did not spell the end of

---

[32] 15 USCA §§ 700 et seq. Pub L 73-67, Statutes at Large 48 Stat. 195.

[33] 15 USCA §§ 41–58, as amended.

[34] Meese, n. 29 at 292, citing Himmelberg, *The Origins of the National Recovery Administration* at 211.

[35] Meese, ibid.

[36] Cole and Ohanian, 'New Deal Policies and the Persistence of the Great Depression' at 784; Taylor, 'Cartel Code Attributes and Cartel Performance' at 602–607 for a statistical analysis of codes' provisions; and Meese, ibid. at 292–296 who cites a litany of examples.

[37] *ALA Schechter Poultry Corp. v. United States*, 295 US 495 (1935).

[38] Ibid. at 541–542.

such practices. In the immediate aftermath of *Schechter Poultry*, the Roosevelt administration weakened its enforcement of the antitrust laws, permitting industry to continue with their Eddyesque codes and practices.[39]

In retrospect, it is clear that the NIRA did not have its desired effect. While the Act raised some wages, this was only in those industries in which a code had been agreed. The coal industries illustrate this. In the bituminous sector (where a code existed), wages rose over 40 per cent during 1932–1939. In the code-free anthracite sector, wages fell over 5 per cent during that period.[40]

Second, wages rose faster than prices. As Temin notes, this had other consequences: '[I]f wages rise relative to the cost of products, employers will reduce the number of employees they hire. . . . The rise in real wages therefore acted to preserve unemployment – not to reduce it.'[41] The result of this was that any wage benefits of 'fair competition' would accrue entirely to employees in code-governed industries. The rise in labour costs would add a barrier to reducing employment, and higher prices would impose additional economic costs on those in code-free industries.[42] In addition to its effect on the labour marker, the NIRA was a failure as a means of increasing production in the code-governed industries covered. Output fell, as would be expected in any cartel.[43]

By 1938, Roosevelt recognised that too little competition may be part of the problem and reversed his administration's policy. He appointed Thurman Arnold to head the Antitrust Division of the Department of Justice in 1938. Arnold soon developed a reputation as a 'trust buster'.

What ended the Great Depression is perhaps more obscure than its causes. Eichengreen describes research in this area as '"normal science". There is now a steady stream of publications adding incrementally to existing knowledge.'[44] What this science has shown us is that whatever ended the Great Depression was not the suspension of competition law.

2.2.3 *Europe before the War*

It would not be an exaggeration to describe pre–World War II Europe as 'the land of cartels'. One commentator remarks:

> When the Second World War began, restrictive business programs sponsored by governments were pervasive in Germany, Italy, and Japan, were broadly authorized

---

[39] Cole and Ohanian, n. 36 at 786, see Posner n. 8 at 366 who notes that the Department of Justice initiated sixteen prosecutions between 1935 and 1938, but 106 in the subsequent three year period.

[40] Cole and Ohanian, n. 36 at 788.

[41] Temin, n. 24 at 322, see also Cole and Ohanian, n. 36 at 792.

[42] Cole and Ohanian, n. 36 at 813.

[43] Taylor, 'The Output Effects of Government Sponsored Cartels during the New Deal' at 8.

[44] Eichengreen, n. 24 at 24.

by law in Belgium, the Netherlands, Latvia and New Zealand, and were in effect in important industries in the United Kingdom and France.[45]

The paradise of cartels was Germany: 1,500 cartels were operating in 1923. This represented 50 per cent of raw steel, 82 per cent of coal and 90 per cent of paper production.[46] Although Germany had cartel control legislation at the time, control was weak as a result of political necessity and subsequent judicial interpretation. Indeed, the subsequent effect of this legislation was to regulate the relationship of cartel members, rather than to prohibit cartels.[47] On this, Feldenkirchen remarks:

> The generally friendly attitude towards cartels was shared by German Courts which in the 1890s held up the principle of liberty of contract, expressly confirming the binding force of cartel agreements under civil law, even in cases involving a restraint of trade. This judgement was in accordance with public opinion that unrestricted competition could be harmful for some lines of businesses and that cartels and similar organizations bore a responsibility for the well-being of the overall economy.[48]

This view of the benign influence of cartels was to have consequences.

Industrial cartelisation allowed for the 'rationalisation' of industry, which aided in insulating it from economic shocks faced by its foreign competitors. For instance, due to cartelisation the German coal industry increased its volume of output and rate of production during the 1925–1926 crisis, when industries in other countries were supported by governmental programmes of subsidies and tariffs.[49] In addition to this use of cartels as economic stewards, these organisations, along with combinations of large companies,[50] would also serve as symbols of the economic power of a post-unified Germany,[51] and would advance the economic aims of the National Socialist regime. Under that regime, '[p]rice fixing was to assure sufficient profitability for important companies and to prevent what was called ruinous competition'.[52] Cartels were viewed as preferable to competition as a means of organising the economy.[53] It would be this use of cartels which would influence how they were perceived post–World War II, and thus also influence how they were subsequently treated by the competition regime.[54]

---

[45] Edwards, *Control of Cartels and Monopolies* at 6.

[46] Wardhaugh, n. 1 at 170 using figures from Djelic, 'Does Europe Mean Americanization? The Case of Competition' at 236–237, see also Schröter, 'Cartelization and Decartelization in Europe, 1870–1995'; Feldenkirchen, 'Big Business in Interwar Germany'; Feldenkirchen, 'Competition Policy in Germany'.

[47] See Wardhaugh, ibid. at 170–171.

[48] Feldenkirchen, 'Competition Policy', n. 46 at 257.

[49] Eastman, 'International Aspects of the European Coal Crisis in 1926' at 233–236.

[50] Feldenkirchen, 'Big Business' n. 46.

[51] Harding and Joshua, n. 1 at 69–73 and Gerber, n. 1 at 69–91.

[52] Feldenkirchen, 'Competition Policy', n. 46 at 260.

[53] Ibid. at 261.

[54] See Harding and Joshua n. 1 at 87.

Europe, of course, did not escape the Great Depression.[55] In addition to the general, global causes which impacted the US economy, Europe faced a set of its own endogenous causes. Demand post–World War I declined to a greater degree than in the USA. The shadow of that war left debts and reparations, and addressing these led – in some economies – to hyperinflation. While monetary policy was a significant factor in Europe's problems,[56] establishing the entire causal chain is part of the incremental scientific endeavour that Eichengreen alluded to earlier.

2.2.4 *Pre-war UK: The Case of Coal*

The change in social and technological structures during the interwar period in Britain required industry to rapidly adapt. The end of the war meant an influx of labour, at the same time that industry was mechanising. Post-war decline in demand further aggravated weak economic conditions; and given that industries were concentrated locally or regionally, the economic effects of decline were seen in regional unemployment. Although all heavy industries were under strain, the coal industry provides '[a]n admirable example of the dilemma confronting inter-war Governments in dealing with the problems of the declining industries'.[57]

Even before the First World War, the British coal industry was in decline.[58] The industry was labour-intensive (but adapting to increased mechanisation). Although World War I created a demand, and there were occasional spikes in demand in the post-war period, production never exceed its pre-war (1913) peak. A leading historian remarks:

> After 1924 the new situation asserted itself decisively: coal-mining entered a prolonged period of stagnation as its excess capacity and superfluity of workers were exposed. A high level of unemployment (between 1928 and 1936 there were never less than 24% of miners wholly or partly out of work) and widespread distress, especially in South Wales, the North East and Scotland, became endemic to the industry. And the benefits of the modest revival of demand in the late 1930s were only feasible because so many miners had left the industry and so many mines had closed. Prosperity never fully returned and, ironically, with the Second World War, in spite of severe shortages of coal and desperate needs, output and employment continued to decline.[59]

---

[55] For an accessible description of the Depression in Europe, see Middleton, 'The Great Depression in Europe' at 179–206.

[56] Wolf, 'Europe's Great Depression'.

[57] Kirby, 'Government Intervention in Industrial Organization'.

[58] See e.g. Greasley, 'Fifty Years of Coal-Mining Productivity' at 877; Supple, *The History of the British Coal Industry*, Volume 4; Supple, 'The British Coal Industry between the Wars'; Court, 'Problems of the British Coal Industry between the Wars'.

[59] Supple, 'Coal Industry', ibid. at 5–6.

Finding a solution to this problem was an exercise which occupied and perplexed governments for decades.

Immediately after World War I, in 1919, the government established a commission headed by Mr Justice Sankey (later Viscount Sankey LC). In their reports,[60] the commissioners were divided as to the solution. Four solutions were proposed; they ran the gamut from complete private ownership[61] to full nationalisation.[62]

Little arose from the Sankey Commission's Report, and in 1925 – in the face of additional stagnation in the industry – a further commission was established.[63] The recommendation of this commission was broadly in accord with what would have been a consensus (or compromise) position that could have arisen from the Sankey Report. The industry was inefficient, much of which resulted from historical ownership and exploitation practices. It was in dire need of restructuring.[64] Outright nationalisation was not seen as either workable or offering a 'clear social gain'.[65]

For present purposes, the key recommendations of the 1925 Report were: (1) that the mineral resources be nationalised, acquired by compulsory purchase (or declaration of ownership for unproven coal without present market value); (2) a Coal Commission be established to administer the newly acquired resource; and (3) the amalgamation of existing mines (compulsory, if necessary) to develop efficiencies.[66]

The legislative response to the 1925 Commission's Report consisted of the *Coal Mines Act* of 1930, which was enacted after 1929's further downturn in the industry.[67] That Act has been described as being 'to the British coal industry what the National Industrial Recovery Act in a less thoro [sic] manner is to American industry'.[68]

Politics had a role in the shaping of the Act, which was designed to promote two goals. Part I (to fulfil Labour promises) attempted to stabilise the industry (including wages) by establishing a regime of cartels in an effort to raise prices. Part II (to capture Liberal support) allowed for the rationalisation of the industry through mergers (compelled, if necessary).[69] These two goals were inconsistent;[70] rationalisation would necessarily bring about unemployment (particularly where labour

---

60 Coal Industry Commission, *Reports and Minutes of Evidence on the First Stage of the Inquiry*; Coal Industry Commission, *Coal Industry Commission Act 1919. Second Stage. Reports.*

61 Balfour's view, see *Second Stage Reports*, ibid. at 29ff.

62 Sankey's view, see ibid. at 5ff.; and *First Stage*, ibid. at viii.

63 Royal Commission on the Coal Industry, *Report of the Royal Commission on the Coal Industry.*

64 Ibid. at 232; see also Lessing, 'Report of the Royal Commission on the Coal Industry' for a contemporaneous analysis.

65 Report, ibid. at 233.

66 Ibid.

67 See Lucas, 'A British Experiment in the Control of Competition' at 418.

68 Ibid.

69 Ibid. at 420; see also Kirby, 'Government Intervention', n. 57 at 160, 162–164; and Kirby, 'The Control of Competition in the British Coal-Mining Industry in the Thirties'.

70 Kirby, 'Government Intervention' at 161.

mobility was low). In addition, the cartel system was designed to protect the industry as it was, yet amalgamation sought to transform it into something else.[71]

The Act established a Central Scheme and twenty-one (later reduced to seventeen) District Schemes (s 1). The Central Scheme (run by the Central Council) was tasked with, *inter alia*, determining the output of each District Scheme and advising District Schemes accordingly (s. 2(2)). District Schemes would establish an output quota for each colliery within the district and fix prices accordingly (s 3(2)–(3)). District schemes could impose penalties on owners who contravened the scheme (s 3(2)(m)). Dispute resolution mechanisms were established at both the central and district levels (s 5). In other words, the Act established a cartel.

In terms of raising miners' pay, the cartel was moderately effective. Wages, adjusted for deflation, dropped 6 per cent between 1926 and 1930. In 1931, they began to increase, and by 1933 had levelled back to their (real) 1926 level (an increase of 6.5 per cent over the 1930 rate). By 1938, they were at 16.8 and 24.1 per cent above their 1926 and 1930 levels, respectively.[72] Miners may have benefited from this arrangement.

However, cartels tend to break down, and this cartel was no exception. In a declining industry, it was difficult to predict needed output. Inter-District competition was inevitable. Lucas reported: 'Control has not eliminated price competition. It has led merely to "price cutting by one district at the expense of another," as *The Economist* puts it'.[73] This was compounded by 'evasion', i.e. production in excess of quota.[74] This experience is entirely consistent with modern analysis of cartel instability.[75]

Industrial 'rationalisation' of the coal and other sectors had to wait until after World War II,[76] when such reorganisation became not just a matter of industrial policy, but also a source of political and social division during this period. The coal industry continued to decline throughout this period,[77] with only one English

---

[71] Ibid. at 172.

[72] These data were derived from the Mines Department's Statistical Summaries from 1926 to 1938 (published by HMSO). These provide a 'summary of output, and of the costs of production, proceeds and profits of the coal mining industry' over the relevant time period, which include a statement of 'earnings per man-shift worked'. (This would be an average cost of labour, as skilled employees would receive a higher wage.) Although there is some regional variance in labour costs, we have used the national data, for Britain as a whole. Inflation (actually deflation, as the period 1926–1938 was marked by deflation, averaging minus 0.8 per cent per year) data were obtained via the Bank of England's inflation calculator.

[73] Lucas, n. 67 at 431, citing *The Economist*, 30 July 1932 at 213; see also Fine, 'Economies of Scale and a Featherbedding Cartel?' at 444–446; Andrew Henley, 'Price Formation and Market Structure' at 265; Court, 'Problems of the British Coal Industry between the Wars' at 15.

[74] Ibid. at 433–434, Lucas's reference to *Hansard* and footnote describing means of evasion (sales to a subsidiary which in turn sells on at a loss) omitted.

[75] See e.g. Levenstein and Suslow, 'What Determines Cartel Success?'

[76] Coal Industry Nationalisation Act 1946 (9 & 10 Geo. 6 c. 59).

[77] O'Donnell, 'Pit Closures in the British Coal Industry'.

mine still operating by late 2020 (and only a handful remaining in Wales and Scotland).[78]

If anything, this discussion of the interwar use of cartels (and cartel-like arrangements) demonstrates that they are far from effective means of rescuing industries in crisis. The American NIRA's reorganisation of industry did not assist in mitigating the consequences of the Great Depression. Rather, it created an in–out, have–have not dichotomy among those who were employed. Wages rose in industries covered by codes, while they did not in uncovered industries, and the increase in wage costs exacerbated unemployment. It was not until the underlying causes of the Depression were addressed that its effects were eliminated.[79]

Statutorily imposed cartelisation in the British coal industry was also no panacea. The goals of the Coal Mines Act (simultaneously cartelising and rationalising) for the industry were inconsistent: cartelisation freezes the status quo, while rationalisation requires moving on. Further, in the face of decreasing demand, mine owners behaved as cartelists would be expected to behave – they cheated on the cartel.

The Continental experience (particularly of Germany) was different. This may have been a result of commercial expectations and practices, where cartelised behaviour was not just condoned but facilitated by the interwar legal regime. In spite of attempts to the contrary, the cartel control regime became a cartel members' dispute resolution regime. This, of course, facilitated rationalisation of industries, protecting them from foreign competition, and aided in the war effort. It was as a result of this latter consequence that those reconstructing post–World War II Europe shaped the post-war legal regime to prevent the re-emergence of such powerful commercial entities.

2.3 THE EU'S PRE-MEA REGIME

2.3.1 *Post-war Background*

The legal regime established by the Treaties of Paris and Rome was described in Chapter 1. We need not go into the historical reasons for how and why this post-war regime arose. It is clear that the purposes of the two Treaties was to go beyond trade facilitation between the members of the EEC (and ECSC), but to integrate their economies. This economic integration would culminate with the Maastricht Treaty.

The competition provisions in both Treaties attempted to foster an environment of genuine, undistorted competition among all industries of the Member States. In addition to attempting to integrate the coal and steel industries of Europe, the

---

[78] Ambrose, 'One of England's Last Coalmines to Close near Durham'.

[79] Likely due to a devaluation of the dollar and pre–World War II influx of capital (gold) into the USA, both permitting the Federal Reserve to increase money supply and the war-driven increase in consumption; see e.g. Temin, n. 24.

ECSC attempted to ensure that there was real, that is unsubsidised, competition in these industries where commercial success would be governed by market forces.[80] Article 4(c) of that Treaty is an absolute prohibition on government subsidies to the coal and steel industry, and Article (d) prohibits restrictive practices designed to share or exploit markets. This is supplemented by Article 65's prohibition on price fixing.

During its first eighteen years the ECSC was successful. The late 1950s was a sellers' market for steel, particularly high-quality European steel, and markets tended to be organised along (traditional) national lines.[81] Only three ECSC state aid cases were brought before the Court of Justice prior to 1970.[82] The situation changed dramatically with the accession of the UK (a major steel producer) and the world-wide recession that began in 1974.[83] This crisis was exacerbated over the following years as a result of competition from abroad. Downsizing the European steel industry was the only commercially viable solution.

It would not be too simplistic to argue that the steel crisis was mitigated through a coordinated downsizing response of national governments organised through the institutional aegis of the ECSC. Post-1970, the Commission's Reports on Competition Policy are replete with accounts of that body's consideration and approval of support programmes for that industry.[84] Additionally, the ECSC Treaty (Article 61) contained provisions to permit the High Authority to establish steel prices. This was done in consultation with the industry.[85] The almost unique position of steel and coal with the political and legal framework of the ECSC permitted the effective mitigation of the downturn in this industry.[86] Most other industries did not have the special status of these two industries.[87]

Rather, competitive conditions for other industries were governed by the provisions of the Treaty of Rome, as enforced by the Commission and the ECJ. Completion of the internal market was the primary goal of both competition and

---

[80] See Schmitt, 'The European Coal and Steel Community'.

[81] Alter and Steinberg, 'The Theory and Reality of the European Coal and Steel Community' at 94–95.

[82] Ehlermann, 'State Aids under European Community Competition Law' at 414–415. Nevertheless, other national policies were the subject of contention. Alter and Steinberg (ibid. at 98, fn. 14) note that '[t]he ECJ heard 226 Coal and Steel cases from 1953 to 1963, and an average of 31 cases per year from 1958 to 1963. The ECJ averaged 5.5 ECSC cases from 1964 to 1969'. See also Gerber, n. 1 at 336ff.

[83] Alter and Steinberg, ibid. at 98–101.

[84] See e.g. *Ist Report on Competition* p 18; *Xth Report* (1980) point 4; and, *XIth Report* (1982) points 186 et seq., for just three such accounts.

[85] Which was done, see as an example Protocol Consultative Committee of the European Coal and Steel Committee, Decision 9394-81 (November 16, 1981).

[86] See e.g. Mestmäcker, 'The Applicability of the ECSC-Cartel Prohibition (Article 65) during a "Manifest Crisis"'; Joliet, 'Cartelisation, Dirigism and Crisis in the European Community'; Kokkoris and Olivares-Caminal, *Antitrust Law amidst Financial Crises* at 274–284.

[87] Ehlermann, n. 82, notes that the agriculture, shipbuilding and transportation sectors also have this sort of preferred status.

state aid policy in the early years of the EEC.[88] Indeed, in *Consten and Grundig*, the first case to consider the import of what is now Article 101, the ECJ was to stress the fundamental importance to the Community of dismantling intra-state trade barriers, whether established by public or private means.[89] Economic integration requires the elimination of trade barriers.

The Commission was to stress this point in its *Ist Report on Competition Policy*.[90] In this regard, the Commission explained its view of its primary purpose of Community competition policy as, 'in the first place, prevent governmental restrictions and barriers – which have been abolished – from being replaced by similar measures of a private nature'.[91] While efficient use of resources to the benefit of the consumer were also goals, the Commission's initial view was that this could be best achieved through dismantling internal trade barriers, i.e. integration of the internal market.

State aid can distort competitive market forces, preventing those forces from ensuring an efficient allocation of resources. It also has a distorting effect, with the potential to establish barriers to trade, as a subsidy to a domestic product has the same consequences as a tariff on an imported one. Thus, formalistically applied, any advantage given to an undertaking or industry can be viewed as establishing a market barrier.[92]

Although state aid to industry, particularly failing ones, was regarded as prima facie contrary to the purposes of the competition rules, the Commission recognised that competition policy could not be indifferent to other concerns. To this end, in the *Ist Report on Competition Policy* (1971), the Commission wrote:

> Furthermore, increased competition and more rapid technological changes have revealed structural weaknesses in a number of sectors and regions of the Community. Neither the national public authorities concerned nor the institutions of the Community can remain indifferent to these weaknesses, either for economic or social reasons.
>
> Although other means of action sometimes provide more appropriate remedies for the problems which arise (whether relating to infrastructures, social policy measures for facilitating occupational training and mobility, etc.), state aid must be considered as a necessary instrument of structural policy.[93]

Temporary, targeted measures to mitigate the harshness of a market solution may be permissible.[94]

---

[88] We should differentiate between policy and goals. The latter are more normative (e.g. promoting freedom, consumer welfare), while the former are instrumental (how these goals are achieved).

[89] Cases 56 and 58–64, *Établissements Consten SàRL and Grundig-Verkaufs-GmbH v. Commission*, ECLI:EU:C:1966:41 at 340.

[90] Commission, *Ist Report on Competition Policy* at 11–13.

[91] Ibid. at 13.

[92] See e.g. Kleiner, 'Modernization of State Aid Policy' at 2–4.

[93] *Ist Report on Competition Policy*, n. 84 at 16–17.

[94] Ibid. at 17–18.

Until the advent of the MEA the Commission took this holistic view of competition and state aid. Although both Treaty provisions had a significant role in the Treaty's internal market goal, neither acted alone or at the expense of other community goals.

The preceding remark regarding the use of aid programmes to support retraining was not a 'one-off' statement.[95] The Treaty sets limits to how any goal may be pursued. As the Commission wrote in 1992:

> As far as the application of Articles 85 and 86 is concerned, it is clear that agreements which restrict competition continue to be prohibited by Article 85(1) even if the parties invoke environmental protection in order to justify them. Article 85(3) may however be applicable. The tests it lays down must of course be satisfied.[96]

That Report makes similar remarks regarding the permitted use of state aid in some environmental matters.[97] But the Commission also noted that, with the Maastricht Treaty's expansion of goals, the link between competition and other Treaty aims becomes more significant.[98] Yet, the Commission warns, the recognition of multiple goals is not carte blanche for these goals to trump competition concerns. It remarks, 'this is not a one-way process: competition policy will also play a fundamental role in the implementation of other Community policies'.[99]

2.3.2 *Twentieth-Century European Crisis Cartels*

The market-based solution to a situation where an industry is in crisis, resulting from overproduction, is to demand that each undertaking assess their own position on the market and determine how to proceed. This mandates that each firm determines their future strategy and the extent to which they should reduce capacity or exit the market independently from others' decisions. However, market failure can hinder this solution. Such failure can arise from pre-existing (or further) state aid, cost advantages arising from a fully depreciated – but inefficient – plant and cross-subsidisation by other divisions of the undertaking.[100] Further, downsizing can produce externalities in the form of the social costs of unemployment, which will be exacerbated if the industry in question is concentrated within a particular region.

One means of addressing these market failures is through so-called 'crisis cartels'. These sorts of arrangements are horizontal agreements among most or all members

---

[95] See e.g. *XXth Report on Competition Policy*, point 280; *XXVIIth Report on Competition Policy* at 8–9; *XXVIIIth Report on Competition Policy*, points 217–220.
[96] *XXIInd Report on Competition Policy*, Commission reference to *VOTOB* omitted.
[97] Ibid. point 75.
[98] *XXIIIrd Report on Competition* Policy, points 90–95.
[99] Ibid. point 95.
[100] See *XIIth Report on Competition Policy*, point 38.

of a particular industry to adopt measures in the face of an industry-wide economic downturn. These measures typically take the form of a reduction in production (or otherwise limit output), increased prices or reduced investment, in the face of an economic downturn in the industry. Put differently, these are hardcore cartels, justified in the face of an industry-wide downturn. The justification proffered is typically that the anticompetitive consequences of the cartel would be less than the economic harm that an uncontrolled shutdown would inflict.

The early practice of the Commission was that crisis cartels could be justified within the competition rules, provided the conditions of Article 101(3) were met. The use and control of crisis cartels would be an ongoing theme of the Commission's Reports on Competition Policy from the late 1970s to the early 1990s; much of this analysis would be shaped by the downturn in the synthetic fibres sector, which is an important illustration.

2.3.2.1 Synthetic Fibres

The European synthetic fibres industry grew significantly in the late 1960s and early 1970s. Between 1967 and 1973, nylon production doubled and acrylic and polyester fibre production tripled.[101] Starting in 1974, as a result of the 'world recession, sharply increased feedstock costs, a change in fashion from some synthetic fibres back towards natural fibres and increasing competition from outside Western Europe',[102] output fell. Ironically, the increased competition from imported, natural textiles was due to the Community's own trade liberalisation policies. By 1977, capacity utilisation rates in that industry dropped to 70 per cent,[103] with some firms accruing multibillion dollar losses during the latter half of the 1970s.[104] The industry was in dire need of restructuring.

However, the structure of the industry and the nature of the product made unilateral restructuring difficult. The industry (like most chemical industries) is characterised by high fixed costs, intensive research and development (and resulting expenditure), and links between the chemical processes of different end products.[105] This required production of large quantities of material, to achieve appropriate economies of scale in order to make production commercially viable.[106] Further,

---

[101] Shaw and Shaw, 'Excess Capacity and Rationalisation in the West European Synthetic Fibre Industry' at 149; *VIIth Report on Competition Policy*, points 203–204.
[102] Shaw and Shaw, ibid. at 151.
[103] *VIIIth Report on Competition Policy*, point 42; see also ibid. at 151.
[104] Shaw and Shaw, ibid.
[105] Kilduff and Jackson, 'The Competitive Characteristics of the Man-Made-Fibre Industry in Western Europe' at 186 and 192.
[106] Typically, capacity had to be operated at 85 per cent for production to be commercially viable: Commission Decision of 4 July 1984 relating to a proceeding under Article 85 of the EEC Treaty (IV/30.810 – *Synthetic Fibres*) [1984] OJ L-207/17, point 16.

as patents on most products had just expired in the 1960s, production plants were new (and undepreciated), so their closing would entail significant write-offs.[107]

Here was an industry in crisis, which was recognised as such by the then commissioner for industrial policy.[108] Indeed, in 1977, the Commission requested that Member States not provide the industry with aid that would have the effect of increasing capacity.[109]

In July 1978, representatives of the fibre producers notified the Commission of their proposals for an orderly reduction of capacity. It formed the opinion that the notified agreement was incompatible with (then) Article 85.[110] The agreement was sent back to the undertakings to be revised, as it 'is not permissible for undertakings to use restrictive agreements or concerted practices to determine the way in which their output or their sales will progress'.[111] In addition, that summer, the commissioner for industrial policy (Viscount Davignon) met with the competition commissioner (Raymond Vouel) to draft a Regulation to exempt the industry (and proposed crisis cartel) from the competition rules. However, the Commission, as a body, did not support the proposed draft regulation.[112]

In spite of not approving either the industry's proposal or a draft regulation, the Commission expressed its concern, wondering whether 'Community Funds or facilities might help support any redeployment, restructuring or conversion activities that might be undertaken, and what other measures might be envisaged to resolve the difficulties facing the European man-made fibres industry'.[113] During 1979, the Commission renewed their request to Member States not to provide capacity-increasing aid, and notify it of all other aid proposed to be granted. As all the proposed aid was targeted to capacity reduction, the Commission approved plans.[114]

This aid code would be extended and formalised,[115] with the Commission's stated intention to:

> [O]ppose any public financial support which would result in the installation of new capacity or even in the maintenance of existing capacity in the synthetic fibres industry. It intends to do this by making its authorization of the grant of aid conditional on a significant reduction in the production capacity of the assisted company.[116]

---

[107] Kilduff and Jackson, n. 105 at 192.
[108] Fiebig, 'Crisis Cartels and the Triumph of Industrial Policy over Competition Law in Europe' at 620.
[109] *Bulletin of the European Communities* 1977(7–8) (July/August 1977) point 1.5.3, and *Bulletin of the European Communities* 1977(11) (November 1977) point 2.1.47.
[110] *VIIIth Report on Competition Policy*, point 42.
[111] Ibid.
[112] Fiebig, n. 108 at 621; Joliet, n. 86 at 412–415.
[113] *VIIIth Report on Competition Policy*, point 42.
[114] *IXth Report on Competition Policy*, point 172.
[115] *XIIIth Report on Competition Policy*.
[116] Code on Aid to the Synthetic Fibres Industry [1992] OJ C-346/2 at 2.

Although the code would significantly aid in alleviating the problem, on its own it was insufficient.

Capacity reduction alone would not mitigate resulting unemployment. In the context of a recession, this was a concern.[117] Reflection on unemployment would lead the Commission body to consider how Article 85(3) might be used in overcapacity reduction.

In this reflection, the Commission stressed that such capacity reduction agreements must comply with the four criteria of 85(3), and provided some suggestions to ensure compliance. In brief, 85(3) could be met by:

1. Improvement in production can arise by a restructured and profitable industry, where 'coordination of closures helps to mitigate, spread and stagger their impact on employment'. Binding restructuring plans are required.
2. Consumers obtain their fair share of the benefit of the restriction through a revitalised industry market by healthy competition.
3. The agreement is targeted at industrial structuring, and its temporally limited restrictions are indispensable to this goal. Exchange of information is limited to verifying capacity reduction, and not for the purposes of coordinating commercial policy.
4. There is certainty that sufficient residual competition will remain after restructuring.[118]

The Commission was willing to consider reciprocal specialisation agreements among a small number of firms, as a further means of capacity reduction.[119] These criteria would influence the Commission's scrutiny of proposed crisis cartels until the turn of the twenty-first century.

This approach was instantiated in the 1984 Decision on Synthetic Fibres.[120] State aid was insufficient to enable the producers to downsize the industry. Accordingly, nine industry members (who among them accounted for 85 per cent of installed capacity in the EEC) entered into an agreement to downsize the industry by 18 per cent. Residual competition remained: not all European producers were signatories to the agreement, and there was competition from outside the EEC.[121] The agreement was concluded in October 1982, approved in July 1984 and would last until the end of 1985.[122]

This agreement was primarily aimed at targeted capacity reduction, aiming to reduce output while maintaining production at or above the commercially viable

---

[117] *XIIth Report on Competition Policy*, point 38.
[118] Ibid. point 39.
[119] Ibid. point 40 (paraphrased).
[120] See n. 106.
[121] *Synthetic Fibres*, ibid. points 6–7.
[122] *XIVth Report on Competition Policy*, point 81.

capacity utilisation ratio of 85 per cent.[123] Hence the parties incorporated a detailed capacity reduction plan into the agreement.[124] Although the agreement came within the scope of Article 85(1), the Commission held that the agreement could be exempted under Article 85(3).[125] Improvements in productivity would result from more intensive (and specialised) operation of the remaining plants, which would aid in the restoration of profitability of the industry.[126] Coordination of closures would aid in alleviating the social and economic problems of unemployment, with arrangements for retaining of redundant workers.[127] Consumers would gain from a revitalised, and hence more competitive, industry once restructuring is complete.[128] As the agreement was focused on capacity reduction, it did not limit parties' choice regarding output or deliveries, it was temporally limited, and clauses that may have been inessential to the agreement's purpose were deleted.[129] Finally, sufficient residual competition remained.[130]

Fifteen days after approving the agreement in *Synthetic Fibres*, the Commission approved a joint venture (JV) between BP and ICI to reduce structural overcapacity in the production of polyvinylchloride and low-density polyethylene.[131] ICI would specialise in the former, with BP on the latter. The Commission's analysis of this agreement paralleled *Synthetic Fibres'*. Efficiencies would ensue from specialised production, meshing with the long-term plans of both undertakings. This would be done through closing older plants and increasing the capacity of more modern ones.[132] Consumers benefited through a more efficiently produced and more secure supply.[133] The agreement was tightly drawn, and non-parties to the agreement provided sufficient residual competition.[134] BP/ICI was not unique. During the 1980s the Commission approved similar JVs focused on specialisation to restructure troubled industries.[135]

The world economy went into recession again in the 1990s. This reinvigorated latent interest in the potential for crisis cartels as a means of mitigating some of the

---

[123] *Synthetic Fibres*, n. 106 point 16.
[124] Ibid. point 17.
[125] Ibid. points 28–52.
[126] Ibid. points 28–36.
[127] Ibid. point 37.
[128] Ibid. point 39, see also *XIVth Report on Competition Policy*, point 82.
[129] *Synthetic Fibres*, ibid. points 42–47.
[130] Ibid. points 50–51, see also *XIVth Report on Competition Policy*, point 82.
[131] Commission Decision of 19 July 1984 relating to a proceeding under Article 85 of the EEC Treaty (IV/30.863 – *BPCL/ICI*) [1984] OJ L-212/1, and *XIVth Report on Competition Policy*, points 83–84.
[132] *BPCL/ICI*, ibid. points 34–35.
[133] Ibid. points 36–36.2.
[134] Ibid. points 37–42, and *XIVth Report on Competition Policy*, point 84.
[135] Notice Pursuant to Article 19 (3) of Regulation No. 17/62 concerning Notification No. IV/30.778 – *Rovin* [1983] OJ C-295/7; Commission Decision of 4 December 1986 (IV/31.055) (*ENI/Montedison*) [1987] OJ L-5/13; and Commission Decision of 22 December 1987 (IV/31.846) (*Enichem/ICI*) [1988] OJ L-50/18.

downturn. In its *XXIIIrd Report on Competition Policy* (1993), the Commission restated its approach to crisis cartels, which was unchanged from that contained in the *XIIth Report on Competition Policy* (1982).[136]

2.3.2.2 The Dutch Brick Industry

This approach was applied to a downturn in the Dutch brick industry. At the turn of the 1990s, the Dutch brick industry was in crisis. This crisis was primarily endogenous to the Netherlands, and not particularly a symptom of global problems. As a result of the introduction of more efficient processes in the production of bricks and a drop in demand arising from competition from other building materials, there was a glut of bricks on the Dutch market.[137]

The industry determined that the most effective means of mitigating this problem was an industry-wide rationalisation plan, which would coordinate capacity. The parties proposed a detailed plan that would reduce capacity and they prohibited themselves from bringing additional capacity on-stream.[138] Significantly, a number of producers agreed to close down permanently seven production sites. Those undertakings which dismantled capacity would be compensated by the other firms. This compensation would include compensation for 'social costs', as part of a social plan negotiated with the relevant trade unions.[139]

The Commission approved this plan, again using reasoning paralleling previous cases. All four criteria of Article 85(3) were met. The downsizing of the industry meant that the more efficient plants would survive, passing on cost efficiencies to consumers and resulting in an industry that was more competitive in the long term.[140] The coordination of closures entailed that 'restructuring can be carried out in acceptable social conditions, including the redeployment of employees'.[141] The system of compensatory payments was viewed as indispensable.[142] The agreement was time-limited, with non-parties (from outside the Netherlands) and alternative types of building material providing residual competitive forces.[143]

In its discussion of the arrangement in the *XXIVth Report on Competition Policy* (1994), the Commission commented on the agreement's contents, which served as further guidance on acceptable restrictions for crisis cartels:

---

[136] Points 85–86 of the *XXIIIrd Report on Competition Policy* repeats verbatim points 39–40 of the *XIIth Report on Competition Policy.*

[137] Commission Decision of 29 April 1994 (IV/34.456) (*Stichting Baksteen*) [1994] OJ L-131/15, point 7.

[138] Ibid. points 8–13.

[139] Ibid. points 11–12.

[140] Ibid. point 26.

[141] Ibid. point 27.

[142] Ibid. point 34.

[143] Ibid. points 35–42.

[T]he agreement contains a closure plan which guarantees that outmoded surplus capacity will be effectively and permanently dismantled, there exists no restriction of the individual freedom of decision of the participating firms other than the coordinated reduction in overcapacity (no output restriction, no price fixing, no market sharing, etc.), there remains effective competition on the market by way of internal competition (coordination limited to reduction of overcapacities) and external competition (alternative building materials and imports).

In addition, the Commission imposed the condition that the participating firms must refrain from divulging any data on individual outputs and deliveries of bricks, either direct between themselves or between some of them, or through a fiduciary or third party.[144]

The significance of these comments is that they emphasise the lines that even a crisis cartel cannot cross. This was a restatement of its earlier approach.[145]

In crisis situations (i.e. where an industrial sector is facing a situation of overcapacity which market forces alone will not correct – or where there may be market failure in such correction) the pre-MEA view was that coordinated capacity reduction was acceptable provided that the conditions of 85(3) (loosely interpreted) were met. In assessing such agreements, the Commission's apparent practice was to take a broad view of what counts as fulfilling 85(3)'s criteria, without demanding the production of significant quantitative evidence. This is evident in the arguments that the Commission accepted about the post-crisis, reorganised industry being more efficient and more competitive to the benefit of consumers. The Commission did not discuss either timescales or details about costs and benefits for consumers in their Decisions. Similarly, in discussing the advantages that the agreement would have for mitigating the social costs of downsizing, the Commission seems to take the benefits as a fact, rather than a proposition requiring data in its support.

Notwithstanding the apparent ease with which the criteria of 85(3) could be satisfied in the pre-MEA era, acceptable crisis cartels could not incorporate so-called hardcore restrictions, e.g. price fixing, quotas or market sharing. Furthermore, the sharing of confidential data is likewise prohibited,[146] even in a crisis. Quotas were rejected in Cementregeling voor Nederland[147] and Cimbel.[148] Coordination of conduct on the market was prohibited, notwithstanding claims of

---

[144] *XXIVth Report on Competition Policy*, point 180.

[145] Points 85–86 of the *XXIIIrd Report on Competition Policy* repeats verbatim points 39–40 of the *XIIth Report on Competition Policy*.

[146] Such data sharing is indicative of a concerted practice, contrary to Article 101 (and its predecessors), see Commission Decision of 17 February 1992 (IV/31.370 and 31.446) (*UK Agricultural Tractor Registration Exchange*) [1992] OJ L-68/19, *subsequently appealed and affirmed*: Case C-7/95P, *John Deere Ltd v. Commission*, ECLI:EU:C:1998:256.

[147] Beschikking van de Commissie van 18 december 1972) (IV/581 – *Cementregeling voor Nederland* – 1971) [1972] OJ L-303/7.

[148] Décision de la Commission, du 22 décembre 1972 (IV/243, 244, 245) (*Cimbel*) [1972] OJ L-303/24.

hard times.[149] Similarly, the Commission was able to see through attempts to 'crisis-wash' hardcore cartel conduct.[150] A global or industry-wide downturn was not to be taken as carte blanche for general anticompetitive conduct.

2.3.3 *Other Appeals to Employment Considerations: 85(3) TFEU and JVs*

The Commission had a further opportunity to consider the relationship of increasing employment and the possibly anticompetitive effect of a JV for the production of multipurpose vehicles (MPVs) by two of Europe's largest automotive manufacturers. In 1991, Ford and Volkswagen agreed to the joint development, engineering and manufacture of such vehicles, and the plant housing the JV would be located in Setúbal, Portugal (a new, and less economically developed, Member State).[151] Article 85(1) would prima facie catch this agreement: not only would it restrict both companies from further independent developments in the MPV market, the JV would also involve sharing technical information, reducing the parties' commercial advantage.[152]

However, the cooperation would lead to technical advances in production and economies of scale (from which consumers would benefit), the restrictions were indispensable and residual competition remained (particularly from Renault and Japanese manufactures).[153]

In assessing the indispensability of restrictions, the Commission noted that the proposed project would directly create 5,000 jobs (and indirectly create another 10,000) and would be the largest single investment in Portugal, facilitating regional development and Community integration.[154] While employment considerations on their own may have been insufficient to justify an exemption under 85(3), at that time they were regarded as relevant to the assessment as a whole, and possibly sufficient to push an otherwise marginal case over the threshold.

2.3.4 *The Early Approach to Control of Dominance in Crisis*

In comparison to the competition provisions governing collective action, merger and state aid, the abuse of dominance provisions have been little used in times of

---

[149] Commission Decision of 11 June 2002 (Case COMP/36.571/D-1) (*Austrian Banks – Lombard Club*) [2004] OJ L-56/1, appealed and affirmed Cases T-259/02 to T-264/02 and T-271/02, *Raiffeisen Zentralbank Österreich AG and Others v. Commission*, ECLI:EU:T:2006:396.

[150] Commission Decision of 23 April 1986 (IV/31.149) (*Polypropylene*) [1986] OJ L-230/1; and Commission Decision of 27 July 1994 (IV/31.865) (*PVC*) [1994] OJ L-239/14, appealed as Joined Cases T-305/94 etc., *Limburgse Vinyl Maatschappij NV et al. v. Commission*, ECLI:EU:T:1999:80, further appeal to the ECJ: Joined cases C-238/99P etc., *Limburgse Vinyl Maatschappij NV et al. v. Commission*, ECLI:EU:C:2002:582.

[151] Commission Decision of 23 December 1992 (IV/33.814) (*Ford Volkswagen*) [1993] OJ L-20/14.

[152] Ibid. points 20 and 21.

[153] Ibid. points 23–38.

[154] Ibid. point 36.

crisis. The abuse of dominance provisions typically have application only in the narrow circumstances when there is an undersupply of a good, by a dominant undertaking. In other words, demand is high, given production. On the other hand, crisis cartels, mergers involving failing firms and state aid to depressed industries occur when there is an oversupply of goods relative to capacity. In these situations production (or production capacity) exceeds demand. These latter situations are the 'bread and butter' of industrial crises.

The 1973 oil shock is the leading example of where a sudden drop in the supply of a crucial commodity placed industries (or significant parts of industries) into a crisis situation. The details of the Commission's response to this crisis are discussed in Chapter 1.[155] Its general warning was published in the *IIIrd Report on Competition Policy* (1973), where it stated:

> If the majors refused to supply independent distributors fairly, they might be caught by the competition rules of the Treaty, in particular Article 86. This could also be the case where the majors apply differing terms to equivalent transactions with other trading parties or make the conclusion of contracts subject to the other parties accepting supplementary obligations.[156]

On 21 December 1973, the Commission announced a market investigation into the industry.

The Commission published its conclusions in a report dated 10 December 1975.[157] Briefly put, the Commission noted that the sudden market changes put the major oil suppliers in a collectively dominant position on the market,[158] and:

> In view of the scarcity of oil products and since dealers and consumers were, as a result, unable to rely on other suppliers even in their own countries, each of the companies with refining capacities in a given country thus became the sole and imposed supplier of all dealers and consumers who were its traditional customers. In the context of their collective dominant position, each of the refining companies was, therefore, in a monopolistic position towards its customers.[159]

Three paragraphs later, the Commission concludes, '[i]t is on this basis that the Commission made its assessment of the companies' behaviour in this field'.[160] This situation of a monopolistic supplier existed in all states but Germany.

Although the Commission was unable to identify cases of the major oil companies abusing their joint dominant position,[161] it was able to identify some cases of

---

[155] Chapter 1, text accompanying nn. 39 to 45.
[156] *IIIrd Report on Competition Policy*, point 15.
[157] Commission, *Report on the Behaviour of the Oil Companies* (Brussels, 1975).
[158] Ibid. at 145.
[159] Ibid. at 146, see also *Vth Report on Competition Policy* at 18.
[160] *Report on the Behaviour of the Oil Companies*, n. 157.
[161] *Vth Report on Competition Policy* at 21.

single-firm dominance.[162] The competition remedy for such abuse was to insist on a fair sharing of oil among customers, on a pro rata basis.[163] It is submitted that this remains good law. A possible non-competition remedy may have been to modify or eliminate the system of price controls, which may have been responsible for impeding an efficient, market-based response to the crisis.

2.3.5 Mergers in Times of Crisis

The FFD, discussed earlier,[164] is an additional sword that undertakings in trouble can bear in times of crisis. However, as we have seen, the Commission has to (and continues to) strictly apply the Kali and Salz[165] criteria, albeit slightly modified. Given the high barriers imposed by these criteria, the defence is of little practical use, and is even less frequently successful. The defence typically fails as a result of the inability to establish that the failing firm would inevitably exit the market,[166] or that the acquiring firm would obtain the failing firm's market share.[167]

Beyond slightly relaxing the three criteria, little has changed in the Commission's application of the failing firm criteria since the 1990s. Of additional significance is the Commission's unwillingness to incorporate a social or economic dimension into its analysis, notwithstanding the exhortation of the recitals to the Merger Regulation. As we explore in Chapter 3, the Commission remains consistent in its exclusion of such goals in evaluating the application of the FFD. This approach to the irrelevance of social considerations was in strong contrast to the broader scope of 85(3) analysis (as seen Section 2.3.3) and to the assessment of state aid, which we consider in Section 2.4.

2.4 STATE AID AND INDUSTRIAL CRISES

Like competition policy, state aid also underwent an economic metamorphosis around the turn of the century. Early seeds of this can be seen in two white papers, the Commission's 1985 White Paper on completing the internal market and its 1999 White Paper in preparation for the next century.[168]

---

[162] Commission Decision 77/327/EEC of 19 April 1977 (IV/28.841) (*ABG/Oil companies Operating in the Netherlands*) [1977] OJ L-117/1-16.

[163] *Vth Report on Competition Policy* at 21.

[164] See Chapter 1, text accompanying nn. 65 to 82.

[165] Commission Decision of 14 December 1993 (Case No. IV/M308) (*Kali/Salz/MdK/Treuhand*) [1994] OJ L-186/38.

[166] E.g. Commission Decision of 2 October 1991 (Case No. IV/M.053) (*Aerospatiale- Alenia/de Havilland*) [1991] OJ L-334/42, and Commission Decision of 4 December 1996 (Case No. IV/M.774) (*Saint-Gobain/Wacker-Chemie/NOM*) [1997] OJ L-247/1.

[167] E.g. Commission Decision of 26 June 1997 (Case No. IV/M.890) (*Blokker/Toys 'R' Us*) [1998] OJ L-316/1.

[168] Commission, 'Completing the Internal Market' COM (85)310 final, 14 June 1985, see paras. 19 and 158; and Commission, 'Growth, Competitiveness, Employment'.

The Treaty provisions force a two-stage analysis of whether a measure is prohibited state aid. The first stage is to determine if the measure counts is aid; and, if so, whether the aid is compatible with the internal market. The Treaty provisions are imprecisely drafted, and as such part of the goal of judicial interpretation (as prompted by Commission enforcement) was to define these provisions in a more precise manner. Also of importance in the development of state aid control was the position into which the Commission was inserted.

State aid control is ultimately about the control of Member State governments' political agendas. Governments could attempt to outbid each other to attract investment, or to attempt to keep national industries afloat; and control by the Commission could be met by similar attempts on the part of Member States to neuter the Commission's powers in this regard.[169] Led by the initial accomplishments of Commissioners Sutherland and Brittan, the Commission was able take steps to expand its ability to control state aid. Indeed, it is likely that much of the Commission's success went hand in hand with a more market-friendly orientation of Member State governments, who would regard state aid as a distortion.[170]

Our concern is state aid and the economic circumstances in which the world found itself in the 1970s and 1980s. At that time the Commission was to find itself considering a wide range of support proposals initiated by Member States. In evaluating these measures, the Commission was caught on the horns of a dilemma. On the one hand, it was sympathetic to alleviating the social and economic problems caused by industrial downturns. Economic crises affecting firms and industries will lead to downsizing (including outright closure of plants and/or industries). This can spill over into other firms and industries (suppliers and communities whose livelihoods are dependent upon the troubled firm, for instance). These effects will be compounded if the affected industry is regionally concentrated and/or if there are few other employers in the region. In addition to offsetting the social costs of wholesale closures, the Commission recognised that a competitive market may require the continued existence of competitors.[171] Hence a case can be made that benefits from supporting an ailing firm or industry can offset these adverse social consequences.

On the other hand, support in crises is among the most distortive forms of state aid. Whatever the reason for the trouble that a firm finds itself in (usually either an increase in costs or a decrease in demand), further subsidisation only jams market signals, and impedes troubled firms' exit from the market. If the firm survives, in a subsidised fashion, this is at the expense of more efficient firms (albeit bankrolled by the taxpayer).

---

[169] Kleiner, n. 92 at 6, citing Cini, 'From Soft Law to Hard Law'.
[170] Doleys, 'Fifty Years of Molding Article 87'.
[171] Commission, Community Guidelines on State Aid for Rescuing and Restructuring Firms in Difficulty [1994] OJ C-368/12.

Attempting to resolve this dilemma, the Commission produced guidance on what it would regard as acceptable Rescue and Restructuring (R&R) aid. The Commission's experience with industries in distress (coal, steel, synthetic fibres, etc.) informed the production and evolution of this guidance. In its *VIIIth Report on Competition Policy* (1978) the Commission consolidated the approach that it had previously taken towards such aids. Rescue aids must consist of only the following features:

(i) they must consist of cash aid in the form of loan guarantees or loans bearing normal commercial interest rates;

(ii) they must be restricted to the amount needed to keep the firms in business (for example, covering wage and salary costs, routine supplies);

(iii) they must be paid only for the time needed (generally six months) to draw up the necessary and feasible recovery measures;

(iv) they must be warranted on the grounds of serious social difficulties, keeping the firm in operation must not have any adverse effects on the industrial situation in other Member States.[172]

Restructuring aid is predicated on the production of a restructuring plan to restore the firm to a viable state. Again, such a plan must not go beyond what is minimally necessary to achieve this, and be limited in time.[173] As a precondition of approving aid, the Commission required that a detailed rescue or restructuring plan be submitted with the (advance) notification.

This consolidation of Commission practice would be codified into its 1994 Guidelines. The above conditions for rescue aid are reproduced in that Guideline, with the added proviso that rescue aid is a 'one-off holding operation mounted over a limited period during which the company's future can be assessed'.[174]

Among the Commission's concerns with restructuring aid are the effects that it may have for (more efficient) competitors in other Member States. Hence, under the Guidelines, the Commission will approve such restructuring only if it is in the Community interest to do so,[175] and is subject to a number of caveats regarding the distortive effect, proportionality, of the aid and the binding nature of the prerequisite restructuring plan.[176] The Commission would also take 'a less restrictive attitude' with small and medium-sized enterprises (SMEs).[177]

---

[172] *VIIIth Report on Competition Policy*, point 228; see also points 177 and 227.
[173] Ibid.
[174] Guidelines on State Aid for Rescuing and Restructuring 1994, n. 171, point 3.1.
[175] Ibid. point 3.2.1.
[176] Ibid. point 3.2.2.
[177] Ibid. point 3.2.4.

These conditions on restructuring aid are imposed to mitigate the distortive effects of granting the support. The Commission is more enthusiastic about state aid granted in the course of restructuring to alleviate the social problems in restructuring. Not only is any contribution that a Member State may make towards an undertaking's legal obligations to compensate displaced workers a form of state aid, state aid can also consist in additional (discretionary) state funding granted to employees for redundancy. However, this aid is compatible with the internal market,[178] and is aid to which the Commission takes favourably. It notes:

> The Commission has a positive approach to such aid, for it brings economic benefits above and beyond the interests of the firm concerned, facilitating structural change and reducing hardship, and often only evens out differences in the obligations placed on companies by national legislation.
>
> As well as to meet the cost of redundancy payments and early retirement, aid is commonly provided in connection with a particular restructuring case for training, counselling and practical help with finding alternative employment, assistance with relocation, and professional training and assistance for employees wishing to start new businesses. The Commission consistently takes a favourable view of such aid.[179]

The Commission's Guidelines for R&R aid have been revised several times; their most recent version was promulgated in 2014.[180] These are considered in Chapter 3, though subsequent developments were fairly minor, further specifying criteria for the acceptability of such aid and tightening the 'one time, last time' requirement in funding.

This initial approach to R&R aid enabled the Commission to walk a very fine political line. A favourable attitude towards the granting of aid to mitigate economic and social consequences, yet at the same time attempting to control within the Community the adverse effects of subsidisation of inefficient, failing firms, seemed to please everyone. Yet this solution brought with it a vexing question: was this aid money well spent? With the shift towards a more economic approach to competition, which included state aid, this question would be one which the Commission was to address but – likely due to political sensitivities – was never able to resolve. We explore this in Chapter 3.

2.5 NON-ECONOMIC CONSIDERATIONS: THE ENVIRONMENT

Employment consequences were not the only non-economic concerns that the Commission considered in its competitive assessments during the pre-MEA era. Since 1970s, the Commission has explicitly recognised environmental concerns as

[178] Commission Decision SG(94) D/8907 of 27 June 1994, see *XXIVth Report on Competition Policy* (1994), point 349; upheld: Case C-241/94, *French Republic v. Commission* ('Kimberly Clark'), ECLI:EU:C:1996:353.

[179] Guidelines on State Aid for Rescuing and Restructuring 1994, n. 171, point 3.2.5.

[180] Guidelines on State Aid for Rescuing and Restructuring Non-financial Undertakings in Difficulty [2014] OJ C-249/1.

also being relevant to this analysis. While environmental considerations are the focus of Chapter 7, we can nevertheless make several preliminary observations.

First, in 1974, the Commission adopted a Framework for State Aid in Environmental Matters,[181] which was extended several times. This framework provided an exemption for environmental aid, subject to some restrictions (the most important of which was a 15 per cent cap on total value of added investment).[182] The 'polluter pays' principle (PPP) adopted by the Single European Act (Article 130 R (2), now Article 191 TFEU), limits the ability to grant aid, as subsidies can have the consequence of preventing the polluter from fully internalising this cost. The *XXth Report* recognised that some exceptions to the PPP may be merited under the Article 92(3)(b) EEC (now Article 107(3)(b) TFEU) rubric of 'an important project of common European interest'.[183]

The Commission also recognised that environmental considerations could extend beyond state subsidies and be a possible point of relevance in justifying joint action among undertakings. Noting that environmental considerations do not eliminate competition concerns, in its 1992 Report, the Commission noted that if the environmentally friendly agreement were to violate 85(1), 85(3) might apply. However, its four tests still need to be satisfied.[184]

In this regard, the Commission referred to its decision in Vereniging van Onafhankelijke Tankopslag Bedrijven (VOTOB).[185] That decision concerned the practices of VOTOB, an organisation of six undertakings offering underground chemical tank storage facilities. To offset the costs of their investments for vapour emission abatement, the undertakings increased their prices by an identical, flat-fee supplement, billed as an 'environmental charge'.[186] The Commission determined that this environmental charge was incompatible with Article 85 for three reasons:

> Firstly, it is fixed. All members are to apply it regardless of their own considerations. Secondly, it is uniform. Though varying from product to product, the increase is identical for all VOTOB members. Thirdly, it is invoiced to customers as a separate item, suggesting it is a 'charge' imposed by the government.[187]

As the fee was fixed, there was no competition around this parameter of competition, and thus no incentive for any of the undertakings to develop more efficient means of abatement and pass the resulting savings on to consumers.

With the Maastricht Treaty, and its associated set of policy clauses, environmental considerations took on a new dimension in their relationship to the Treaty's other

---

[181] *IVth Report on Competition Policy*, points 175–183.
[182] *XVIth Report on Competition Policy*, point 259.
[183] *XXth Report on Competition Policy*, point 284.
[184] *XXIInd Report on Competition Policy*, point 77.
[185] Ibid. points 177–186.
[186] Ibid. point 179.
[187] Ibid. point 180.

policy and market goals. The Commission recognised this.[188] It noted (following past practice) that the provisions of Article 85(3) are sufficiently broad to capture other objectives, including environmental objectives.[189]

However, the Commission warns, taking account of other objectives is a two-way street. While competition will take account of the other objectives, the pursuit of these other objectives must be done in a manner consistent with competition policy, and this requires the use of a market mechanism.

The Commission notes that this is already in effect with the PPP; its explanation is worth considering in detail:

> In the first place, one of the fundamentals of Community environmental policy is the 'polluter pays' principle. When applied, this allows the price mechanism, which ought to translate into costs the negative effects of a particular process or good on the environment, to perform its signalling function which forms the basis of a market economy. This pushes firms to convert environmental costs into financial terms. The pressure of competition will therefore be one of the mechanisms which will prompt businesses to reduce emissions in particular by using less-polluting production and disposal techniques. In the longer term these price incentives stimulate research to develop environmentally friendly products or production technologies, thereby putting the economy on a structurally less polluting path.[190]

The quid pro quo for competition policy recognising and accounting for other policies is that these policies – whenever possible – play by market rules.

This market approach is apparent in the Commission's 1999 decision in *CECED*.[191] This case concerned an agreement among the manufacturers, importers and distributors (and their trade association) of domestic clothes washers to phase out the import, manufacture and sale of the least energy-efficient models.[192] Although this was a clear breach of Article 81(1) of the Treaty, there were significant benefits, both collectively and to individual consumers, which would result from the scheme.

On an individual basis, although the initial price for an efficient washer was higher than an inefficient one, this would be made up within nine to forty months by consumers' savings on energy costs.[193] The collective benefits consist in the (monetised) savings in carbon damage.[194] These savings entailed that a fair share of the benefits of the agreement would accrue to consumers. As the Commission was able to determine that 81(3) other conditions were met, the agreement was exempted.

---

[188] *XXIIIrd Report on Competition Policy*, point 162.
[189] Ibid. point 91.
[190] Ibid. point 164.
[191] Commission Decision of 24 January 1999 (Case IV.F.1/36.718) (*CECED*) [2000] OJ L-187/47.
[192] Ibid. points 19–20.
[193] Ibid. points 52–54.
[194] Ibid. point 56, Commission's reference omitted.

The CECED decision likely marks a turn in Commission thinking. Environmental considerations are now explicitly taken into account in assessing the competitive benefits of a proposed commercial arrangement that is prima facie anticompetitive. However, and foreshadowing the methodological approach to come,[195] these benefits must be expressed and evaluated in market terms.

2.6 CONCLUSION

This chapter has provided us with a number of results about the use of competition law and thus its appropriate role in situations of economic crises. We began by considering the Great Depression and how normal competition rules were disapplied during this crisis. The US system provides an ideal point of comparison. Prior to 1927, that system was fairly robust, with fairly clear lines drawn between permitted and prohibited conduct. Hardcore cartel conduct was in the prohibited category.

Yet law and policymakers were not unanimous as to whether or not a strict competition regime was an appropriate means for organising the economy, particularly in the face of a crisis. Many thought that 'ruinous competition' was part of the problem; and if industry were permitted to aid in organising and coordinating production and employment, this could alleviate some of the economic problems that the American economy faced. The NIRA was an experiment with this belief. By suspending the application of the antitrust laws, it permitted the cartelisation of certain industries, with the proviso that some of the benefits of these cartels would accrue to those employed in the industries.

But the NIRA was a failure. Not all industries could agree on code of practice. In industries which were able to agree to a code, the employees gained; but given this increased cost of labour, employment in the industries did not increase. Further, employees working in similar, code-free industries did not share their gains. The NIRA fostered a sense of 'in' versus 'out' among labour, and those who were 'in' code-governed industries were the beneficiaries.

The reason the NIRA was a failure is that it was the wrong solution to the problem. The problem was a significant drop in demand, across all sectors of the economy, fuelled by fears of deflation. This drop in demand had a number of causes: fiscal and monetary policy and the dollar's tie to gold being likely causes. There is no consensus among economists as to what eliminated the Depression. In any event, the suspension of antitrust laws was not the solution; and by raising labour costs, it may have exacerbated the problem.

Similarly and simultaneously in the UK, the coal industry was cartelised via legislation. That industry was facing a decline in demand, and having developed piecemeal over centuries, it was inefficient. Yet cartelisation was not the panacea

---

[195] As exemplified by the Commission's Guidelines on the Application of Article 81(3) of the Treaty [2004] OJ C-101/97, discussed in Chapter 3.

that Westminster first thought it would be. While miners' real wages increased over time, industry cartels broke down for the very reason that cartels traditionally fail: their members cheat. In the absence of a strong body capable of overseeing cartel participants' behaviour and sanctioning non-compliance, participants will engage in opportunistic behaviour. The pre-war coal industry was no exception.

It took the organisation of the war effort and post-war nationalisation to address the coordination problem within the coal industry. But demand problems were another set of issues, which were neither solved by pre-war cartelisation nor post-war nationalisation. Again, suspension of the competition regime was not the solution.

Cartelisation, on the other hand, seemed to work when it was part of an existing industrial culture (and perhaps judicially enforced), as we saw in the examination of the pre-war German experience. While such means of organisation provide a bit of a cushion to allow the industries to weather economic shock, so organised industries were able to be co-opted into a war effort. And it was this unfortunate legacy which the drafting of the competition provisions of the Treaties of Paris and Rome sought to prevent.

These Treaties prohibit anticompetitive conduct (whether joint or unilateral); and to protect a competitive European market, they prevent the use subsidies or other forms of aid which would distort competitive conditions in that market. The European project has evolved since the 1950, with subsequent Treaties reflecting this development. Although the competition provisions have been unaltered since the Treaty of Rome (and the state aid aspects only slightly altered), the (now) Union's policy priorities have evolved.

Notwithstanding such evolution, community actors recognised that the competition regime worked in concert with other policy goals. In particular, both the Commission and Court applied Article 85 (now 101) and the state aid provisions with sensitivity for non-economic considerations, particularly in employment and environment matters. The limited acceptance of the FFD seems to be an outlier to this otherwise universal sensitivity towards employment concerns. Further, the Commission's sensitivity to such concerns was also tempered by the need to display some scepticism, to enable it to distinguish cases where employment and environmental concerns were legitimate from other cases dressed up so that they appear to involve these non-economic concerns.

In the early stages of the development of EU competition policy, up to at least the turn of the century and the MEA, competition policy did not appear to significantly hinder how the Community advanced other, non-economic goals. This, of course, leads to the question of a more refined competition (or market-based) analysis of the problem could have led to a better outcome. Further, the MEA itself raises the question of whether a competition policy backboned by this approach helps or hinders the pursuit of other Union goals. Chapter 3 considers recent developments in EU competition policy, and in doing so, addresses these two concerns.

3

The Post-MEA Relationship between Competition Law and Crisis Management

3.1 INTRODUCTION

Starting roughly at the turn of the twenty-first century, European competition law took a turn towards an MEA to competition analysis. This approach consists of two, related strands. The first is that in competition matters, only the economic consequences are of concern. The second is that orthodox economic analysis, particularly (but not necessarily strictly limited to) traditional prices theory, is the appropriate methodology to assess the competitive consequences of a given arrangement.

The immediate advantage of the MEA is that by focusing solely on advancing consumer welfare, competition policy could promote economic growth by attempting to control those market failures which prevent consumers from obtaining quality goods at price set by the market. However, this approach, and more specifically its apparent focus on economic considerations at the expense of other policy goals, particularly those found in the policy (or linking clauses) of the Treaties, has been subject to criticism, as it apparently 'ring-fences' competition considerations from other Union aims.[1] And by not taking the full Treaty context (and its case law) into account, this approach also raises rule of law concerns.[2]

The purpose of this chapter is not to mount a full-frontal attack on the MEA; this has been done elsewhere.[3] Rather, the present purpose is to examine how competition law (as evolved under the MEA) has responded to economic crises and shocks. This initially involves examining how the MEA has shaped the interpretation of the

---

[1] See e.g. Kingston, 'Competition Law in an Environmental Crisis'.
[2] See e.g. Witt, *The More Economic Approach to EU Antitrust Law* at 289–294; Wardhaugh, *Competition, Effects and Predictability*.
[3] In addition to the works cited in the two monographs ibid., see also e.g. Witt, 'Public Policy Goals under EU Competition Law'; Maziarz, 'Do Non-economic Goals Count in Interpreting Article 101(3) TFEU?'; Hodge, 'Compatible or Conflicting'; Witt, 'The European Court of Justice and the More Economic Approach to EU Competition Law'; Townley, 'Is There (Still) Room for Non-economic Arguments in Article 101 TFEU Cases?'.

competition, merger control and state aid regimes, in an effort to determine their present efficacy as a means (or as adjuncts to a means) of reducing the impact of economic crisis, whether at the firm industry level or economy wide.

To do this we first briefly consider the origin of the MEA, then show how it has altered the interpretation of the EU competition rules. This is done in Sections 3.2 and 3.3, respectively. This then allows us to consider, in Section 3.4, three cases (*BIDS*,[4] *UK Dairy*[5] and the Dutch CoT initiative[6]) in which non-economic considerations may have been relevant. The CoT case involved animal welfare concerns; the others involved some form of economic crisis. These three cases well illustrate how the MEA has remoulded how competition law can respond in times of crisis.

3.2 THE ORIGINS OF THE MEA

One part of the story behind the MEA's origins involved the need for the Commission to improve the rigour of its analysis in the face of embarrassing defeats in the Court of First Instance, and with a desire for a less formalistic approach to this analysis, which converges with that used in other jurisdictions. This history,[7] and its summary, has three elements: academic criticism of the nature of the Commission's reasoning; a transatlantic divergence in merger analysis, which led to the collapse of some significant transactions; and the Commission's own failure before the European Courts.

Although the Regulation 17[8] regime required Commission clearance of agreements as a condition of receiving the benefit of Article 85(3), in practice this process was aided through the use of Bock Exemption Regulations (BERs) promulgated by the Commission. If the parties could fit a proposed agreement within a BER, that agreement would not need to be notified to the Commission.[9] BERs, as Witt notes, 'tended to be tailored to highly specific forms of agreements, which were often even further limited to specific industries'.[10] Because of their number and broad coverage,

---

4   Case C-209/07, *Competition Authority v. Beef Industry Development Society Ltd and Barry Brothers (Carrigmore) Meats Ltd* (BIDS), ECLI:EU:C:2008:643.
5   *Tesco et al. v. OFT* [2012] CAT 31, and UK Dairy Industry Case, OFT Case CE/3094-03 (Decision of 10 August 2011).
6   See ACM's analysis of the sustainability arrangements concerning the 'Chicken of Tomorrow'; Bos, van den Belt and Feindt, 'Animal Welfare, Consumer Welfare, and Competition Law'; Monti and Mulder, 'Escaping the Clutches of EU Competition'.
7   See e.g. Witt, *More Economic Approach*, n. 2 at 7–39; Wardhaugh, *Competition, Effects and Predictability*, n. 2 at 92–95.
8   Regulation No. 17: First Regulation implementing Articles 85 and 86 of the Treaty [1962] OJ 13/204 (English special edition: Series I, Volume 1959–1962 at 87–93).
9   See e.g. Règlement n° 67/67/CEE de la Commission, du 22 mars 1967, concernant l'application de l'article 85 paragraphe 3 du traité à des catégories d'accords d'exclusivité [1967] OJ 57/849 (OJ English special edition [1967] Series I, p 10), Recital 16.
10   Witt, n. 2 at 202.

these regulations were formalistic in their treatment of the various practices that they considered. This did not go unnoticed, or uncriticised.[11]

Second, starting in about 1997, a gulf emerged between the Commission and the American authorities in their analytic approaches in merger cases and antitrust investigations. This divergence came to a head in two merger cases (Boeing/McDonnell Douglas[12] and GE/Honeywell[13]) and the antitrust investigation of Microsoft.[14] The former merger involved Boeing's proposed purchase of McDonnell Douglas. This would have reduced the global number of manufacturers of large passenger jets to two, and result in significant consolidation of defence manufacturing (particularly in the American defence industry). American authorities approved the merger, but the Commission was initially sceptical of its competitive consequences. Although the Commission was to eventually approve the merger subject to commitments, transatlantic recriminations were to flow, accusing the Commission of domestic protectionism and scepticism about its methodological approach to merger analysis.[15]

If Boeing/McDonnell Douglas was to spark the flames of controversy, GE/Honeywell unleashed a firestorm. That case involved two manufacturers active in, *inter alia*, the aviation and avionics industries. While the US authorities had concerns about overlap in the manufacturing of military helicopter engines, they cleared the transaction subject to divesture of this division and other assurances regarding the servicing of Honeywell aircraft engines. The Commission, on the other hand, blocked the merger (thereby collapsing the transaction) on the basis of a controversial theory of leveraging.[16]

The Commission's main concern was not that the transaction would merely strengthen the merged entity's position in (some) aircraft engine markets.[17] Its more significant concern was Honeywell's presence on markets for avionics and GE's financial strength and integration into financial services markets. Given this, the

[11] See e.g. Hawk, 'System Failure'.

[12] Commission Decision of 30 July 1997 (Case No. IV/M.877) (*Boeing/McDonnell Douglas*) [1997] OJ L336/16.

[13] Commission Decision of 3 July 2001 declaring a concentration to be incompatible with the common market and the EEA Agreement (Case No. COMP/M.2220 – *General Electric/Honeywell*).

[14] Commission Decision 2007/53/EC of 24 March 2004 (Case COMP/C-3.37.792) (*Microsoft*); appealed to the Court of First Instance under Case T-201/04 *Microsoft Corp v. Commission*, ECLI:EU:T:2007:289.

[15] See e.g. Kovacic, 'Transatlantic Turbulence' at 808–811 and 833–838; Witt, *More Economic Approach*, n. 2 at 11–14.

[16] See, *inter alia*, Pflanz and Caffarra, 'The Economics of GE Honeywell'; Kolasky, 'Conglomerate Mergers and Range Effects'; and Reynolds and Ordover, 'Archimedean Leveraging and the GE/Honeywell Transaction'.

[17] Particularly the markets for 'large commercial' and 'large regional jet' engines, and to create dominance in the market for 'corporate jet' engines and in marine gas turbines: see *GE/Honeywell*, n. 13 paras. 341, 489 et seq., 566 et seq. and 587 et seq.

merged entity could use this portfolio to leverage itself into a dominant position in avionics and engine markets offering bundled products (including financing) to airframe manufacturers and their customers.[18]

The European Courts' somewhat muted criticism of the quality of the Commission's economic analysis was to increase in volume in 2002, when the Court of First Instance (CFI) annulled three merger decisions: Airtours, Schneider Electric and Tetra Laval.[19] The Commission's analysis of the collective dominance in Airtours was so poor that the CFI was scathing in its criticism.[20] The Court voiced similar criticisms in Schneider Electric and Tetra Laval.[21]

In response, the Commission took measures to improve the quality of its economic analysis.[22] These measures would include the appointment of a chief economist, supported by a team of specialised economists.[23] It is likely no coincidence that the competition commissioner at the time, Mario Monti, was himself the first PhD economist to act in that role.

But this is only part of the story. On 1 May 2004, ten new countries joined the EU; that date was also the effective date of Regulation 1/2003,[24] and hence the start of the modern EU competition regime. The need for the Commission to adopt new procedures for the assessment of agreements had been apparent for a number of years. Due to a high workload, the approval process was slow. A movement towards a self-assessment regime would free up Commission resources from the notification assessment process. This would permit the deployment of these resources to other tasks that would provide greater benefit to the economy as a whole, e.g. cartel control.

In addition to self-assessment by undertakings, the modernisation programme would also bring in decentralised enforcement of EU competition law. This required National Competition Authorities (NCAs) and Member State courts to enforce EU competition law.[25] Although consistency in interpretation of EU law is ensured through the Preliminary Reference procedure of Article 267 TFEU (and its predecessors), such references are the exception rather than the day-to-day norm in competition enforcement.

The day-to-day task of evaluating commercial practices was complicated by the apparent polycentric nature of competition law during the pre-MEA era. Earlier

---

[18] Ibid. paras. 342–458.
[19] Case T-342/99, *Airtours plc v. Commission*, ECLI:EU:T:2002:146; Case T-310/012, *Schneider Electric SA v. Commission*, ECLI:EU:T:2002:254; and Case T-80/02, *Tetra Laval BV v. Commission*, ECLI:EU:T:2002:265.
[20] *Airtours*, ibid. para. 294.
[21] *Schneider Electric*, n. 19 paras. 404 and 411; and *Tetra Laval*, n. 19 paras. 140 and 336–337.
[22] XXXIInd *Report on Competition Policy* at 4.
[23] XXXIIIrd *Report on Competition Policy* at 5.
[24] Council Regulation (EC) No. 1/2003 of 16 December 2002 on the Implementation of the Rules on Competition Laid Down in Articles 81 and 82 of the Treaty [2003] OJ L 1/1, Article 45.
[25] Regulation 1/2003, Articles 3, 5–6 and 16.

Commission decisional practice recognised the importance of non-economic values such as the environment, and social concerns such as the alleviation of the effects of unemployment. The Commission needed to use non-economic considerations to balance (or assess) these competing values.

When the Commission had a monopoly on assessing agreements which were potentially restrictive of competition, yet advanced a desired non-economic goal, objectivity and consistency in assessing these arrangements could be assured. The Commission's experience and institutional memory could ensure this.[26] However, with the decentralisation that flowed with the modernisation programme, there was no longer a single assessor operating at the day-to-day level. Accordingly, this guarantor of consistency was lost.

Affected parties would now be in a position of uncertainty in the application of the rules. Further, given the need for self-assessment, in the absence of an objective metric, the system may be open to being 'gamed', possibly with the assistance of national authorities.

The use of an economic approach, with its consumer welfare backbone, could provide this objective metric. The Commission would provide additional assistance in the assessment process by promulgating Block Exemption Notices, Regulations and Guidelines. In the mind of the Commission, this would assist in the task of self-assessment.[27] Further, in novel cases, the Commission undertook to provide guidance letters to undertakings that feared their practices would infringe the competition rules.[28] However, this 'use' of comfort letters was illusory. The first letter issued was in April 2020 during the Covid-19 pandemic.[29]

Yet the story has a coda. This new approach may not be entirely consistent with the Treaties or with the case law of the Courts; and the approach may stymie the implementation of genuinely beneficial arraignments. In Sections 3.3 and 3.4 we examine how the MEA altered the application of the competition rules, and then observe the application of this new approach in three case studies.

3.3 THE MEA AND MODERN CRISES

In this section we show how the MEA has affected how the completion rules can be used and adapted in times of crisis. Our approach considers restrictions on competition and the reinterpretation of Article 101(3), a brief account of Article 102, a

---

[26] See further Wardhaugh, n. 2 at 93–95.

[27] See e.g. *XXXIVth Report on Competition Policy*, point 1, and Commission Notice on Informal Guidance Relating to Novel Questions concerning Articles 81 and 82 of the EC Treaty that Arise in Individual Cases (Guidance Letters) [2004] OJ C-101/78, points 3 and 4.

[28] Commission Notice on Informal Guidance, ibid.

[29] Commission (DG Comp) to Medicines for Europe, Comfort Letter; see also De Stefano, 'Covid-19 and EU Competition Law' and Buhart and Henry, 'COVID-20: The Comfort Letter Is Dead'.

discussion of the present use of the FFD in merger control and the Commission's new approach to state aid. The discussions of 102 and the FFD are brief.

We note that although the switch to an MEA approach was Commission-driven, the Courts also adopted this approach in a somewhat tempered manner. This is no surprise, as in at least merger matters, the Courts had been demanding more robust economic analysis; yet at the same time recognising the stability of previous case law, which recognised goals beyond consumer welfare.

3.3.1 *The MEA and Article 101*

The most significant influence of the MEA in Article 101 analysis was the determination of whether or not a given arrangement is restrictive of competition and in the application of the four criteria of 101(3).

3.3.1.1 Restrictions on Competition

For a practice to be caught by Article 101, it must prevent, restrict or distort competition in the internal market. As there are no Treaty definitions of these concepts, this phrase is given meaning through case law. Even prior to the MEA, the Courts recognised the need not just to look at a particular arraignment in the abstract; rather, the agreement needs to be considered in its full commercial context.[30] Central to this is determining what counts as a restriction within a given context, i.e. determining the theory of harm that 101 was designed to remedy.

Pre-MEA both the Commission and Court(s) shared a very wide view of the nature of harm. The first major competition case, *Consten and Grundig*,[31] concerned market division. In view of the importance of internal market considerations and the early drive towards market integration, this is no surprise.[32] Additionally, the Commission would consider limits to the parties' freedom of commercial action as restrictions of competition.[33] Adverse effects on consumer welfare might be a part of the operative theory of harm, but it often took a back seat to other factors.[34]

---

[30] Case 56-65, *Société Technique Minière v. Maschinenbau Ulm GmbH* (STM), ECLI:EU:C:1966:38 at 250.

[31] Cases 56 and 58–64, *Établissements Consten SàRL and Grundig-Verkaufs-GmbH v. Commission* ECLI:EU:C:1966:41.

[32] These concerns still play an important role today, see e.g. Ibáñez Colomo, 'Article 101 TFEU and Market Integration'.

[33] See Wardhaugh, n. 2 at 80–84, Witt, *More Economic* Approach, n. 2 at 111–118 and the cases cited in both.

[34] Witt, ibid. at 268, who cites, *inter alia*, Commission Decision of 21 December 1976 (IV/28.8) (*Theal/Watts*) [1977] OJ L 39/19, affirmed in Case 28/77, *Tepea BV v. Commission*, ECLI:EU:C:1978:133, which nicely illustrates the role played by commercial freedom in the theory of harm.

However, post-MEA the Commission shifted towards a consumer welfare stand-ard of harm. This is best seen in its Guidelines on 81(3),[35] discussed in Section 3.3.1.2. The Courts appear to have adopted this view, at least in part. Unfortunately, no extended judicial discussion regarding what constitutes harm under 101 has been produced in the MEA era. While the Courts' discussions of the object/effect distinction show a need to consider 'harms to competition', to determine if given restrictions are by their very nature harmful to competition (hence a by object restriction)[36] or whether they merely restrict some competition while providing other market benefits. However, all of this definition is somewhat circular: restric-tion of competition is defined in terms of harms to competition.

An ostensive definition may be better. With the Courts, these harms seem to be wider than a detriment to consumer welfare. While consumer welfare losses are one consideration (and indeed, these may be the key markers of by object restrictions, which are well known to produce harmful effects to consumers[37]), the Court recognises other competitive harms. These include removing uncertainties of com-petition (and thus the requirement for market participants to determine their own commercial strategy)[38] and altering the structure of the market.[39] This is wider than the Commission's view.

3.3.1.2 The 101(3) Exemption

The most striking change in the Commission's approach to interpreting Article 101 rests in its Guidelines on the Application of Article 81(3) of the Treaty.[40] This Guidance was included in the first set of publications issued by the Commission as part of the modernisation programme. The Guidelines take the explicit position that consumer welfare is the goal of competition policy.[41] Considerations of 'fair compe-tition' are viewed as irrelevant.[42]

With a consumer welfare goal in mind, the Guidelines build on existing case law. They recognise efficiencies arising through cooperation between undertakings, and note that 101(3) serves as a defence when a proposed agreement triggers Article 101(1). The defence will be successful if all four of its conditions are (cumulatively) met.[43]

---

[35] Commission, Guidelines on the application of Article 81(3) of the Treaty [2004] OJ C-101/97, particularly para. 33.

[36] E.g. Case C-67/13 P, *Groupement des cartes bancaires (CB) v. Commission*, ECLI:EU: C:2014:2204, paras. 51, 83–87.

[37] See ibid., paras. 50–51.

[38] Case C-8/08, *T-Mobile Netherlands BV et al. v. Raad van bestuur van de Nederlandse Mededingingsautoriteit*, ECLI:EU:C:2009:343, paras. 41, 43.

[39] Case C-209/07, BIDS, n. 4 paras. 4 and 31.

[40] See n. 35, supra.

[41] Ibid. paras. 13 and 33.

[42] Ibid. para. 47.

[43] Ibid. paras. 40–42.

Assessment of agreements is done in the economic and commercial context in which the agreement appears.[44] Moreover, the assessment of gains and losses must be made on the same relevant market.[45] The immediate consequence of this is that although the conditions of 101(3) cannot be used to justify a wealth transfer between two groups (e.g. producers and consumers), this interpretation likely precludes justifying intergenerational transfers, where one group makes savings to benefit another.[46] Proposed environmental arrangements may possess this characteristic. However, a time lag on a particular market, where (a group of) consumers 'pay' before receiving the benefit of the arrangement, is acceptable so long as the discounted value of the benefits compensates for the loss.[47]

All purported benefits must be objectively justified and weighed against the anticompetitive results of the arrangement.[48] Additionally, in this weighing and balancing process, those making efficiency claims need to objectively quantify these claims and do so in a manner which permits independent verification.[49] Qualitative efficiencies (and other non-cost savings) are not excluded from consideration, but their economic benefits must be explained and justified.[50]

Article 101(3) requires that consumers receive a 'fair share of the resulting benefit'. This is an inherently non-economic concept, and 'fairness' may require wealth transfers from one group to another.[51] Rather than tackling this directly, the Commission excludes the intra-group balancing of benefits; and, perhaps less controversially, it demands that future benefits be appropriately discounted. However, central to this understanding of fairness is that consumers, as a group, are compensated for the agreement's anticompetitive effects, in the sense that a '"fair share" implies that the pass-on of benefits must at least compensate consumers for any actual or likely negative impact caused to them by the restriction of competition found under Article 81(1)'.[52] Each and every affected consumer need not receive a share of each and every benefit; rather, it is merely required that sufficient compensatory benefit is passed on.[53] Finally, although the Commission will not *a priori* exclude any form of agreement from the scope of Article 101(3), it notes that hardcore restrictions of competition are unlikely to fulfil its criteria. Hardcore restrictions tend to transfer value from consumers without producing countervailing benefits.[54]

---

[44] Ibid. paras. 43–44.
[45] Ibid. para. 43.
[46] Wardhaugh, 'Crisis Cartels' at 323.
[47] Guidelines on 81(3), n. 35 paras. 87–88.
[48] Ibid. paras. 51–58.
[49] Ibid. para. 56.
[50] Ibid. para. 57.
[51] This serves as a foundation for wealth redistribution though taxation.
[52] Ibid. para. 85.
[53] Ibid. para. 86.
[54] Ibid. para. 46.

Whether or not the Commission's interpretation of 101(3) is consistent with the Treaty's words or Court of Justice of the European Union (CJEU) case law is an open question.[55] Nevertheless, because of its position as the enforcer of the European Treaties, with a right to act as *amicus curiae* in competition matters before national courts,[56] this reading of 101(3) is nevertheless influential. This influence, as we will see in Section 3.4, not only influenced the outcome of the Irish Beef case (*BIDS*), but also defined the Commission's views of crisis cartels, and shaped European (i.e. including Member State) responses to collective responses to crises generally.

3.3.2 *Article 102: Dominance*

Article 102 was the last element affected by the MEA. This was done in the Commission's 2009 Guidance on the Commission's enforcement priorities in applying Article 82.[57] There the Commission announced that it would focus its efforts on exclusionary abuses, as this is the most efficient means of protecting consumers.[58] By definition, exclusionary practices prevent or deter the entry of competitors into a market. Preventing entry is one main market failure preventing pricing at a competitive level – collusion is another.[59] The Guidance enumerates a number of practices which may give rise to exclusionary effects and provides details of how the Commission proposes to analyse these practices to identify their exclusionary effects.

The Guidance has been criticised on a number of grounds, in particular that the conception of anticompetitive foreclosure is 'uninformative and potentially over-inclusive',[60] and although they purport merely to provide guidance, they in fact change substantive 101 policy,[61] doing so in a manner which oversteps the Commission's powers.[62] But these important criticisms aside, the new approach announced in the Guidance paper reorients 102 analysis into a more effects-based approach, consistent with the methodological approach used in other areas of competition policy.[63]

This new, effects-based approach to 102 changes little for our purpose. The Dutch Petroleum case (examined in Section 1.3.3) was a clear case of exclusionary conduct, and the competition remedy for which was a pro rata allocation of supplies. Under

---

[55] Witt, *More Economic Approach*, n. 2 at 261–295; Wardhaugh, n. 2 at 113–115.
[56] Regulation 1/2003, Article 15(3), see also Section 3.4.1, 'The Irish Beef Case'.
[57] Guidance on the Commission's Enforcement Priorities in Applying Article 82 of the EC Treaty to Abusive Exclusionary Conduct by Dominant Undertakings [2009] OJ C-45/7.
[58] Ibid. Articles 6–7 and 19.
[59] Ibid. Articles 11 and 16–20.
[60] O'Donoghue and Padilla, *The Law and Economics of Article 102 TFEU* at 101.
[61] Ibid. at 97.
[62] Witt, *More Economic Approach*, n. 2 at 293–294.
[63] See also, Wardhaugh, n. 2 at 111–113.

the MEA regime, the result would almost certainly be the same. As we explore in Chapter 7, environmental arrangements often require infrastructure and network access; again, it is not evident that a shift to the MEA would have any significant enforcement or policy consequences in these matters.

3.3.3 *Merger Control: Failing Firms in Crises*

The Commission's failure in litigation in Airtours, Schneider Electric and Tetra Laval was significant for the development of the MEA. Its subsequent use of more refined economic analysis in assessing potential mergers is a specific application of this approach. Additionally, the 2004 Merger Regulation,[64] promulgated by the Council, and the Commission's corresponding soft law guidance, show a move towards a more robust, effects-based analytical method.

The significant change brought by the 2004 Regulation was its new test for intervention. The previous Regulation[65] used 'creation or strengthening of a domination position'[66] as the test, and in 2004 the test became whether or not the proposed concentration would 'significantly impede effective competition in the common market or in a substantial part of it, in particular as a result of the creation or strengthening of a dominant position'.[67]

Creation of or strengthening of a dominant position is now a sufficient, but not necessary, condition for prohibition. The concern addressed oligopolistic markets, where a merger may not result in the creation of a dominant player, but would eliminate an important competitive constraint, thereby reducing competitive pressure on remaining competitors.[68] The Council requested the Commission 'to publish guidance which should provide a sound economic framework for the assessment of concentrations with a view to determining whether or not they may be declared compatible with the common market'.[69]

Horizontal Guidance was published in 2004,[70] and Non-horizontal Guidance in 2008.[71] The latter recognises the benefits that such mergers can bring, with the result the Commission modified its approach from that used in TetraLaval/Sidel and GE/Honeywell. The former explicitly includes merger-specific efficiencies into the

---

[64] Council Regulation (EC) No. 139/2004 of 20 January 2004 on the Control of Concentrations between Undertakings (ECMR) [2004] OJ L-24/1.

[65] Council Regulation (EEC) No. 4064/89 of 21 December 1989 on the Control of Concentrations between Undertakings, as corrected, [1990] OJ L-257/13 (First Merger Regulation).

[66] Ibid. Article 2.

[67] EU Merger Regulation, n. 64 Article 2(2).

[68] Ibid. Recital 25; this is a response to *Airtours*.

[69] Ibid. Recitals 28 and 29.

[70] Guidelines on the Assessment of Horizontal Mergers under the Council Regulation on the Control of Concentrations between Undertakings, [2004] OJ C-31/5.

[71] Guidelines on the Assessment of Non-horizontal Mergers under the Council Regulation on the Control of Concentrations between Undertakings, [2008] OJ C-265/6.

evaluation process but requires any such efficiency claims to be verifiable and evidenced with sound data.[72]

The Horizontal Guidance also recognises the FFD.[73] In so doing, it explicitly appeals to the Kali and Salz criteria as modified in BASF/Pantochim/Eurodiol. The methodological turn manifested by the MEA did not alter the Commission's interpretation of the defence. A successful use of FFD would continue to remain a rare event in the post-MEA era.[74]

But the FFD is not without controversy. Posner has described it as 'one of the clearest examples in antitrust law of a desire to subordinate competition to other values'.[75] The non-competition values to which Posner refers are those social considerations which flow from the economic and social consequences of market exit on other stakeholders (e.g. employees, suppliers, members of communities in which the failing firm is located) affected by the failure.

Competition scholars frequently see the FFD as a merger control issue. In focusing only on this aspect of the transaction, they fail to see the larger perspective, namely that these transactions normally occur within the context of restructuring driven by insolvency (or its threat).[76] But the insolvency process is not value neutral itself.[77] Given that there are numerous parties with different interests in any corporate bankruptcy these are balanced within the insolvency regime, and explicit trade-offs are frequently made. These trade-offs are value judgments and are varyingly resolved in different insolvency regimes. The English regime heavily favours creditors. But the French model, for example, is balanced towards keeping a firm in operation to support employment.[78] The policy choices underlying a particular statutory regime will influence the actions of firms both before and during the insolvency process.[79] Indeed, a too lenient bankruptcy code may keep inefficient companies in the market, in either a trimmed down incarnation or as a 'zombie' firm,[80] resulting in an inefficient deployment of assets.

The FFD makes its own policy choices based on a set of assumptions that may not be true.[81] In particular, as a defence, the burden rests with those proposing the merger to produce evidence of the competitive effects of the proposed merger. However, competition agencies have better expertise to make such assessments,

---

[72] Horizontal Merger Guidelines, n. 70, Articles 76–88.
[73] Ibid. Articles 89–91.
[74] One successful use of the FFD in the MEA era, and within the context of a financial crisis, is: Commission Decision of 9 October 2013 (Case No. COMP/M.6796) (*Aegean/Olympic II*).
[75] Posner, *Antitrust Law* at 472.
[76] Kokkoris and Olivares-Carminal, *Antitrust Law amidst Financial Crises* at 103 is an exception.
[77] See Finch and Milman, *Corporate Insolvency Law* at 26–52.
[78] Davydenko and Franks, 'Do Bankruptcy Codes Matter?'; see also La Porta et al., 'Law and Finance' (for a comparative discussion of European legal regimes).
[79] Oxera, *Should Aid be Granted to Firms in Difficulty?*
[80] OECD, 'Background Note', FFD at 34.
[81] Ibid. at 34–35.

and have the ability to obtain information from other market players, who have every reason not to cooperate with the merging parties.

Some of the FFD's preconditions, particularly the requirement that the merging firm (and its assets) will – absent the merger – exit the market, may not be justified. The Organisation for Economic Co-operation and Development (OECD) succinctly identifies two fallacious assumptions in this requirement. First:

> [T]he presumption that having a financially distressed firm in the market, possibly gambling for resurrection or crippled after restructuring, is better for consumers than the proposed merger. This presumption is not justified: the presence of a handicapped, financially distressed firm in the market is likely to distort productive efficiency and may crowd out relatively efficient firms to the ultimately detriment of long-run consumer welfare.[82]

And second:

> [T]he presumption that the market structure that will result from the merger will necessarily be less competitive than a market structure where the assets of the failed firm are shared among a number of actual and/or potential competitors. But this need not be the case: a market with a few large symmetric players and multiple minnows may be less competitive than a market with fewer minnows if the large players become less symmetric.[83]

In short, it is conceivable that the conditions imposed by the FFD will block mergers which are the least anticompetitive remedy for a failing firm,[84] and in so doing may also exacerbate (or at least hinder the mitigation of) other averse consequences of business failure.

3.3.4 *The MEA and State Aid*

The publication of the Commission's 2005 State Aid Action Plan (SAAP)[85] marked the start of that body's MEA approach to state aid. After the 2005 spring (Lisbon) Council's conclusion,[86] the Commission undertook to reform the process by which the consistency of state aid programmes was measured against the Treaties' provisions. This document announced that the new state aid approval programme would contain four elements:

- less and better-targeted state aid;
- a refined economic approach;

---

[82] Ibid. at 35.
[83] Ibid.
[84] Ibid.
[85] State Aid Action Plan: Less and Better Targeted State Aid: A Roadmap for State Aid Reform 2005–2009.
[86] Ibid. paras. 13–14; cf. Kaupa, 'The More Economic Approach' at 320.

- more effective procedures, better enforcement, higher predictability and enhanced transparency;
- a shared responsibility between the Commission and Member States.[87]

To implement this programme, the Commission declared that it would take an explicitly economic approach in examining state aid proposals.[88]

In its new efforts, the Commission indicated that it would focus (albeit not exclusively) on state aid as a means of resolving market failure, when there are common interests that cannot be achieved through a strict market mechanism.[89] The implementation of a 'refined economic approach' would allow for better-targeted state aid to address these failures while avoiding the market distortions.[90] To aid in this effort, the Commission undertook to publish guidelines and communicate the criteria it would use in its assessment.[91]

This refocused analytic approach is a prima facie improvement over the regime it replaced. The former regime, with its roots in a conception of state aid control as a means to prevent the consequences of trade distortion in the internal market caused by subsidy wars, was little used, formalistic and unclear in its parameters.[92] Within six weeks of the announcement of the SAAP, Commissioner Kroes would note the advantages of the economic approach of the new regime: 'Adopting an economics-based approach is about identifying why certain desirable economic objectives are not met naturally by markets – and what can best be done to attain these objectives. It is far from true that state aid will be the best or most effective solution in all cases.'[93] The details of the new regime, and its balancing test, were to be published in the Commission's 2009 document on the Common Principles for Assessment of State Aid.[94]

Presented as a consultation document, these Common Principles would shape the Commission's analytical method. In particular, it formalised the balancing test in the following terms:

1. Is the aid measure aimed at a well-defined objective of common interest?
2. Is the aid well designed to deliver the objective of common interest, i.e. does the proposed aid address the market failure or other objectives?
   i. Is the aid an appropriate policy instrument to address the policy objective concerned?

---

[87] Ibid. para. 18.

[88] Ibid. para. 19.

[89] Ibid. para. 23.

[90] Ibid. para. 22.

[91] Ibid. paras. 20–47.

[92] See e.g. Coppi, 'The Role of Economics in State Aid Analysis and the Balancing Test' at 67.

[93] Neelie Kroes, 'The State Aid Action Plan'. This was followed by a further speech: Neelie Kroes, 'The Law and Economics of State Aid'.

[94] Common Principles for an Economic Assessment of the Compatibility of State Aid under Article 87.3.

   ii. Is there an incentive effect, i.e. does the aid change the behaviour of the aid recipient?

   iii. Is the aid measure proportionate to the problem tackled, ... ?

3. Are the distortions of competition and effect on trade limited, so that the overall balance is positive?[95]

The Commission recognised that equity objectives are included in the 'well-defined objectives of public interest', and these would further include aid to employees who may have (long-term or chronic) difficulties in obtaining employment, and R&R aid.[96]

The aid must first address an objective, typically by identifying the market failure of concern. Then the aid will be scrutinised for whether or not it is appropriate to address this failure. Proportionality, selectivity and incentive-shaping are key to this assessment. The first two determine if the proposed state aid is an appropriate means of addressing the problem (or whether the problem can be remedied through a different policy instrument). The Member State must also demonstrate that the proposed measure alters market incentives in an appropriate manner to address the problem of concern – in other words, to correct the relevant market failure.[97]

The third step is an explicit balancing test, to determine whether the benefits of the aid programme exceed the competitive distortions caused by the aid. State aid can distort competition by subsidising production, thereby encouraging overproduction of a good (static or allocative inefficiencies)[98] and/or by shifting the incentives to compete by altering behaviour in a market (e.g. the creation of moral hazard by altering the parameters of commercial responses).[99]

The Commission adopts a 'social welfare standard' as its metric for the balancing test.[100] This standard is problematic. This is a different standard from the consumer welfare standard used in all other areas of competition policy. It is also neither a strictly economic standard, nor necessarily capable of producing a determinate outcome. If the standard is total welfare, that is, the sum of consumer and producer surplus, this is readily measurable; and although it is a different standard from the norm of EU competition policy, it is a standard that is both in used in another jurisdiction's merger policy[101] and has been suggested as appropriate for merger analysis generally.[102]

However, a social welfare standard which includes total welfare plus distributional and equity concerns is entirely different. In a very real sense, equity and distributive

---

[95] Ibid. para. 9.

[96] Ibid. para. 28.

[97] Ibid. para. 32–36.

[98] Ibid. para. 44; see also Coppi n. 92 at 73.

[99] Principles, ibid. paras. 44 and 47, and box 1; and Coppi ibid.

[100] Principles, ibid. para. 58 and fn. 41.

[101] Canada uses total welfare in merger analysis, see Chapter 1, n. 6.

[102] This originates from Williamson, 'Economies as an Antitrust Defense'; see also Blair and Sokol, 'The Rule of Reason and the Goals of Antitrust'.

considerations are of little concern in economic analysis; and that discipline has yet to develop a means of measuring these qualities. Additionally, the mandate to maximise welfare and integrate this with distributional concerns will likely not yield a unique outcome.

Indeed, this challenge is reminiscent of early utilitarian thinkers who unreflectively claimed that their ethical goal was to maximise good (or happiness) for the greatest number.[103] This maxim was soon regarded as ambiguous (as between the greatest amount of good, or as maximised over the largest set of people) and replaced with other statements. The ambiguity is exemplified by a request to buy 'the best book possible at the cheapest price'.

These problems aside, equity concerns must remain at (or at least close to) the heart of state aid policy, as state aid is a part of the 'tax and transfer' redistributive regime. Hence it is impolitic for the Commission to crack down too vigorously on equitable (or distributive) uses of state aid, given their use as a political instrument by Member States.

The problem with so-called equitable state aid is not market failure, but 'government failure'.[104] These are failures resulting from effective, rent-seeking political lobbying and/or the fear of the electoral consequences of non-intervention.[105] The set of equitable uses for state aid is large, of which R&R aid is the main focus of our attention, as this is the primary assistance used by Member States to subsidise firms and industries which are in crisis.

Historically, the Commission has taken a mildly favourable approach to R&R aid. The Commission's approach to R&R aid was published in a series of Guidelines, the first of which was published in 1994; its post-MEA approach to R&R was first set out in the 2004 Guidelines.[106] The most recent set, the 2014 Guidelines,[107] were written to bring them in line with the Commission's recent modernisation plan.[108] The substantive content of the 2014 guidance does not vary much from 2004's.[109] The 2014 Guidelines were set to expire on 31 December 2020; as a result of the Covid-19 crisis their validity was extended to 31 December 2023.[110]

These Guidelines permit Member States to grant aid to firms in difficulty, subject to certain limits. The firm must be in 'material difficulty', measured by losses, in

---

[103] See Francis Hutcheson, *Inquiry Concerning Moral Good and Evil* (1725), sect. 3.

[104] Buelens et al., 'The Economic Analysis of State Aid'.

[105] Ibid. at 8; see also Dewatripont and Seabright, 'Wasteful Public Spending and State Aid Control'.

[106] Community Guidelines on State Aid for Rescuing and Restructuring Firms in Difficulty [2004] OJ C-244/2.

[107] Commission Communication Guidelines on State Aid for Rescuing and Restructuring Non-financial Undertakings in Difficulty [2014] OJ C-249/1 (2014 Guidelines).

[108] Ibid. para. 2.

[109] Jones and Sufrin, 'State Aid' Supplementary Chapter at 208.

[110] Communication from the Commission Concerning the Prolongation and the Amendments of the Guidelines on Regional State Aid for 2014–2020, ... [2020] OJ C-224/2, point 12.

insolvency proceedings (or fulfils the criteria for entry into insolvency) or by falling below certain accounting metrics.[111] If an undertaking meets this financial test, then a Member State can (subject to other conditions of eligibility) grant aid in the form of rescue aid, restructuring aid and temporary restructuring support.[112] As such, reorganisation frequently requires (mass) reduction in employment, and the Commission is sympathetic towards schemes which allows state contributions towards what would otherwise be the employer's legal obligation,[113] and to programmes which provide retraining and other assistance for those made redundant.[114] R&R aid is then approved subject to tests for consistency with the internal market.[115]

Additionally, Guidance is sympathetic to the position of SMEs. While the Commission no longer recognises the special role that SMEs play in the economy,[116] the Guidelines recognise that SMEs can be more susceptible to liquidity problems, and their exit may eliminate an innovative force or have a negative impact on other local or regional undertakings.[117] Thus, aid to SMEs will be looked on more favourably than aid to larger enterprises, and with a simplified approval procedure.[118]

However, R&R aid interferes with the market signals that the troubled firm's assets are more efficiently used elsewhere.[119] In contrast to cases where aid may be granted to promote (unpatentable) research and development, or provide a public good or service of general economic interest, there is no market failure to be addressed by aiding a failing firm. Preventing exit aid to the firm is distortive to the market process; and, by prolonging such a firm's market presence, such aid contributes to a form of market failure.

Hence, there is no sound economic argument in support of R&R aid.[120] Rather, the justification for R&R aid rests on equitable or redistributive considerations, i.e. that granting aid to firms in difficulty will alleviate the social and economic problems that would otherwise result from closure. These problems include mass unemployment, with the resulting knock-on effect on dependent communities, up- and down-stream suppliers and customers.

It is therefore quite legitimate to ask if the aid is appropriate and/or proportionate (in the Commission's terms[121]). In other words, could these adverse consequences be

---

[111] 2014 Guidelines, n. 107, points 20–21.
[112] Ibid. points 26–28.
[113] Ibid. points 32–34.
[114] Ibid. point 35.
[115] Ibid. points 38 et seq.
[116] See 2004 Guidelines, n. 106, point 8.
[117] 2014 Guidelines, n. 107, points 104 and 107.
[118] Ibid. points 104–108.
[119] See e.g. EAGCP Commentary on European Community Rescue and Restructuring Aid Guidelines at 2; Oxera, n. 79, point 1.3.4; and, Bolsa Ferruz and Nicolaides, 'An Economic Assessment of State Aid for Restructuring Firms in Difficulty'.
[120] See, in particular the EAGCP Commentary, ibid. at 1–5.
[121] See 2014 Guidelines, n. 107, points 38 (c) and (e).

mitigated or eliminated at less cost and without the trade distorting effect of subsidies?

Heim et al.[122] examined fifty-six cases where the Commission had approved such aid between 2003 and 2012. They found 'that restructuring aid increases a firm's average survival time by approximately eight to fifteen years or, putting it differently, decreases the exit rate by 58 percent to 68 percent'.[123] Hence, '[f]rom a policy perspective, our empirical results directly support the conclusion that the European Commission's R&R aid policy is effective in significantly increasing both the probability that firms in difficulty will survive as well as the probability that they return to a status of financial viability (in the long-term)'.[124] However, these authors note that although recipient firm survivability is increased, this is a different question from the ultimate question of whether or not this is the best expenditure of funds, i.e. 'whether such government policies are likely to generate positive or negative net total effects on social welfare'.[125]

This is consistent with Nulsch's 2014 results, which considered 190 cases where firms sought R&R aid between 2000 and 2010 and compared their long-term survival.[126] Firms which received restructuring aid were more likely to survive than non-supported firms or firms which received only rescue aid.[127] There may be external factors present, as the difficulties facing non-supported firms may have been too severe to justify funding. Firms that receive only rescue aid are not required to produce a detailed restructuring plan; hence their prospects may be less viable than those in need of (and with a rigorous plan for) restructuring. Her results show that 'despite this financial support business failure is still high in the group of funded firms and the market exit is often only post-poned [*sic*]. The highest survival rates have companies that get long-term support, enterprises in transition economies as well as small and new firms.'[128] Again, these results do not show whether such aid represents an efficient use of state resources. Nulsch is aware of this, and notes, '[h]owever, these results do not illustrate whether the public resources that were invested in the ailing companies was the best solution in terms of the allocation of resources'.[129]

There are few studies on the efficacy of this resource allocation problem. What exists shows that R&R aid could be better spent on directly addressing the social problems arising from restructuring, rather than restructuring as a mediated effort to

---

[122] Heim et al., 'The Impact of State Aid'.
[123] Ibid. at 40.
[124] Ibid.
[125] Ibid.
[126] Nulsch, 'Is Subsidizing Companies in Difficulties an Optimal Policy?'
[127] This point is consistent with London Economics, 'Ex-post Evaluation of the Impact of Rescue and Restructuring Aid'.
[128] Nulsch, n. 126 at 6.
[129] Ibid. at 24; she refers to Schweiger, 'The Impact of State Aid for Restructuring on the Allocation of Resources' (2004 version); a later (May 2011) version appears in our bibliography.

mitigate social costs. Bolsa Ferruz and Nicolaides' study[130] is the most comprehensive analysis of this issue. It examined 114 R&R aid cases between January 2000 and April 2013 to consider the economic value of subsidising employment in troubled firms. Their data show 'that the average cost of saving a job, EUR 49,293, was 1.7 times larger than the average annual salary, EUR 29,400'.[131] In spite of differences among Member States, Bolsa Ferruz and Nicolaides observe:

> In more than half of the cases, the aid clearly exceed 100% of the average annual salary .... We find ratios reaching up to 900%, which means that the amount of state aid used to save a job was larger than the production that one of this saved jobs could generate over nine years. Surely, any worker could be retrained and gainfully employed elsewhere in a period of nine years. And for those workers over 55 years of age, it would be cheaper for society to pay them to take early retirement and avoid the distortions of competition from keeping their otherwise inefficient employer artificially alive.[132]

The result of this aid is a transfer of wealth from the state (that is, taxpayers) to owners and creditors of recipient firms, and not to employees or others who would otherwise bear the social costs of business failure. In addition, these data also show that SMEs receive a greater per worker amount of aid. Given that the social consequences of the failure of an SME are less than those occasioned by a large firm's failure, this result, too, makes little sense.[133]

Our view is that if the Guidelines for granting R&R were to be rewritten to ensure consistency with the MEA-driven state aid modernisation programme, the considerations of the appropriateness and proportionality of the aid programme (in considering the programme's consistency with the internal market) need to be revised. We propose that a new counterfactual test be added in future R&R assessment guidance, which would consider whether social costs resulting from closure could be more efficiently addressed through direct payment to those affected.

State aid for restructuring is a legally viable option to assist failing firms. Viewed from the perspective of orthodox economic theory, R&R aid has little to recommend it. It jams market signals indicating that the firm's capital is better deployed elsewhere, it distorts the conditions of competition within a market and it can be a source of moral hazard. From the perspectives of social equity and political expediency, such aid is prima facie appealing. Yet, R&R aid may not be efficient: directly aiding those affected may be a better use of funds. This may be the most salient result of our consideration of the new approach to state aid and serve as a lesson for the future.

---

[130] Supra n. 119.
[131] Ibid. at 224.
[132] Ibid. at 227.
[133] Ibid. at 227–231.

With this consideration of how the MEA has shaped the present approach to competition and state aid policy, in Section 3.4 we turn to four recent (i.e. post-MEA) cases to assess the responsiveness and efficacy of the competition regime to challenges posed by economic and social crises.

3.4 THE MEA IN MODERN CRISES

Although the discussion in Section 3.3 of R&R aid might be an outlier,[134] it is a reasonable suggestion that one consequence of the MEA is that the Commission and NCAs have become reluctant to take factors which are not supported by detailed economic evidence into account in their competition assessments. As social considerations may not be quantifiable to the degree demanded, it is reasonable to argue that as a result, the MEA approach discounts or ignores such values in these assessments. As such, modern EU competition law is unresponsive to these socially and legally significant values. There is some truth to this argument.

Yet not every claimed social benefit is truly a benefit. An effective, economics-based competition regime can show this, and thus prevent undertakings from disguising anticompetitive behaviour as some form of noble social good. We next consider three recent cases that show the response of the modern competition regime to economic (and social) crises.

3.4.1 *The Irish Beef Case*

The litigation surrounding the Irish Competition Authority's assessment of the Beef Industry Development Society's proposals to rationalise production in that country's beef industry marks a turning point from earlier decisions regarding cooperation in industries in crisis. It appears to have signalled the death knell for (legal) crisis cartels in the EU. This litigation[135] arose as a result of an industry-wide agreement to reduce structural capacity in the beef processing industry that existed in Ireland during the late 1990s and early 2000s.

The facts of this case are presented in some detail in Mr Justice McKechnie's judgment,[136] and it is appropriate to provide some background. The beef industry is and has been a significant contributor to Ireland's economy. In 2006, it contributed

---

[134] This can be explained by viewing R&R aid as part of a second-stage tax and transfer regime.

[135] Relevant documents can be found on the Irish Competition and Consumer Protection Commission's website: www.ccpc.ie/business/enforcement/civil-competition-enforcement/civil-court-cases/agreements-reduce-capacity-irish-beef/. See also Case C-209/07, *Competition Authority v. Beef Industry Development Society Ltd and Barry Brothers (Carrigmore) Meats Ltd.* AG's Opinion, ECLI:EU:C:2008:467.

[136] *Competition Authority v. Beef Industry Development Society Ltd & Anor* [2006] IEHC 294, paras. 8–31; see also Odudu, 'Restrictions of Competition by Object'; Talbot, 'Finding a Baseline for Competition Law Enforcement during Crises'.

€3 billion and employed over 10,000 people.[137] Although there is a domestic market for beef, the bulk of production is exported. Until the mid-1960s the industry norm was that live cattle were exported to Britain for slaughter there.[138] The mid-1960s marked a change in the industry towards slaughtering and processing beef in Ireland, with resulting meat being exported.[139] Further change occurred with the entry of Ireland to the EEC in 1973.

As a Member State, Ireland (hence its farmers) could obtain the numerous benefits of the Common Agricultural Policy (CAP).[140] Among these benefits, the CAP provided for price supports and grants to construct slaughterhouses. McKechnie J describes the net effects of the CAP's price support as guaranteeing a floor price for farmers, which was exacerbated by overcapacity with meat production caused by the availability of grants to fund construction of 'factories'.[141]

Traditionally, cattle were slaughtered in the months of September, October and November, reflecting the cycle of breeding and outdoor grazing, requiring plants to have sufficient peak capacity for production during these months.[142] There was thus an early incentive to build for these peaks. But as part of the 1992 reforms to the CAP, farmers received financial incentives to reduce delivery of cattle during peak periods, smoothing out demand (and need for capacity) in production, entailing that capacity designed for peak periods would be superfluous.[143]

This led to a situation where the incentives for beef production were divorced from market realities.[144] By the late 1990s the severity of the situation was apparent.[145] Representatives of the industry and government engaged the consulting firm McKinsey to produce a report on the state of the industry.[146] The Report noted severe overcapacity and resulting unprofitability. McKechnie J summarises these points:

> In 1997, with thirty-two plants operating, the industry had an estimated capacity to kill 66,000 head of cattle per week. This compares with an actual maximum throughput of 45,000 and an average throughput of 32,000 per week. In addition,

---

[137] *BIDS* (High Court), ibid. para. 13.

[138] Ibid. para. 8.

[139] In 2002, domestic consumption accounted for only 12.75 per cent of production, with the export industry valued at €1.185 billion. See (Ireland) Competition Authority, Merger Determination M/03/029p2, the proposed acquisition of Galtee Meats (Charleville) Ltd by Dawn Meats Limited (20 November 2003), para. 2.18 available at: www.ccpc.ie/business/mergers-acquisitions/merger-notifications/mo3029-dawn-meats-galtee-meats/.

[140] *BIDS* (High Court), n. 136 para. 9.

[141] Ibid.

[142] Ibid. para. 17.

[143] Ibid.

[144] Ibid. para. 11.

[145] But the poor state of the beef industry resulting from interventions had been noticed earlier. See Sheehy, 'The Impact of EEC Membership on Irish Agriculture' at 310.

[146] *BIDS* (High Court), para. 13–26 (this contains a good summary of the Report's details), see also Talbot, n. 136 at 56–57.

there were a number of dormant plants which if activated would add to this overcapacity.[147]

And:

> The report then identifies the financial prize, as it terms it, which would be available if the sector could move forward. Firstly, by removing plants with a throughput of 420,000 animals per annum, the report estimates a resulting saving of IR £18 million per annum. This is calculated by subtracting the sum of IR £21 million, being the marginal cost to the stayers of slaughtering the additional 420,000 animals, from the sum of £39 million which is calculated as being the current cost of processing such numbers; hence a net saving per annum of £18 million. Secondly, if plants could become more efficient and fifth quarter realisations increased, there would be additional revenue of IR £14 million per annum.[148]

The McKinsey Report recommended coordinated action to reduce total capacity by 430,000 head (or 32 per cent) per annum, with those remaining in the industry ('stayers') compensating those leaving ('goers'). Appendix II to the Report contained a set of proposals for the rationalisation of the industry. These proposals served as the foundation of the industry (BIDS) plan.[149] Other stakeholders commissioned additional reports.[150] These concurred with the McKinsey Report's conclusions on the state of the industry and need for rationalisation. In turn, the government recognised the need for rationalisation and provided indications of its support.[151]

In May 2002 the Beef Industry Development Society Limited (BIDS) was established to implement the rationalisation strategy suggested by the McKinsey Report. Its members were responsible for the production of approximately 93 per cent of Irish beef.[152] The plan proposed by BIDS is reproduced in paragraph 31 of McKechnie J's judgment. Its salient features included:

- a reduction in production capacity (maximum reduction 420,000 head/ year);
- a levy on production would be instituted, which would be used so that stayers would compensate goers;
- the levy would consist of €2/head on the traditional percentage of kill, and €11/head of kill over that percentage;
- goers would decommission their plants and undertake to sign a two-year non-compete agreement (with a geographical scope of the island of Ireland);

---

[147] Ibid. para. 18.
[148] Ibid. para. 19.
[149] Ibid. paras. 23 and 31.
[150] Ibid. paras. 25–28; and Talbot, n. 136 at 57.
[151] *BIDS* (High Court) ibid. para. 28.
[152] *The Competition Authority v. Beef Industry Development Society Ltd and Barry Brothers (Carrigmore) Meats Ltd* [2009] IESC 72 (BIDS (Supreme Court)), per Kearns P at 2.

- land associated with decommissioned plants would not be used for beef processing for a period of five years (enforced by restrictive covenant);
- equipment from decommissioned plants could only be sold to stayers for use only as back-up/spare parts; and,
- '[t]he freedom of stayers in matters of production, pricing, conditions of sale, imports and exports, deliveries, mergers and acquisitions and other commercial activity would not be affected by the Programme. In particular, no plant would be prohibited from increasing capacity and there would be no understanding that animals previously slaughtered by a Decommissioned plant would be secured or slaughtered by any given stayer.'[153]

After the BIDS programme was agreed, its members informed the Competition Authority of the programme, and provided submissions as to the programme's compatibility with Irish and EC competition law. BIDS and its members attempted to engage with the Competition Authority (and cooperated with it throughout its investigation).

The plan was proposed prior the self-assessment regime of Regulation 1/2003, and BIDS sought clearance (under the domestic equivalent of Regulation 17) of the programme. Yet, the Authority did not vet these proposals and 'declined to engage in this way'.[154] The Competition Authority took the view that these arrangements were contrary to domestic provisions mirroring Article 81(1), and could not benefit from the equivalent of 81(3).[155] In the end, the Authority commenced proceedings.

In the High Court, McKechnie J held that these restrictions were not restrictive of competition by their object. Taking a narrow view of the notion of a 'by object' restriction, he concluded:

> I cannot see any provision or clause which could be said to fix prices or share customers. Nor do I believe that the arrangements can in any way be described as plainly or evidently limiting output, sharing markets or prohibiting investment. In addition, there is no injunction on those who might remain in the industry to reduce output or indeed even to freeze it at a certain level. There is no question of production quotas. Such players and each one of them, would be entirely free to increase production within their plants if they so wished. Unless therefore, a reduction per se in capacity must necessarily be equated with a limitation on output, which in my view is unlikely, ... then I cannot see how the arrangement is objectionable in this regard; which is of course the major suggested violation by object restriction.[156]

---

[153] *BIDS* (High Court), n. 135 para. 31.
[154] Ibid. para. 87.
[155] These provisions are Ireland, *Competition Act* 2002 (No. 14 of 2002), ss. 4(1) and 4 (5), respectively.
[156] *BIDS* (High Court), n. 135 para. 98; references omitted.

Not only were these arrangements not restrictive by object, McKechnie J also found that the Competition Authority had failed to demonstrate that they were unlikely to produce appreciable anticompetitive effects.[157]

Strictly speaking, this conclusion should end the legal analysis. However, McKechnie J also considered the Article 81(3) justification for the programme. McKechnie J found that the arrangements would provide some economic gains, which were 'not scientifically quantified'.[158] Article 81(3)'s first condition was thus met. The lack of precise quantification precluded the second condition from being satisfied. As that condition mandates that consumers receive a fair share of that benefit, without quantification, it is impossible to know whether the balance of consumer gain and loss is 'fair'.[159] Thus, BIDS did not provide the evidence to establish that this condition had been met.

Given the market failure which resulted in the crisis, McKechnie J held that incumbent operators would remain in business, albeit in survival mode, rather than exiting the industry as a result of market forces. He described the true test of the indispensability and its relationship to market failure thus:

> On the issue of market failure, which is relevant to the indispensability require-ment, the true test is not whether normal attrition will ever achieve a rationalisation of the industry; if that was correct then the Commission could never have given its decisions in the *Dutch Bricks* case and in the *Synthetic Fibres* case. Rather it is whether a normal market can correct this excess in a timely manner. There is no evidence whatsoever that it can do so.[160]

Hence the restrictions are indispensable, satisfying the third criterion.[161] As the restrictions would not eliminate all overcapacity, since remaining overcapacity will ensure that there is residual competition (and the market will be sufficiently fragmented, so that tacit collusion will not occur), the final criterion was met. The Competition Authority's application was thus dismissed.

McKechnie J's judgment was appealed to the Supreme Court, which made a reference to the ECJ for a preliminary ruling. At issue was whether agreements possessing features of the BIDS arrangements are anticompetitive by object alone, or whether it is also necessary to demonstrate the anticompetitive effects of the agreements.[162]

The ECJ held that the BIDS arrangements had as their object the restriction of competition. The Court held that there were two purposes to the arrangements: to increase the concentration in the beef processing sector, by reducing the number of

---

[157] Ibid. paras. 99–117.
[158] Ibid. para. 127.
[159] Ibid. para. 131.
[160] Ibid. para. 83; McKechnie J discusses (albeit descriptively) *Synthetic Fibres* and *Dutch Bricks* in paras. 38–40 and 41–46 of the judgment (respectively).
[161] Ibid. para. 132–134.
[162] *BIDS* (ECJ), n. 135 para. 14.

undertakings in that sector; and to reduce overcapacity by about 75 per cent.[163] The agreement would change the structure of the market,[164] by implementing a common policy which interferes with undertakings' ability to compete. This, the Court held:

> [C]onflicts patently with the concept inherent in the EC Treaty provisions relating to competition, according to which each economic operator must determine independently the policy which it intends to adopt on the common market. Article 81(1) EC is intended to prohibit any form of coordination which deliberately substitutes practical cooperation between undertakings for the risks of competition.[165]

In addition to this overall anticompetitive common policy, the Court was of the view that certain measures contained in the agreement also restricted competition by their object.

In particular, the €11/head levy on overpercentage slaughter would act as a deterrent to the market development, as it would dissuade stayers from exceeding their traditional volume;[166] and the agreement's restrictions on disposal of disused processing plants would act as a barrier to market entry.[167] That such restrictions were time-limited is irrelevant for 81(1) analysis, i.e. whether they are restrictive by object or effect. Rather, they may be relevant to 81(3) analysis.[168]

In this regard, the Court followed the opinion of the advocate-general. However, the advocate-general went slightly further, and made it explicit that in sectorial crises (whether cyclical or structural) or whether the parties intended to pursue a legitimate objective will not entail that the arrangement falls outside of 81(1).[169] Further, in her view, reduction of total capacity is a restriction of competition by object.[170] Although the Court did not explicitly follow her on these points, it would a reasonable interpretation of the judgment to accept that agreed reductions of capacity (irrespective of the economic circumstances motivating the agreement) are by object restrictions under 81(1).[171]

Hence the compatibility of this crisis cartel with EU competition law relied on a 101(3) justification. The Irish Supreme Court referred the case to the High Court to consider the 101(3) issue *de novo*, and in light of the ECJ's judgment.[172]

---

[163] Ibid. para. 32.
[164] Ibid. para. 31.
[165] Ibid. para. 34.
[166] Ibid. para. 37.
[167] Ibid. para. 38.
[168] Ibid. para. 39.
[169] *BIDS*, AG's Opinion, n. 135, paras. 98–99.
[170] Ibid. paras. 105–108.
[171] They interfere with the goal of offering the product to consumers at the lowest possible price (Opinion, para. 106); or, following the Court, they interfere with independent determination of commercial policy.
[172] *BIDS* (Supreme Court), n. 135.

The High Court heard these arguments in 2010. It did not issue a ruling, as in January 2011 BIDS withdrew its action against the Competition Authority. At the hearing stage, the Commission used its right to submit *amicus curiae* observations to a national court.[173] This submission reflects the Commission's post-MEA thinking on crisis cartels, and would additionally serve as the basis of a 2011 submission to the OECD on crisis cartels.[174] The tenor of the *amicus* submission was shaped by the 2004 Guidelines on 81(3), whose wording is repeated (often verbatim) in the submission.

The underlying axiom behind the Commission's approach to crisis cartels is explained in paragraph 33 of the *amicus* submission. There it remarks:

> The Commission wishes to emphasise that so-called '*crisis cartels*' which aim to reduce industry capacity cannot be justified by economic downturns and recession-induced falls in demand. As a general rule in a free market economy, market forces should remove unnecessary capacity from the market. Prices should amortise the changing relationship between supply and demand. Indeed, when demand falls, it is only natural that price should follow. In such circumstances, it is for each undertaking to decide for itself whether, and at which point, overcapacity becomes economically unsustainable and to take the necessary steps to reduce it.

In its submission, the Commission addressed three of 101(3)'s four points. It did not address this issue of elimination of competition; and we only need to consider one of the points – crisis cartels.

The Commission noted that crisis cartels could improve production or distribution in two ways: by the elimination of the least efficient producers;[175] and by allowing the most efficient to increasing their utilisation (by capturing shares of the inefficient and passing on these savings to consumers).[176] Rather, the Commission's concern with crisis cartels centres on its preference that market forces, rather than industry agreement, determines the outcome. Quoting paragraph 75 of its Guidelines on 83(3), the Commission notes that crisis cartel agreements are indispensable only when there are 'no other economically practicable and less restrictive means of achieving the efficiencies'.[177] Nevertheless, the Commission also recognises that in some instances, market forces will not solve the problem in a reasonable time.[178]

After the case concluded, the Irish Competition Authority published its Guidance on agreements to reduce capacity,[179] which provides that Authority's interpretation

---

[173] Under Article 15(3) of Regulation 1/2003.
[174] Contribution of the European Union, OECD, *Policy Roundtable: Crisis Cartels* at 109–120.
[175] Amicus Submission, paras. 20–21, available at: https://ec.europa.eu/competition/court/amicus_curiae_2010_bids_en.pdf, paras. 20–21.
[176] Ibid. paras. 24–25.
[177] Ibid. para. 30 and Contribution, n. 174, quoting Guidelines on 81(3), n. 35 para. 75.
[178] Amicus Submission, ibid. paras. 35–38.
[179] Competition Authority (Ireland), Notice on Agreements to Reduce Capacity (N/11/001 16 June 2011).

of the litigation's outcome. In it the Authority suggests that the *Synthetic Fibres* and *Dutch Brick* decisions are no longer good law, in the sense that they 'should no longer be regarded as indicative or representative of the Commission's current approach to the application of Article 101(3) to agreements to reduce capacity'.[180] The Competition Authority gives five reasons for this.[181] (1) The decisions contain little discussion. (2) They rely on a now abandoned distinction between cyclical and structural overcapacity, which suggests that in situations of structural overcapacity national courts should be more generous in their assessment. (3) The decisions do not use the MEA approach. (4) The Guidelines do not cite either decision. And (5) the Decisions contain 'inaccurate statements of the law on Article 101(3)'.[182]

This latter point is somewhat disingenuous, as 'the law' cited by the Authority consists merely of the Commission Guidelines on 81(3). It is one thing to state that the decisions no longer reflect current thinking; it is another to imply that they have been overruled by the CJEU. Nevertheless, the Competition Authority is correct in maintaining that the Commission has changed its thinking towards crisis cartels. There is no doubt that the MEA played a role here, particularly in the preference for market-driven solutions to overcapacity.

In concluding our discussion of *BIDS*, we make three points. First, to a large degree, the cause of the overcapacity was a result of the distortive effects of subsidies. Subsidies created an artificial floor for beef prices, underwrote the cost of expansion of processing plants and smoothed out the demand for capacity during the year. In such circumstances, it is hardly a surprise that the industry acquired too much capacity.

Second, the Commission's approach in this case is a repudiation of *its* light-touch analysis found in *Synthetic Fibres* and *Dutch Brick*. The new approach is clearly a result of the MEA and that approach's use as a methodology in shaping the Guidelines on 81(3). Commission Guidelines are not binding on national courts or NCAs – although there is an obligation (on all parties) to ensure a consistent application of EU law.[183] It is, however, the job of the ECJ to ensure this consistency. At this point, there is no comprehensive, authoritative statement from the Court regarding how 101(3)'s conditions are to be interpreted, particularly in regard to either non-economic considerations or as applied to crisis cartels. While the Commission left open the possibility of a further reference to the ECJ in *BIDS* (presumably on the interpretation of 181(3)),[184] due to the resolution of the matter, no such reference was could be made.

---

[180] Ibid. para. 6.11.
[181] Ibid. paras. 6.12–6.16.
[182] Ibid. para. 6.16.
[183] On the difficulties associated with ensuring a consistent interpretation of 101(3), see Brook, 'Struggling with Article 101(3) TFEU'.
[184] Amicus Submission, n. 175 para. 48.

Finally, *BIDS* does not rule out the use of crisis cartels. The Commission's *amicus* submission recognises that there may be situations where the market forces will not remedy structural overcapacity within a reasonable period. But the submission implies that such cartels are a last resort – after other, more 'economically practicable and less restrictive means of achieving the efficiencies'[185] are available. The ECJ's judgment holds that such cartels are 'restrictions by object'. As such, they must satisfy the four conditions of Article 101(3), with the burden of proof falling on the relevant undertaking(s). While not an impossible burden, it is a difficult hill to climb, and rightly so – given the practice of 'crisis-washing'.

3.4.2 *The UK Dairy Case*

UK Dairy[186] involved a purported crisis resulting from overcapacity resulting in low revenues for British dairy farmers. The products in question were fresh liquid milk (FLM) and other dairy products (cheese, milk powder, butter, yoghurt and condensed/UHT milk). In 2002–2003 (the relevant period for this cartel), approximately half of all British raw milk was used to produce FLM, a quarter was used in cheese production and 12.5 per cent for milk powder, with the remainder used for other dairy products.[187] During the 1980s, customers switched away from the doorstop delivery of milk (which in 1980 accounted for 90 per cent of household milk sales) to buying milk from the four major grocery multiples (Tesco, Asda (Walmart), Sainsbury's and Morrisons). By 2002 the four accounted for 80 per cent of UK household milk purchases, and 65 per cent of UK liquid milk purchases.[188]

However, contemporaneous with this switch to milk distribution via the multiples, demand for milk dropped, productivity of dairy herds increased and the industry was liberalised. Since the 1950s, demand for milk had been decreasing at a rate of 1 to 2 per cent per year,[189] and yields increased.[190] The industry's liquid milk output was approximately double the amount of domestic consumption.[191]

The key mechanism for market management was intervention purchases under the CAP. When prices fell below certain, pre-set levels, the EU bought butter and skimmed milk powder at the floor prices, so farm gate prices (i.e. the price paid to

---

[185] See n. 177.

[186] *UK Dairy Industry Price Initiative (Dairy) UK Dairy and Tesco v. OFT*, n. 5.

[187] See Competition Commission, Arla Foods amba and Express Dairies plc A Report on the Proposed Merger, para. 3.13; *UK Dairy*, ibid. para. 4.12.

[188] *UK Dairy*, ibid. paras. 4.15–4.16; see Arla/Express, ibid. figure 3.7 illustrating the trend away from doorstop sales; see also House of Commons Environment, Food and Rural Affairs Committee, Milk Pricing in the United Kingdom, paras. 16–27.

[189] Arla/Express, ibid. para. 3.44.

[190] House of Commons Environment, Food and Rural Affairs Committee, Milk Pricing in the United Kingdom, n. 188 para. 16.

[191] See ibid. para. 4.6.

the farmer for the milk) were driven (if not determined by) by the intervention price.[192]

Consumers' switch to grocery chains for milk influenced the supply chain. The multiples require a constant supply of milk (daily delivery to stores) and assurance of quality (milk is typically sold as 'own label', with corresponding reputational risks for a poor-quality product). This entailed that only a few (four) milk processors could supply the chains, and prospects for other processors entering the market to supply the multiples were poor.[193]

Because of the homogeneity of the product, overcapacity in the industry and the transparency of the farm gate price, the multiples had significant buying power.[194] Further, demand for FLM (and other dairy products) is inelastic.[195] Consequently, retailer margins on milk and dairy have increased since 1994.[196] Nevertheless, the dairy market was highly competitive: no retailer wanted its prices to be higher than the others'.[197] Hence, raising prices to pass on the additional revenue to farmers would have would have a first-mover disadvantage: none of the multiples wished to be the first to raise prices and be seen as non-competitive with regard to milk or cheese.

In spite of the increase in the chain's margins, little revenue trickled up the chain towards the farmers.[198] The farmers were in effect being squeezed, and further reforms to the CAP were threatening to exacerbate this squeeze.

These reforms would decouple support from production to encourage the dairy industry to produce 'for the market' (i.e. not overproduce due to subsidy). This decoupling depressed farm gate prices, by eliminating the linkage with the intervention price. The multiples would opportunistically use this to their advantage and further depress farmers' revenue.[199]

By 2002, the farmers believed that effective lobbying (of both the multiples and Parliament) and protests would be effective means of raising the farm gate price.[200] The protests proved popular with the public and were noticed by politicians.[201]

As part of their campaign, one pressure group, the Farmers For Action, sought to obtain letters from the multiples which would commit them to raise the retail price of milk, with the resulting increase passed on to farmers, on the condition that the other multiples would follow suit. These letters would in turn be disclosed to the

---

[192] Ibid. para. 4.11.
[193] Arla/Express, n. 187 paras. 3.24, 5.17–5.22.
[194] *UK Dairy*, n. 5 para. 4.28.
[195] Ibid. paras. 4.57–4.60.
[196] Ibid. paras. 4.63–4.65 and 5.3.
[197] Ibid. paras. 4.50–4.54.
[198] See House of Commons Environment, Food and Rural Affairs Committee, Milk Pricing in the United Kingdom, n. 188, para. 24.
[199] Arla/Express Report, n. 187 paras. 3.88–3.91.
[200] *UK Dairy*, n. 5 paras. 5.4–5.5.
[201] See e.g. 'Dairy Farmers Rally in London' and 'Milk Protests Continue across Wales'.

other retailers in an attempt to gain their commitment.[202] There appeared to be some initial, albeit uneasy willingness among the multiples to proceed with the plan, until one retailer informed the Office of Fair Trading (OFT) about these discussions. The OFT in turn wrote to the multiples to inform them that this plan was likely a breach the UK's domestic analogue to Article 101.[203] As a result of this correspondence, the plan was abandoned, at least with respect to FLM in 2002.[204]

However, the industry implemented other initiatives: in 2002 and 2003 regarding cheese and in 2003 regarding FLM. The goal was to pass back to the farmers 2 pence per litre (ppl) for milk and £200/metric ton of cheese (i.e. approximately 2 ppl for the milk used in the cheese production). These initiatives were popular. On 16 October 2002, Parliament passed an early-day motion in support. The motion originally read:

> That this House welcomes the decision taken by ASDA and Tesco to give an extra two pence per litre direct to dairy farmers for their milk; acknowledges the help and support given by these two supermarket chains; and looks forward to the same initiative to be taken by other supermarket chains to help dairy farmers through these difficult times and help to ensure British dairy farming has a sustainable future.

It was amended as follows:

> [A]fter 'milk', leave out to end and add, 'regrets that this increase has not yet reached the farm gate; believes that only when this happens can the action be judged a success; acknowledges the need to review the huge influence of the supermarkets over commodity prices; calls on the Government to do this; and looks forward to action by all supermarkets to support UK farming'.[205]

This was not all that was done in Parliament.

In November 2003, the Common's Environment, Food and Rural Affairs Committee appointed a subcommittee to conduct an inquiry into whether (and to what extent) increases into retail prices of FLM and cheese had been passed back to farmers. The increases, of course, were a result of the 2003 initiatives. It concluded:

> We accept Defra's [Department for Environment, Food and Rural Affairs] evidence that, although retail prices for liquid milk rose by 2 ppl between October 2002 and October 2003, the average farmgate price in fact rose by 1.46 ppl, as against the 0.6 ppl that might be expected. We therefore conclude that the July and September 2003 retail price increases were transmitted to farmers.[206]

---

[202] *UK Dairy*, n. 5 para. 5.5.

[203] Ibid. paras. 5.6–5.12.

[204] Ibid. para. 5.12.

[205] Early Day Motion 1764 of 2001–02, tabled 16 October 2002.

[206] House of Commons Environment, Food and Rural Affairs Committee, Milk Pricing in the United Kingdom, n. 188 para. 40.

However, the opacity and delays in the transmittal of revenue led to suspicion that this was not occurring. The OFT concluded that the purpose of the 2002 cheese and 2003 FLM initiatives was to aid the farmers; but the 2003 cheese initiative's purpose was to 'stabilise' the margins of McLelland – a cheese producer.[207]

These initiatives were implemented by hub and spoke (or 'A-B-C') cartels, with the multiples using the processors/dairies to coordinate the strategy.[208] This was, of course, contrary to the UK Competition Act's analogue to 101. The participants were fined. It is also surprising that the illegality of the scheme went unnoticed in, and was encouraged by, Parliament.

It is true that the farm gate price of milk was depressed, and there was sympathy among the British public and political class to see an increase in revenue for these producers, so it could be said that there was a crisis in the industry. The response was not to address the structural causes of the crisis and reduce capacity. Rather, it was to seek a means to increase prices. This appropriation of consumer surplus, although popular, was done without any of the usual quid pro quo offered by crisis cartels, or corresponding benefits which were passed on to consumers. In this regard, the OFT noted that at the relevant time, the parties could have applied for an exemption from the Chapter I prohibition. Yet, no such exemption was sought. There were no improvements in terms of resulting efficiencies in production or distributions, and consumers had to pay more for FLM and cheese.[209]

We make two final points First, subsidies and resulting market distortions were the source the problem (industry overcapacity). Second, and perhaps more significantly, this case offers an illustration of how a well-organised and politically popular interest group can 'crisis-wash' a situation. Here the public and Parliament developed the misperception that this rent-seeking arrangement was benign, if not in the public interest. If anything, the initial increase in milk prices merely delayed the need for structural reform of the industry.[210]

3.4.3 *The Dutch Chicken of Tomorrow Initiative*

The Dutch CoT (in Dutch, 'Kip van Morgen') initiative arose from a February 2013 agreement among Dutch poultry farmers, processors and supermarkets to enhance sustainability and welfare in broiler chicken production.[211] This was not a 'crisis cartel' in the standard sense. It was a buying arraignment among Dutch

---

[207] *UK Dairy*, n. 5 para. 5.14.
[208] See the conclusions, ibid. paras. 5.487 (2002 cheese), 5.638 (2003 cheese) and 5.863 (2003 FLM), though the OFT's findings regarding Tesco's participation in these were set aside in part: see CAT judgment, n. 5, points 485–488.
[209] Ibid. paras. 6.15–6.17.
[210] See Wardhaugh, 'Crisis Cartels' at 338–339.
[211] Autoriteit Consument en Markt, 'Welfare of Today's Chicken and That of the "Chicken of Tomorrow"' at 3.

supermarkets, motivated by the non-economic concerns of enhancing welfare and environmental sustainability in chicken production. This initiative is regarded as a test case for competition law's ability to take into account non-economic values.

The goal of the CoT agreement was to phase out entirely the sale of regularly produced broiler chicken by 2020, in an effort to replace it with meat produced according to the CoT standard. The immediate consequences of this would be that supermarkets would pay more for such chicken, with these costs passed on to consumers.[212]

This initiative was popular with the Dutch public.[213] According to the Dutch Competition Authority (ACM), this minimum standard would be achieved by:

- 'The introduction of a new, slower growing chicken breed for the basic chicken meat varieties. ... A slower growing chicken is able to move more, and needs less antibiotics.'
- 'Fewer chickens per square meter in broiler chicken barns.'
- More straw and more distractions for the chicken barns, as straw reduces foot pad lesions.
- 'Strict enforcement of compliance with legal animal welfare standards, thereby keeping the number of injuries to the foot pads and breasts to a minimum.'
- Chickens provided with six consecutive hours of darkness to allow natural circadian rhythm.
- Antibiotics used only as treatment, not for prophylaxis.
- Exclusive use of soy feed.
- Incorporating environmental measures, e.g. reduction of ammonia and particulate emissions, manure processing, reducing the CO_2 footprint, and use of sustainable energy, into the process.[214]

Pricing was not part of the standard.

This was a buying arrangement for Dutch supermarkets. It would not have affected meat sold to (and by) butchers, poulterers and market traders, or for export. The latter accounts for 70 per cent of Dutch chicken production.[215] Nevertheless, in the Netherlands, supermarkets sell 95 per cent of chicken meat for household consumption.[216]

---

[212] Bos et al., 'Animal Welfare, Consumer Welfare, and Competition Law: The Dutch Debate on the Chicken of Tomorrow', n. 6 at 20.
[213] See e.g. Gerbrandy, 'Solving a Sustainability-Deficit in European Competition Law' at 540; Schinkel and Toth, 'Compensatory Public Good Provision by a Private Cartel' at 6; Lianos, 'Polycentric Competition Law'; Holmes, 'Climate Change, Sustainability, and Competition Law'.
[214] Sustainability Arrangements, n. 6 at 2–3; see also Bos et al., n. 6 at 20.
[215] ACM, ibid. at 4.
[216] Ibid.

The ACM was asked to provide an informal opinion (similar to a comfort letter[217]) regarding this initiative. The Authority opined that the arrangement would deny customers the freedom of choice regarding their chicken purchases and would 'have a considerable effect (real or potential) on the consumer market for chicken meat'.[218] Further, given that supermarkets would sell only chicken which was raised according to the CoT standard, this would preclude the sale of chicken imported from neighbouring Member States.[219]

The measures violated both the national analogue of 101(1) and Article 101(1).[220] As such, the compatibility of the initiative with Dutch and European competition law rested with whether or not they could be exempted under Article 101(3) TFEU (and its domestic analogue). The ACM's analysis found that the proposed CoT standard would not satisfy any of the 101(3) criteria.

The starting point of the ACM's analysis of Article 101(3)'s first criterion (improvement in productive or distributive efficiencies) is that any such efficiencies are efficiencies only to the extent that customers are willing to pay for them. Accordingly, the Authority collected data to determine consumers' willingness to pay for the animal welfare, environmental and public health benefits which would accrue from the arrangement.[221] The results of the ACM's study showed that:

> [C]onsumers are only willing to pay a small amount for the animal welfare measures as agreed upon in the 'Chicken of Tomorrow' arrangements, which is 68 eurocent per kilo of chicken filet. In addition, it turns out that the environmental effects have a positive effect, which is 14 eurocent per kilo of chicken filet. Finally, public health has no positive effect, which is 0 eurocent per kilo of chicken filet. The latter is because the objective of reduced use of antibiotics will already be achieved irrespective of the sustainability arrangements concerning the 'Chicken of Tomorrow'. Therefore, the total benefits of the 'Chicken of Tomorrow' are: 82 eurocent per kilo of chicken filet. On the other hand, there are costs, which are the additional costs that consumers are charged for chicken in the supermarkets. These costs are estimated at EUR 1.46 euro per kilo of chicken filet.[222]

As the costs of the initiative to the consumer exceed its benefits, it could not be said to improve the production or distribution of a good. In light of this cost–benefit balance, the initiative also failed the second criterion (consumers obtaining a fair share).

[217] Gerbrandy, n. 213 at 541 fn 6; see also ACM, 'ACM Procedure Regarding Informal Opinions'.
[218] ACM, Sustainability Arrangements, n. 6 at 4.
[219] Ibid.
[220] Mededingingswet (22 May 1997) Article 6(1) and ACM, Sustainability Arrangements, n. 6 at 4.
[221] Mulder et al., 'Economische effecten van "Kip van Morgen" Kosten en baten voor consumenten van een collectieve afspraak in de pluimveehouderij'.
[222] ACM, Sustainability Arrangements, n. 6 at 6, the Conclusion of the Economic Study, ibid. at 26 provides more detail. See also Mulder and Zomer, 'Dutch Consumers' Willingness to Pay'.

The ACM also had concerns about the necessity and proportionality of the programme. It was clear that consumers were willing to pay (to some extent) for chicken which had been produced in accord with sustainability and welfare considerations. However, supermarkets had been selling meat produced in this manner for several years. There was no 'first-mover disadvantage' in doing so. Indeed, supermarkets were using sustainability and welfare concerns as a marketing advantage – setting their products apart from their competitors'. These considerations indicate the need for a more robust proportionality of the arrangements, which had not been provided to the ACM.[223] Finally, the CoT arrangements covered approximately 95 per cent of the market for household chicken consumption. The initiative would leave only a small amount of residual competition for less expensive (non-CoT) chicken, but would permit greater competition among chicken produced in accord with sustainability/animal welfare concerns. As a result, the ACM had reservations about the initiative's computability with the fourth criterion of Article 101(3).[224]

As the ACM noted, its findings were subject to criticism and discussions from all corners, domestically and internationally.[225] There were two consequences arising from this decision. The first and broader issue was the consequences such analysis might have for sustainability concerns. The decision is often cited as evidence of a sustainability deficit in competition law. Though there may be an element of truth to this, the ACM subsequently published guidance on the relationship between competition law and sustainability matters.[226] In addition, the Dutch government has directed the ACM to take long-term benefits into account in its assessment of the application of Article 6(3) (the 101(3) analogue) of the Dutch Competition Act.[227]

The second consequence of this 'negative decision' was that it forced the supermarkets and producers to work, without colluding or otherwise restricting competition, to improve the chicken welfare standards of their product. In May 2014, the largest Dutch supermarket chain, Albert Heijn, became the first chain to introduce higher-welfare chicken. Jumbo (the second largest) followed suit in October 2014.[228] In August 2020, the ACM published a stock-taking exercise to assess the extent to which sustainability and welfare goals had been achieved in the absence of the CoT initiative.

The results of the study showed:

> [T]he welfare conditions of the current selection of chicken meat sold in Dutch supermarkets more than exceeds the minimum requirements of the Chicken of

---

[223] ACM, Sustainability Arrangements, n. 6 at 7.
[224] Ibid. at 8.
[225] ACM, n. 211 at 3.
[226] ACM, Vision Document on Competition and Sustainability; and ACM, Draft Guidelines 'Sustainability Agreements'.
[227] Netherlands, Decision of the Minister of Economic Affairs of 6 May 2014, No. WJZ/14052830 (Government Gazette, 8 May 2014, 13375).
[228] Swormink, 'Chicken of Tomorrow Is Here Today'.

Tomorrow. Fresh meat from chicken that were raised under conditions that the Chicken of Tomorrow wanted to abolish can almost no longer be found in Dutch supermarkets. Supermarkets offer differentiated levels of animal welfare, based on welfare classifications of their own, and also based on market-wide labels using three different levels. Consumers pay more for higher levels of animal welfare.[229]

There is competition among the main supermarkets (representing over 97 per cent of the market) over chicken welfare standards. Though these vary, all are in excess of those that the CoT programme would have established.[230] In addition to these own-brand standards, supermarkets also sell chicken certified under market-wide labels (the Better Life Label – with three levels, initiated by the Dutch Society for the Protection of Animals – and organic), which also exceed the CoT standard. The participation of organisations focused on animal welfare added trust and made consumers more willing to pay for the more sustainable, higher-welfare product.[231]

The study could not establish whether the present state of the market would have developed sooner (or later) had the ACM cleared the CoT initiative.[232] That initiative could have served as a starting line for a race to greater welfare, or as a position from which no one sought to depart. Nevertheless, the study shows that sustainability and animal welfare programmes can be effectively implemented in a manner that is consistent with the competition regime.

3.5 CONCLUSION

This chapter illustrates how the post-MEA regime has altered competition authorities' responses to industrial crises. The first conclusion we can draw is that the relaxed application of the 101(3) criteria found in, e.g., *Synthetic Fibres* and *Dutch Brick* is no more. Rather, the authorities will insist on the production of robust evidence to defend a practice. This is consistent with the approach mandated by the Commission's Guidelines on 81(3) – one of the first guidance documents published as part of the modernisation programme.

This is significant. Our analysis of *BIDS* has shown that any agreement, particularly in the context of an industrial crisis, which restricts output is a by object restriction of competition. As such, any industry-wide agreement to reduce capacity in an orderly manner (the hallmark of a crisis cartel) can only be justified via the 101 (3) route.

Yet, this requirement may in fact be beneficial. The CoT case showed that upon closer analysis, the popular, industry-wide proposal was unnecessarily restrictive of competition, and its goal could be better implemented through alternative, less

---

[229] ACM, Memo: Welfare of Today's Chicken, n. 211 at 2.
[230] Ibid. at 5–8.
[231] Ibid. at 15.
[232] Ibid. at 3–4.

collusive measures. The grocery chains' reaction after the ACM's negative assessment shows that in the right circumstances, uncoordinated private actions can bring about social goods.

In this regard, the contrasting approaches of the Dutch and Irish competition authorities are worth noting. In the chicken case, the Dutch authorities were in a position to provide an informal opinion to the industry about the legality of the proposed arrangements, and – when they determined that the proposal likely contravened the competition rules – to engage with them and provide suggestions as to how to move forward. Eventually the industry, likely heeding these suggestions, developed a solution.

In *BIDS*, there was no such engagement, despite the old (notification) regime not expiring. This was a cause for comment by McKechnie J in the High Court. One can only speculate as to what the eventual outcome may have been, had the Authority engaged. Indeed, to go forward, this difference between the two cases demonstrates the need for competition authorities to engage with stakeholders in times like this.

The *UK Dairy* case is another nice example. It is illustrative of dressing up an overcapacity problem as a crisis, and then – with popular support – using the 'crisis', not to reduce capacity, but to extract consumer surplus. The OFT saw through this 'crisis-washing' and treated the arrangement as it should: as an illegal cartel.

The influence of the MEA on the state aid regime is also clear – the Commission's goal is to ensure that such measures are better used, i.e. more effective. But, in supporting firms that need rescue and/or restructuring, there has been a divide between what the Commission desires and what the Member States have done. Aid, in these cases, seems to have been distributed too generously, supporting firms in a manner which appears to transfer tax revenues to owners of capital, rather than to (ex-)employees and other stakeholders in the community, who are viewed as the appropriate recipients of such aid.

Yet this is not to say that all forms of assistance to such firms is suspect. Chapter 4 considers the financial crisis of 2008. Here a significant amount of state aid was provided to financial (and other) firms in trouble. In approving this support, the Commission showed flexibility, and may well have mitigated an even larger economic crisis.

4

The Financial Crisis of 2008

4.1 INTRODUCTION

While 24 October 1929 – the day that the Dow Jones lost 11 per cent – might serve as a convenient (but inaccurate) point to mark the beginning of the Great Depression, there is no similar date which could serve as a starting point for the financial crisis of 2008. Searching for a definitive date would be futile, as the crisis was an evolving problem, marked by three stages.[1] Stage one consists of the regime which permitted the crisis to occur: this is the shift towards the securitisation model of mortgage financing and the corresponding easing of credit standards. This ended some time during the late summer of 2007. Stage two, from (approximately) August 2007 to September 2008, was a period in which individual institutions found themselves facing problems with liquidity and with the resulting access to financing. At this point, the view was that the problems were isolated and confined to particularly exposed institutions, i.e. there was no systematic threat or risk. The final stage began in mid-September 2008 (here the bankruptcy of Lehman Brothers could be used as an appropriate starting point), when both the scope of the crisis and the threat it posed to the financial system became apparent.

The consequences of the 2008 financial crisis were profound, both for the financial industry and for those operating in the real economy. In the USA and the UK this crisis led to the deepest recessions since the end of World War II. Unemployment rose to levels almost unseen since the 1930s. By 3 October 2008, American authorities had underwritten a $700 billion bank rescue and some months later a $787 billion fiscal stimulus package.[2] In the three-year period from 1 October

---

[1] We have based this staged view of the crisis's development on Pisani-Ferry and Sapir, 'Banking Crisis Management in the EU'; a timeline of significant events beginning March 2007 can be found in the Appendix to Bank of England, *Financial Stability Report: June 2009*.

[2] Emergency Economic Stabilization Act of 2008 (Public Law 110–343) and American Recovery and Reinvestment Act of 2009 (Public Law 111–115), respectively.

2008, the European Commission approved state aid of €4.5 trillion to the financial sector (representing 36.7 per cent of the EU's GDP).[3] In addition to such state aid packages, governments, at times, relaxed the strictness of merger control to permit transactions that pre-2008 would be regarded as unthinkable, due to their concentrative effect on the market.

This chapter considers the response of European authorities (both EU and Member State) to this crisis. To do so in an appropriate manner, we briefly consider the origins of the crisis. We suggest that governmental responses to mitigate the consequences of the programme, via aid packages, were the appropriate responses to mitigate the effects of this failure. However, a more lenient approach to merger control in the financial sector, which was seen in some Member States, was an inappropriate response. This led to significant decline in competition in the market for financial services, with the result of the loss of consumer welfare. We will not consider the efficacy of the post-crisis regulatory reforms implemented to prevent similar crises from occurring, as this is beyond this work's mandate.

This chapter contains four further substantive sections. In Section 4.2 we consider the background to the financial crisis, particularly in how banks and other financial institutions shifted in the way in which mortgages were sold (and their risks distributed) throughout the financial system. This led to uncertainty about the extent of exposure to these assets. This reassessment of risk caused a freeze in the financial market, culminating in the 2008 crisis.

Section 4.3 considers the events of 2007. We use the failure of the UK's Northern Rock as an illustration, as it was typical of the problems faced by small banks in the EU. The problems which these institutions faced were not just harbingers of things to come, but also provided small-scale lessons for the authorities (both competition and financial) in how to deal with crises of these sorts.

This provides a springboard for Section 4.4, which considers the events of autumn 2008. After briefly outlining the events of the crisis, in Section 4.4.1 we consider the state aid and forced merger regimes which were put in place not only to reintroduce stability into the financial system, but also to aid the recovery of the real economy. Our conclusion about the state aid response is generally favourable: the competition authorities acted with flexibility and sufficient speed to mitigate the worst of the crisis.

This contrasts with the results of our discussion in Section 4.4.2 regarding merger policy in the financial crisis. In two Member States, the UK and the Netherlands, the competition authorities approved mergers which further concentrated an already concentrated market. Indeed, in the UK, this was a political decision, requiring statutory amendment to do so. The net result in both cases was an increase in harm to consumers of banking products.

---

[3]   See European Commission, 'Tackling the Financial Crisis'.

This allows us to use Section 4.5 to evaluate these responses. The lesson which we draw from this is that the merger rules are in place to ensure that some form of market failure will not arise as a result of a concentration. The financial crisis arose from market failure which was aggravated by significant, systematic moral hazard in the business model incorporated into the financial sector. The crisis manifested itself as an undersupply of liquidity in the financial markets and a sudden loss of capital by financial institutions. In the real economy, the crisis manifested itself in a sharp reduction in credit and lending. Some of consequences of this market failure were mitigated via well-designed state aid programmes. However, some regulators attempted to use merger as a means to resolve the crisis. This, we suggest, added further market failure to the situation, and did more harm than good.

4.2 THE BACKGROUND TO THE FINANCIAL CRISIS

The conventional folklore describing the background to the financial crisis is a story of a change in mortgage origination and distribution practices, with a corresponding expansion of credit fuelling a housing bubble that ultimately burst, resulting in the crisis of 2008. Although any such story risks an element of oversimplification, there is a significant element of truth to this lore.

The structural and regulatory conditions in the first part of the twenty-first century set the foundation for the financial innovations that fuelled the American sub-prime crisis of 2007. These would culminate in the crisis of 2008. The global microeconomic conditions were of low interest rates and high liquidity (*inter alia*, resulting from China building up significant foreign currency reserves and pursuing a monetary policy to maintain low exchange rates). As a result, this was a period in which credit was readily available.[4]

Deregulation of the American securities market added a contributing factor to the crisis. In 2004, the US Securities Exchange Commission (SEC) relaxed its rule regarding the debt–equity ratio applied to broker-dealers (including investment banks).[5] The traditional rule[6] permitted a maximum indebtedness to capital ratio of 15 to 1. The new rule[7] allowed for the 'use [of] mathematical models to calculate net capital requirements for market and derivatives-related credit risk'.[8]

---

[4] Barrell and Davis, 'The Evolution of the Financial Crisis of 2007–8' and Goodhart, 'The Background to the 2007 Financial Crisis' at 332–334.
[5] See Labaton, 'Agency's '04 Rule Let Banks Pile up New Debt'.
[6] 17 CFR § 240.15c3–1 (a)(1)(i).
[7] See Securities and Exchange Commission, 'Final Rule: Alternative Net Capital Requirements for Broker-Dealers that Are Part of Consolidated Supervised Entities' 17 CFR Parts 200 and 240 [Release No. 34-49830; File No. S7–21–03] RIN 3235-AI96.
[8] Ibid.

The largest investment banks (Merrill Lynch, Goldman Sachs, Morgan Stanley, Lehman Brothers and Bear Stearns) chose to be governed under the new rule as Consolidated Supervised Entities (CSEs).[9] By autumn 2008, none of these institutions were operating as investments banks in their original form.[10] But while deregulation may have been part of the problem, it was unlikely to be the sole cause.

A transformation of the manner in which mortgages were sold and held was also a contribution to the crisis. Prior to 2003,[11] financial institutions would originate mortgage lending using customers' deposits (and small amounts of short-term borrowing) to fund mortgages. Mortgages would be held as assets on the other side of the banks' balance sheets. This model would be backed by deposit insurance and liquidity assistance through lenders of last resort. This model is iconically captured in the movie *It's a Wonderful Life*, when the banker (played by James Stewart) in part averts a bank run by explaining that clients' deposits are not held in the safe, rather are used to fund mortgages held by others in the depositor's community.

Starting in 2003, financial institutions developed an 'originate to distribute' model.[12] Mortgages would now be converted (or 'wrapped up') into securities. The underlying mortgages served as collateral. These securities would then be sold on. Banks would rely upon credit-rating agencies to evaluate the pool of assets on which the security was based, and this rating would – at least initially – be a determinate of the value and liquidity of the security. As a result, moral hazard and informational asymmetries would creep into the system.

Selling-on mortgages allowed banks to obtain origination fees from the sale; and banks now did not need deposits to cover the mortgages.[13] Once the mortgages were sold, originating banks had no incentive to monitor these loans. In turn, those who bought these securities could use them in the leveraging process as collateral to obtain further funding to support other market activities.[14] For instance, when the investment bank Bear Stearns collapsed in March 2008 it had an indebtedness–capital ratio (leverage) of approximately 33:1;[15] nevertheless, it was compliant with the capital and liquidity rules of the 2004 CSE Program.[16] This raised concerns about the adequacy of the CSE Program's requirements, as the SEC later admitted.[17]

---

[9]   Coffee, 'What Went Wrong?' at 10–11.

[10] Ibid. at 10.

[11] Levitin and Wachter, 'Explaining the Housing Bubble' at 1181–1184.

[12] See e.g. Goodhart, n. 4 at 334–337 for more details.

[13] Barrell and Davis, n. 4 at 6.

[14] See Shin, 'Reflections on Northern Rock' at 111.

[15] United States Securities and Exchange Commission Office of the Inspector General (Office of Audits), SEC's *Oversight of Bear Stearns and Related Entities: The Consolidated Supervised Entity Program* at 19.

[16] Ibid. at 10.

[17] Ibid. at 13.

The limiting principle to leveraging (borrowing to buy and/or lend) model of financing is the 'haircut' administered to the security, i.e. the difference between the market price and the sale price of that security.[18] As Shin remarks:

> For example, if the haircut is 2 percent, the borrower can borrow $98 for every $100 worth of securities. ... The arithmetic of the borrowing multiplier is that if the haircut is 2 percent, then the maximum permissible leverage – ratio of assets to equity – is 50 (the reciprocal of the haircut ratio). In other words, to hold $100 worth of securities, the borrower must come up with $2 of equity.[19]

Haircuts vary with the security's underlying rating and fluctuated with market conditions. Securities were 'marked to market', that is their value depended on what they would be worth if sold on the market. Both market conditions and the haircut it would face would affect the security's utility as collateral. Given the global nature of finance, financial institutions throughout the world were exposed to the risks of ownership and of these securities.

As a result of this new model of financing, lending (primarily for residential mortgages) expanded. This expansion occurred particularly in the USA, Spain and the UK. The lending market expanded to include 'types of borrower (notably sub-prime and buy-to-let borrowers) who had been previously excluded or quantity rationed, especially in the US, and to a lesser extent in the UK'.[20] This, of course, drove up prices for housing,[21] inflating a bubble where a significant part of the bubble rested with riskier borrowers. Others have demonstrated the relationship between this expansion of the availability of credit to those unable to afford it, and their subsequent default.[22]

In addition, the credit-rating agencies must – in part – share the blame for the crisis. The US's Financial Crisis Inquiry Commission concluded that '[t]he three credit rating agencies were key enablers of the financial meltdown. The mortgage-related securities at the heart of the crisis could not have been marketed and sold without their seal of approval.'[23]

The imprimatur of a credit-rating agency was crucial to a security's utility as collateral in the leveraging process, as the rating was determinative of the extent of the haircut that was applied to the security. Accordingly, the credit-rating agencies (of which there were only two – Moody's and Standard & Poor's – until the late 1900s, when Fitch expanded from London to challenge this status quo) acted as 'gatekeepers'[24] in the system. But they failed in this function.

---

[18] Shin, n. 14 at 111.
[19] Ibid. at 111–112 .
[20] Barrell and Davis, 'The Evolution of the Financial Crisis of 2007–8'; see also Coffee, n. 9 at 5.
[21] Barrell and Davis, ibid. at 7.
[22] Mian and Sufi, 'The Consequences of Mortgage Credit Expansion: Evidence from the U.S. Mortgage Default Crisis'.
[23] Financial Crisis Inquiry Commission, *Final Report* at xxv.
[24] See Coffee, n. 9 at 7–10.

There are a number of explanations for this failure. The most significant of these causes was the business model of, and competition among, the ratings agencies. The ratings agencies worked on an 'issuer pays' model of remuneration, entailing that the security's issuer paid for the rating. This was an obvious conflict of interest, which was exacerbated by: (1) the revenue for rating such offerings constituted around 40 per cent of the agencies' earnings; (2) the fees for evaluating each security was itself significant (five times the revenue of a government security of equal value); and (3) as the five investment banks generated this revenue for the agencies, they would have had power over the agencies.[25]

As Coffee notes, the consequence of (3) was that 'the client had at last acquired power over its gatekeeper and could adroitly exploit it to obtain inflated rating'.[26] The entry of Fitch appears to have exacerbated the banks' capture of the ratings agencies, by causing the agencies to recognise their dependence on their custom-ers – the banks – and not investors, thereby inflating ratings.[27] Coffee adds two additional contributing factors to explain the rating agencies' behaviour: the agen-cies had no fear of liability (there had been no successful lawsuits or settlements against an agency), and the agencies – unlike auditors – were 'not required to verify information ... , but rather simply express' their opinion on the facts as given by their client (i.e. the banks).[28]

The above story is necessarily incomplete. For instance, it fails to provide a comprehensive account of securitisation in the market, and it does not give details regarding the various vehicles developed to achieve this. Others have done so.[29] For present purposes it is sufficient to outline the structure of the new financial model in a manner that allows for an understanding of its failure, which the above does.

But the story is also one of endemic moral hazard. Given the profits that could be realised from the securitisation of a pool of mortgages, there were few incentives for the mortgage originators to verify the employment and income status of mortgage applicants. When buying a home with cheap money was less expensive than renting, there was every reason to obtain a mortgage; and, if necessary, to be less than forthright about one's economic circumstances. 'Stated income loans', i.e. loans which relied on the borrower's (unverified) statement of income (aka 'liar loans'), were used as a means of obtaining mortgages by those who otherwise did not qualify (and likely should not have qualified on risk grounds).[30] Pools of these mortgages were 'wrapped up' as securitised packages. These securities were in turn treated

[25] Ibid. at 8–9.
[26] Ibid. at 9.
[27] Ibid. at 9–10.
[28] Ibid. at 7–8.
[29] See e.g. Ashcraft and Schuermann, 'Understanding the Securitization of Subprime Mortgage Credit' and Levitin and Wachter, n. 11.
[30] Black, 'When Liar's Loans Flourish'.

generously by credit-rating agencies, and then used as collateral to leverage additional funds, thereby generating their originators further income streams.

So long as the economic environment remained stable, this system was fairly sustainable. However, both demand- and supply-side shocks destroyed any equilibrium that this market may have had. US interest rates began to rise in July 2004.[31] This would increase mortgage payments for those holding variable (floating) rate mortgages, when their interest rates reset.[32] In turn, this would change the homeowner's rent–buy decision. As Goodhart notes, 'when the value of the mortgage rises above the value of the house there is a clear economic benefit to the mortgager in handing the keys to the house back to the lender'.[33]

Additionally, supply-side factors caused a drop in house prices. During the initial (boom) phase, developers began expanding house building, by acquiring land (or options to purchase) and entering into projects which would involve rezoning and planning approvals and the construction of infrastructure.[34] These would be difficult to reverse. Projects that had been in the pipeline during boom times came on-stream just as demand was dropping. Increased supply further exacerbated a decline in house prices, reducing any equity held by those who borrowed at the margin, further incentivising them to walk away from their homes.

It is therefore no surprise that the 'credit challenged' were more likely to default on their mortgages,[35] or that house prices rose faster, and crashed further, in areas populated by sub-prime borrowers.[36] And although sub-prime mortgage lending was not a new phenomenon, it grew substantially between 2003 and 2005.[37] This correlated with a rise in delinquency rates of sub-prime mortgages.[38] Sub-prime defaults started increasing in February 2007, and the largest American provider of sub-prime mortgages, New Century, filed for bankruptcy on 2 April 2007.[39]

The drop in housing value and increase in mortgage default had immediate consequences for the value of the paper secured by the pooled mortgages. The value would have dropped, but also the amount of the drop would be difficult to measure, particularly on a mark to market basis. Hence the value of the security would be uncertain, and possibly unsaleable (or at least not at above 'fire sale' prices).

This sets off a chain reaction. Krugman writes:

---

[31] Federal Reserve Bank of St. Louis, 'Interest Rates, Discount Rate for United States', available at https://fred.stlouisfed.org/series/INTDSRUSM193N, and Labonte and Makinen, 'Federal Reserve Interest Rate Changes: 2000–2008'.

[32] International Monetary Fund, *Global Financial Stability Report: April 2007* at 4–10.

[33] Goodhart, n. 4 at 338.

[34] Haughwout et al., 'The Supply Side of the Housing Boom and Bust of the 2000s'.

[35] See Mian and Sufi, n. 22 passim.

[36] Pavlov and Wachter, 'Subprime Lending and Real Estate Prices'.

[37] Mayer, Pence and Sherlund, 'The Rise in Mortgage Defaults' at 28.

[38] Ibid.

[39] Scholtes and Beales, 'New Century Files for Chapter 11'; see New Century Financial Corporation, New Release, 'New Century Financial Corporation Files for Chapter 11; Announces Agreement to Sell Servicing Operations' (April 2, 2007).

When liquidity dries up, ... it can produce a chain reaction of defaults. Financial institution A can't sell its mortgage-backed securities, so it can't raise enough cash to make the payment it owes to institution B, which then doesn't have the cash to pay institution C – and those who do have cash sit on it, because they don't trust anyone else to repay a loan, which makes things even worse.[40]

He was speaking in the context of BNP Paribas' announcement on 9 August 2007 that it was suspending redemptions of three funds, on the basis that it was unable to fairly value them.[41] The bank was to 'unfreeze' these funds two weeks later, as it subsequently developed a mechanism to value the funds.[42] However, BNP Paribas' actions were a sign of things to come.

If one of the largest banks in the world was unable to value its own securities, how could other banks value these (and other) securities? And if these securities could not be adequately valued, why should they be accepted as collateral? While the credit-rating agencies may have subsequently downgraded a significant amount of the securities,[43] this would have simultaneously decreased their mark to market value and increased the haircut that would have been applied to them. This fuelled the chain reaction Krugman describes.

The market response was to lower the mark to market value of collateral, increase the haircut applied[44] and to hoard cash (on the basis that the hoarding institution may suddenly need the cash and be otherwise unable to raise it).[45] An increased haircut entails reduced leverage. These responses forced a reduction in lending.

Reduced lending had two consequences. First, as a systematic response, this further decreased liquidity by shrinking the pool of available funds. Second, this shrinking pool of funds reduced the support available to the real economy through lending. It is with this background that the events of 2007 and 2008 should be understood.

4.3 THE FAILURE OF NORTHERN ROCK

On Friday, 14 September 2007, Britain saw something it had not seen since the nineteenth century – a bank run.[46] Customers queued up outside branches of Northern Rock to withdraw their money.[47] The BBC television news had

---

[40] Krugman, 'Very Scary Things'.
[41] BNP Paribas, 'BNP Paribas Investment Partners Temporally Suspends the Calculation of the Net Asset Value of the Following Funds ... '.
[42] BNP Paribas, 'BNP Paribas Investment Partners Resumes Calculation of the Net Asset Values of the Three Funds Temporarily Suspended on 7 August'; see also Burgess, 'BNP Reopens Funds that Sparked Crisis'.
[43] International Monetary Fund, *Global Financial Stability Report: October 2007* at 2.
[44] Shin, n. 14 at 112.
[45] Ibid. at 3–4.
[46] House of Commons, Treasury Committee, *The Run on the Rock* at 8–9.
[47] See e.g. Weale, 'Northern Rock: Expert Views'.

announced at 8.30 the previous evening that Northern Rock had sought liquidity support from the Bank of England. The details of the support were finalised thereafter, and announced at 7.00 am on the 14th. The bank's website crashed and customers were unable to get through on the phone.[48]

At the time, the UK's deposit insurance scheme only covered 100 per cent of a depositor's first £2,000 and 90 per cent of the next £33,000. In the absence of information about the cause of the bank's problems, it would be rational for a depositor to switch banks, particularly if others are seen removing funds. The average retail bank customer would be unaware of the difference between their bank's liquidity and solvency concerns and the implications that this would have for their deposits.

At 4.00 am on Monday, 17 September, depositors began to line up to withdraw funds. Fears of contagion spread to other financial institutions.[49] Although the government was to guarantee all deposits in Northern Rock (and other banks in a similar position) on that day, this did not stop the outflow of funds from Northern Rock. By the time that the guarantee was announced its depositors had withdrawn over £2 billion.[50]

Until it went public in 1997, Northern Rock was a mutually owned building society (created by the merger of two other building societies, both of Victorian origin[51]), located in the north-east of England.[52] Prior to floatation (and until 1999), Northern Rock financed its activities (primarily the origination of residential mortgages) through the traditional 'originate to hold' model of financing, raising funding through deposits, which would be used to lend and these loans would be held to maturity, rather than sold on. It would rely on wholesale funding only to manage the liquidity gap between short-term liabilities of deposits and the longer-term maturity of loans and mortgages.

In 1999, Northern Rock switched its mortgage distribution model to the 'originate to distribute' model. This permitted the bank to grow rapidly.[53] In August 2007, it was the UK's fifth largest mortgage lender. Unlike American banks, which funded their lending with short-term paper (maturing in months, thus requiring rolling over several times a year) and shifted this off their balance sheet,[54] Northern Rock used longer-term paper.[55]

---

[48] House of Commons, Treasury Committee, *The Run on the Rock*, n. 46, para. 1.
[49] Eaglesham et al., 'UK to Guarantee Northern Rock deposits'; Collinson, 'Government Guarantees Northern Rock deposits'.
[50] Eaglesham et al., ibid.
[51] Ibid. 103.
[52] Ibid.
[53] House of Commons, Treasury Committee, *The Run on the Rock*, n. 46 para. 12.
[54] Shin, n. 14 at 106–107.
[55] House of Commons, Treasury Committee, *The Run on the Rock*, n. 46 para. 16.

It was this shift in the funding model which led to Northern Rock's demise, not poor lending. Northern Rock did not lend to sub-prime borrowers.[56] This casts doubt on the commonly held view that Northern Rock was responsible for its own demise by incurring this risk.[57] Rather, Northern Rock's problems stemmed from a liquidity crisis, arising from its funding model and the market conditions in which it found itself in the late summer of 2007.

On 9 August 2007 (the same day that BNP Paribas announced a freeze on some of its funds), 'Northern Rock's traders noted a "dislocation in the market" for its funding. This dislocation was the result of a global shock to the financial system, with the American sub-prime mortgage market as its centre.'[58] This took the bank by surprise. It had assumed that the quality of its assets and its diversification in funding sources would insulate them from such shocks.[59]

But Northern Rock was wrong. From 9 to 16 August, Northern Rock sought alternative (private) sources of funds; and on the 17th, it approached the UK's tripartite authority (the Bank of England (BoE), the Financial Services Authority and the Treasury) for assistance.[60] At that time, the BoE confirmed that liquidity assistance would only be provided if it could not obtain private investment. Beginning on 17 August, Northern Rock attempted to find further sources of liquidity and/or a buyer.[61] Those attempts were abandoned on 10 September;[62] on the 13th it turned to the BoE for emergency assistance.

On 14 September, the BoE granted Northern Rock support in the form of loan facilities against a charge over mortgage loans and a repurchase facility in respect of securities. These were repayable upon demand, and each drawdown required Northern Rock to provide high-quality collateral. The BoE would apply haircuts to the collateral, and the value of the collateral would be adjusted daily. The interest rate on the agreement and facility was (a confidential amount) in excess of the BoE's reference rate.[63]

This set of rescue measures provided a lifeline to Northern Rock. They were allowed to continue operating, subject to restructuring. In its consideration of this support, the European Commission agreed with the UK and held that the measures taken by the BoE on 14 September (the loan agreement and Repo facility) did not

---

[56] Ibid. para. 13.
[57] This explanation is implied by, e.g., 'Timeline: The Northern Rock Crisis'.
[58] House of Commons, Treasury Committee, *The Run on the Rock*, n. 46 para. 23.
[59] Ibid. paras. 24–25; Northern Rock was sufficiently confident in these assumptions that they did not extensively insure itself against this risk, ibid. para. 26. Northern Rock was not alone in this assumption, see House of Commons, Public Accounts Committee, *The Nationalisation of Northern Rock*, para. 16.
[60] Commission, Decision of 5 December 2007 (State aid NN 70/2007 (ex CP 269/07) – United Kingdom) (C(2007) 6127 final) (*Northern Rock Rescue*), para. 5.
[61] House of Commons, Treasury Committee, *The Run on the Rock*, n. 46 para. 27.
[62] Northern Rock Rescue Decision, n. 60 paras. 5–9; and 'Timeline: The Northern Rock Crisis', n. 57.
[63] *Northern Rock Rescue*, ibid. paras. 11–14.

constitute state aid.[64] The support of 17–20 September (the deposit guarantee) and 9 October (additional liquidity provisions) were viewed as state aid, as no market economy investor would have provided such measures.[65] This aid was compatible with R&R aid pursuant to Article 87(3)(c) (now 107(3)(b)) and the 2004 Guidelines and was authorised until 17 March 2008.[66]

Northern Rock's problems arose from the difficulties in renewing its wholesale borrowing (accounting for 25 per cent of its funding). The bank was fishing from the same pond of funding as every other bank. As a result of market-wide conditions, by August 2007 the fishing pond was frozen over. Hence market failure in or of the market for liquidity was the likely proximate cause of Northern Rock's failure, not the sudden withdrawals, i.e. the 'run' on the bank. In this regard, as Shin notes, Northern Rock's problems fell outside the usual explanation of a bank run.[67] Rather than depositors who fear a solvency event of *one* institution and rationally withdraw their funds before others do, Northern Rock's problem was a symptom of a liquidity problem facing *all* institutions.[68]

The rescue of Northern Rock would be followed by its restructuring. The Treasury's objectives in this process, which it announced in October 2007, were threefold: to 'protect the taxpayers' interest; to protect consumers; and to maintain financial stability'.[69] There were four prima facie options: closure (either solvent or insolvent); or maintaining a viable business, either owned by (and hence later sold to) the private sector or the public sector. There were number of unsuccessful proposals,[70] of which the two most appealing were from Northern Rock's own management and from Virgin Group.[71] These latter bids would serve as the counterfactual for the Commission's analysis of the need for and efficacy of the restructuring measures. The Treasury initially[72] took the bank into public ownership, pending a sale to the private sector. While the bank was publicly owned, it was operated on an arm's length basis from the government.[73]

Once the bank had entered post-rescue public ownership, the Treasury prepared a business plan with the aim of turning it into a 'viable private sector entity'.[74] To achieve this goal, the Treasury sought to grow retail deposits, but to reduce assets, new mortgage lending and running costs.[75] On 17 March 2008, the UK notified the

---

[64] Ibid. paras. 32–33.
[65] Ibid. para. 35.
[66] *Northern Rock Rescue*, n. 60 paras. 39–53.
[67] But see Diamond and Dybvig, 'Bank Runs, Deposit Insurance, and Liquidity' at 418.
[68] Shin, n. 14 at 110.
[69] HM Treasury, *The Nationalisation of Northern Rock* para. 2.2.
[70] See ibid. at 24, figure 8.
[71] See Decision of 2 April 2008 State Aid C 14/2008 (ex NN 1/2008) (Decision C(2008)1210 final of 2 April 2008) (*Northern Rock Restructuring*), paras. 26–44.
[72] Ibid. para. 2.47.
[73] Ibid. paras. 3.2–3.7.
[74] Ibid. para. 3.9.
[75] HM Treasury, n. 69 para. 3.9; see also *Northern Rock Restructuring*, n. 71 paras. 48–83.

Commission of its restructuring plan. This was the date of the expiry of the rescue aid decision, and the Commission's deadline for providing a restructuring plan.[76] By letter of 2 April 2008, the Commission informed the UK that it had reservations about the compatibility of some of the plan's points, and accordingly it initiated proceedings under Article 88(2) EU Treaty (now TFEU 108(2)). It also reminded the UK of the suspensory effect of that Article, and the requirement for recovery of any illegally granted aid.[77]

As a result of changed economic circumstances and revisions to the original restructuring plan, the Commission extended the deadline under Article 88.[78] The procedural history indicates a close dialogue between the Commission and the UK government. This appears to be reflected in the Commission's approval of the restructuring plan, albeit subject to some conditions (which were unlikely to have been a surprise; and were likely imposed to ensure enforceability – the decisional equivalent of a consent judgment).

The change in economic conditions was significant. By the time that the Commission adopted its Decision on 28 October 2009, the full effect of the 2008 meltdown of financial markets had been felt. As a result, the legal basis for the measures had shifted from Article 87(3)(c) (R&R aid) to Article 87(3)(b) (aid 'to remedy a serious disturbance in the economy of a Member State').[79] In addition, the global financial crisis forced coordinated action by both Member States and the Union to remedy the disturbance it caused to European economies, most of which involved state aid. Accordingly, the Commission developed a set of guidelines and communications governing its approach to the assessment of this sort of aid. These were applicable to Northern Rock's restructuring.

Northern Rock was not unique. German Landesbanken were particularly hit, due to their activities: they tended to operate on wholesale markets, and were susceptible to liquidity problems.[80] On 17 August 2007, the German savings bank association (Sparkassen-Finanzgruppe) bailed out Sachsen Landesbank, as a result of the bank's inability to maintain a credit facility that it had arraigned with a special investment fund (SIF) that the bank funded and managed. The SIF required access to the facility as other commercial paper investors were unwilling to refinance the SIF.[81]

---

[76] Pursuant to *Northern Rock Rescue*, n. 60 at 9.

[77] Ibid.

[78] See the procedural history described in Decision of 7 May 2009, Letter Extending the Article 88(2) Procedure (C(2009)/3743 final), paras. 1–6, and Commission Decision of 28 October 2009 on the State Aid N° C 14/2008 (ex NN 1/2008) implemented by the United Kingdom for *Northern Rock*, paras. 1–14 (*Northern Rock Restructuring II*).

[79] *Northern Rock Restructuring II*, ibid. para. 103.

[80] But they were not alone; private banks (including those supporting medium-sized companies – the *Mittelstand*) also faced difficulties. See e.g. Commission Decision of 21 October 2008 on State aid measure C 10/08 (ex NN 7/08) implemented by Germany for the restructuring of IKB Deutsche Industriebank AG (notified under document C(2008) 6022) [2009] OJ L-278/32 (this case originated from IKB's liquidity problems in July 2007, see points 14–18).

[81] Simensen, 'Sachsen Falls Victim to Credit Crisis'.

Sachsen was sold to Landesbank Baden-Württemberg (LBBW) nine days later,[82] in a process that was held not to involve state aid.[83] However, this had a knock-on effect for LBBW. It required a bailout of its own (in the form of a capital injection and asset relief) in 2009. This need was caused by the fall in value of assets it acquired in the rescue of Sachsen that was in turn exacerbated by the market conditions of 2008–2009.[84] Liquidity problems and the resulting inability to access wholesale funding (including rolling over existing funding) affected banks elsewhere in Europe during late 2007.[85]

When the crisis first emerged, from what we can see, the UK financial regulators did not see Northern Rock's problems as a sign of a systematic failure. Rather, the focus was (quite rightly) to deal with Northern Rock's problem in a manner which prevented contagion to the financial system generally, i.e. to prevent a run on Northern Rock (and similar institutions) by depositors. In this respect, the measures put into place to support Northern Rock accomplished this goal.

While post-crisis hindsight is easy, the financial regulators' exclusive focus on Northern Rock meant that it might have missed opportunities to view the wider picture. This was in spite of the reports in the financial press of other European banks facing similar liquidity problems. And it would be these problems, compounded by the drop in value of opaque securities backed by difficult to value assets, which would lead to even larger problems in 2008.

The positive lesson from Northern Rock is not just a 'need for speed' in acting, but also the willingness of both the UK government and the Commission to work together to find an acceptable solution in a short period of time. This allowed both to work jointly to immediately fight the fire, before it got out of control. The procedural history described in the Northern Rock Restructuring Decision illustrates this well. It was well known that the Commission and the UK government were in constant contact over this time, and this appeared to become a standard practice in the post-2008 efforts to stem the larger crisis.[86]

4.4 THE FINANCIAL CRISIS OF 2008

The 15 September 2008 bankruptcy of the investment bank Lehman Brothers represented a turning point. It was not the start of the crisis. What the collapse of

---

[82] Clark, 'German State-Run Bank, Caught in Subprime Mess, Is Sold'.

[83] Commission Decision of 4 June 2008 on state aid implemented by Germany for Sachsen LB Notified under No. C 9/2008 (ex NN 8/2008, CP 244/2007).

[84] Commission Decision of 15 December 2009 on State aid C 17/09 (ex N 265/09) by Germany for the restructuring of Landesbank Baden-Württemberg (notified under document C(2009) 9955) (*LBBW*) [2010] OJ L-188/1.

[85] See e.g. Commission Decision of 31 July 2008 not to raise objections (NN36/2008 – *Roskilde Bank*) (C(2008)4138 final); Hellwig, 'Germany and the Financial Crises 2007–2017'; Hodson and Quaglia, 'European Perspectives on the Global Financial Crisis: Introduction'; and Hardie and Howarth, '*Die Krise* but not *La Crise?*'

[86] See e.g. LBBW, n. 84 point 5.

Lehman Brothers represented was a fundamental change in the understanding of how widespread and profound a threat to the financial system the underlying problem was. On 15 September 2008, it was clear that the threat was not merely about the liquidity problems facing the occasional bank. Rather, the market predicated on financing via liquid assets had failed, due to a global realisation that the collateral that was used in that market was impaired, worthless or otherwise opaque in value.

This bankruptcy did not happen overnight: directors of large companies do not wake up one morning and decide to put their firms into insolvency proceedings for no reason. The signs of Lehman's bankruptcy could be seen earlier in 2008. The March collapse of Bear Stearns (and subsequent purchase by JP Morgan with the assistance of the New York Federal Reserve Bank), as a result of its problems with liquidity was an obvious premonition. Market signals were another, as 'on March 18, the day after JP Morgan announced its acquisition of Bear Stearns, the market ... put the cost of insuring $10 million of Lehman's five-year senior debt at $310,000 annually; for Merrill Lynch, the cost was $241,000; and for Goldman Sachs, $165,000'.[87] Stress tests were yet another signal.[88] Lenders became reluctant to deal with the bank, which was a problem, as Lehman was reliant upon Repo funding[89] secured by non-traditional securities.[90]

At the beginning of September, Lehman recognised that it would have to write down $3.9 billion. Its exposure was approximately $200 billion (in contrast to Bear Stearns' 'limited' exposure of $50–$80 billion); and although it was seeking support by way of investment from other (overseas) sources, none would be found.[91] On 9 September, when it was announced that this support would not materialise, Lehman's share price dropped 55 per cent, and later that day the Treasury began planning for a bankruptcy, as nightmarish as that outcome then appeared.[92] However, by Saturday, 13 September, it appeared that a lifeline had been thrown to Lehman.

The British bank Barclays proposed to buy the bulk of Lehman, and a private consortium had been found to buy the remainder. But as part of the terms, 'the NY Fed required Barclays to guarantee Lehman's obligations from the sale until the transaction closed, much as JP Morgan had done for Bear Stearns in March'.[93] UK law required a shareholder vote to authorise such a guarantee, which would take 30–60 days to arrange. While the UK's Financial Services Authority could waive this

[87] Financial Crisis Inquiry Commission, n. 23 at 325–326 and 324–343.

[88] Ibid. at 328.

[89] A 'Repo' agreement is an agreement to sell and later repurchase (at a premium over the sale price) a security.

[90] Ibid.

[91] Ibid. at 330.

[92] Ibid.

[93] Ibid. at 335.

requirement, they were unwilling, and suggested that the NY Fed provide the guarantee instead. The Fed was unwilling to act as guarantor.[94]

Lehman filed for bankruptcy on 14 September. That and the news that Bank of America would take over Merrill Lynch would be announced before markets opened in London on Monday the 15th. If the crisis had been a smouldering fire, the events of 15 September 2008 poured accelerant on it. Three days later, two of the UK's largest banks, Lloyds and HBOS, whose combined market capitalisation stood at over £134 billion on 2 April 2007, announced a 'merger of convenience' to keep HBOS in business. Also in the UK, on 29 September, Bradford and Bingley, a building society, was part nationalised and other assets transferred to Abbey National.[95] Other building societies followed suit. And the problem extended beyond the UK; other banks in Europe (including the European Economic Area (EEA)) were pushed to (or over) the edge. Hypo Real Estate (Germany), Dexia (France/Belgium), Fortis (Belgium), Dresdener Bank (Germany) and the Anglo Irish Bank (Ireland) and numerous Icelandic banks were institutions on this list. By the time the crisis had abated in 2017, the Commission's list of state aid measures (both initial and their extensions) to financial firms ran to thirty-four pages.[96]

Governmental responses were on two fronts: granting state aid to institutions in trouble and allowing (or encouraging) mergers to take place. In the UK's case, this included legislative changes to permit an otherwise uncompetitive merger. We discuss this merger of Lloyds and HBOS, and its competition consequences, in Section 4.4.2. State aid approval required significant support from Member State governments. Before concluding this chapter, we examine these two responses.

4.4.1 *State Aid to Banks as a Crisis Containment Measure*

The initial response by Member States was to direct funding to individual institutions, with the Commission regarding such aid as R&R aid to individual undertakings. However, by late September 2008 it was clear to all that the crisis affecting financial markets was a threat to the financial system and the real economy. The above discussion of earlier bank failures shows where and how help was needed to restructure affected banks in an effort to restabilise the financial system.

The measures needed were: (1) liquidity assistance; (2) aid with recapitalisation of affected institutions; (3) measures for dealing with impaired assets held by these institutions; (4) directions for the use of aid in restructuring financial institutions;

---

[94] Ibid.

[95] Bradford and Bingley's problems were liquidity and accessing wholesale funding with exposure to sub-prime and buy-to-let mortgages, see House of Commons Treasury Committee, *Banking Crisis*, para. 26.

[96] European Commission, Memo, 'State Aid: Overview of Decisions and On-going In-Depth Investigations of Financial Institutions in Difficulty'.

and (5) support to the real economy – which was affected by the inability of financial institutions to finance commerce.

The need for liquidity assistance was obvious. As trading losses had reduced banks' capital, many institutions – including large and systematically important banks – found that their capital holdings were below the minimum level required by regulation. Accordingly, these institutions needed a further capital injection to allow them to continue operating. Assisting banks with 'impaired' or 'toxic' assets removes uncertainty about the quality of a bank's assets expressed in its accounting statements and allows for the development of confidence in the institution and sector as a whole.[97] Although the Commission had promulgated general R&R guidance, the production of additional and specific guidance for the financial sector was merited given the systematic importance of these institutions within national and European economies. Finally, banks were hoarding cash, therefore reducing the availability of credit. Hence support to the real economy was necessary to facilitate recovery.

The European Council (in the configuration of ECOFIN, i.e. the Economics and Finance Ministers) met on 6–7 October 2008 to coordinate the political response to the crisis.[98] Its Final Communication noted that the priority would be to preserve the confidence and stability of the financial system by ensuring liquidity and protecting depositors' interests through the recapitalisation of vulnerable financial institutions. While the ministers agreed that they would take 'all necessary measures' to address the problem, such measures would be taken within the confines of EU Common Principles.[99]

On 13 October, the Commission published its initial guidance on how Member States would be able to provide aid to support troubled financial institutions.[100] This Communication ('the Banking Communication') recognised the severity of the situation, shifting the legal basis for aid to Article 87(3)(b) (disturbance in the economy), rather than Article 87(3)(c) and the R&R Guidelines.[101] The Commission drew a distinction between illiquid but otherwise sound institutions, and those institutions whose problems arose from inefficiency and/or excessive risk taking. Support for the former would 'normally be more limited and require less substantial restructuring'.[102] But support for the latter would need to be granted with

---

[97] See e.g. Communication from the Commission on the Treatment of Impaired Assets in the Community Banking Sector, [2009] OJ C-72/1, para. 7.

[98] Council of the European Union, 'Immediate Responses to Financial Turmoil Council Conclusions – Ecofin Council of 7 October 2008'.

[99] Ibid. at 2–3.

[100] Commission, Press Release, 'State Aid: Commission Gives Guidance to Member States on Measures for Banks in Crisis'. The guidance was published on 25 October: Communication from the Commission, 'The Application of State Aid Rules to Measures Taken in Relation to Financial Institutions in the Context of the Current Global Financial Crisis' [2008] OJ C-270/8.

[101] State Aid Communication, ibid. points 6–13.

[102] Ibid. point 14.

a careful eye to the principles found in the R&R Guidelines.[103] Additionally, given the need for prompt action and the requirement for *ex ante* approval of aid, the Commission undertook 'to ensure the swift adoption of decisions upon complete notification, if necessary, within 24 hours and over a weekend'.[104]

The Commission released guidance on measures to support access to finance in January 2009 (with retroactive effect from 17 December – the date the Commission had agreed its content).[105] This latter guidance followed from the Commission's November economic recovery plan. The plan was designed to develop a large and coordinated economic response aimed at stimulating consumer and business confidence, post-crisis.[106]

On 5 December, the Commission issued a Recapitalisation Communication.[107] This consolidated the Commission's practice.[108] Although the Commission identified benefits associated with recapitalisation,[109] it noted that recapitalisation was not without competitive concerns. In particular, it gave an advantage to less sound banks over those that did not require support.[110] This point is significant, as otherwise unchecked, '[t]his will distort competition on the market, distort incentives, increase moral hazard and weaken the overall competitiveness of European banks'.[111] To get the balance right,[112] the Commission mandated that no aid be granted 'for free'. Hence, there is a need to find a market-based solution where the risk profiles of the beneficiary, the risk of the support instrument chosen, incentives for exiting the scheme and risk-weighted interest are considered in pricing the aid.[113]

---

[103] Ibid.

[104] Ibid. point 53.

[105] Communication from the Commission, Temporary Community framework for state aid measures to support access to finance in the current financial and economic crisis [2009] OJ C-16/1, point 7.

[106] Communication from the Commission to the European Council, A European Economic Recovery Plan Brussels, 26 November 2008 COM(2008) 800 final.

[107] Communication from the Commission, The Recapitalisation of Financial Institutions in the Current Financial Crisis: Limitation of Aid to the Minimum Necessary and Safeguards against Undue Distortions of Competition [2009] OJ C-10/2 published in consolidated form: [2009] OJ C-83/1 (Recapitalisation Communication).

[108] Commission Decision of 13 October 2008 (Case N 507/08) (*Financial Support Measures to the Banking Industry in the UK*) [2008] OJ C-290/4; Commission Decision of 27 October 2008 (Case N 512/08) (*Support Measures for Financial Institutions in Germany*) [2008] OJ C-293/2 and Commission Decision of 19 November 2008 (Case N 560/08) (*Support Measures for the Credit Institutions in Greece*) C(2008) 7382; Commission Decision of 12 November 2008 (Case N 528/08) (*Aid to ING Groep N.V.*) [2010] OJ L-274/139; and Commission Decision of 25 November 2008 (Case NN 68/08) (*Latvian State Support to JSC Parex Banka*) [2009] OJ C-147/01.

[109] Recapitalisation Communication, n. 107 points 4–6.

[110] Ibid. points 8–10.

[111] Ibid. point 9.

[112] Ibid. points 11–12.

[113] Ibid. points 23 and 28.

The Commission applied a stricter regime to unsound banks, requiring fundamental restructuring (under new management, if necessary) or liquidation.[114] Finally, the Communication stresses a point made in the Banking Communication: there is an obligation on Member States to report to the Commission on the implementation of the measures.[115]

On 25 February 2009, the Commission published its Communication on the treatment of impaired assets (the 'Impaired Assets Communication').[116] Like the US Troubled Asset Relief Program,[117] the objective of the EU's programme was to enhance the flow of credit to the real economy by reducing uncertainty about the value and location of toxic assets.[118] Although recapitalisation of the banks aided in making credit available, recapitalisation alone was insufficient. In it, the Commission noted that as a result of the crisis, European banks wrote-down $293.7 billion, and that the International Monetary Fund (IMF) suggested that bank losses resulting from write-downs could approach $ 2,200 billion. These write-downs (reflecting losses or potential losses) would necessarily reduce banks' abilities to extend credit at any level of the market.

In the Communication, the Commission again noted that crafting measures to reduce the uncertainty of the value of the banks' assets again requires the need for economic stimulus provided by an asset relief programme, and that this must be balanced against its potentially anticompetitive consequences, but also done within the context of a Member State's budgetary constraints. Further, while asset relief programmes can stimulate the flow of credit to the real economy, they can distort competition not just in the relevant Member State's financial sector, but also in the Community's, due to cross-border activity. These distortions of competition, and associated moral hazard, may result in situations where governments may be periodically called upon to (re)intervene.

The Banking, Recapitalisation and Impaired Asset Communications were directed to Member States' treatment of systematic problems in the financial sector. The Commission's Restructuring Communication of 23 July 2009[119] was aimed at parallel measures by Member States to restructure individual institutions with the goal of their return to long-term viability. While the then in-force R&R Guidelines provided direction on the need for and contents of an acceptable restructuring plan, this Communication added specific guidance for aid to financial institutions, by

---

[114] Ibid. point 44.
[115] Ibid. point 40.
[116] Communication from the Commission on the Treatment of Impaired Assets in the Community Banking Sector [2009] OJ C-72/1.
[117] Emergency Economic Stabilization Act of 2008 (Public Law 110–343).
[118] Impaired Assets Communication, n. 116 point 6.
[119] Commission Communication on the Return to Viability and the Assessment of Restructuring Measures in the Financial Sector in the Current Crisis under the State Aid Rules [2009] OJ C-195/9.

indicating how the Commission approached its assessment.[120] In particular, it provided guidance on: the contents of a restructuring plan, own resource contributions and effective measures to prevent distortions of competition as a result of the granted support.[121] This Communication was modified in December 2010 (with effect from January 2011)[122] to encourage the phasing out of such assistance and tightening-up of the conditions for governmental guarantees, and to remove the distinction between sound and unsound banks in the analysis of support measures.[123]

To address the difficulties that undertakings (particularly SMEs) in the real economy had in accessing credit in December 2008, the Commission adopted a temporary framework to support access to finance ('Temporary Framework').[124] This framework followed from the European Economic Recovery Plan it had announced the previous month.[125] The Framework made it easier for Member States to direct smaller amounts of aid to undertakings which required liquidity assistance or credit. (It also contained provisions to encourage the investment in 'green' or sustainable products, which was a part of the Recovery Plan.) The Framework built upon the *de minimis* Regulation,[126] and expanded the amount and type of aid which could be provided by a Member State. In particular, the Framework's adoption now meant that Member States could now provide, *inter alia*, a lump sum of aid up to €500,000 per company for the next two years, to relieve them from current difficulties and state guarantees for loans at a reduced premium.[127]

The framework did not modify the *de minimis* Regulation, thus Member States were required to notify the Commission of aid in excess of the *de minimis* Regulation's limits.[128] However, the Commission would regard aid granted under the framework (provided its conditions applied[129]) as compatible with the common market (pursuant to Article 87(3)(b) of the Treaty). The Commission also undertook to ensure swift authorisation, upon receipt of a complete notification. In the expectation that financial markets would return to normality, this framework expired on 31 December 2010.

It must be remembered that granting aid to troubled financial institutions was (and remains) the prerogative of the Member States. The Commission's role is

---

[120] Ibid. point 7.

[121] Ibid. points 11–12, 22–27 and 28–45, respectively.

[122] Communication from the Commission on the Application, from 1 January 2011, of State Aid Rules to Support Measures in Favour of Banks in the Context of the Financial Crisis [2010] OJ C-329/7.

[123] Ibid. points 9, 10 and 12–16, respectively.

[124] Recapitalisation Communication.

[125] See n. 106 supra.

[126] Commission Regulation (EC) No. 1998/2006 of 15 December 2006 on the application of Articles 87 and 88 of the Treaty to *de minimis* aid [2006] OJ L-379/5 (now replaced).

[127] Commission, 'The Commission Launches a Major Recovery Plan'.

[128] See Commission, The Effects of Temporary State Aid Rules Adopted in the Context of the Financial and Economic Crisis (Commission Staff Working Paper) (October 2011) at 34.

[129] See Temporary Framework, n. 124 sections 4.2.2–4.5.2.

merely to examine the measures to determine their consistency with the Treaties, and the presumption against granting aid. In spite of the general negative presumption, Member States are able to grant aid in limited, specific circumstances. The Commission was able to assist Member States by promulgating appropriate guidance.

Member States used this ability to support their financial systems. With the exception of Bulgaria, the Czech Republic, Estonia, Malta and Romania (whose institutions, combined, accounted for less than 1 per cent of the assets of European financial institutions), all Member States implemented at least one support measure.[130] Between September 2008 and December 2010, Member States had committed almost €4,300 billion in aid.[131] Although not all that was committed was used, the commitment to grant large sums of support sent a signal to the markets, and more importantly to the public, that national governments would intervene to prevent a liquidity problem from evolving into a greater systematic crisis in the financial system.

These measures put pressure on the public finances of Member States. This was not unforeseen, as in the Impaired Assets Communication the Commission explicitly noted that Member States' budgetary constraints could affect their ability to extend these measures.[132] The Commission's responsibility in assessing the measures extended only to determining their compatibility with the Treaties. 'Stress testing' Member States' budgets to determine if the proposed aid was 'affordable' was not part of the state aid approval process. There is a separate Treaty provision to monitor Member States' budgets, which is conducted by the Commission and Council.[133]

For some Member States, granting this aid may have aggravated pre-existing economic imbalances, culminating in a sovereign debt crisis. However, it is easy to overstate the relationship between the support measures and a sovereign debt crisis. While the increase in public debt due to the measures would have aggravated pre-existing deficits and increased risk premiums on sovereign debt, the immediate fallout of the banking crisis on the real economy would also have had a significant effect, particularly on already precarious economies. To ease these sovereign debt problems the Council (acting with the cooperation of the IMF and World Bank) established the European Financial Stability Mechanism to support Member States in difficult financial situations which arose from circumstances outside their control.[134]

[130] Commission, The Effects of Temporary State Aid Rules, n. 128 at 36.

[131] Vives, *Competition and Stability* at 206, see also Commission, The Effects of Temporary State Aid Rules, n. 128 at 36–42.

[132] Impaired Assets Communication, n. 116 point 12.

[133] The Treaty basis is TEU Article 104 (now TFEU Article 126), see Wardhaugh, 'Chapter 23: Economic and Monetary Union' in Vaughan and Robertson (eds.) *Law of the European Union* ¶¶ 23.333–23.706, which discusses the then existing monitoring process and its development since the financial crisis.

[134] See ibid. ¶¶ 239–244; the European Financial Stability Mechanism was given a more permanent basis via the European Stability Mechanism Treaty of 2 February 2012 (ibid. ¶¶ 23.301–23.332).

4.4.2 *Bank Merger as a Crisis Containment Measure*

A jurisdiction's merger regime is complementary to its insolvency regime. To the extent that the insolvency or merger regime reduces fixed costs in the event of market exit, these regimes reduce entry barriers and thus promote a more competitive environment. At the same time, an effective competition regime must also prevent mergers which are likely to impair competition. Permitting troubled financial institutions to merge with stronger ones is consistent with this model of exit. An initial response of a failing institution is to look around for a buyer in the hope of preserving some value for its shareholders.

Yet, as banking markets in Europe tend to be concentrated, such mergers may be harmful to consumer interests. In particular, as a result of lack of competition, consumers of financial products may pay too much in interest or service charges, have a reduced range of products from which to choose or receive a reduced rate of return on their savings. It is appropriate to examine the use of merger as a response to the financial crisis. Here we consider the Lloyds/HBOS (in the UK) merger of 2008 in the immediate face of the crisis, and the Fortis/ABN AMRO (in the Netherlands) merger during the aftermath of that crisis. The Dutch case is interesting, as its shows a clear post-merger diminution of consumer surplus. In Lloyds/HBOS the UK government altered legislation to permit the merger. The merger was likely costly for the consumer, as other measures – in particular the recapitalisation of both institutions – would have maintained more effective competition in the market.

By way of background, in April 2007, HBOS and Lloyds TSB were the fifth and sixth largest UK banks by market capitalisation; although their capitalisation declined, they were the fourth and fifth largest in April 2008.[135] Lloyds TSB arose from the 1995 merger of the Trustee Savings Bank with Lloyds Bank. Similarly, HBOS resulted from a 2001 merger of Halifax Bank and the Bank of Scotland.

In 2000, Lloyds TSB proposed merging with Abbey National. Abbey National was formed in 1944 through a merger of two building societies. Abbey National was the first building society to demutualise (in 1989), and by 2001 had developed into a large full-service retail and wholesale bank.[136] It provided an important source of competition for the (then) 'big four' UK banks (Barclays, HSBC, Lloyds TSB and Royal Bank of Scotland/NatWest).[137]

At the time of the proposed Lloyds TSB/Abbey National merger, there was substantial overlap between the two banks in the product markets for: '(a) markets for financial products sold to personal customers; (b) markets for financial products

---

[135] Commons Treasury Committee, *Banking Crisis*, n. 95 para. 1. (table 1).
[136] Competition Commission, Lloyds TSB Group plc and Abbey National plc: A Report on the Proposed Merger (July 2001), para. 2.7.
[137] Ibid. para. 5.118.

sold to SMEs; (c) markets for financial products sold to larger firms; and (d) wholesale banking'.[138] There was sufficiently strong competition from other players in the last two markets to alleviate competition concerns.[139]

The merger would have resulted in a diminution of quality (the products offered by the merged entity would be more closely aligned with Lloyds' offering[140]) and service (approximately 600 'overlapping' branches would close[141]), and would concentrate the market. The merger would result in a Herfindahl-Hirschman Index (HHI, a measure of market concentration) for current accounts of 1,849 (delta of 318).[142] As no proposed remedy could rectify the problems, the Competition Commission blocked this merger.

In 2008 the situation was as follows: HBOS held 20 per cent of the UK mortgage market and 16 per cent of its savings market.[143] Its growth over the five previous years was rapid, but made extensive use of wholesale financing to support this business model.[144] HBOS had two divisions responsible for property lending, with the commercial property arm of its corporate division (catering to businesses with annual turnovers in excess of £1 million) responsible for much of the bank's losses in 2008.[145] The bank's response to 2007's problems was to expand corporate lending (increasing loans by 22 per cent).[146] Additionally, HBOS had governance problems, with a centralisation of its risk, hence allowing its divisions to externalise risk in their strategies.[147] In retrospect, there is little doubt how or why HBOS reached the weakened position in which it found itself in September 2008.[148] Lloyds, on the other hand, was in an apparently more solid position in 2008. It had no direct exposure to the US sub-prime market, had a strong liquidity position[149] and was profitable.[150]

On 18 September 2008, HBOS and Lloyds announced that they had reached a merger agreement. The secretary of state issued an intervention notice that day, and requested a report by the OFT by 24 October.[151] Subsequent to this report, two

---

[138] Ibid. para. 2.17.

[139] Ibid.

[140] Ibid. para. 5.115.

[141] Ibid. para. 5.114.

[142] Ibid. para. 5.117.

[143] Commons Treasury Committee, *Banking Crisis*, n. 95, para. 39.

[144] Ibid. para. 43.

[145] Ibid. para. 40.

[146] Ibid. para. 41.

[147] Ibid. paras. 41–47, see also Financial Conduct Authority (Bank of England) and Prudential Regulation Authority, *The Failure of HBOS plc (HBOS)*, paras. 76–93.

[148] See ibid. passim.

[149] Commons Treasury Committee, *Banking Crisis*, ibid. para. 51 provides a more detailed analysis of HBOS's failure.

[150] Ibid. para. 52.

[151] Office of Fair Trading, Anticipated Acquisition by Lloyds TSB plc of HBOS plc: Report to the Secretary of State for Business Enterprise and Regulatory Reform (24 October 2008), paras. 20–21.

events occurred. The conditions of the financial system further weakened, and the government added[152] a new public interest provision, as Section 58(2D) of the Enterprise Act 2002, to specify that 'the interest of maintaining the stability of the UK financial system' was a ground for intervention by the secretary of state to approve a merger.

As part of its efforts to strengthen the financial system, on 13 October 2008, the government announced a set of support measures.[153] In particular, and of relevance to this merger, the Treasury 'announced that it was making capital investments in HBOS and Lloyds, conditional on completion of their proposed merger'.[154] It was also announced that these 'investments' (recapitalisation) would amount to £37 billion.[155] Although these announced support measures changed the terms of the merger agreement, they did not alter the competitive situation.

In assessing the competitive harms that could result from the merger, the OFT counterfactual did not consider the failure of HBOS. Given announced governmental support, failure would be inconceivable. Hence, its assets would not leave the market, so an appeal to an FFD was inappropriate.[156]

The most realistic scenario, according to the OFT, was the following sequence of events. Immediate governmental intervention, including some recapitalisation (the precise amount would be speculative).[157] If aid to other banks could serve as an indication, this recapitalisation would allow it to remain competitive on the market (particularly to households and SMEs) for three years.[158] This would be followed by withdrawal of governmental support. This was a question of when, not if.[159] Withdrawal would entail the government selling off its shareholding or brokering the sale to a third party. If the latter, then this would be done to a 'no overlap' purchaser, to avoid competition concerns.[160]

The OFT Report noted that the merger would have the consequence of significantly lessening competition in some of the markets in which both parties were active, and in particular markets for 'current accounts, banking services to small and medium enterprises, and mortgages'.[161] The lessening of competition in the market

---

[152] Enterprise Act 2002 (Specification of Additional Section 58 Consideration) Order 2008, SI 2008/2645.

[153] Notified to the Commission on 12 October and approved the next day: Decision not to raise objections (State Aid N 507/2008 – *UK Financial Support Measures to the Banking Industry in the UK*) (Brussels, 13 October 2008 C(2008)6058).

[154] OFT, Anticipated Acquisition by Lloyds TSB plc of HBOS, n. 151, para. 25.

[155] See ibid. para. 51 and the HM Treasury's Press Release of 13 October 2008 (Statement re. Banking Industry, RNS Number: 6665F).

[156] OFT Lloyds-HBOS, n. 151 paras. 55–60.

[157] Ibid. paras. 71–77.

[158] Ibid. para. 75.

[159] Ibid. paras. 78–84.

[160] Ibid. para. 79.

[161] Treasury's Press Release of 13 October 2008, n. 155 para. 384.

in Great Britain (and in Scotland in particular) was significant. The details from the OFT's Report are worth quoting in detail:

> [T]he merged entity will be the clear market leader in terms of stock of PCAs in
> Great Britain, with a combined market share of 33 per cent (increment 14 per cent).
> The next three players (RBSG [Royal Bank of Scotland Group], HSBC and
> Barclays) have market shares between 14 and 17 percent, and the concentration
> ratio of the top four players in the market (C4) is increased by the merger from
> 67 per cent to 80 per cent. All other players have shares of less than ten per cent
> each. The post-merger HHI is 1950, which indicates that this is a highly concen-
> trated market, with an increment of almost 500.[162]

The competitive situation was worse for the Scottish market.[163] Further, the merger would remove HBOS from its status as a 'challenger bank' to the big four.[164]

Several parties provided representations regarding need for the merger and the stability of the UK's financial system, i.e. a public interest consideration. The merging parties and the tripartite authorities (the Treasury, the Financial Services Authority and the BoE) argued that the merger was necessary on financial stability grounds, and this outweighed competition considerations.[165] Competitors saw the need for financial stability, but had concerns about the long-term effect on compe-tition.[166] Consumer interest groups and others (including the Scottish government) expressed similar concerns.[167]

The OFT referred the merger to the Competition Commission for a full-scale inquiry. However, the secretary of state intervened on the new grounds of maintain-ing financial stability in the UK's banking system and cleared the merger on 31 October, creating the Lloyds Bank Group (LBG). There were suggestions that the merger was a 'done deal' brokered by then Prime Minister Brown the Monday before the announcement. The alleged quid pro quo for permitting the deal was that LBG would continue to provide mortgage funding for first-time buyers.[168]

As a condition of approval, LBG was required to submit a restructuring plan, which included divestment of over 600 retail branches, on the assumption that this addressed some of the competition concerns associated with the merger.[169] LBG attempted to sell these branches and business to the Co-op Bank in spring 2013, but

---

[162] Ibid. paras. 106–107; 'C4' denotes the aggregate market share of the largest four firms in the market.

[163] Ibid. the figures for the Scottish market were redacted by the OFT.

[164] Ibid. paras. 109–110.

[165] Ibid. paras. 356–362.

[166] Ibid. paras. 363–367.

[167] Ibid. paras. 368–373.

[168] Treanor, 'Lloyds TSB Chairman Struck HBOS Deal with Brown at City Drinks Party'; see, however, Croft, 'Lloyds Not "Compelled" by Government to Acquire HBOS'.

[169] Commission, Decision not to raise objections (State Aid No. N 428/2009 – *United Kingdom Restructuring of Lloyds Banking Group*) (Brussels, 18.11.2009) C(2009)9087 final, points 76–77; see also Trustee Savings Bank, *Annual Report 2014* at 3.

that transaction fell through. Divesture only occurred in April 2014, with the spin-off of TSB as an independent bank.[170] Nevertheless, irrespective of how the original merger decision was made and/or brokered, it is the competitive consequences of the merger, and the support the merging parties received, which matter for our purposes.

It is trite to note that as markets become more concentrated, and as 'challengers' are edged out, taken over or otherwise eliminated, competition in these markets becomes worse. The clear conclusion from the OFT reports in both Lloyds/Abbey National and Lloyds/HBOS was that further amalgamation of the 'big four', and Lloyds in particular, would lead to an anticompetitive outcome. Yet, in the circumstances of 2008, the then government made a *political* decision to permit such a merger.

The Dutch government made a similar political decision in 2010, regarding the merger of Fortis Bank and ABN AMRO. This merger was the culmination of a three-year process involving the aborted takeover of ABN AMRO. That process began in the spring of 2007, when ABN AMRO entered talks with Barclays Bank regarding a merger, which was followed several weeks later by an announcement that a consortium of Fortis, Royal Bank of Scotland and Santander would also seek to take over the underperforming bank and divide its assets among them.[171] In October 2007, Barclays abandoned its efforts and the consortium bid was accepted.[172] However, the financial crisis intervened, and on 3 October 2008, the Dutch government ended up nationalising the Dutch assets of both Fortis and ABN AMRO.[173] In spite of the crisis, the Dutch government went ahead with the merger. To facilitate the transaction, the Dutch government aided in the recapitalisation of and the provision of liquidity facilities to ABN AMRO. As this constituted state aid, the Commission was notified, and the transaction was approved in April 2011.

The Dutch banking market was already one of the most concentrated banking markets in Europe,[174] and this merger exacerbated that phenomenon. The 2011 merger enhanced market concentration and, as expected, reduced consumer surplus. One consequence of the merger was a drop in competition in the Dutch market on interest paid to savings accounts. In their study of this merger, Hellwig and Laser note that ABN AMRO and Fortis decreased their rates by 3 to 5 per cent (from what would be expected in a no-merger situation, corrected for market

---

[170] TSB, ibid. at 17.

[171] See Hellwig and Laser, 'Bank Mergers in the Financial Crisis' at 5–7.

[172] Notified as: Case No. COMP/M.4844 *Fortis/ABN AMRO Assets*; Case No. COMP/M.4843 *RBS/ABN AMRO Assets* and Case No. COMP/M.4845 *Banco Santander/ABN AMRO Assets*.

[173] See Commission Decision of 05 April 2011 on the Measures No. C 11/2009 (ex NN 53b/2008, NN 2/2010 and N 19/2010) implemented by Dutch State for *ABN AMRO Group NV*, points 1–49 for details of the situation in which the banks and Government found themselves.

[174] De Nederlandsche Bank, Perspective on the Structure of the Dutch Banking Sector, point 1.2; see also ACM, Barriers to Entry into the Dutch Retail Banking Sector.

conditions). The interest rates of non-merging banks dropped by about 1 per cent.[175] This equated to a reduction of €69 million in interest payments in 2010.[176] The impact was felt primarily by customers of the merging banks, who received €36.2 million less than they would have otherwise obtained.

This impact was not evenly distributed among account holders. Hellwig and Laser performed consumer-level welfare analysis to identify those groups most affected by the decrease in interest rates. They found that this had a disparate impact on 'less educated consumers with lower savings'.[177]

The lesson from these two mergers is clear: mergers and state aid to achieve systematic stability comes at a cost, the imposition of which has distributive consequences. These consequences need to be considered and addressed when competition is reduced and done so particularly when this choice is made as a deliberate political decision.

4.5 CONCLUSION: THE RESPONSE AND ITS EFFICACY

The efforts of Member State governments, guided by the Commission, appeared to be successful in mitigating the worst of the crisis. Of course, the worst counterfactual – a dystopian scenario of the collapse of the financial system – did not occur, and to this extent the problem was solved. In assessing these efforts, the Commission remarked, 'the worst case scenario was avoided: as of end 2010, there has been no uncontrolled collapse of European financial institutions, no systemic crisis of the financial system and no long-lasting drying-up of financing flows to the real economy'.[178]

Success may be one thing, but an examination of this response and the efficacy of the measures adopted is still merited. The results of this examination may provide a lesson for those who must respond to future crises (which, it is to be hoped, are less severe than 2008's).

4.5.1 *Systematic Risk and Apparently Unlimited Aid*

In assessing the response to the financial crisis, the unique nature of banks and the financial system must be kept in mind. Financial institutions have a different place in the economy than other commercial organisations, and the crises that affect them are different. With an 'ordinary' business, failure will not have an impact on customers' perceptions of the health of other undertakings in the same industry. When a large department store closes down, this does not cause people to line up in

---

[175] Hellwig and Laser, n. 171 at 29.
[176] Ibid. at 34.
[177] Ibid. at 35–36.
[178] Commission, The Effects of Temporary State Aid Rules, n. 128 at 76, the Commission's emphasis omitted.

front of its competitors to do business (or terminate their business) with them. People may line up in front of the exiting store to take advantage of 'clearance' prices, aiding in the liquidation of the store. In contrast, people line up in front of failing banks to remove their funds, possibly aggravating the situation.

When a bank is perceived to be exiting the market, this affects the confidence of all customers of the banking system.[179] This leads to the view that support to the financial system is merited on the (assumed) basis that the benefits to society of granting such support outweighs any anticompetitive effects produced by that support.[180] In other words, the consequences of not granting aid to support the financial system are dire, and any alternative outcome, including those which result in anticompetitive markets, is to be preferred.

This view seems to be a crude one, holding that any aid, no matter of what amount or where targeted, is better than no aid.[181] This is clearly a false dichotomy. The nature and scope of the aid matter – as better-targeted and limited aid may prevent the exacerbation of anticompetitive outcomes. Better, smarter state aid – of the sort advocated by the Commission – may be part of the solution, and certainly provides an alternative to a false dichotomy.

Further, anticompetitive outcomes have distributive consequences. Robust policymaking acknowledges and identifies these consequences and takes them into account when the policy is designed and implemented – in an effort to prevent their worst effects. The cost in mitigating the financial crisis was significant, yet there was limited consideration about how, or by whom, these costs should be paid.

The Commission's Guidance on aid to the financial sector may have limited excessive award of aid. Yet there never appeared to be discussion of the distributive effects of these measures. Member States (or more precisely, national taxpayers) had to pay for these measures: taxes would rise and services would be cut (or both). It is likely no coincidence that in a few Member States, state aid measures were followed by a sovereign debt crisis, necessitating a bailout and economic measures of a different sort. While causality is difficult to establish, it would be reasonable to suggest that the state aid measures may have added sufficient additional stress to some national finances to push them beyond the breaking point.

---

[179] See e.g. Vives, n. 131 at 38–44 and Stephan, 'Did Lloyds/HBOS Mark the Failure of an Enduring Economics-Based System of Merger Regulation?'

[180] This view is shared by some academics and financial regulators, see e.g. Ahlborn and Piccinin, 'The Great Recession and Other Mishaps' at 143, and the views of the tripartite authorities in the Lloyds/HBOS merger, see n. 166 supra.

[181] Ahlborn and Piccinin (ibid.) seem to express this when they note, without qualification, that 'it is clear that aid to banks in the financial crisis provides large enough social benefits to outweigh any competition distortions that may arise', and (at 151), 'aid to banks in the financial crisis is unambiguously beneficial even without any compensatory measures'.

4.5.2 *The 'Too Big to Fail' Problem*

Additionally, larger financial institutions can take on a significant role in the functioning of the financial system, and as such they become 'too big to fail' (TBTF). The failure of such an institution would impose significant negative externalities on the entire financial system (and hence the economy as a whole), such that regulators will do what it takes to ensure the survival of these institutions. Given the stakes, political considerations point towards support of TBTF institutions.[182] However, the difficulty is to determine which institutions (or which institution(s) in a given set of circumstances) is TBTF. Given the consequences of a Type II error, regulators are likely to be overinclusive in their determination that an institution is TBTF.

This response injects a further element of moral hazard into the system, compounding the competitive environment in which these institutions operate. Being perceived as TBTF acts as an implicit governmental guarantee. This reduced risk entails the TBTF institutions pay a lower cost for their funds, impeding the efficient allocation of assets on the market and providing TBTF institutions with an advantage over smaller institutions. It allows such institutions to engage in riskier activity by externalising risk onto the government (or, more precisely, taxpayers).[183]

Although shareholders may suffer a loss (or their holdings are wiped out) by a bailout, the institution's governance structure may be such that the shareholders are diffused and thus not having the incentive to monitor risk, or the details of the institution's activity are too opaque to provide a basis for shareholder action. The pre-merger activities and governance of HBOS seem to demonstrate this point. This suggests that TBTF or other systematically important institutions should be subject to heightened governance and regulatory measures, as a trade-off for their possession of systematic importance.

4.5.3 *Merger, TBTF and Consolidation*

An immediate lesson from this is the danger of TBTF institutions. It is inevitable that these institutions will exist and thus pose a systematic risk in any economy. However, regulatory policy, and particularly competition policy as applied to the financial sector, should seek to prevent the development of such institutions – particularly by 'forced' merger. Further, even if amalgamation does not create a TBTF institution, consolidation in times of crisis may be an inappropriate policy choice.

---

[182] Morrison, 'Systemic Risks and the "Too-Big-to-Fail" Problem' at 500.
[183] Office of the Special Inspector General for the Troubled Asset Relief Program, Quarterly Report to Congress (January 26, 2011) at 6.

The analysis of the Fortis/ABN AMRO merger demonstrated the consequences that bank consolidation had on the market. In this case, fewer players led to weakened competition, which in turn led to consumer harm: all banks (not just the merging banks) paid less on their savings interest rates. Further, the Lloyds/ HBOS merger removed a challenger to the 'big four'. The OFT's finding was that the merger would substantially lessen competition (the UK's criterion) in the UK's banking market. The market shares in question were greater than those in the 2001 Lloyds/Abbey National merger that the Competition Commission blocked.

Further, it was well known that the UK's market in banking services, particularly to consumers, was highly concentrated and uncompetitive. This was a finding of the 2000 Cruickshank Report,[184] and later confirmed in the 2011 Independent Commission on Banking's Report.[185] In fact, the latter Commission noted historically that challenger banks had exerted competitive pressure on the larger banks,[186] and the loss of challenger banks during the financial crisis 'can therefore be expected to reduce levels of competition and lead to worse outcomes for consumers'.[187]

Yet, on the same day that the OFT released its Report on the proposed merger, the UK government altered the relevant legislation to permit intervention to approve mergers on the grounds of maintaining the stability of the UK's financial system. The hasty process by which this new ground was introduced and used gives rise to real concerns not just of politicisation of competition policy, but also for opening the door to rent-seeking activity.[188]

While the merger did increase (or at least maintain) confidence in the financial system for a while, the underlying problems remained. The difficulty was that HBOS's problem stemmed from undercapitalisation and associated liquidity concerns. These problems were addressed not by the merger, but by the government's subsequent provision of a support package (that was available to all similarly situated institutions) to address liquidity problems and capital shortages.[189] The merger itself did not address these concerns. Indeed, the merged group required a further recapitalisation of £17 billion.[190]

The merger was almost certainly a serious mistake. In its immediate aftermath, Sir John Vickers was to remark:

> It has potentially high costs in terms of a serious risk of an irreversibly less-competitive banking services market in Great Britain, especially in Scotland, for

---

[184] Cruickshank, *Competition in UK Banking*, paras. 4.83–4.85.
[185] Independent Commission on Banking, *Final Report* at 153–230.
[186] Ibid. para. 8.4.
[187] Ibid. para. 8.5.
[188] Vives, n. 131 at 217, and Vickers, 'The Financial Crisis and Competition Policy' at 550–553.
[189] See also Vickers, ibid. at 7–9.
[190] Commission, Restructuring of Lloyds Banking Group, n. 169 point 50.

the long term. If these costs do materialize, they will, however, be borne by future consumers, not current political decision-makers.[191]

Consolidation tends to bring a reduction in competition. As in our earlier discussion of the use of cartels (a form of consolidation) in the Depression, concentrating industry in a crisis can aggravate the situation. There is no reason to believe that concentration in the financial sector is any different. In fact, the evidence suggests not only a direct harm to consumers by a reduction in competition, but also a greater threat to the stability of the financial system by allowing consolidating institutions to become greater systematic risks.

4.5.4 *The Causes of the Crisis and State Aid Remedies*

The causes of bank crises are different from the causes of crises in other industries. The causes of industrial crises stem from overcapacity, resulting from a decrease in demand. Thus, the restructuring of these industries involves an orderly reduction of capacity. With the financial crisis, however, the problem was *undersupply*. In the financial economy, this was an undersupply of liquidity and a significant loss of capital. In the real economy, the crisis induced an undersupply of credit.[192] Hence, the restructuring and rescue response to the financial crisis needed to be of a different sort than the norm.

In the regular course of events, inefficient or otherwise uncompetitive undertakings would exit the market. Support for such firms therefore distorts this process. This was well recognised by the Commission in its analysis of the state aid regime for rescuing and restructuring such firms; as such, the Commission will impose post-restructuring remedies upon recipient firms. The restructuring of failing financial undertakings was no exception – the Commission imposed both structural and behavioural remedies on aided financial institutions.

But the Commission's choice of remedies seemed to follow the approach it took with earlier R&R cases. In particular, frequently imposed remedies included a prohibition on price leadership, the reduction of balance sheets and the sale of non-core businesses.[193] In an industry characterised by oversupply, where firms' response is to reduce capacity, such remedies are appropriate as a quid pro quo for receiving restructuring support. However, in markets characterised by undersupply, the situation is different, and these remedies may not be appropriate.

Divesture, whether of core or non-core assets or businesses, raises a number of problems. First, it may be difficult to segregate one part of a financial institution's business from others. Service industries are different from, say, manufacturing industries. Selling a factory or the machinery contained within may be an easier

---

[191] Vickers, n. 188 at 9.
[192] See e.g. Ahlborn and Piccinin, n. 180 at 163.
[193] Ibid. at 152–155.

task than cleaving off some aspects of a well-integrated enterprise, given the syner-
gies and economies of scale and scope that the institution has developed. As banking
markets in Europe tend to be national, spin-offs of non-core businesses were often
determined by geography.[194] However, divesture along geographic lines would often
make little sense from an integrated, internal market perspective.

Disposals of assets, in normal circumstances, may be unproblematic. During and
in the immediate aftermath of the crisis, however, dozens of institutions required
restructuring, many of which were required to divest parts of their operations as (part
of) the quid pro quo. The state aid rules imposed tight windows for such divestment.
The consequence of this was that a large number of businesses were placed on the
market at the same time. As Ahlborn and Piccinin note, 'the effect is that a
significant number of banking businesses will be sold in "fire sales" at approximately
the same time'.[195]

Further, they note that even when the Commission approved longer divesture
periods, this may not have helped, '[i]f a business were earmarked now for divestment in up to four years' time, it is not clear that even the appointment of a powerful
monitoring trustee could prevent the loss of morale, staff and customers as a result of
the uncertainty over the future'.[196] The result of this is that these 'leaner' institutions
may well be weaker institutions, operating with reduced size, possibly less capital
and fewer resources than they otherwise would in the absence of such remedies. If
so, the ability of such institutions to act in the real economy, by providing credit, was
likely impaired, resulting in welfare losses.

There seemed to be little reason behind the imposition of many of these remedies
upon aided financial institutions. The explanation for their imposition likely rests in
an attempt at consistency. In past crises, R&R aid required some form of 'own
contribution' or quid pro quo from the recipient firm. The remedies imposed during
the financial crisis are consistent with this earlier practice. That the crisis had its
origins in another sort of market condition that was either unnoticed or was regarded
as irrelevant.

4.6 FINAL CONCLUDING REMARKS

This chapter has only considered the *ex post*, and fairly immediate, response of
Member States and the Commission to the problems which rapidly unfolded in the
financial system after August 2007. It is not the chapter's purpose to examine or
advocate a regulatory structure to prevent a reoccurrence of the crisis. The literature
is replete with such discussions. To use a metaphor, our task is to examine how the

---

[194] See e.g. the case of Fortis: Commission, Decision not to raise objections (State aid NN 42/
2008 – Belgium, NN 46/2008 – Luxembourg NN 53/A/2008 – *Netherlands Restructuring Aid to
Fortis Bank and Fortis Bank Luxembourg*) Brussels, 3 December 2008 C(2008) 8085.
[195] Ahlborn and Piccinin, n. 180 at 155.
[196] Ibid.

fire was extinguished, and not to prevent future fires. However, we note, the accelerant that encouraged the fire was the endemic moral hazard which had entered the financial system since securitisation altered the mortgage distribution model.

The lessons that this chapter shows is that the competition rules themselves did not prevent an appropriate response to the crisis. At times, particularly in the case of state aid remedies, the rules appeared to be applied in a formalistic manner – demanding a remedy because such remedies had been required in the past – without realising that the present situation may be vastly different from the past.

Similarly, at times the political choice of rules was incorrect. The choice of merger over state aid as a solution was almost certainly incorrect. The financial crisis arose out of, and was exacerbated by, market failure. The purpose of state aid is to correct market failure. On the other hand, merger control, and in particular the prohibition of anticompetitive mergers, is designed to prevent market failure. Hence, any political decision to let an anticompetitive merger proceed, thereby overruling a competition authority's assessment, introduces further market failure into the system. These mergers harmed consumers, as they did in both the UK and Netherlands. This harm was preventable, and provides further evidence that consolidation, collusion and other sorts of 'collective' activity in markets are not solutions in crisis situations.

5

The Covid-19 Crisis

5.1 INTRODUCTION

By December 2019,[1] physicians in China had noticed patients presenting with flu/pneumonia-like symptoms in the Wuhan area of Hubei, China. On 31 December 2019, Chinese authorities reported this outbreak to the World Health Organization (WHO) as cases of 'pneumonia of unknown etiology'.[2] By January 2020, subsequent laboratory investigation and gene sequencing identified the cause as a novel corona virus, which was given the identifier '2019-nCoV' (hence 'Covid-19').[3]

Initial risk assessments suggested that there was little indication that this virus could be transmitted from human to human in a sustained manner. The European Centre for Disease Prevention and Control noted:

> As of 16 January 2020, there is no clear indication of sustained human-to-human transmission. The report of two small family clusters in Wuhan and the exposure history of the imported Japanese case (history of contact with a person with an acute, not laboratory-confirmed, respiratory infection in Wuhan) suggest that person-to-person transmission may have occurred. In the absence of detailed information from the ongoing studies in China, it is impossible to quantify the potential of the 2019-nCoV for human-to-human transmission.[4]

This initial assessment was unfortunately very wrong, as experience was to show.

---

[1] The precise date of the first case is unknown; however, the first documented case was identified on 1 December 2019, but patients presented with Covid-19-like symptoms before that date. See Allam, 'The First 50 Days of COVID-19'; Bryner, '1st Known Case of Coronavirus Traced Back to November in China'; and Wang et al., 'A Novel Coronavirus Outbreak of Global Health Concern'.

[2] World Health Organization, 'Pneumonia of Unknown Cause – China Disease Outbreak News'.

[3] See Zand and Hackenbroch, 'A Failed Deception'.

[4] European Centre for Disease Prevention and Control, 'Cluster of Pneumonia Cases Caused by a Novel Coronavirus, Wuhan, China'.

On 16 and 17 January, cases had been identified in Japan and Thailand, and the USA began screening arrivals from Wuhan at three airports (SFO, LAX and JFK).[5] By the end of January, cases were identified throughout the globe, including the EU (and the UK), the USA, the UAE, Iran, the Philippines and Russia. By this time, epidemiologists had confirmed that human-to-human transmission had occurred since the middle of December 2019.[6] By 15 February, China reported 1,500 deaths and 66,000 cases.[7] Some governments took the outbreak seriously.[8] South Korea imposed lockdowns on 21 February,[9] Italy imposed a national lockdown on 9 March. Other governments did not. Former President Trump famously stated (on 10 February), 'I think the virus is going to be – it's going to be fine' and '[l]ooks like by April, you know in theory when it gets a little warmer, it miraculously goes away'.[10] He could not have been more wrong. On 11 March 2020, the WHO declared the situation to be a pandemic. In its final weekly epidemiological update for 2020, the WHO noted that there had been more than 79.2 million cases and in excess of 1.7 million deaths reported to it since the start of the pandemic.[11]

The public health measures and private actions taken to contain the disease (Covid-19) caused by the virus caused significant asymmetric shifts in consumer demand. In the early days of the disease's spread, demand for some foods and consumer goods increased (pasta and toilet paper in the UK, for example), while others declined (e.g. international travel and restaurant meals).

This shift in demand had at least two immediate economic consequences, both with implications for the application of competition law. First, the asymmetric shift in demand put pressure on those supplying demanded goods to meet the demand, and for state-backed support for those who produced goods and services which were no longer in demand (at least in the short to medium run). Second, consumption patterns were significantly disrupted to the point that most major economies entered into a sharp recession.

In addition to calls for governmental assistance to undertakings (and individuals) affected by the impact of declines in demand, there were calls to relax competition laws (or at least their enforcement), so that businesses could cooperate to supply

5   Allam, n. 1 at 5.
6   Li et al., 'Early Transmission Dynamics in Wuhan, China, of Novel Coronavirus–Infected Pneumonia'.
7   Safi, 'Coronavirus from Unknown Virus to Global Crisis – Timeline'.
8   A good account of the initial outbreak of the virus and the UK's response can be found in *Financial Conduct Authority (Appellant) v. Arch Insurance (UK) Ltd and others* [2021] UKSC 1 [6]–[35].
9   Newey et al., 'Coronavirus: Chance to Contain Outbreak is "Narrowing" Says WHO'.
10 Rep Lloyd Doggett (D-TX 35 District), 'Timeline of Trump's Coronavirus Responses'.
11 WHO, 'Weekly Epidemiological Update – 29 December 2020'.

goods to meet demand[12] or merge with one another in an effort to save jobs.[13] Given increases in demand for some products (particularly face masks and antiviral sanitiser), their prices rose – thus leading to predictable calls that in these circumstances, competition (or consumer protection laws) should be strictly enforced to prevent this sort of price gouging.[14]

This chapter considers these calls and the responses of the antitrust authorities. We do this in the following four sections. These sections (respectively) examine the calls for permitting greater collaboration among competitors (Section 5.2), the need for and efficacy of controls on price gouging (Section 5.3), the merits of relaxing the strictness of merger control regimes and relaxing the conditions for a successful FFD (Section 5.4), and the use of state aid to alleviate some of the more severe economic consequences (Section 5.5).

Our argument is sceptical about the need to relax or reform the antitrust response to such arrangements. In particular, we are of the view that other than the magnitude, there is nothing special or unique about the drop or shift in demand resulting from changed behaviour during the pandemic. This does not merit alteration of the antitrust regime or its enforcement as a response. In fact, we further suggest that any such changes, even if 'temporary', may have a lasting effect on the behaviour of market actors, and that their anticompetitive consequences will be felt well after the pandemic's effects have subsided. These anticompetitive effects may have the result of retarding subsequent economic recovery. In this regard, we recall the consequences of the American experience with cartel-like activity encouraged by the NIRA, and how it prolonged the Great Depression.[15]

We are more sanguine about the use of state aid. The decrease in demand required a degree of economic support to undertakings, to ensure that they could remain viable in a post-pandemic environment once demand returned. However, this optimism does not extend to unreserved enthusiasm. The use of such aid, while needed, was – frequently – suboptimal, and thus was not 'smarter aid'. In many respects, significant amounts of taxpayers' funds could have been put to more effective use, had they been directed elsewhere.

Before turning to the competition law issues, we point out the obvious. This chapter is not a discussion of public health, or the best means to control a pandemic. While it is legitimate to debate matters of the efficacy of governments' responses to the control of epidemics, this is not the point of this chapter.

---

[12] See e.g. Eley, 'Supermarkets Take Measures to Control Panic Buying'; Eley and Evans, 'Supermarkets Raid Restaurants to Restock Shelves'; and also Odudu, 'Feeding the Nation in Times of Crisis'.

[13] Discussions of this have tended to stem from law firms' newsletters, see e.g. White and Case, 'A Re-awakening of the Failing Firm Defence in the EU in the Aftermath of COVID-19?'

[14] See, as an example: Young, 'Third of Shoppers Stung by Price-Gouging'.

[15] See Sections 2.2.1, 'American Antitrust and the Great Depression' and 2.2.2, 'American Antitrust Responses to the Great Depression'.

5.2 COLLABORATION AS A CRISIS MITIGATION STRATEGY

The spread of Covid-19 had an asymmetric effect on consumer demand. In the time preceding the lockdown, demand for travel and hospitality declined, yet demand for other goods increased. As the pandemic took hold, health authorities faced shortages of specialised medical equipment (particularly ventilators), and there was increased institutional and individual demand for personal protective equipment and antiviral products (including hand sanitiser). In addition, given the possibility of disruptions in the global supply chain, there were fears of shortages of pharmaceuticals.

The response among consumers was a predictable panic buying/hoarding strategy. O'Connell, de Paula and Smith note:

> Rapidly rising COVID cases and the expectation of curbs on movement in the early stage of the Pandemic provided a rationale for consumers to build up their stocks as a precautionary measure against, for instance, the need to quarantine or significant supply disruptions. In addition, knowledge that other consumers were in a similar position provided an additional incentive to purchase before stock ran out.[16]

In the UK, this translated into varying spikes in demand:

> Spending on staples (such as canned goods, pasta, rice and grains) rose sharply at the end of February, peaking on March 14 at over 80% of the January–February daily average. A similar pattern is evident for non-food household supplies (such as soap, cold treatments, and toilet tissue), with demand peaking at over 70% of January–February levels on March 14. Spending on the remaining set of fast-moving consumer goods (discretionary calories and perishable foods) increased much more gradually into March, and continued to rise as the UK entered the lockdown period [announced 23 March, in force 26 March].[17]

This behaviour manifested itself in incremental purchasing, that is buying 'slightly more' than the usual quantity of goods (rather than a smaller number of extremely large purchases).[18] This pattern was present in all socio-economic groups, with the wealthiest showing the greatest increase in purchases.[19]

The most visible effect of this behaviour was a shortage of goods on supermarket shelves, which fed into the perceived need to hoard. As the *Financial Times* reported on March 20:

> Retailers have repeatedly assured consumers that there is enough food for everyone. However, the daily experience of many shoppers remains one of heavily depleted

---

[16] O'Connell, de Paula and Smith, 'Preparing for a Pandemic'.
[17] Ibid. at 2.
[18] Ibid.
[19] Ibid. at 3.

shelves – not just in items like toilet roll and pasta, but increasingly in meat, poultry and vegetables.[20]

Putting more goods on supermarket shelves would address the demand problem, and simultaneously assuage the need to hoard.

To this end, the UK's supermarket industry lobbied the government to modify the competition rules to permit cooperation in an ostensible effort to ensure effective and timely production and distribution of goods. Again, as reported in the press:

> Industry figures also said that the relaxation of competition rules confirmed by the government on Thursday should help them co-ordinate supplies better.
>
> 'It just means [for instance] that people from Tesco and Sainsbury's could sit and talk to Kimberly-Clark about toilet rolls without the fear of being prosecuted for collusion,' said one.[21]

The purported justification of this request was that coordination would allow for better-managed coordination of manufacturing, supply and distribution chains. By sharing stock information, the retail industry would better know where shortages existed and could coordinate their supply lines to supply additional products. In addition to information sharing and coordination in distribution, the industry proposed sharing the workforce.[22]

The UK government's response to this took the form of a public policy exclusion, exempting certain agreements in the groceries sector from the prohibitions of Chapter 1 of the Competition Act, i.e. the UK law which mirrors Article 101 TFEU.[23] This exclusion exempted some forms of coordination and information sharing among industry members, to purportedly address these supply and distribution issues. The government provided a similar exemption to the dairy industry.[24] These exemptions were subject to a notification requirement.[25]

---

[20] Eley and Evans, n. 12.

[21] Ibid.

[22] See also Ormosi and Stephan, 'The Dangers of Allowing Greater Coordination between Competitors during the COVID-19 Crisis' at 299.

[23] The Competition Act 1998 (Groceries) (Coronavirus) (Public Policy Exclusion) Order 2020 SI 2020 No. 369; see also the Explanatory Memorandum. SI 2020 No. 369 was repealed on 8 October 2020 (The Competition Act 1998 (Coronavirus) (Public Policy Exclusions) (Amendment and Revocation) Order 2020 SI 2020 No. 993). On 17 December 2020 a similar exception, The Competition Act 1998 (Groceries) (Public Policy Exclusion) Order 2020 SI 2020 No. 1568, was laid before Parliament; it came into force on 11 January 2021 and expired on 31 March 2021.

[24] Competition Act 1998 (Dairy Produce) (Coronavirus) (Public Policy Exclusion) Order 2020 SI 2020 No. 481, repealed 8 October 2020, by SI 2020 No. 993; other industries provided exemptions were Isle of Wight Transport Services and Health Service Bodies and Private Health Care Providers.

[25] The notifications can be found at: www.gov.uk/guidance/competition-law-exclusion-orders-relating-to-coronavirus-covid-19 The details of the notified agreements are thin, consisting of general, boilerplate statements. No precise details of either the terms of any agreement or minutes or notes of any discussions appear to be in the public domain. This would have made

The UK was not alone in granting these sorts of exemptions. Some Member States provided exemptions,[26] or comfort letters relating to proposed cooperative practices.[27] In fact, the European Commission provided its first 'comfort letter'[28] to Medicines for Europe, a representative of the European generic and biosimilar pharmaceutical industry. That industry noted a need to increase production of certain medicines used to treat patients (particularly those in intensive care). To address this, they proposed cooperation to 'identify production capacity and existing stocks, and to adapt or to reallocate, based on projected or actual demand, production and stocks, and to potentially also address the distribution of Covid-19 medicines'. And:

> [T]o coordinate available industry production capacity throughout Europe and identify means to optimise the use of resources available in the industry. In particular, the coordination may need to include cross-supply of API(s) (active pharmaceutical ingredient(s)), possibly including intermediates, and jointly identifying where to best switch production of a certain production site to a certain medicine and/or to increase capacity, so that not all firms focus on one or a few medicines, whilst others remain in under-production.[29]

This was the first comfort letter that the Commission issued in the post-Regulation 1/2003 regime.[30] The European Competition Network (ECN) (the EU's network of NCAs) issued a more general statement that its members would not 'actively intervene against necessary and temporary measures put in place in order to avoid a shortage of supply'.[31]

The difference between an exemption (of the UK sort) and a comfort letter is significant. The latter indicates that the practices envisaged are consistent with the competition rules.[32] A comfort letter merely remedies a possible deficiency with

---

the arraignments proposed and discussed among these parties transparent and demonstrated that they were truly in the public interest.

[26] E.g. Autorità Garante della Concorrenza e del Mercato (Italy), 'Comunicazionedell'Autorità Garante della Concorrenza e del Mercato sugli accordi di cooperazione e l'emergenza COVID-19' (24 April 2020).

[27] E.g. Bundeskartellamt (Germany), 'Crisis Management Measures in the Automotive Industry – Bundeskartellamt Supports the German Association of the Automotive Industry (VDA) in Developing Framework Conditions under Competition Law Aspects' (9 June 2020).

[28] EU Commission DG Comp, 'Comfort Letter: Coordination in the Pharmaceutical Industry to Increase Production and to Improve Supply of Urgently Needed Critical Hospital Medicines to Treat COVID-19 Patients', Brussels, 08/04/2020 COMP/OG – D(2020/044003).

[29] Ibid. at 3.

[30] Buhart and Henry, 'COVID-20: The Comfort Letter Is Dead – Long Live the Comfort Letter?' and De Stefano, 'Covid-19 and EU Competition Law'.

[31] ECN, 'Antitrust: Joint Statement by the European Competition Network (ECN) on Application of Competition Law During the Corona Crisis' (23 March 2020).

[32] As is made clear in Commission's letter (n. 28) at 2, 'the Commission considers that in the present exceptional circumstances the cooperation practices as set out above do not raise concerns under Article 101 of the Treaty on the Functioning of the European Union'.

self-assessment, given uncertainties about activities at the margin. Undertakings contemplating a given arrangement may, in their self-assessment, have determined that their proposed course of action is consistent with the competition rules. However, because of the novelty of the situation and/or arrangement (or the possibility of a significant fine), the undertakings nevertheless may have residual doubt, and in the absence of such a 'clearance' may forego the activity. This would come at the cost of any benefit that the agreement would produce. A comfort letter merely confirms the practice's legality, and hence that the proposed is not anticompetitive.

On the other hand, a public policy exemption, such as granted in the UK, is a different matter. On one view, such an exemption recognises that the proposed practice, in the absence of the exemption, would be illegal, and hence is anticompetitive. And the practice remains anticompetitive, notwithstanding any declaration about its legality.[33]

Another view championed by Odudu[34] is that such exemptions do not necessarily legalise an otherwise illegal practice. Rather, they confer, *ex ante*, the certainty that those engaging in such practices will not be prosecuted under Chapter 1 of the Act. Hence, parties do not have to undertake the legal or economic analysis required by the self-assessment process. Further, the involvement of governmental entities such as the relevant minister ensures political accountability for the decision to disapply competition law.[35]

While there may be an appeal to this view of such exemptions, telling against it is the limited utility of the 'simplified' self-assessment process.[36] These orders also require that certain commercially sensitive information (price and cost) not be shared and that the agreements are for only a limited purpose. The undertakings involved will still need to vet the agreements for these features and purposes. Further, if the proposed practices were actually efficiency-enhancing (and

---

[33] The Memorandum to SI 2020 No. 369 notes that '[s]uch coordination as explained above would ordinarily breach domestic competition rules' (para. 7.3). And, '[t]his Order is intended to disapply competition law only in respect of agreements needed as a result of coronavirus'. This recognises the otherwise illegal nature of the groceries arrangements.

[34] Odudu, n. 12 at 75.

[35] Ibid. at 78. The lack of transparency concerning the precise details of the agreements or discussions (see n. 25) does not instil great confidence that those responsible for the disapplication of competition law (or the consumer welfare consequences resulting from this) will be held accountable.

[36] Odudu notes (ibid. fn. 54) that the Explanatory Memoranda are 'ambiguous'. This is not the case. After noting the Memorandum to SI 2020 No. 369 (cited above, n. 33), Odudu cites the Memorandum to the Competition Act (Public Policy Exclusion) Order 2012 SI 2012 No. 710 which concerned the petroleum industry. The Memorandum noted that these arrangements would receive the benefit of Section 9 of the Competition Act. The arrangements under the 2012 Order were subject to a government–industry protocol which would have incorporated the Section 9 provisions.

consistent with the competition regime) – why did the undertakings not engage in them prior to the crisis?

Nevertheless, the difference between the two approaches (exemptions versus comfort letters) raises the question of how an anticompetitive arrangement that is predicated on collaboration between (former) competitors solves the problems more effectively than a competitive, market-driven solution.[37]

The market is a very effective means of distributing goods and services. Where demand is high, prices will rise or goods will be brought in to satisfy the demand.[38] If prices rise as a result of scarcity, this serves as a signal and incentive for others to enter the market and alleviate the scarcity, competing the price down. Cartels and cooperative activity among competitors do not have this effect. Cartel behaviour creates artificial shortages and the resulting scarcity to exploit higher prices. Cartelists will tend to erect market barriers to prevent other parties from entering the market and compete the cartelists' prices down.

Where supply problems are caused by a shortage of goods, suppliers have an incentive to seek new supplies from elsewhere or increase production, and to do so before their competitors do. When competitors cooperate, this race to supply is eliminated, and there is no fear that the resulting higher prices will subsequently be competed down to a competitive price. As Ormosi and Stephen note with reference to the UK food industry:

> The relaxing of the present rules may even cause supermarkets to close some stores, to concentrate supply where it is needed most. Coordination will ensure that those closures do not overlap with each other (thereby ensuring that at least one supplier remains in each geographic location). But ensuring that there is at least one supplier in any area does not equate to ensuring that there is a sustained supply of food in these areas. On the contrary, economic theory would suggest that reduced competition is unlikely to lead to a sustained supply of food.[39]

---

[37] See Ormosi and Stephen, n. 22 at 300, and Schinkel and d'Ailly, 'Corona Crisis Cartels: Sense and Sensibility'.

[38] The UK experience showed that there was some diversion of food supplies from the restaurant industry to grocery supplies. There was also diversion of distilled alcohol towards the production of hand gels. The food diversion was limited by packaging (the quantities purchased by the catering industry were far larger than those needed by households), logistics and labelling issues. These concerns would not be mitigated by reduced competition. Indeed, enhanced competition (e.g. providing retail-sized packaging and more agile logistics) is likely to solve the problem. See Wentworth, 'Rapid Response: Effects of COVID-19 on the Food Supply System'. The diversion of alcohol towards antivirals was constrained by requirements in the production of ethanol and of hand sanitisers. This is not a competition law issue but may be an argument for the general reduction of the regulatory burden. See Health and Safety Executive (UK), 'Manufacture and Supply of Biocidal Hand Sanitiser Products during the Coronavirus Pandemic'.

[39] Ormosi and Stephen, n. 22 at 301.

Indeed, they could have added that this sort of coordinated strategy in store closing will ensure a set of geographical monopolies – with corresponding prices, lack of choice and resulting consumer harm.

A belief that the competition rules prohibit all cooperation or coordination between competing undertakings is false. There is no binary choice between competition and cooperation. Rather, the rules prohibit cooperative action when that activity is likely to lead to consumer harm. Beneficial cooperation is entirely consistent with the EU's (and other jurisdictions') antitrust regime(s); and – to this end – the Commission has promulgated a set of exemptions and guidelines on cooperation. It is noteworthy that the Oxford/AstraZeneca, Moderna and Pfizer-BioNTech vaccines (the first approved) are collaborative efforts, produced within a competitive environment of (consortiums of) undertakings developing competing products.[40] The design and production of ventilators, which were in short supply in the early stages of the pandemic, provides another illustration of this point.[41]

During the Covid-19 pandemic, when the public interest required collaboration among competitors, that collaboration was often deemed not contrary to the competition regime. This strongly suggests that the disapplication of the competition rules via a so-called public policy exemption (introduced after the initial stages of the pandemic) was not in the consumer interest.

Other considerations also tell against setting aside the rules. First, a public policy exemption, and the ability of undertakings to take advantage of this exemption, is predicated on the view that the undertakings will act strictly in the public interest in their collaboration. This is not necessarily the case.[42] Firms are motivated by profit, and it is the pursuit of profit which drives their activities.[43] On this point, Schinkel and d'Ailly correctly note:

> Altruistic initiatives are fragile. The problem is that in a corporate context, the profit motive is never far away. Even the most benevolent manager will have to report to the owners and shareholders, funders and lenders of his company, who require a rate of return on their investments. Before a company can sacrifice profit, these financially interested parties would need to agree to accept a lower rate of return than they can earn elsewhere in the economy. That is complex enough to achieve

---

[40] As a coda, one might consider the dangers of industry-wide cooperation in developing this vaccine. The success of the project may have been delayed if industry-wide cooperation steered research towards one (or a very limited set of) direction(s), had the preferred direction turned out to be a 'dead end'.

[41] On ventilator production and procurement in the time of Covid-19, see Scott Morton, 'Innovation Incentives in a Pandemic'.

[42] This point thus asks whether we can trust those granted an exemption to act in the public interest. The two UK industries that were the main beneficiaries of exemptions during the Covid-19 pandemic (the grocery and dairy industries) have a history of collusive activity (however, prosecution of this activity has not always been successful). See e.g. OFT Case CE/3094-03 (Decision 10 August 2011); *Tesco et al. v. OFT* [2012] CAT 31.

[43] On this point, see Ormosi and Stephen, n. 22 at 300.

for a single firm, let alone for all involved in a cooperation. Rent seeking capital has the tendency to undermine low rate of return corporate social responsible activities, by management interventions and ultimately capital flight.[44]

The opportunities for activity that is both eleemosynous and simultaneously successfully profit-seeking is, at best, limited, as those interested in an adequate return on capital will note.

A second, related, point is that anticompetitive collaboration typically results in a reduction in output. This is the main driver of the price increase which leads to extra profit. A purported reason for enhanced collaboration during the pandemic is that this will stimulate additional production of needed goods. This justification is unsound. As cartels lead to reduced output, there is no good reason to believe that cartel activity will increase the supply of goods in the face of a shortage.[45] In fact, if anything collaboration in production and supply – including, as envisaged, determining which goods should be produced and stocked – is likely to prioritise production of those goods with the highest profit margins.[46] The literature which appears in business and marketing journals seems to suggest this point.[47]

Finally, the post-pandemic effects of anticompetitive collaboration must be taken into account. The US experience in using cartels to combat the economic consequences of the Great Depression did more harm than good by prolonging its effects. Once the public health consequences of the pandemic are brought under control, the economic consequences of the pandemic and the measures taken to control it will need to be addressed. Policymakers will need to use many tools to heal the economy. One of these tools should be ensuring competitive markets, which will aid businesses and the economy generally to rebound, and provide consumer confidence in promoting demand.[48] While exempted collusion is time- and purpose-limited to the pandemic, it may have lingering after-effects. It allows undertakings to glean information about their competitors' businesses that they would not have otherwise known. But further, it marks a cultural change in the industry to one

---

[44] Schinkel and d'Ailly, n. 37 at 9.

[45] See Ormosi and Stephen, n. 22 at 301 who title the fourth part of their paper: 'If Output under Competition Was Not Sufficient, Why Would Cartel Output Be Any Better?'

[46] In March 2020, one UK manufacturer of own-brand toilet and kitchen paper reduced its range of production 'from 120 to 30 so more can be manufactured quickly. Each supermarket it supplies now gets one type of kitchen roll and two of toilet roll' (Eley, supra, n. 12). One need not be overly cynical to ask whether the least profitable lines were reduced, particularly given other industry statements assured that the Covid-19 outbreak had no effect on the UK's production and supply of toilet paper; see Devlin, 'Don't Panic: Toilet Roll Production and Distribution Normal, Say Suppliers'.

[47] See e.g. Crick and Crick, 'Cooperation and COVID-19', who suggest (at 211) that '[i]f competition laws are relaxed, firms should capitalise on the increased freedom to share resources and capabilities with their trustworthy and complementary industry rivals for mutually-beneficial outcomes'. Given that the publication is directed towards the business community, we presume that 'mutually-beneficial' is a euphemism for 'mutually-profitable'.

[48] See e.g. Tyrie, 'How Should Competition Policy React to Coronavirus?'

where regular sharing of information is permitted, or even encouraged. As noted in an academic marketing journal:

> Owner-managers are encouraged to acknowledge that once this global pandemic is over (and the regulation of certain forms of coopetition [*sic*] are potentially enforced), it might be challenging to end their partnerships with rivals. Thus, they should agree on the extent to which they will cooperate, vis-à-vis, compete with their rivals in advance of changing circumstances.[49]

Nevertheless, it is not clear that post-pandemic this information can be 'unlearned' or that the culture will return to the 'old ways'.[50]

To conclude, relaxing or 'disapplying' the competition rules to permit collusion between competitors is unlikely to be a solution to remedying shortages resulting from pandemic-induced spikes and shifts in demand. If cooperative activity could remedy these shortages without harming the public interest (i.e. diminishing consumer welfare), that activity would not be precluded by the rules. But more significantly, the encouragement of anticompetitive activity may well leave a post-pandemic hangover that could hinder an effective recovery for the economy.

This said, there might be room for greater use of comfort letters or other forms of informal guidance to direct undertakings on how to ensure that their goals are consistent with the competition rules. But the need for this sort of guidance extends to matters other than the Covid-19 pandemic. The Commission's use of a comfort letter in these circumstances was a welcome development. This should serve as a precedent, and not be a one-off.

5.3 PRICE GOUGING AS A COMPETITION PROBLEM

Economists and the general public tend to have different views towards price increases in the immediate aftermath of a crisis or other emergency. The popular view of those who increase prices is that these individuals and firms are opportunistic price gougers, seeking to enrich themselves from the unfortunate predicament and suffering of others. To the economist, on the other hand, these people are merely transmitting market signals, being receptive to the increase in price given an increased demand for, and shortage of, the good. High prices act as market signals, indicating an opportunity for other players to bring the scarce goods to the market, which will eventually drive the price down to near its pre-crisis level.[51] Competition

---

[49] Crick and Crick, n. 47 at 211.
[50] Ormosi and Stephen, n. 22 at 301 remark: 'It is very hard to monitor coordination and allowing competitors to share key data will bestow a level of familiarity about one another that did not exist before. This means that even after the relaxing of competition rules ceases, there will still be an increased ability to continue colluding tacitly. This sort of behaviour has been observed in the past.'
[51] See Salinger, 'Price Gouging and the Covid-19 Crisis – This Time Is (a Little) Different'.

lawyers seem to occupy a position between the two (albeit one closer to the economists'), recognising that while shocks to consumption can cause spikes in demand, driving prices up, there may be market barriers which can retard entry, hence there may be opportunities for these actors to acquire some extra profit (or rent). But, the competition lawyer is not a consumer lawyer – her concern tends only to focus on large, dominant entities (or groups of entities acting as a dominant entity) when they engage in these practices.

The early days of the Covid-19 pandemic were marked by sudden demand for some consumer goods that were part of the standard grocery purchase (e.g. toilet paper and pasta) and others that were not (e.g. hand sanitiser and face masks). Demand for the former, and supermarkets' unwillingness to increase prices, led to a shortage. This was alleviated somewhat by the industry imposing rationing of purchases of these products. In the case of the latter set of goods, we witnessed – quite notoriously – substantial increases in their prices.[52] The UK's Competition and Market Authority opened a Chapter II (the mirror of Article 102) investigation into the practices of four pharmacies and convenience stores regarding their pricing of sanitiser. These investigations were closed within three months of being opened.[53] The UK's authority was not the only NCA to open an investigation; others did – but typically did so in their other role as a consumer protection authority.[54]

Excessively high prices can infringe European competition law. Article 102 TFEU (and its national counterparts) prohibit 'directly or indirectly imposing unfair purchase or selling prices'. In spite of this prohibition, since the advent of the MEA, the Commission's enforcement focus has been directed towards exclusionary practices – i.e. the erection of market barriers which prevent the entry of competitors whose activities can drive down prices.[55] Although there has been some enforcement by NCAs of excessive pricing,[56] it is nevertheless easier (and, if the Commission is correct, more effective for competition in the long run) to pursue exclusionary conduct.

There are two threshold problems associated with excess pricing claims. The first is that EU competition law prohibits abusive practices by *dominant* undertakings. Hence the pricing must occur in a market in which the undertaking in question is dominant. Second, enforcers must determine some threshold of 'excessive'.

---

[52] Hegarty, 'Coronavirus: Where Has All the Hand Sanitiser Gone?'

[53] See CMA Case Page, 'Hand Sanitiser Products: Suspected Excessive and Unfair Pricing', www .gov.uk/cma-cases/hand-sanitiser-products-suspected-excessive-and-unfair-pricing.

[54] See e.g. Italian Competition Authority (ICA), 'ICA: Coronavirus, the Authority Intervenes in the Sale of Sanitizing Products and Masks'.

[55] See Guidance on the Commission's Enforcement Priorities in Applying Article 82 of the EC Treaty to Abusive Exclusionary Conduct by Dominant Undertakings [2009] OJ C-45/7.

[56] See e.g. Case C-177/16, *Autortiesību un komunicēšanās konsultāciju aģentūra/Latvijas Autoru apvienība v. Konkurences padome* (AKK/LAA), ECLI:EU:C:2017:689, and *Competition and Markets Authority v. Flynn Pharma Ltd and Anor (Rev 3)* [2020] EWCA Civ 339.

In dealing with the latter problem, EU law prohibits dominant entities from charging an excessive price when the price has, for instance, no relationship to the economic value of the product in question.[57] This was the holding in the pivotal *United Brands* case. However, that case does not provide an exhaustive recipe for competition agencies to positively identify 'excessive' or 'unfair' prices. And, in spite of the large arsenal of potential tests that a competition authority could use to detect and prove excessive pricing,[58] such proof remains a difficult task. The difficulty is exacerbated in times of sudden, acute shortages, particularly when arbitrageurs or other producers/distributors of goods have yet to enter the market. The 'broad terms' test of reaping benefits in conditions outside of workable competition is inapplicable in these circumstances. In fact, it is these sorts of price signals which stimulate the market entry associated with 'workable competition'.[59]

In the best of times, it is very difficult to calculate a firm's costs of producing a product. As Giosa notes:

> This is because the calculation of the difference requires the identification of the producer's costs, which is a complex, demanding and time-consuming operation .... Nevertheless, 'firms' diverse production and market operations incur various categories of costs' e.g. marginal cost, long-term average cost, total cost etc., which makes it difficult to decide which of the dominant firms' costs should be considered for the analysis of the excessive pricing.[60]

In a crisis situation, these costs will likely vary from those incurred in the normal course of business.

In addition to assessing costs, determining whether a price is 'fair' also requires the assessment of the appropriate level of return (i.e. 'profit', in the accounting sense) to which a firm is entitled. This requires examining a myriad other factors such as the enterprise's level of risk, and the availability and opportunity costs of capital.

It is not clear that competition authorities are best placed to make these sorts of assessments of cost and return, and thus serve as generic price regulatory agencies – particularly if drafted into service during a crisis. This is especially so if the problem is approached from an error–cost framework.

The main danger of false positives (type I errors) in the assessment of 'fair prices' is that this undermines the investment incentives of those seeking to enter the market.

---

[57] See Case 27/76, *United Brands Continentaal BV v. Commission*, ECLI:EU:C:1978:22, paras. 250–253.

[58] *Flynn Pharma*, n. 56 para. 97.

[59] On the notion of 'workable competition', see Baumol, Panzar and Willig, *Contestable Markets* and e.g. Brock, 'Contestable Markets and the Theory of Industry Structure'. The 'broad terms test' is likely applicable to those practices which reap the benefits of high prices while erecting market barriers to prevent workable competition.

[60] Giosa, 'Exploitative Pricing in the Time of Coronavirus' at 503; the internal quotation is from Pozdnakova, 'Excessive Pricing and the Prohibition of the Abuse of a Dominant Position under Article 82 EC' at 121.

It is well known that the imposition of rent controls in the interests of fairness results in an undersupply of rental accommodation.[61] The example of rent control is part of the introductory cannon of microeconomics, and it provides a lesson for the understanding of the price regulation of other goods and services.

In a crisis situation, underinvestment in entry incentives translates to possibly deterring those who may wish to mitigate the shortage through arbitrage or by producing substitutes.[62] The effect of price controls is that entry may not occur. On this point, Culpepper and Block note:

> Anti-gouging legislation reduces incentives for stores to open or outside sellers to come to the disaster area. Sellers do not want to enter a market in which there is little or no opportunity to earn a profit. It is price that rations the scarce resources and calls forth supply. All other things being equal, production increases as a result of price increasing. Implicit in this is that if prices are not allowed to increase due to government regulation, production will not increase.[63]

Further, controls on prices, whether exercised as competition regulation or anti-price-gouging consumer protection legislation, may have other perverse effects.

Such controls can discourage entry to mitigate a present crisis, and successful prosecutions will have consequences for the future. Salinger provides the following account:

> After hurricane Wilma [in 2005], which hit Miami about a month after hurricane Rita (and two months after Katrina), a Miami man drove his flatbed truck to North Carolina – several hundred miles away – and purchased a set of portable generators, paying roughly $300 for some and $500 for others. He drove the truck back to Miami and sold the generators for approximately double what he had paid for them. The Florida Attorney General sued him for price gouging.
>
> The initiative shown by this truck owner helped alleviate the shortage of generators, since more Floridians were able to acquire generators than if the truck owner had not driven to North Carolina. We do not need to give him an award for his initiative. The market did that, or at least would have if he had not had to pay a fine to the state. It would be interesting to know what that truck owner did the next time a hurricane hit Miami. Perhaps he was civic-minded enough to act to ease the impending shortage without profiting from it. More likely, the lesson he learned was not to show so much initiative.[64]

These type I errors (particularly when translated into legislation) will deprive consumers of needed goods.

---

[61] See Olsen, 'An Econometric Analysis of Rent Control' and Glaeser and Luttmer, 'The Misallocation of Housing under Rent Control'.

[62] Motta and de Streel, 'Excessive Pricing in Competition Law' at 17–19.

[63] Culpepper and Block, 'Price Gouging in the Katrina Aftermath: Free Markets at Work' at 514.

[64] Salinger, n. 51 at 10.

Further, the imprecision of the appropriate cost test to use, and how a competition authority will apply it, produces additional uncertainty. In addition to the controlled price possibly being insufficient to attract entry, lack of clarity over legal standards of conduct may further dissuade involvement in the market. Not only will this further deter entry, but it may be a rule of law problem if the conduct is subsequently subject to investigation and prosecution.

However, most significantly, price controls have a strong political appeal to them.[65] There is a political interest in seeing that prices of basic goods do not rise. This is understandable, as an increase in prices for goods entails that consumers' real incomes (i.e. the amount of goods that consumers can buy) have dropped. There is thus political incentive to keeping prices under control, particularly in the aftermath of a sudden crisis, where prices increase due to decreased supply and/or increased demand when delays to a wage-based response (if they in fact do occur) make consumers poorer. However, this is a political response to the phenomenon of high prices, not a response to the phenomenon of market conditions or failure.

The solution to this is to bring in more goods, which will cause a drop in prices. The market failure that may prevent price-reducing arbitrage or production of goods is often associated with the erection and maintenance of entry barriers. Competition authorities have (through their work in dominance and merger cases) an understanding of how such barriers can be constructed. It is here where their expertise lies, and where their efforts should be focused – not with price controls.

Consumer law restrictions on price gouging tend to focus on elevated prices simpliciter. In contrast, the focus of EU competition law where high (or 'exploitative') prices are present is on the dominance or market power of the undertaking involved. In this regime, high prices are not necessarily contrary to the competition rules, as Article 102 TFEU only prohibits unfair pricing by *dominant* undertakings.

As *United Brands* teaches us, an undertaking exhibits dominance if it has sufficient economic strength (market power) such that it can act independently of its competitors, customers and consumers.[66] Subsequent case law shows that market shares can be used as evidence to establish dominance;[67] however, other indicia can be used to establish dominance.[68] Nevertheless, the need to define a market and assess an undertaking's power and behaviour within the market so defined is essential for this sort of analysis.

---

[65] Motta and Streel, n. 62 at 19.

[66] Case 27/76, n. 57 para. 65.

[67] Case 85/76, *Hoffmann-La Roche & Co. AG v. Commission*, ECLI:EU:C:1979:36, paras. 40, 59; Case 322/81, *NV Nederlandsche Banden Industrie Michelin v. Commission* ('Michelin I'), ECLI:EU:C:1983:313, para. 52; Case C-62/86, *AKZO Chemie BV v. Commission*, ECLI:EU:C:1991:286, para. 60.

[68] See e.g. Lianos, Korah and Siciliani, *Competition Law Analysis, Cases, and Materials* at 844–858; and Jones, Sufrin and Dunne, *EU Competition Law* at 300–306, 331–355.

Defining the relevant market and assessing the market position of the undertaking in question are the two hurdles which Article 102-based assessment must overcome. These two tasks are related – if the market definition is incorrect, the authorities may draw incorrect conclusions regarding the undertaking's power within it. The OECD notes:

> Even in normal circumstances this is a challenging proposition, requiring the identification of the relevant market, followed by an in-depth analysis to ascertain that the investigated company does possess the requisite level of market power . . . . These challenges are exacerbated in a crisis, where market power may disappear as suddenly as it appeared, and where the traditional evidence of market power concerning matters such as market shares, entry barriers, buyer power, etc., may be difficult to come by.[69]

In addition to presenting difficulties in obtaining evidence, the disruption caused by the pandemic altered supply and demand patterns.

From the supply side, disruptions to the usual supply chains can add entry barriers. From the demand side, restrictions on movement shrink the set of suppliers from which consumers can obtain goods. This causes disruptions to the chain of substitution,[70] where overlap in geographic and product markets permit a wider market definition. The overlap shrinks, narrowing markets. As the OECD remarks:

> Limitations in supply and stringent restrictions of circulation may prevent effective 'chains of substitution' within the relevant product markets, making geographic markets smaller than usual. Further, from a supply perspective, the closing of factories, the severing of value chains and the reduction in international trade levels can lead to a supplier becoming essential to the provision of necessary goods in certain areas. On the demand side, confinement may severely limit the ability of consumers to move around to purchase goods and services. In this context, even a local shop may acquire substantial market power, and become able to significantly increase prices even if it enjoys abundant supply.[71]

In both cases, this may narrow the geographical market.[72]

A small geographical market may give an undertaking an opportunity to develop sufficient market power to raise prices to an exploitative level. Costa-Cabral et al. provide the example of 'a single outlet being the only one still selling face masks during a weekend and therefore able to charge exorbitant prices'.[73] They rightly note that this behaviour is usually within the ambit of price-gouging laws, to which we add, 'and the problems associated therewith'.

---

[69] OECD, 'Exploitative Pricing in the Time of COVID-19' at 5.
[70] Commission, Notice on the Definition of Relevant Market for the Purposes of Community Competition Law [1997] OJ C-372/3, paras. 56–58.
[71] OECD, n. 69 at 7, citing Motta, 'Price Regulation in Times of Crisis Can Be Tricky'.
[72] See OECD, ibid. and Costa-Cabral et al., 'EU Competition Law and Covid-19' at 11.
[73] Ibid.

Notwithstanding the usual deference to consumer protection law, there has been some – though limited – competition law analysis of these so-called 'situational monopolies'. The oil supply crisis of 1973 led the Commission to investigate the Dutch oil market and the inability of smaller players to obtain petroleum from their usual suppliers.[74] In this situation, the Commission held that each of the major oil suppliers was in a dominant position relative to their regular customers.[75] (The decision was later annulled on the basis that the undertaking in question was an occasional and not a contractual customer and hence a dominant position did not exist.[76]) This is a fairly untested antitrust concept, and it may be dangerous to use in a crisis situation.

Although the theoretical appeal of situational monopolies is attractive – and they are certainly consistent with the microeconomics used in antitrust analysis – enforcers should be cautious about applying this concept.[77] At present it is not clear whether or not competition authorities have sufficiently robust data to determine if situational monopolies existed as a result of the crisis; and if they did, their extent.

A crisis will serve as a catalyst for cries to 'do something'. There are resulting political and social pressures for agencies to somehow act in the perceived public interest. In cases where high prices are a concern this often translates into demands to act against purported price gougers. At best this is a consumer protection concern. The involvement of competition authorities, using obscure theories in a politicised, crisis situation is institutionally inappropriate at best, and a rule of law problem at worst.

Competition law does not deal well with price shocks associated with crisis-induced demand shifts and spikes, nor does it – on its own – have the ability to immediately 'smooth out' prices. This should not be a surprise – this is the way that competition law should operate. These price increases are a result of the normal functioning of the market, not a result of some market failure. If market failure existed in this situation, it is with the existence of entry barriers that prevent prices from dropping. Identifying and suggesting means for the elimination of such barriers is the appropriate role of competition authorities.

---

[74] Commission Decision 77/327/EEC of 19 April 1977 (IV/28.841) (*ABG/Oil companies operating in the Netherlands*) [1977] OJ L-117/1, discussed in Sections 1.3.3, 'Article 102: Control of Unilateral Action' and 2.3.4, 'The Early Approach to Control of Dominance in Crisis'.

[75] Ibid. at 8–9.

[76] Case 77/77, *Benzine en Petroleum Handelsmaatschappij BV and others v. Commission*, ECLI: EU:C:1978:141, para. 29.

[77] The South African competition authority successfully prosecuted a number of firms, under competition law, for price gouging. Section 7 of the South African statue (Competition Act No. 89 of 1998, as amended) permits a firm to be regarded as dominant if it has market power, even if it has a low market share. See Ratshisusu and Mncube, 'Addressing Excessive Pricing Concerns in Time of the COVID-19 Pandemic – A View from South Africa'; First, 'Robbin' Hood'; and Boshoff, 'The Competition Economics of Excessive Pricing and Its Relation to the Covid-19 Disaster Period'.

5.4 THE FFD AS A RESPONSE

In every economic crisis or downturn, antitrust authorities are faced with calls to relax their enforcement of the competition rules. Such calls extend to merger control. As one former American Federal Trade Commission (FTC) official remarked:

> This is not the first time, even in recent memory, that large numbers of firms in our economy suffer from a severe economic downturn. During the Great Recession that began in 2008 a similar situation arose. At that time, many observers were calling for more lenient treatment of mergers proposed by firms in economic distress. Today, some in Congress are arguing for the exact opposite.[78]

While the calls in Congress are for enhanced scrutiny of mergers in the big data/big tech sector, crisis-motivated calls for lenient merger treatment focused on the desirability to relax scrutiny in merger control to giver greater leeway for firms which are in difficulty to merge. In the UK, Lord Tyrie remarked, 'the crisis may prompt an increasing number of mergers in which the parties argue that one of them is a failing firm, which would otherwise leave the market'.[79] In other words, these are calls for a relaxation of the criteria for the application of the FFD.

In brief, the FFD is a defence which allows for an otherwise anticompetitive merger to be consummated if three conditions are met:

1. The acquired firm is failing, i.e. would exit the market if it were not taken over by another firm.
2. The acquiring firm would take over the market share or assets of the acquired (failing) firm.
3. There is no less anticompetitive acquirer.

These criteria must be considered in the context of the impending insolvency of the failing firm. If the firm is inevitably exiting the market, and if, upon exit, the acquiring firm were a candidate to obtain the failing firm's market share or assets, then a 'pre-failure' merger could not be said to be the cause of the subsequent anticompetitive situation.

This context is important and should be kept in mind in assessing suggestions that the FFD criteria be relaxed. First, this is a defence; hence, the burden of proving each of the three conditions rests on the merging entities. However, competition agencies have an obligation to consider all arguments proffered by the firms. Second, the FFD is mounted within the context of an insolvency process. The insolvency process is one of the features of a market economy and allows for the exit of inefficient firms from the market, with their assets being put to alternative

---

[78] Heyer, 'Failing Firm Analysis and the Current Economic Downturn' at 15.
[79] Tyrie, n. 48 at 14.

uses – in most cases by different purchasers. Third, the defence requires that the firm be failing, i.e. its market exit is inevitable. These contextual elements are clearly related.

Calls for making the defence more generally applicable in times of crisis often are directed at suggesting agencies reduce their scrutiny of the financial state of the firm which is purported to be failing or of the competitive conditions of the market, post-merger. It would be a mistake to accept either suggestion. The FFD is often an inferior alternative to the insolvency process. If the firm were healthy it would not enter the insolvency process. Reduced scrutiny of the purported 'failing' firm's financial position increases the probability that the agency will approve an anticompetitive merger between two healthy undertakings.

Second, if the merger were not in fact anticompetitive, the defence would not need to be invoked. From the perspective of ensuring a competitive economy, the FFD is inferior to the insolvency process as a means of firm exit. Costa-Cabral et al. succinctly make this point:

> If we compare the welfare effects of merger and insolvency, the latter is preferable: assets are allocated among different purchasers, avoiding the risk of one player gaining pre-eminence over others. Furthermore, an effective insolvency regime is also a stimulus to enter markets in the first place, thus stimulating competition. This is why the failing firm defence tolerates an otherwise troublesome merger only when the assets would otherwise disappear: insolvency is the preferred option, merger is a second-best.[80]

The insolvency process, by dissipating the failed firm's assets (and market share) among that firm's competitors, is less likely to enhance the concentration of the market in question.

Competition agencies have correctly exhibited scepticism about reducing scrutiny in these cases in a pandemic economy. The Competition and Markets Authority (CMA) remarks:

> The coronavirus (COVID-19) pandemic has not brought about any relaxation of the standards by which mergers are assessed or the CMA's investigational standards. It remains critical to preserve competition in markets through rigorous merger investigations in order to protect the interests of consumers in the longer term.
>
> The CMA needs to ensure its decisions are based on evidence and not speculation, and will carefully consider the available evidence in relation to the possible impacts of coronavirus (COVID-19) on competition in each case.[81]

An American FTC official advises those making such claims in merger submissions, in the following – and perhaps – more cynical terms: 'Candor before the agency

---

[80] Costa-Cabral et al., n. 72 at 18.
[81] CMA, 'Summary of CMA's Position on Mergers Involving "Failing Firms"', Annex to *Guidance on Merger Assessments during the Coronavirus (COVID-19)*.

remains paramount, and it has been striking to see firms that were condemned as failing rise like a phoenix from the ashes once the proposed transaction was abandoned in light of our competition concerns.'[82] The fear is that affected firms will 'crisis-wash' their evidence, which – without appropriate scrutiny by authorities – will produce an anticompetitive outcome to the detriment of consumers.

The relaxation of the merger, or, more generally, the competition regime, in times of crisis is something to be resisted. The historical evidence shows that the relaxation of competition rules to counteract crises does not achieve this goal. If anything, the evidence shows that weakening competition will hinder recovery. The former chair of the CMA writes:

> Coronavirus may well lead to reduced competition; increased product market competition [concentration?]; increased gatekeeper power over suppliers; and a stronger position in digital advertising. This all suggests that at least as much regulatory scrutiny will be required, in future.[83]

This is particularly the case with mergers. The effects of an anticompetitive merger (e.g. increased concentration in the relevant market, the existence of a firm with greatly enhanced market power) will persist after the crisis has ended. The Lloyds/HBOS and ABN AMRO/Fortis mergers discussed earlier provide evidence of the lasting effects of mergers forced through for political reasons.[84]

Notwithstanding these concerns about the use of Covid-19 (or any other crisis) as a 'free pass' to avoid close scrutiny of competition regulators, there is no doubt that the pandemic had an adverse effect on many undertakings. Although support programmes somewhat mitigated the economic fallout, the Covid-19 pandemic pushed numerous undertakings into the insolvency process. This will certainly continue post-pandemic as a result of market and consumption changes. It is therefore appropriate that the competition authorities take into account the disruptions caused by the pandemic in their analysis. They need to demand robust data from the parties, and subject them to the usual vigorous scrutiny – and use equally as robust data in their own analyses.

Here lessons can be learned from the UK's CMA in two mergers considered during the pandemic: Amazon/Deliveroo and JD Sports/Footasylum. In both cases the mergers were contemplated before the outbreak. (Indeed, the latter was consummated prior to the pandemic.) During the investigations of the two mergers, the economic effects of the pandemic became apparent.

The former case concerned a transaction which would give Amazon a 16 per cent holding in Deliveroo (a food delivery services sourcing from local restaurants). This transaction was a result of a successful, pre-pandemic round of funding to raise

---

[82] Conner, 'On "Failing" Firms – and Miraculous Recoveries'.
[83] Tyrie, n. 48 at 19.
[84] Discussed in Section 4.4.2, 'Bank Merger as a Crisis Containment Measure'.

capital. Although it was (at the time) a negative cash-flow company, relying on ongoing raising of capital, Deliveroo was not a failing firm, given its success in raising capital.

However, in the immediate aftermath of the outbreak of the pandemic, this situation changed. Demand for food deliveries dropped, and restaurants (from which deliveries were made) closed. In effect, in March 2020 Deliveroo was 'on the ropes', and without additional funding it would exit the market, as the CMA provisionally concluded.[85] After examining other potential sources of funds, the CMA concluded that there was no likelihood of Deliveroo receiving funding other than through Amazon, and unfunded it would exit the market.[86] The CMA also found that if Deliveroo exited the market, the market would be in a weaker competitive position over time.[87] On this basis, the CMA's provisional decision was to approve the transaction, subject to comments.

In the interim, however, Deliveroo's fortunes changed, and its cash position dramatically improved in late March through June 2020.[88] It would now be unlikely to exit the market and could likely rely on the market to raise funding. It would therefore not be treated as a failing firm, and the CMA conducted a substantive assessment of the impact of Amazon's acquisition of this shareholding. The CMA concluded that at that level, this would not lead to a substantial lessening of competition in the affected markets and cleared the transaction in August 2020.

This robust use of data (including views of competitors), which was acquired on an ongoing basis during the approval process, contrasts with the CMA's practice in the JD Sports/Footasylum merger. There, the CMA initially failed to gather sufficiently robust data regarding the effect of Covid-19 on the relevant markets, hence any conclusions it drew about the economic effects of the pandemic were highly speculative. As a result, the Competition Appeal Tribunal (CAT) required the CMA to revisit their assessment.[89] However, the new evidence showed that notwithstanding the effects of Covid-19, the merger would result in an anticompetitive outcome.[90] Again, this shows the importance of robust and critical examinations about purported commercial damage occasioned by a crisis.

Finally, while it is important to consider the effects that the Covid-19 pandemic, or the impact that any other crisis or economic downturn might have on the viability of a business (or industry), a crisis should not be used as a 'free pass' to escape competition analysis. We again restate the point that the financial crisis has provided instances of

---

[85] Anticipated Acquisition by Amazon of a Minority Shareholding and Certain Rights in Deliveroo Provisional Findings Report (16 April 2020) para. 4.44.

[86] Ibid. paras. 4.64–4.65.

[87] Ibid. paras. 4.79–4.80.

[88] Anticipated Acquisition by Amazon of a Minority Shareholding and Certain Rights in Deliveroo Final Report (4 August 2020) paras. 6.27–6.40.

[89] *JD Sports Fashion PLC v. CMA* [2020] CAT 24 paras. 137–186.

[90] CMA, Completed Acquisition by JD Sports Fashion plc of Footasylum plc Provisional Report (3 September 2021).

anticompetitive mergers and their lingering consequences. These cases should be taken as cautionary notes when listening to calls for the relaxation of the competition rules, and particularly merger standards. The effects of mergers can be very long lasting. If merger control rules are relaxed to 'deal with' a crisis and thus permit otherwise anticompetitive concentrations, the damaging consequences often survive the crisis. To paraphrase a Christmas slogan of the Dogs Trust:[91] 'A merger is for life, not just a crisis'.

5.5 STATE AID AS A PANDEMIC RESPONSE

During the Covid-19 pandemic, public health measures caused significant shifts in demand in all major economies. Some sectors gained as a result of increased demand; for example, streaming entertainment and, after the initial stages of the pandemic, home food delivery from restaurants and supermarkets come to mind; and as people were unwilling or unable to leave home, the large technology companies (e.g. Amazon, Google, Netflix, Apple and Facebook) saw an increase in demand for their services. However, the majority of sectors were hit with sudden and sharp drops in demand. Among the hardest hit were the travel and transport, hospitality, entertainment and (in person) retail sectors. To provide support for those industries, and those employed or economically dependent upon them, governments devised numerous programmes to support people and businesses whose livelihoods were threatened by the economic fallout from Covid-19. Many such programmes had the character of state aid.

The first state aid package was approved by the Commission on 12 March 2020.[92] This was a Danish programme to compensate for losses resulting from the cancellation of public events with more than 1,000 participants. The Commission approved this programme within a day of receiving the Danish government's notification. By the end of 2020 the Commission had approved several hundred initiatives affecting almost every area of the economy.[93]

The Commission initially approved measures under Article 107(2)b TFEU ('aid to make good the damage caused by natural disasters or exceptional occurrences'). As the scale of the pandemic, and its economic consequences, became more grave, the legal basis soon shifted to Article 107(3)b TFEU ('aid to promote the execution of an important project of common European interest or to remedy a serious disturbance in the economy of a Member State').[94] To aid national governments in the design of these programmes (and facilitate their rapid approval) the

---

[91] Given the popularity of adopting pets during the Covid-19 lockdown, the Trust diversified its portfolio of slogans/campaigns. See Woodmansey, 'A Dog Is for Life, Not Just for Lockdown'.

[92] State Aid SA.56685 (2020/N) – *Denmark* – *Compensation scheme for cancellation of events related to COVID-19* (12 March 2020) C(2020)1698 final.

[93] The Commission's list of such approvals on 15 September 2021 extended to over fifty pages.

[94] The first approval under the latter ground occurred on 11 April 2020: State Aid SA.56819 *Belgium* – *COVID-19* – *Loan Guarantee Scheme in Response to the COVID-19 Crisis* (11.04.2020) C(2020) 2364.

Commission developed a Temporary Framework to support the economy in the context of the Covid-19 pandemic.[95] Paragraph 21 of that Framework identified the conditions under which support could be granted; the main requirements were:

- the aid does not exceed EUR 800 000 per undertaking;
- the aid is granted on the basis of a scheme with an estimated budget;
- the aid may be granted to undertakings that were not in difficulty on 31 December 2019; and
- it may be granted to undertakings that are not in difficulty and/or to undertakings that were not in difficulty on 31 December 2019, but that faced difficulties or entered in difficulty thereafter as a result of the Covid-19 outbreak.

The framework was approved on 17 March 2020. It has been modified subsequently.[96] The 8 May modification to the Framework permitted public recapitalisation of companies in trouble as a result of the pandemic. This was subject to some conditions, particularly:

- proof of the need for state support;
- that it is in 'the common interest to intervene. This may relate to avoiding social hardship and market failure due to significant loss of employment, the exit of an innovative company, the exit of a systemically important company, the risk of disruption to an important service';
- the inability of the beneficiary to obtain market-based funding;
- the beneficiary was not in difficulty pre-pandemic.[97]

In addition, the Framework included provisions regarding repayment to the Member State, managerial remuneration, etc. similar to those found in the R&R Guidelines.

As was the case with the last severe pan-European crisis – the financial crisis – the Commission was able to 'fast track' its scrutiny of proposed aid measures, often approving programmes overnight. This meant that support could be delivered in an expedited manner, hence providing rapid financial support to enable the early mitigation of commercial difficulties.

This governmental support seems reasonable at first glance. Faced with significant falls in demand across almost all sectors of the economy, resulting in hardship for the vast majority of businesses, opening the Treasury's coffers to provide this aid appeared to be an appropriate decision for politicians to make in the midst of a crisis.

---

[95] Communication from the Commission Temporary Framework for State Aid Measures to Support the Economy in the Current COVID-19 Outbreak [2020] OJ C-91 I/01.

[96] On 3 April, 8 May, 29 June and 13 October 2020.

[97] Communication from the Commission, Amendment to the Temporary Framework for State Aid Measures to Support the Economy in the Current COVID-19 Outbreak [2020] OJ C-143/04, para. 49.

However, this is not to say that it was a 'smart decision', particularly in the context of smarter state aid – a goal of the Commission's state aid modernisation plan.[98]

The demand shocks which resulted from the pandemic were not homogenous throughout an economy or even within a sector. Some firms will not survive the pandemic, some were unviable before the pandemic, others may survive with or without altering their business practices and models. The same observations apply to industries.

Generous support to unviable firms and industries (whether they were unviable before or as a result of the pandemic) is not only an inappropriate use of governmental funding, but it interferes with market processes that encourage failing or otherwise insolvent firms to exit the market, and their assets to be put to more productive and efficient use. Governmental aid to such firms only prolongs their existence, perpetuating their static and dynamic inefficiencies. There were more than a few businesses and industries that fell into this category.

Where the firm or industry is viable, different considerations apply. If it is assumed that, post-pandemic, demand for the firm in question's product will return, and what is needed is merely liquidity or financial support to enable restructuring for the post-crisis world, the argument is different. In this case, the competition-distorting effects of the aid are less pronounced than in the former, and there is a significant argument to grant this sort of support.

But it must be emphasised: this argument is not 'Covid-19 specific'. These considerations (and this argument) apply to all firms and industries facing downturns, whatever the cause or extent of the downturn. The magnitude of the crisis should not result in a weakening of the scrutiny applied to the measures or conditions for aid eligibility.[99] Inefficient, 'zombie firms' are 'zombies', irrespective of their cause or the economic environment in which they operate.

There are error costs associated with attempting to determine which firm or industry might be viable post-crisis. Given that it is difficult to foresee what the post-crisis demand patterns might be,[100] there is significant room for error. In the face of this uncertainty, the choice appeared to be between granting wasteful aid

---

[98] See Communication from the Commission to the European Parliament, the Council, the European Economic and Social Committee and the Committee of the Regions, State Aid Modernisation, COM/2012/209 final.

[99] Of course, the magnitude of the crisis may have an effect on post-crisis recovery. However, this would go to the assessment of the viability of the firm post-crisis and not on the scrutiny of the measures or conditions for aid eligibility during the crisis.

[100] This is particularly difficult when the cause of the crisis is not exclusively economic. In the context of the post-Covid-19 economy, it is difficult to know, in advance, what the future for large-venue entertainment (concerts, stage and cinema) or the hospitality industry will look like. Making such determinations is difficult 'part way' through the pandemic; making such determinations at the start of the crisis would have required an almost superhuman degree of prescience.

(thereby extending the life of zombies) or failing to provide aid (thereby hastening the exit of otherwise viable firms).

If markets were operating as they should, we should be sceptical about grants of aid and more concerned about grants to zombies. If a zombie firm is granted aid this perpetuates inefficiencies; if an otherwise viable firm is not rescued, market forces will operate to ensure that its assets will return to their best use – in this case restoring the firm's viability. However, markets may not operate this way.

The survivability of firms is dependent upon their access to capital. An inefficient form which is part of a larger conglomerate may have better access to additional capital than a similar, independent (but possibly slightly more efficient) firm.[101]

There is also a set of evidence suggesting that less efficient firms which are already on a 'lifeline' may continue to receive support, while more efficient competitors do not. This is particularly exacerbated in crisis situations. Fumagalli, Motta and Peitz note:

> This apparently paradoxical result is the result of banks' incentives. Banks have to satisfy capital requirements, and in times of crisis, when non-performing loans increase, raising capital also becomes more difficult. As a result, banks prefer to avoid writing off their capital. When faced with the choice between rolling over the loan to otherwise insolvent (or 'zombie') firm or recognising this loan is non-performing and hence writing off capital), the bank will tend to prefer the former.[102]

They cite evidence from the Japanese depression of the 1990s and of the global financial crisis in support.

Further, risk aversion in the market may play a role in limiting access to funds. In theory, a well-functioning financial market should be risk neutral, factoring risk into expected return (e.g. interest on debt, capital gain or dividends for equity). But this theoretical point may not hold, particularly in times of crisis. In situations where the economy is in a downturn, banks will fear loss of capital, due to the insolvencies of their debtors. In response to this, to preserve their capital cushions, banks may reduce lending, thereby hoarding cash.[103]

This suggests that market mechanisms may fail, or at least be imperfect in their response to the funding needs of otherwise efficient firms in the face of such crises, pointing towards limited state aid. The Framework attempts to provide these limits by imposing limits on the time frame for support and its requirement that aid is

---

[101] Fumagalli, Motta and Peitz, 'Which Role for State Aid and Merger Control during and after the Covid Crisis?' at 296.

[102] Ibid. at 296–297.

[103] Although in the UK, bank lending to businesses increased during the pandemic, this was a result of a government-guaranteed loan scheme (state aid) designed to keep smaller businesses solvent. See Ernst and Young LLP, 'Bank Lending to Firms Surges to a 13-Year High as COVID-19 Leads to UK Businesses Borrowing More'; 'Business Borrowing from Banks "Up Fivefold" amid Coronavirus'; and McCormick, 'Investors Hoard Cash to Ward off Worst Effects of Coronavirus Crisis'.

granted only to viable undertakings. It is in assisting in the determination of viability of firms and industries that competition agency expertise is germane. Although accountants and other business analysts may have expertise at the firm level, competition agencies – through their merger control work – have experience in the analysis of the competitive situation in a given market.

The use of these state aid programmes has also opened a European dilemma. The Treaties create a presumption against the use of such governmental aid. Among the justifications for this presumption is that aid can have a distortive effect on competition within the internal market. Aid can be used to subsidise inefficient production and attract production to areas which have no comparative advantage in their production. A prohibition on (or at least limits to) state aid ensures a so-called level playing field. However, the considerable use of state aid in the context of Covid-19 has opened the door for an unlevelling of this playing field. Wealthier Member States, or those more amenable to protecting their jurisdiction's businesses, were more willing and able to provide support. This of course provides an advantage to their domestic industries, the consequences of which will likely survive the pandemic.[104]

This points towards the need for a pan-European scheme. The Commission proposed (in May 2020) a Recovery and Resilience Facility to 'mitigate the economic and social impact of the coronavirus Pandemic and make European economies and societies more sustainable, resilient and better prepared for the challenges and opportunities of the green and digital transitions'.[105] The approval of this facility was mired by political considerations by attaching rule of law considerations to Member State eligibility.[106] A political agreement of sorts was achieved in December 2020. However, it should be noted that this is a recovery programme, not a support programme, and it is designed to assist in the funding of programmes to enable the European economy to recover post-pandemic.[107] There is thus a strong

---

[104] There are also budgetary implications to this. Member States have made commitments about their financial planning, which are enshrined in, *inter alia*, the Stability and Growth Pact (SGP) and the Treaty on Stability, Coordination and Governance in the Economic and Monetary Union (to which all EU Members, save the Czech Republic and Croatia, are parties) that imposes limits on a Member State Government's budgetary 'freedom'. This Treaty nominally requires a balanced budget and automatic debt reduction, if a Member State's GDP-to-debt ratio exceeds a given threshold. However, on 20 March 2020, the Commission and Council activated the General Escape Clause of the SGP to give Member States greater financial flexibility in their response to Covid-19. See Communication from the Commission to the Council, On the Activation of the General Escape Clause of the Stability and Growth Pact, Brussels, 20.3.2020 COM(2020) 123 final. This will be subject to ongoing review. On Member State budget discipline and oversight, see also Chapter 4, nn. 133. and 134.

[105] European Commission, 'Recovery and Resilience Facility'.

[106] See e.g. Editorial Board, 'EU Should Resist Blackmail over Recovery Fund'.

[107] As the Commission notes, '[i]t will play a crucial role in mitigating the economic and social impact of the coronavirus Pandemic and making European economies and societies more sustainable, resilient and better prepared for the challenges of the green and digital transitions'. Press Release, 'Commission Welcomes Political Agreement on Recovery and Resilience Facility'.

argument that should there be a future crisis of such an extent, a recovery response should be initiated at the pan-European level. However, at present there is no legislative scheme, or budgetary provision, to allow for such a response. Going forward, this may be something to consider.

Ultimately, the extent and depth of governmental support programmes was a matter of political choice, albeit somewhat constrained by the state aid rules. As matters of political choice, the usual influences may have been applied to and felt by those making the choices. Hence, although passing the tests established by the Framework, support may not have been directed to its best use. Indeed, some support programmes may have been counterproductive, not just in ensuring the viability of competitive undertakings but also in controlling the public health problem.

An illustration of the latter might be found in the UK's 'Eat-Out-to-Help Out' programme, designed to aid the hospitality industry. The hospitality sector was suffering from a drop in demand – in the UK such undertakings were closed from the lockdown in March until 4 July, when they were reopened with limited capacity and 'social-distancing measures'. This programme offered a subsidy of 50 per cent for all meals and non-alcoholic drinks (to a limit of £10 per person) on Mondays through Wednesdays during August 2020. There was no limit on how often an individual could use the scheme. The scheme cost the UK Treasury £849 million (the initial estimate of the cost was £500 million).[108] While the programme did offer some support for this month, initial evidence suggested that consumption of such meals increased in August (unsurprisingly as they were subsidised) but this demand may have shifted from the weekends to mid-week.[109]

However, increased socialisation in restaurants likely contributed to the spread of Covid-19. Econometric modelling suggests that this programme may have had an effect in subsequently exacerbating the spread of the disease. Fetzer writes:

> The most prominent point of divergence between the UK's fiscal response and that of other countries was a large scale demand-inducing measure aimed at the hospitality sector – specifically, restaurants and cafes. A total of GBP 500 million was spent to subsidize the cost of eating out in restaurant by up to 50% in the month of August. At the time, evidence of the likely spread of COVID19 in hospitality settings was already paramount. ... [T]he Eat-Out-to-Help-Out scheme, hailed as an economic cure for the ailing sector, may have substantially worsened the disease. The paper documents that the scheme had a substantial and causal impact leading to new spatially spread out COVID19 infections in the weeks during which the scheme was active. The estimates suggest that the scheme is responsible for around 8–17% of all infections during the summer months and likely, many more non-

---

[108] House of Commons Library, 'Eat out to Help out Scheme' Briefing Paper.
[109] Ibid. at 5; see also Plummer and Read, 'Eat out to Help out Will Definitely Affect the Weekend'.

detected asymptomatic infections, that may have substantially contributed to accel-erating the second wave of the pandemic.[110]

On 18 September 2020, the UK prime minister remarked that the country was now facing a second wave of Covid-19.[111] As a result, the UK government introduced additional public health measures (some of which affected the hospitality industry) on 22 September.

When made (August 2020), the decision to subsidise consumption in restaurants was a popular decision. It was also an effective means for the chancellor of the exchequer to raise his profile and better position himself in any prime ministerial succession contest. However, from the perspectives of public health and economic benefit, the programme appears to have been a disaster. It is likely that the funds could have been better spent directly supporting those employed in the hospitality industry.

Fetzer's study shows the likely contribution of this programme to the September second wave. There are, of course, other factors which contributed to that wave (holiday travel, incaution in adherence to public health/social-distancing measures, etc.). There is room for further analysis of the extent of the programme's contribu-tion to this wave. Second, once this contribution is determined, and if the economic costs of the second wave can be established, these additional costs can be added to the £849 million in direct costs[112] to determine if the programme provided effective value for money. The likely conclusion is negative, since – even without taking into consideration any detrimental effect on public health measures to control the pandemic – the UK's Treasury was uncertain about how effective the scheme would be and thus whether it represented 'value for money'.[113] The Treasury required a political direction to proceed with the scheme.

One conclusion that can be drawn from this, is that the support programme which was extremely popular at its inception, which actually magnified the crisis whose effects it was intended to mitigate. This may be a public health analogue to the cartel behaviour encouraged by the American NIRA. This too was an initially popular programme, brought in by a politician to curry favour at the beginning of his influence, but which resulted in exacerbating and prolonging the problem it was meant to solve.

This section has shown that the state aid response to alleviating the economic fallout of Covid-19 may have been effective, but it was far from ideal. Although significant sums of money were shifted to support businesses and stimulate con-sumer spending, the jury is still out on the extent to which aid was smartly deployed.

---

[110] Fetzer, 'Subsidizing the Spread of COVID19' at 26–27.
[111] 'Covid: UK Seeing Second Wave, Says Boris Johnson'.
[112] And any additional deaths calculated.
[113] See letter from Jim Harra (chief executive and first permanent secretary HM Treasury) to Rt Hon Rishi Sunak MP (chancellor of the exchequer) dated 7 July 2020 at 2–3.

The Commission's Framework was based around a paradigm of R&R aid, and most aid was delivered on this basis. While this paradigm was likely the most appropriate paradigm drawn from existing models, it is not clear whether (or to what extent) such aid is an effective use of funds. As we saw earlier, it is often the case that directing funding to affected (ex-)employees may be a more cost-effective use of funds when an undertaking (or industry) is faced with terminal decline.

State aid is only one of a number of measures which can be used to support the economy. Unfortunately, in a crisis situation – where those in charge of the economy need to be seen to be doing something – it can be a default solution. As a default solution, it has its advantages. It may distort competition less than other proposed solutions. State aid programmes have limited duration; there is also no hangover of post-crisis, lasting collusion or efficient entry deterred by threats of prosecutions for 'price gouging', or the effects of anticompetitive mergers causing consumer welfare losses years after the crisis has ended.

Yet, state aid programmes – particularly those involving the R&R of undertakings and industries – are inherently a gamble. They bet that the plan will be workable, that is, that the undertaking or industry will exit the process in a healthy condition and be more able to effectively compete afterwards. However, it is not clear that R&R bets are the best uses of funding – that the adverse social consequences of failure could not be mitigated in a less expensive manner.

5.6 CONCLUSION AND EVALUATION

The Covid-19 pandemic which began in 2020 resulted in significant drops in demand in most economic sectors throughout the world. Given this economic effect, there were almost immediate calls for the relaxation of the competition rules as a means of mitigating these economic effects. However, as we have argued, these calls were misguided, and listening to them would have been a mistake.

The only exceptional characteristic of the economic consequences of Covid-19 was its scale. The drop in demand was deep; however, early indications show that the Great Depression of the 1930s may have been worse.[114] The Great Depression provides a point of illustration. The NIRA, as part of Roosevelt's strategy to deal with the effects of the Depression, permitted wholesale collusion among firms. As we saw in Sections 2.2.1 and 2.2.2, this had the effect of thwarting market-based responses to the problem, thereby aggravating and prolonging the Depression. There is no reason to suppose that a collusive strategy misguidedly implemented to mitigate the consequences of the pandemic would not have had a similar effect.

The purpose behind the competition and state aid regimes is to address market failure. In particular, the competition regime addressed those market failures associated with monopoly, i.e. firms acting as a monopoly or firms in a monopoly position

---

[114] Wheelock, 'Comparing the COVID-19 Recession with the Great Depression'.

abusing the associated market power; and merger control prevents 'marriages' of firms which result in a risk to competition. The EU's state aid is designed to prohibit aid which distorts competition, and yet permit granting aid in circumstances where market failures may preclude efficient financing of firms or projects. The drop in demand caused by Covid-19 is not a market failure caused by monopoly. Hence, there is no reason to adjust the competition rules to mitigate the crisis or aid in recovery from it. There is a case for the use of state aid to assist in the R&R of viable undertakings and industries. However, granting aid – particularly in the context of a national or global crisis – is an inherently political decision. It is clear that not all funds were wisely spent, in the sense of the Commission's desire for 'smarter' aid. Some was poorly spent – the UK's attempt to stimulate the hospitality industry in August 2020 is a case in point.

Not only is relaxing the competition rules not an acceptable means of addressing the immediate effects of the pandemic (or any other crisis). It can also lead to a hangover, affecting competition well after the consequences of the crisis have subsided. If collusion is (misguidedly) permitted on a 'temporary basis' to deal with a crisis, it may be difficult to unlearn the information shared in the crisis or change collusive behaviour (or culture) within an industry. 'Temporary' price-gouging laws can deter those who may wish to enter a market or engage in arbitrage during the next crisis. A merger that was otherwise anticompetitive but 'waived through' in the midst of a crisis (e.g. as a result of political considerations) is still anticompetitive. Its effects will be felt well after the crisis has ended. To address a crisis by relaxing the regime is an easy political 'sound bite' providing an apparent immediate remedy, but it will only aggravate the consequences in the long term.

6

Brexit

Squandered Opportunities?

6.1 INTRODUCTION

This chapter considers the implications of Brexit for the development of the UK's competition and industrial policy. As will be seen, among the supposed advantages that could occur by the UK leaving the EU was that it could obtain (or regain) more control over its own laws, and hence shape these to its advantage in the pursuit of a new, and independent, industrial and trade strategy. As this chapter is being written in the immediate aftermath of Brexit, its conclusions are necessarily tentative. However, it is apparent that although the government's ability to develop such policies is slightly less constrained after Brexit, it is not clear whether or not the government will choose wisely in using this 'freedom'. In particular, its proposals surrounding its ability to grant business subsidies (or 'state aid') appear to be a retrograde step. If this is indeed the case, as we fear, then rather than improving the development of the British economy, these measures – by allowing unchecked governmental intervention in the economy – may prove to be costly to the taxpayer and hinder an efficient development of the UK's post-Brexit economy. In fact, the initial signals that the present government is sending give every indication that its post-Brexit industrial policy will go beyond intervention to address market failure and will use measures which are ultimately costly to a competitive economy (and taxpayers).

This chapter proceeds as follows. In Section 6.2 we introduce three issues that were totemic in shaping the UK's attitude in the negotiations of its future relationship with the EU. These were 'sovereignty', fisheries and trade policy. This last concern included competition and state aid policy, and it is on this that the remainder of the chapter is focused. State aid and prospects for an improved regime post-Brexit took on additional significance during and in the immediate aftermath of the Brexit referendum's campaign. This significance was a result of campaigners' misunderstandings regarding the nature of the EU's state aid regime and how it did (or did not) fetter a government's ability to pursue its own industrial policy.

Section 6.3 considers the two agreements between the parties which established the foundation for their future relationship. These were: (1) a withdrawal agreement which set out some principles of the EU's and UK's future relationship[1] (and also determined the relationship between the two up to 31 December 2020, though this latter aspect of the agreement is irrelevant to our focus); and (2) a EU–UK Trade and Cooperation Agreement[2] (TCA) to govern the two parties' post-Brexit relationship. The former agreement contains a Protocol on Northern Ireland (NI). This Protocol was designed to respect the Good Friday Agreement, which was implemented to end 'the Troubles': the period of sectarian civil strife in NI, the Republic of Ireland (RoI) and the UK. Key to the Good Friday Agreement was the end to a hard border between NI and the RoI. In the context of Brexit, and the Withdrawal Agreement, respecting the Good Friday Agreement meant that NI remained in the EU's internal market, required a border between it and the rest of the UK. The implementation of the latter agreement on 1 January 2021 has led to a significant disruption in trade between the UK and the EU and between Great Britain and NI, as a result of the Protocol. This trade disruption is one of the costs of Brexit.[3]

This is followed by Section 6.4, which suggests what the UK's competition provisions might look like post-Brexit. The TCA establishes a framework for the post-Brexit regime. This framework can be (and, to an initial extent, has) been built upon by a regime of domestic legislation. Our analysis shows that there is little that has or can be gained through this 'new regime'. Although it is not entirely clear what the present government's intentions are, it is also reasonably apparent that much of what could be accomplished post-Brexit could have been achieved under the pre-Brexit EU regime.

Section 6.5 discusses the state aid, or 'subsidy' (the term the UK's government now prefers), provisions which are contained in the TCA. These provisions give the government greater scope to subsidise firms, industries and regions in the name of industrial policy and regional equity.

It is not clear how the government will use its new-found freedom to develop a subsidy-based industrial policy. However, it has provided some strong hints, in the form of consultation and briefing papers culminating in a Subsidies Control Bill introduced at the end of June 2021, and statements in its post-Brexit budget. These

---

[1]	Agreement on the Withdrawal of the United Kingdom of Great Britain and Northern Ireland from the European Union and the European Atomic Energy Community [2019] OJ C-384 I/01 (agreed to 17 October 2019, entering force 1 February 2020).

[2]	Trade and Cooperation Agreement between the European Union and the European Atomic Energy Community, of the One Part, and the United Kingdom of Great Britain and Northern Ireland, of the Other Part [2020] OJ L-444/1.

[3]	To which one can add the social and political costs of a perceived internal border within the UK. In the context of NI's fragile peace settlement, this has the potential for undermining the progress made since the 1998 Good Friday Agreement.

hints suggest that the UK's future regime will be driven by light-touch oversight of subsidies. In Section 6.6 we provide an initial evaluation of the government's proposals.

The government has also announced that it will use Freeports to stimulate regional development. These Freeports, a pet project of the chancellor of the exchequer since (at least) the time he was a backbench Member of Parliament,[4] consist of zones within the de facto territory of the UK, but de jure outside of its customs zone. While the EU's existing regime permits such arrangements, albeit to a more limited extent than UK's proposals, the current government's initiative proposes the provision of subsidies to these entities via tax breaks. Section 6.7 expresses our scepticism regarding the need for Freeports and our view that any benefit which accrues to a region as a result a Freeport locating in that region as likely a result of displacement – attracting employment and investment from other areas of the UK. This displacement is identical to the displacement that occurs when subsidies or state aid are used to attract investment to a given region (irrespective of how developed that region may be).

In fact, as this chapter's conclusion suggests, we are sceptical about the utility of the anticipated post-Brexit industrial policy and competition regime. It appears that the new regime will incorporate many elements against which we have cautioned in this work. Rather than using a crisis of the sort we have seen throughout this work to alter the competition rules, usually to the detriment of the consumer, in this case the government has chosen Brexit to make a similar adjustment which is neither in consumers' nor taxpayers' favour.

6.2 THE BACKGROUND TO BREXIT

On 23 June 2016, the citizens of the United Kingdom voted by a narrow margin to leave the European Union. Those advocating that the UK leave, did so on several grounds. They presented a case which included claims that outside of the constraints imposed by EU law the UK could be the master of its own destiny in the international sphere, and negotiate trade agreements with other sovereign equals, thus prospering as 'Global Britain'. This, of course, is not to exclude other planks in the Brexit platform, which included such disingenuous claims that net savings from not paying into the EU's budget could (and would) be better invested in the UK[5] and fears about possible mass immigration from the EU and candidate Member States.[6] These claims played well to an audience which had been subjected to five

---

[4] See Rishi Sunak MP, 'The Free Ports Opportunity'.

[5] The infamous 'Brexit Bus', used by leave campaigners, promised to spend £350 million a week 'saved' by not contributing to the EU on the National Health Service. This money was spent many times over by the leavers in their promises.

[6] The notorious 'Breaking Point' billboard is a case in point. See Stewart and Mason, 'Nigel Farage's Anti-migrant Poster Reported to Police'.

years of governmental austerity.[7] The precise reasons why the public voted to leave are beyond the scope of this work. An examination of what Brexit has done, and how competition and state aid policy could be reshaped in post-Brexit Britain, is the focus of this chapter.

Any individual who objectively analysed the claims made by the leave side would see the dubious, if not false, nature of many of these claims. Nevertheless, popular sentiment prevailed over sense. But not only did the British public vote to leave, the UK government chose to leave under very 'hard' terms, to protect its 'sovereignty', a view discussed next. On 29 March 2017, the UK government notified the EU that it was triggering Article 50 TEU and would leave the EU. The UK left the EU on 31 January 2020. During this process of departure, the UK and EU negotiated the two agreements mentioned here and described in Section 6.3.

In attempting to carve out the UK's role in the post-Brexit world, the UK's negotiators focused on three totemic issues. The first was the UK's need for 'sovereignty', in the sense that henceforth it would be bound only by 'its own' laws (and not, in the minds of those whose political agenda informed the UK's negotiating agenda, 'imposed by an external body'). The second was fisheries: any proposed deal must advance the interests of the UK's fishing industry and give it greater control over its waters and fish stocks. The final totemic issue was the ability for the UK to be able to set its own rules for competition and particularly state aid. This would enable the UK to develop its own post-Brexit industrial policy, allowing it to be successful and capitalise on these successes abroad because of promised trade opportunities.

As with much of the pro-Brexit rhetoric, the significance of these issues was divorced from reality. The talk about 'sovereignty' confused that concept with autonomy. Sovereignty is the ability of a state or body to enter into binding agreements with other sovereign parties. As a result of such agreements, parties' ability to act is limited: they agree to rules and obey them. They may also agree upon an arbiter and a set of permissible sanctions to govern compliance. This is the structure of most trade agreements, particularly those which the UK was attempting to replicate with other jurisdictions. Autonomy, on the other hand, is the ability to act without constraint in a given situation. There are few, if any, autonomous states

---

[7] It is significant to note that this austerity came as a result of a change in government. The new government (led by David Cameron) was ideologically committed to a 'smaller state'. It altered the narrative about the solution to the 2008 financial crisis and suggested that the implementation of austerity measures (which involved 'shrinking the state') was the necessary means to 'pay off' the costs of mitigating the financial crisis. Austerity, of course, had its consequences – an economic crisis of sorts – from which many regions of the UK had failed to recover by the time of the Brexit referendum. One commentator noted that '[a]n anaemic and deeply geographically unequal recovery from protracted economic crisis mediated the political support for the 2016 referendum vote to leave the European Union'. Montgomerie, 'Austerity and the Household' at 419.

(in this sense) in the international community; and the more a state acts in an unconstrained manner, the closer it is to becoming an international pariah.[8]

The fisheries issue made for nice headlines in the domestic press. Those in the fisheries industries voted quite heavily in favour of Brexit. Their vote had to be respected, notwithstanding that the industry – which was heavily dependent on the ability to rapidly export their product, free of trade barriers[9] – only contributed 0.02 per cent of the UK's gross value added (similar to GDP).[10] In 2019, UK fishing vessels landed catches worth £987 million.[11] In contrast, the department store Harrods had a turnover in excess of £2 billion in 2016 and therefore contributed more to the UK's economy.[12] However, in an island state, the symbolic nature of the fisheries industry was to give rhetoric over fish and the fishing industry a significance of its own, disproportionate to the value of its economic contribution. A statement made in Parliament by the government's leader of the house (Jacob Rees-Mogg) on 14 January 2021 perhaps best exemplifies this: 'The key is that we have our fish back: they are now British fish, and they are better and happier fish for it.'[13]

The rhetoric around state aid was felt from both ends of the political spectrum. The right argued that a new state aid regime would allow the UK government to champion and support people and industries in the post-Brexit global environment.[14] Paradoxically, those advocating this position tended to come from the Thatcherite and libertarian 'free market' branches of the Conservative Party – for

---

[8] During the period in which the EU–UK TCA was being negotiated the UK acted autonomously in this negative sense, by introducing a draft Internal Market Bill which – had it passed in an unamended form – would have unilaterally overridden the withdrawal agreement's provisions regarding NI signed less than nine months earlier. The UK government recognised that this breached international law in a 'limited and specific way'. The offending clauses were dropped from the final Act. See 'Northern Ireland Secretary Admits New Bill Will "Break International Law"' and Merrick, 'Brexit: Peers Inflict Heaviest Defeat for More than 20 Years over Bill that Will Break International Law'.

[9] The post-Brexit need for new sorts of paperwork to allow catch landed in the UK to be sold and sent to the EU made it more difficult for industry members to get their catch to market, leading to inevitable criticism and cries of betrayal. See e.g. Parker and Dickie, 'Boris Johnson Accused of Betraying Fishing Industry over Brexit Disruption'.

[10] See Uberoi et al., 'UK Fishery Statistics' at 4.

[11] UK Marine Management Organisation, 'Fishing Industry in 2019 Statistics Published'.

[12] Giles, 'May's Brexit Dividend and Other Myths Worth Exploding'.

[13] UK Parliament, *Hansard*, Business of the House, Volume 687, 14 January 2021. It appears that a part of the 'Brexit Dividend' (ibid.) is an endless stream of misguided to idiotic utterances emanating from the mouths of the political classes.

[14] See e.g. '[o]f course inside the EU, rules on state aid have prevented us from investing in broadband in a way that is best for the UK', Rt Hon Michael Gove, PC, MP (then secretary of state for environment, food and rural affairs) 'A Brighter Future for Farming'. Like so many claims made during the course of the Brexit campaign and subsequent domestic processes, *this was false*. See, *inter alia*, Commission Decision of 22 May 2016 (SA.40720) (*National Broadband Scheme for the UK for 2016–2020*) in which the Commission raised no objections to UK proposal with a £500 million maximum budget to support the roll-out of high-speed broadband, and Commission Decision 20 November 2012 (SA.33671) (*Broadband Delivery UK*) [2013] OJ C-16/1 (which approved aid of a total value estimated at €1.8 billion).

whom state intervention in the market (and hence state subsidies to market players) was otherwise anathema.[15] The left saw Brexit as providing an opportunity for the post-Brexit government to intervene in the market to support favoured industries. Jeremy Corbyn, the then leader of the opposition Labour Party (who lukewarmly campaigned for the UK to remain in the EU, but was suspected of harbouring longstanding Euroscepticism), summarised the left's view on this point in a 2018 speech:

> We cannot be held back inside or outside the EU from taking the steps we need to support cutting edge industries and local business, stop the tide of privatisation and outsourcing or from preventing employers being able to import cheap agency labour to undercut existing pay and conditions.[16]

Both the right and left were wrong in their respective assertions.[17]

From the right, many of their claims about the EU's rules somehow stymieing the UK government were demonstrably false.[18] In 2016, the year of the Brexit referendum, the UK was near the bottom of the EU in Member State expenditure on state aid, spending only 0.49 per cent of its GDP on non-railway state aid.[19]

A good deal of the left's claims were also false. As an example, the above speech by Corbyn was immediately fact-checked by Peretz. He has pointed out that nothing mentioned in Corbyn's speech was impermissible under the existing EU regime.[20] Further, the Labour Party Manifesto for the 2017 election suggested that some of the policies it would implement were incompatible with EU state aid, providing further reason to depart from the Union. These claims were again later fact-checked, and only two of the twenty-seven proposals in the Manifesto would have required clearance from the Commission – the remainder were either not aid or consistent with existing Guidelines.[21] This suggests either a negligent or a wilful misunderstanding, and a subsequent misrepresentation of the role of aid in the EU and its effect on the UK.

---

[15] See e.g. Peretz, 'State Aid and Brexit' at 81.

[16] Corbyn, 'Britain after Brexit'.

[17] See Peretz, n. 15 at 80–81.

[18] See e.g. Michael Gove's claim about broadband, n. 14. This claim was either negligently or deliberately made, and either reflects poorly on the truthfulness of the government's statements during the Brexit process. This statement appears never to have been retracted – again a poor reflection on the government's concern for truth and accuracy.

[19] Only Ireland, Portugal, Spain, Italy, Greece, Belgium, Luxemburg and Slovakia spent less. See EU Commission, 'State Aid Scoreboard 2017' (COMP.A3 Brussels, 29 November 2017), Annex 2 at 31.

[20] Peretz, 'Corbyn on State Aid'.

[21] Tarrant and Biondi, 'Labour's Programme and EU Law', who at 84 remark, '[n]either EU state aid rules, nor other EU rules which are distinct from state aid rules but sometimes considered in the same bracket, provide any obvious barrier to the implementation in the UK of the economic policies contained in Labour's 2017 election manifesto'.

That these inaccurate claims were made (whether negligently, disingenuously, mendaciously or otherwise) is a damning indictment of the UK's political class but is now almost irrelevant. The view that the UK could somehow improve its ability to support industries (particularly at the cutting edge), regions and workers became part of the negotiating framework for the agreement that would define the UK's and EU's future relationship.

In light of the TCA signed on 24 December 2020, the nature of the UK's regime and the extent to which it differs from its EU-based predecessor is a very real question. Although perhaps preliminary, such an analysis will serve as an initial guide in assessing whether and to what extent the TCA achieves its mandate. This, in turn, may serve as a starting point to any ultimate analysis of the 'deal', and whether or not the price of the Brexit project as a whole is worth its benefits.

6.3 THE TWO AGREEMENTS

In the course of the UK's departure from the EU, the parties concluded two agreements to serve as the foundation for their future relationship. These were the 2019 Withdrawal Agreement and the December 2020 TCA.[22] The Withdrawal Agreement governed the conditions for the UK's orderly withdrawal from the EU. It includes provisions regarding citizenship (and the possibility for EU citizens to remain in the UK, and vice versa), a financial settlement regarding the UK's obligations to the EU's budget, a transition period extending the application of EU law to the UK until 31 December 2020 and Protocols on NI, Cyprus and Gibraltar. The first of these three protocols is significant.

6.3.1 *The Withdrawal Agreement and the Protocol on Northern Ireland*

NI and its peoples' interests were never at the forefront of the minds of those advocating Brexit and particularly its hard version. The citizens of NI voted to remain in the EU. The key stumbling block in any orderly exit from the EU is the Good Friday Agreement. As noted, the goal of that agreement was to put an end to the civil strife of the Troubles. It attempts to do so by providing for, *inter alia*, an open border between NI and the RoI and a power-sharing agreement in the Northern Irish Legislature. The agreement's arrangements are overseen, in part, by the EU.[23]

To respect the Good Friday Agreement's provisions, requiring an open border with the RoI, the Withdrawal Agreement's Protocol on Northern Ireland keeps that

---

[22] See nn. 1 and 2, respectively.

[23] There is a substantial literature on the Good Friday Agreement; see, for instance, Doyle and Connolly, 'Brexit and the Northern Ireland Question' and Tannam, 'Intergovernmental and Cross-Border Civil Service Cooperation: The Good Friday Agreement and Brexit'.

nation of the UK within the EU's internal market for goods. This has the consequence of imposing a customs and regulatory border between NI and Great Britain (i.e. the rest of the UK). This regulatory border has immediate implications for any state aid regime which can apply to NI: given the internal market considerations, it will necessarily be governed by EU law. Other regulatory requirements (which include Sanitary and Phytosanitary (SPS) checks) added further trade barriers between NI and Great Britain.

6.3.2 *The Trade Provisions of the TCA*

The trade provisions of the TCA provide for access by each party to the other party's markets on a duty-free, quota-free (DFQF) basis, for most goods. As such, trading takes place under General Agreement on Tariffs and Trade (GATT) Article XXIV's[24] provisions for customs unions and free trade areas, rather than the Most Favored Nation provisions of GATT Article I.1. Although this was the result of the agreement which cumulated in the TCA, a trade agreement was not the purpose of Brexit. After all, with membership, the UK had the best possible trade agreement with the EU. Rather, the totemic issues of 'taking back control' and immigration weighed more heavily in Brexiteers' psyches. In particular, to some – possibly just a noisy minority, but noisy and influential nonetheless – a trade agreement was almost surplusage. They would accept a 'no deal scenario' with trade taking place 'under World Trade Organization (WTO) rules'. Presumably under this scenario, this meant that GATT Article I:1 would govern the terms of trade in goods. However, it was not evident whether those espousing a 'no deal' scenario were aware of this or the consequences of other WTO rules that would govern the UK's trade relationship with the EU in the event of no deal.

The DFQF basis of the future trade arrangement is set out in Part Two, Heading One, Title 1, Article GOODS.6(1) of the TCA:

> A Party may not adopt or maintain any duty, tax or other charge of any kind imposed on, or in connection with, the exportation of a good to the other Party; or any internal tax or other charge on a good exported to the other Party that is in excess of the tax or charge that would be imposed on like goods when destined for domestic consumption.

For reasons already seen, mutual restrictions on the use of subsidies which would have a detrimental effect on the other's market are necessary to preserve the integrity of the DFQF system of market access.

Differences in competition and, particularly, subsidy regimes between countries that choose to trade on a DFQF basis will affect the efficacy of the trade agreement.

---

[24] General Agreement on Tariffs and Trade 1994, 15 April 1994, Marrakesh Agreement Establishing the World Trade Organization, Annex 1A, 1867 UNTS 187, 33 ILM 1153 (1994) Article XXIV.

In particular, a subsidy can have the same effect as a tariff in altering consumption patterns in the 'subsidising' economy and thus altering demand from the trading partner. Given the volume of trade (at least prior to Brexit) between the UK and the EU, it is no surprise that the parties would wish to incorporate strict provisions on the use of subsidies in their DFQF-based trade agreement.[25] We examine these competition and subsidy provisions of the TCA in what follows.

6.3.3 Non-tariff Barriers and Trade

Although the TCA provides for DFQF trade in goods between the UK and EU, it does not eliminate all barriers to trade between the two parties. The UK made the choice to leave the EU's internal market to grant itself greater 'regulatory freedom', which would include the ability to develop its own health and technical standards, which would include an independent SPS regime. This meant that as of 1 January 2021, goods imported into the EU's internal market would require certification that EU standards were met. Given that NI is included in the EU's internal market, this entailed a similar requirement for trade between Great Britain and NI.

The immediate effect of this was a significant drop in trade between the UK and EU. In January 2021, according to Office of National Statistics records, 'UK goods exports to the EU fell 40.7 per cent in the month and imports dropped 28.8 per cent, the largest declines since comparable records began in 1997'.[26] The impact of this drop in trade was disproportionately felt by some industries, particularly those in the food sector (including fisheries) and smaller undertakings.[27]

As NI remained within the EU's internal market, goods imported into that part of the UK had to meet the EU's regulatory requirements, including SPS requirements on foodstuff, resulting in delayed shipments.[28] There are other anecdotal reports that this led to food shortages in some areas of NI.[29] Although in December 2020 the UK and the EU had agreed to a temporary waiver of some of the Protocol's provisions as a transition measure, this was obviously insufficient to prevent the above described shortages. On 21 March 2021, the UK unilaterally extended this waiver, which was

---

[25] Given the UK's publicly expressed willingness to use subsidies as an important element of its post-Brexit industrial policy, the EU had every reason to be concerned that this could undermine any DFQF trade agreement between the parties.

[26] Giles, Foster and Romei, 'UK Exports to EU Slump as Brexit Hits Trade'. See also Office of National Statistics, UK Trade: January 2021.

[27] See e.g. Giles, Foster and Romei, ibid.; Kollewe, 'Brexit Problems Halt Some Scottish Seafood Exports to EU'; O'Carroll, 'Cheshire Cheesemaker Says Business Left with £250,000 "Brexit Hole"'.

[28] See e.g. O'Carroll, 'Eight Days for Carrots to Get to Belfast with Complex Brexit Checks' and O'Carroll, 'Crisps Lorry Held Up for Two Days by Northern Irish Brexit Checks, MPs Told'.

[29] 'Food Supply Problems in NI Clearly a Brexit Issue – Coveney' and Ferguson, 'Food Shortages as Northern Ireland Nears New Brexit Deadline'. The latter article includes the (now iconic) photograph of an empty-shelved Belfast supermarket.

due to end on 31 March, until at least 1 October 2021.[30] In response to this unilateral action the EU commenced an infringement action against the UK.[31]

These initial problems at the NI-Great Britain border were dismissed by the prime minister as 'teething problems'.[32] However, in other statement in Parliament, other cabinet ministers admitted that these issues were bigger than minor, initial 'teething problems'.[33] However, in typically Panglossian fashion, the prime minister, even weeks later, was still maintaining that these problems remained teething problems that could be sorted out through goodwill and imagination.[34] Yet these disruptions to the flow of trade between NI and Great Britain, whether 'teething problems' or something more severe, are only part of the problems which this version of Brexit has unleashed on NI. A border, whether between NI and the RoI, or – as now – between NI and Great Britain, will act as a flashpoint for long-simmering sectarian tensions, which the Good Friday Agreement may have prevented from boiling over. In the first weeks of 2021, threats had been made to those staffing these control points.[35]

This drop in trade and the imposition of new trade barriers, not just between former 'barrier-free' trading partners, but between one constituent nation of the UK and the rest of the country, and the possibility of renewed sectarian tensions in that nation, are all part of the costs of Brexit. Border checks are also required on goods flowing between the UK and EU. To alleviate some of the problems associated with this (at least for those importing goods into the UK), the UK government suspended such checks until mid-2022.[36] These checks are conducted on the EU side. Additional costs can be found in labour shortages affecting supply chains and some (lower-paid) service industries, which had pre-Brexit relied on the availability of EU citizens to perform these tasks.[37] Given that closing the borders to such labour was also part of the Brexit manifesto, these problems could have been anticipated. While

---

[30] See Leahy, Staunton and McClements, 'Government Brands UK Move to Delay Checks on Goods Entering North from Britain "Deeply Unhelpful"'.

[31] Commission Press Release, 'Withdrawal Agreement: Commission Sends Letter of Formal Notice to the United Kingdom for Breach of Its Obligations under the Protocol on Ireland and Northern Ireland'.

[32] Rt Hon Boris Johnson MP PM in response to Sir Jeffrey M. Donaldson, *Hansard*, 13 January 2021, Volume 687, Column 290.

[33] 'In the short term, there are a number of issues that I would not describe as teething problems; they are significant issues that bear on the lives of people in Northern Ireland, which do need to be resolved'. Rt Hon Michael Gove MP in response to Sir Iain Duncan Smith MP, *Hansard*, 2 February 2021, Volume 688, Column 837.

[34] Dickson, 'Boris Johnson: "Goodwill" and "Imagination" Can Fix post-Brexit Border Problems'. See also our final sentence in n. 13.

[35] Parker et al., 'Gove Urges Brussels to Take Action as Northern Ireland Tensions Rise'.

[36] Parker and Foster, 'UK Postpones Imposing Checks on EU Goods Until 2022'.

[37] Parker and Pfeifer, 'UK Rejects Industry Plea for Visas for EU Truck Drivers' and Partington, 'Business Leaders Call for Relaxation of post-Brexit Visa Rules'.

it may be too early to precisely assess these costs, they are likely higher than those which the leave side represented to the public during the referendum campaign.

6.4 THE COMPETITION PROVISIONS IN THE TCA

In this section, we outline the competition provisions in the TCA, in conjunction with relevant domestic primary and secondary legislation used to implement the TCA and post-Brexit competition policy. Most of the latter is still very nascent, suggesting that the government's priorities in this regard lie elsewhere, likely in the implementation of a new industrial policy with state aid as one of its foundational elements. This outline is fairly descriptive. Its purpose is to show that the limits imposed by the TCA provide little scope for independent alteration of the UK's competition regime, and that – at least in the short to medium term – little will change.

Part Two, Title XI of the TCA, entitled 'Level Playing Field for Open and Fair Competition and Sustainable Development', contains the TCA's competition and state aid provisions. Its title has significance, to which we will return in the discussion of state aid. The provisions of this international agreement must be read alongside the UK's domestic legislation implementing the withdrawal from the EU in order to understand the agreement and its implications for the UK's future domestic competition regime.

Chapter Two of this Title sets out the competition regime. Its first two Articles recognise the need for a competition regime to prevent market distortion and underscore the parties' agreement to maintain a competition law which 'effectively addresses' the problems associated with collusion, dominance and mergers. These practices are the sorts described by Articles 101 and 102 of the TFEU and the existing merger regimes and describe the parties' existing regimes. It is worth noting that the TCA makes some attempts to avoid what might be regarded as EU terms of art. Hence, in Article 2.1(2) the TCA uses 'economic actor' to describe what European (and UK) competition lawyers term an 'undertaking'. Such rules are to be enforced against all economic actors, 'irrespective of their nationality or ownership status' (Art. 2.2(2)). Article 2.1(3) permits either party to carve out 'public policy' exemptions from their competition law. This merely reflects existing practice.

Article 2.3 recognises the parties' intention that the competition regimes will be enforced by an 'operationally independent' authority (or authorities), and that this should be done in a transparent and non-discriminatory manner. Article 2.4 opens the door for future cooperation. This Article recognises the advantages of a coordinated approach in new policy developments and enforcement activities and recognises both parties' willingness to cooperate. Such cooperation can include the sharing of confidential information, to the extent permitted by each party's law. To this end, Article 2.4(4) lays the ground for a future, and possibly more comprehensive, cooperation agreement.

The utility of such an agreement would be significant, for both sides. With the UK's withdrawal from the EU, it lost its place in the ECN.[38] The ECN is a network of the Commission and Member State NCAs, which coordinated the application of competition policy and investigations within the EU. One of the roles of the Commission is to aid in the consistent application of EU competition law through-out the Union. Post-Brexit there is no longer a legal reason compelling the UK to apply its competition law consistently with EU law.[39] However, there may be good commercial reasons for the UK's regime to remain as consistent as possible with the EU's, as it is easier for an undertaking to self-assess the consistency of its actions against a single set of rules than with an additional (and inconsistent) set.

However, in addition to reducing transactions costs for undertakings there are other reasons for European cooperation in competition matters. Large cartels do not respect international borders. Experience of cartel activity prior to the UK joining the EEC showed that large cartels existed and affected both markets.[40] During the UK's EU membership, the UK was affected by European cartels (and abusive conduct of dominant undertakings). There is absolutely no reason to suppose that such behaviour ceased with Brexit. A means by which the UK and EU can share information and coordinate their responses will, of course, aid in the investigation and (it is to be hoped) prosecution of entities engaging in such activities. The threat of prosecution may deter this sort of activity, and thus have consumer welfare–enhancing consequences.

The competition provisions of the TCA, taken by themselves, do not appear to depart from the status quo to any significant degree. However, when read in conjunction with domestic legislation which implements Brexit, there may be room for departure. It may be the case that the government could use this as an oppor-tunity to tweak the competition regime to ensure that the rules promote the production of consumer or total welfare; but this goal needs to be balanced against the transaction costs borne by undertakings due to divergence.

As mentioned in Section 6.1, one of the totemic issues in the Brexit campaign and post-referendum process was for the UK to remove itself from the jurisdiction of 'Brussels' laws'. Indeed, the slogan 'Take Back Control' became a mantra of the leave movement.[41] Eliminating the binding nature of retained EU case law was central to the implementation of this programme. To this end, Section 6 of the European Union (Withdrawal) Act 2018 states that the UK Supreme Court (or, in

---

[38] See https://ec.europa.eu/competition/ecn/index_en.html; see also Commission Notice on cooperation within the Network of Competition Authorities [2004] OJ C-101/43; and Council Regulation (EC) No. 1/2003 of 16 December 2002 on the Implementation of the Rules on Competition Laid Down in Articles 81 and 82 of the Treaty [2004] OJ L-1/1, Articles 11 and 12.

[39] Articles 3 and 16 of Regulation 1/2003 (ibid.) require NCAs to apply the EU competition rules consistently.

[40] See e.g. Case 48-69, *Imperial Chemical Industries Ltd. v. Commission*, ECLI:EU:C:1972:70.

[41] On this see e.g. Wolf, 'The Brexit Delusion of Taking Back Control'.

Scotland, the High Court of Justiciary in devolved or Scots law matters) is not bound by retained EU case law. In departing from EU case law, these courts are required, however, to apply the same test that they would apply in departing from their own case law.[42]

Historically, the Appellate Committee of the House of Lords (the predecessor to the Supreme Court) did not overrule its own decisions. If it incorrectly stated the law, it was Parliament's responsibility to rectify this. However, in 1966, the Lords issued a Practice Direction modifying it practice.[43] While the Lords (now the Supreme Court) has the ability to overrule itself, it is a power which is rarely exercised – due to considerations of legal certainty. These considerations are equally germane to competition matters.

There are few cases in which the Court has exercised this power. The most notable is the 2016 judgment in *Knauer*,[44] where the Court reasoned that although it should be 'circumspect' in overruling past precedent, it may do so when there has been 'a change in the relevant legal landscape' since the precedent or if subsequent litigation shows that the precedent is being distinguished on inadequate grounds.

In the summer of 2020, the government engaged in a consultative process regarding the status of retained EU case law. The outcome of this consultation was to recommend that the power to depart from retained EU case law be vested in lower courts, including (and germane for our purposes) the Court of Appeal.[45] This recommendation has been incorporated into UK law.[46]

However, it is unlikely that this will have a significant effect on the day-to-day application of UK competition law. At the Supreme Court level, it remains to be seen what would be regarded as a sufficiently significant change in the legal landscape to alter past ECJ decisions. At the lower level, there is likely to be little effect.

The UK's NCA is the CMA. It not only investigates anticompetitive behaviour, but issues infringement decisions in the first instance. The CMA's decisions can be appealed to the CAT, whose decisions can be appealed to the Court of Appeal, and then only very exceptionally to the Supreme Court.[47] As such, the CAT fits in the judicial hierarchy at the level of the High Court (indeed, its judicial members are

---

[42] On this test see: *Practice Statement* [1966] 1 WLR 1234, and *Knauer v. Ministry of Justice* [2016] UKSC 9.

[43] *Practice Statement*, ibid.

[44] *Knauer*, n. 42 at 23.

[45] Ministry of Justice, *Government Response to Consultation: Response to the Consultation on the Departure From Retained EU Case Law by UK Courts and Tribunals*.

[46] The European Union (Withdrawal) Act 2018 (Relevant Court) (Retained EU Case Law) Regulations 2020, SI 2020 No. 1525.

[47] In recent years, only one substantive competition matter (this involving merger) has been appealed to the UK Supreme Court: *Société Coopérative de Production SeaFrance SA v. CMA* [2015] UKSC 75. In December 2020, the UK Supreme Court handed down a judgment in *Mastercard Incorporated v. Merricks* [2020] UKSC 51. The latter case concerned the criteria for the certification of an opt-out collective action in a competition matter. This was a procedural

drawn from that court). As such, existing case law will be binding on it (and the CMA). It remains a question of whether the Court of Appeal will have an appetite to diverge from CJEU jurisprudence.

We suggest that considerations of certainty and transaction cost reduction suggest convergence with the EU regime. It is likely that the judiciary will also be sympathetic to these concerns. Thus, the greatest threat to divergence comes from Parliament itself, which, if the Brexit saga is of any educational value, may not act in a manner that is in the UK's best economic interests.

The regime as provided for in the TCA preserves both the best and worst of the UK's existing regime. The Chapter I and II provisions of the Competition Act are unaffected. Additionally, the government retains its ability to provide 'public interest' exemptions for individual or types of arrangements and mergers. Leaving the EU did not provide any added scope or freedom of action in this regard. In fact, as discussions in this book have repeatedly shown, the 'freedom' for governments (or, more accurately, ministers) to craft exemptions to the competition is a dangerous freedom. These exemptions, frequently made in the name of 'solving' a problem, have had a tendency to exacerbate the very problem, as we have seen. Any wider scope, or more frequent use of such exceptions, may have long-term and damaging consequences for consumers and a competitive market within the UK.

6.5 THE STATE AID PROVISIONS OF THE TCA

Subsidies and state aid have an odd place in a competitive economy. In a well-functioning market, they are unnecessary. It is fairly axiomatic among competition and trade lawyers and economists that a (or an ideal) market, if left to its own devices, will achieve the optimal allocation of goods and resources ensuring that consumers will have a choice of competing products available to them at competitive prices (i.e. at the marginal cost of their production). Adam Smith's 'invisible hand' will ensure this.[48] A subsidy to a given industry or producer artificially alters the quantity produced of the good or service in question, affecting the optimal level of production and allocation of resources.

But not all markets function well. Those conditions that the ideal market requires to effortlessly produce an optimal outcome are almost never realised. As a result of these failures, markets may not function efficiently.[49] Further, markets are process-oriented rather than end state–oriented. As a result, considerations of equity or fairness in a market outcome are irrelevant. It is at this point where some intervention in the market in the form of subsidies may be relevant. Subsidies can be used to

---

concern regarding the interpretation of a domestic statute, and Brexit would (did) not affect the outcome of the case.

[48] See e.g. Rubini, *The Definition of Subsidy and State Aid* at 25–26.

[49] Ibid. at 26.

promote the production of public (or public-like) goods and address distributional concerns.

Militating against the use of state aid is that it can create market failures of its own. State aid can be used in a subsidy war, as a means of attracting a particular firm or set of firms to a given region.[50] This distorts any comparative advantage possessed by existing regions, and may often saddle taxpayers in the 'winning' region with an industry that costs more than the benefits it generates. Such inefficiencies can result when firms relocate to deprived regions, as a result of subsidies.

But more significantly, for the future of the UK–EU trade relationship, state aid can act as a tariff substitute, eliminating the benefits of tariff-free trade and markets with tariff barriers. A subsidy to a domestic firm acts to reduce that firm's costs, enabling it to sell its product less expensively in comparison to the products of non-subsidised, foreign firms. A tariff has the same effect by raising the relative price of imported (foreign) goods.

This section briefly outlines the TCA's provisions on state aid. The discussion in this section is somewhat descriptive, in order to provide a starting point for the analysis found in Sections 6.5.1–6.5.3. The TCA's substantive provisions on subsidies do not materially differ from the EU's state aid regime. There is a slight difference with regard to the ceilings of permissible aid. The most significant difference between what the TCA permits and the EU's regime rests in procedural concerns. These are in regard to actionable aid (i.e. when a party can invoke the dispute resolution provisions of this part of the TCA), the procedure for approving aid and the dispute resolution process. It is differences with these three elements where the TCA's regime differs from the EU's. This, of course, lays the ground for the UK's post-Brexit regime. Section 6.5.4 is a brief coda on state aid and NI. That coda shows there is little benefit in this regard for the citizens of that nation, who may well pay a high price for Brexit in the form of trade disruption and renewed sectarianism.

6.5.1 Subsidies: Substantive Matters

The TCA's state aid/subsidies provisions are contained in Part Two, Heading One, Title XI, Chapter Three, which sets out the regime in one, albeit lengthy, Article. The substantive provisions contained in the TCA almost perfectly mirror those of the existing EU regime. It is the new procedural and dispute resolution system in which the greatest departure from that previous system can be found.

Other provisions of the TCA mirror the existing regime. One slight distortion in the TCA's reflection of the EU's regime is the *de mimimis* threshold. The TCA provides that its provisions do not apply to support to an undertaking of fewer than

---

[50] American practices of using subsidies (tax incentives, publicly financed construction of private infrastructure or facilities) are illustrative of this. See e.g. Glaeser, 'The Economics of Location-Based Tax Incentives', compare Greenstone and Moretti, 'Bidding for Industrial Plants'.

325,000 special drawing rights over a three-year period.[51] The corresponding EU threshold is €200,000 (or, in the case of a road freight transport firm, €100,000).[52] Although this does represent an increase in the amount, it is nevertheless insignificant, particularly when viewed in the context that future increases to this ceiling are permissible, albeit by agreement of the 'partnership council', i.e. one of the committees that oversees the administration of the TCA.[53] It would be unlikely that this body would countenance the renegotiation of such minutia in the first years of the TCA's existence – hence a need to build in a cushion for inflation into that Agreement's provisions.

6.5.2 *Subsidies: Procedural Matters*

6.5.2.1 Material Effect

The significant difference between the TCA's and the EU's regimes rests in two, procedural features. The first consists in the threshold for the subsidy to be actionable under the agreement; the other lies in the regime that governs the notification/approval process of the subsidy.

Although Article 3.1(1)(b) of the TCA provides a broadly encompassing definition of 'subsidy', this is in contrast with the sort of subsidies that are actionable. Article 3.4 (2) specifically notes that, for the purposes of the agreement, '[w]ithout prejudice to paragraph 1, each Party shall apply the conditions set out in Article 3.5 [prohibited subsidies and subsidies subject to conditions], where relevant, if the subsidies concerned have or could have a material effect on trade or investment between the Parties'. Under Article 3.8(1), if either party is of the view that a measure of the other party has 'a negative effect on trade or investment between the Parties, it may request the other Party to provide an explanation of how the Principles referred to in Article 3.4 [Principles] have been respected with regard to that subsidy'. Key in the understanding of this is the purpose of the TCA's provisions, set out in Article 3.4(2). The purpose of the agreement is therefore limited to the prohibition of those subsidies which have a *material effect* on investment or trade between the parties.

The threshold for a material effect is higher than that found in the EU's regime. Under the EU regime, the concern is with aid that 'distorts or threatens to distort competition' (Article 107(1)). This is a very low threshold, as the EU Courts have

---

[51] TCA Article 3.2(4), as of 15 September 2021, 1 SDR = €1.206020, see IMF, website: 1. www.imf .org/external/np/fin/data/param_rms_mth.aspx.

[52] Commission Regulation (EU) No. 1407/2013 of 18 December 2013 on the application of Articles 107 and 108 of the Treaty on the Functioning of the European Union to *de minimis* aid [2013] OJ L-352/1, Article 3(2)–(3).

[53] There is a 'Partnership Council' which has oversight of the TCA. It, along with a Trade Partnership Committee, takes input from eighteen specialised committees and four working groups. See House of Commons Library, The UK–EU Trade and Cooperation Agreement: Governance and Dispute Settlement.

held. Any strengthening of an undertaking's position is sufficient to satisfy this test. The ECJ noted this in *Philip Morris*: 'When state financial aid strengthens the position of an undertaking compared with other undertakings competing in intra-Community trade the latter must be regarded as affected by that aid.'[54] Indeed, the EU's test is sufficiently low (but not so low to allow the Commission to omit this from their market definition[55]) that in most cases, it is not necessary to perform a detailed second test to determine if the aid has the potential to distort competition, once aid has been identified.[56] Almost any aid satisfies this test.

'Material effect' is a vague term, like a fair amount of the language incorporated in the TCA. But as vague as it may be, it points to a threshold above that defined by EU law. Hence, successfully challenging a subsidy will be a more demanding effort under the TCA than under the EU's regime. Proof of a material effect on trade or investment will not be a pro forma matter.

6.5.2.2 Notification Requirement

In contrast to the EU's regime, the TCA does not require any *ex ante* notification of aid measures. In its place, the TCA substitutes a transparency obligation, requiring each party to make available – in a publicly available form (website or official database) – information about each subsidy that has been granted. This is to be done within six months of granting aid (or one year from when the tax was due, in the case of a tax measure) (Article 3.7).

Article 3.9 provides the requirement that each party 'shall establish or maintain an operationally independent authority or body with an appropriate role in its subsidy control regime. That independent authority or body shall have the necessary guarantees of independence in exercising its operational functions and shall act impartially.' In the EU's case, this is the Commission. It is widely assumed that the UK's national competition authority, the CMA, will take on these tasks. However, the exact nature of these tasks has yet to be determined, pending the outcome of a consultation process (discussed in Section 6.6).

In addition, Article 3.7(5) imposes a further duty on the UK for its authority to provide an 'interested party'[57] who may be applying for a review of the legality a subsidy 'within 28 days of the request . . . information that allows the interested party to assess the application of the principles set out in Article 3.4 [Principles], subject to

---

[54] Case 730/79, *Philip Morris Holland BV v. Commission* ECLI:EU:C:1980:209, para. 11; see also Case C-305/89, *Italian Republic v. Commission* (Alfa Romeo), ECLI:EU:C:1991:142, para. 26.

[55] Cases 296 and 318/82, *Netherlands and Leeuwarder Papierwarenfabriek BV v. Commission*, ECLI:EU:C:1985:113, para. 24.

[56] Commission Notice on the Notion of State aid, [2016] OJ-C 262/1, para. 187.

[57] Further defined in Article 3.7(6) as 'any natural or legal person, economic actor or association of economic actors whose interest might be affected by the granting of a subsidy, in particular the beneficiary, economic actors competing with the beneficiary or relevant trade associations'.

any proportionate restrictions which pursue a legitimate objective, such as commercial sensitivity, confidentiality or legal privilege'. This requirement would presuppose that the UK's authority could rapidly access this information and could provide a redacted version within the twenty-eight-day deadline. As also explored in Section 6.6, a regime which approves, on an *ex ante* basis, subsidies, may be better placed to more effectively comply with this obligation.

6.5.3 *Subsidies: Dispute Resolution*

The TCA provides for two routes of dispute resolution, one apparently designed to address concerns by aggrieved competitors, the other to address any cross-border externalities resulting from subsidies, whether considered individually or as part of a regime.

6.5.3.1 The Court-Based Approach

Article 3.10(1) of the TCA requires that each party ensure that its courts are competent to review the decisions of the granting authority or independent body (including that body's failure to act) and impose appropriate remedies (including award of damages or ordering the repayment of a subsidy). Article 3.11(1) further requires each party to have in place 'an effective mechanism of recovery in respect of subsidies in accordance with the following provisions, without prejudice to other remedies that exist in that Party's law'. An all-important footnote to this indicates that this requires the UK to develop 'a new remedy of recovery which would be available at the end of a successful judicial review, in accordance with the standard of review under national law'. The Article then provides that:

> [R]ecovery may be ordered if a court or tribunal of a Party makes a finding of a material error of law, in that:
>
> (a) a measure constituting a subsidy was not treated by the grantor as a subsidy;
> (b) the grantor of a subsidy has failed to apply the principles set out in Article 3.4 [Principles], as implemented in that Party's law, or applied them in a manner which falls below the standard of review applicable in that Party's law; or
> (c) the grantor of a subsidy has, by deciding to grant that subsidy, acted outside the scope of its powers or misused those powers in relation to the principles set out in Article 3.4 [Principles], as implemented in that Party's law.

However, though the TCA requires that this new juridical competency be established, the actual use of this means of recovery may be difficult, as review of the granting of subsidies will be constrained by Article 3.4's requirement that, to be actionable, subsidies must have a material effect on trade or investment between the parties. Article 3.11(3)–(4) sets out a very short limitation period (in the UK's case, one month after publication of details on the database) for an aggrieved party to commence an action for recovery.

6.5.3.2 Party-to-Party Dispute Resolution/Arbitration

Articles 3.12 and 3.13 of the TCA provide for the means by which the two parties can resolve disputes if either is of the view that a subsidy 'causes, or there is a serious risk that it will cause, a significant negative effect on trade or investment between the Parties'. The process is initiated by a request for information, with the goal that mutual consultation/discussion of the problem will constitute the first step in its resolution.

Article 3.12(2)–(4) establishes a time frame for exchange of information and consultation, which – if unsuccessful – allows for the aggrieved party to implement remedial measures, which 'shall be restricted to what is strictly necessary and proportionate in order to remedy the significant negative effect caused or to address the serious risk of such an effect' (Art. 3.13(8)). The party on whom such remedial measures have been imposed can, under Article 3.13(9), request the establishment of an arbitration tribunal under the dispute resolution provisions of the TCA.

The Tribunal is limited to determining under Article 3.12(9), in the first instance, whether: (1) the remedial measure taken by the requesting Party is inconsistent with the requirements that the subsidy pose a serious risk of a significant negative effect on trade or investment (i.e. the requirements of paragraphs 3 and 8); (2) whether or not the requesting party participated in consultations; and (3) if there was a failure to notify the subsidy within the stipulated timeframe. If the Tribunal finds against the responding party, that party has thirty days from the time of the ruling to notify the complaining parties of its compliance measures (Article 3.12(11)). If the Tribunal finds against the responding party:

> The complaining Party may request the arbitration tribunal, within 30 days from its ruling, to determine a level of suspension of obligations under this Agreement or a supplementing agreement not exceeding the level equivalent to the nullification or impairment caused by the application of the remedial measures, if it finds that the inconsistency of the remedial measures with paragraphs 3 or 8 is significant. (Art. 3.12(12))

The principles for determining the level of suspension of obligations are set out in more detail in other provisions of the TCA and is limited by the provisions of Article 3.12(13)–(17).

The substantive provisions of the TCA in determining what counts as a subsidy, and delineating the acceptable subsidies from the unacceptable, are virtually

identical to the existing EU provisions. The significant difference is in the actionability of a subsidy that 'crosses the boundary'. Under the EU regime, the threshold
for actionability is low, requiring only that it 'distorts or threatens to distort competition'. Almost every instance of state aid, unless it is specifically targeted towards a
market failure, will have this effect. The TCA, however, requires that the subsidy
have a 'material effect' or pose a 'significant negative effect' on trade or investment
between the two parties. This is a higher and less precise set of standards. As such, it
will be a more difficult point to establish in subsequent proceedings.

The ability of an 'interested party' to have access to national courts to challenge
subsidies that put this party at a competitive disadvantage is not a new invention.
Although underdeveloped, private enforcement of state aid law is and has been part
of the EU's regime, certainly since the SAAP of 2005.[58] The part-party arbitration
procedure is, of course, new – necessitated by Brexit.

The lesson of this part is that substantively, the TCA's provisions governing state
aid look very much like those found in the existing EU regime. Given the reasons
for which the EU controls such aid, explored in the introduction to Section 6.5, the
reasons why the EU would insist on similar requirements in any DFQF trade
agreement should be obvious. Nevertheless, there may be greater space in the
TCA's provisions for the UK's government to provide greater state aid. This is
the result of the joint consequences of the higher threshold for actionability and
the requirement of transborder effects on trade an investment, the proof of both of
which will rest on the complaining party.

6.5.4 *State Aid in Northern Ireland Post-Brexit: A Coda*

Significant in resolving the Troubles, and a key element of the Good Friday
Agreement, was the elimination of a hard border between the RoI and NI. A hard
Brexit, of the sort desired by those in government (particularly those with whom
Prime Minister Johnson surrounded himself, and to whom he owed his political
ascent) would require removing the UK from the EU's customs union, and reim-
posing a hard border between it and the EU. This would breach the UK's international commitments,[59] and would likely reopen the somewhat healed wounds of
the Troubles, since it would require the reimposition of border infrastructure
between the RoI and NI.[60]

[58] See Commission Notice on the Enforcement of State Aid law by National Courts [2009] OJ
C-85/1, Wollenschläger, Wurmnest and Möllers (eds.), *Private Enforcement of European
Competition and State Aid Law* and Pastor-Merchante, *The Role of Competitors in the
Enforcement of State Aid Law*.

[59] During negotiations of the Brexit agreements, the UK government appeared indifferent at
times regarding its obligations under international law, see n. 8.

[60] It is worth noting that border infrastructure was a common target of paramilitary attacks during
the height of the Troubles.

To mitigate these problems flowing from NI's status, the UK–EU Withdrawal Agreement contained a Protocol on NI. Article 1(3) notes:

> This Protocol sets out arrangements necessary to address the unique circumstances on the island of Ireland, to maintain the necessary conditions for continued North-South cooperation, to avoid a hard border and to protect the 1998 Agreement in all its dimensions.

These arrangements mandate that NI be aligned with EU regulation for a certain set of activities, which would include alignment with the EU's customs code (including relevant SPS checks) and state aid provisions. In this regard, Article 10(1) of the Protocol provides:

> The provisions of Union law listed in Annex 5 to this Protocol shall apply to the United Kingdom, including with regard to measures supporting the production of and trade in agricultural products in Northern Ireland, in respect of measures which affect that trade between Northern Ireland and the Union which is subject to this Protocol.

Annex 5 explicitly enumerates the TFEU's provisions on state aid (Articles 107–109) along with what appears to be the entirety of the EU's Regulations and soft law on state aid. Pursuant to Article 12(4) of the Protocol, the ECJ still retains jurisdiction in interpretation of these areas of EU law in the context of NI.

The Commission, in a Notice to Stakeholders, succinctly states the legal status of state aid in NI as follows:

> This means that EU State aid rules will continue to apply to the EU Member States, as well as to the United Kingdom in respect of aid that has an effect on the trade between Northern Ireland and the European Union that is subject to the IE/NI Protocol. In this context, the Protocol foresees that these rules shall apply to trade in goods and to the wholesale electricity market. The European Commission, as well as the CJEU and the General Court ('the Union Courts'), will remain competent as regards such aid.[61]

The significance of this is that NI is bound by the presently existing EU rules on state aid. Any aid granted to an undertaking in NI, which has an effect on trade between NI and the EU (which, as seen in Section 6.5.1, is a low threshold), will be subject to the entire spectrum of EU rules – including the procedural requirement of *ex ante* notification. And as the Withdrawal Agreement has not crystallised the rules, EU law will apply to (and the CJEU will continue to have jurisdiction over) NI. Any hope of using Brexit to forward a new industrial policy in NI, which due to the historical legacy of the Troubles has only recently seen an influx of new investment, is an illusion. Similarly, the mantra of 'take back control' seems not to have

---

[61] Commission, 'Notice to Stakeholders: Withdrawal of the United Kingdom and EU Rules in the Field of State Aid' (Brussels, 18 January 2021) at 3–4.

been uttered in the NI context.[62] And Brexit offered little to NI fishers.[63] There appears to be no benefit to NI from these new provisions.[64]

6.6 THE BREXIT BENEFIT? A SUBSIDIES-DRIVEN INDUSTRIAL POLICY

The TCA establishes a framework under which the UK can construct a new regime to aid undertakings (at least those in the British market). The government's thinking on this point was revealed in early 2021 via a consultation process and a draft Subsidies Control Bill,[65] the latter introduced on 30 June 2021.

The Bill's introduction was preceded by a consultation on the UK's new state aid regime announced in February 2021.[66] While policy consultations have an avowed purpose of seeking views from stakeholders and developing the ensuing policy with these views in mind, consultations can often be used to collect evidence in support of a position on which the government has settled.[67] This consultation had all the hallmarks of the latter, given the questions asked and the manner of their asking.

The Consultation boldly announced that the proposed new regime will allow for the possibly contradictory goals of permitting devolved governments (including NI's)

---

[62] Arguably NI received the worst from the so-called freedom from EU law that the rest of the UK obtained. As NI remained in the EU's customs union (to protect goods that may enter the EU via the RoI), goods being shipped from the UK to NI must comply with, *inter alia*, the EU's SPS requirements (and be accompanied by the relevant paperwork and subjected to appropriate inspection). This led to supply chain difficulties leading to food shortages – 'Food Supply Problems in NI Clearly a Brexit Issue – Coveney' – and renewed tension at borders (this time with the NI/rest-of-UK border), see Foster, Payne and Beesle, 'Northern Ireland Ports to Resume Checks after Security Fears'.

[63] It is likely that given the very small size of the NI fishing industry, any concerns they had fell on deaf ears in Westminster. The Common's Northern Irish Affairs Committee reports that in 2016 the NI fleet 'landed fish worth approximately £42 million into UK ports and abroad, representing 4.4% of the total value of fish landed by UK vessels'. House of Commons, Northern Ireland Affairs Committee, Brexit and Northern Ireland: Fisheries, para. 2.

[64] The immediate consequence of this was that NI business could not obtain (on the same terms as businesses in Great Britain) financial relief to mitigate the economic consequences of Covid-19. See Thomas and Pickard, 'Northern Ireland Firms Hit by EU State Aid Restrictions on UK Covid Loans', who report that '[o]fficials have warned lenders that local companies may be "ineligible" for the new scheme in the latest unexpected consequence from Britain leaving the EU'. However, this consequence is only unexpected for those who had failed to read the Withdrawal Agreement's Protocol on NI (and understood the EU position about the distortive effects of subsidies on the internal market) and/or the TCA's own provisions on NI. See e.g. Vickers, 'Spokesman Indicates Boris Johnson Has Not Read Brexit Trade Deal Text'.

[65] Subsidy Control Bill, Bill 135 2020–21 (First Reading 30 June 2021).

[66] Department for Business, Energy and Industrial Strategy, Subsidy Control: Designing a New Approach for the UK.

[67] See e.g. House of Lords, Select Committee on the Constitution, The Legislative Process, paras. 48–50.

to be the masters of their own spending decisions in a constructive manner for the whole of the UK. The Consultation announces, '[i]n this way we will secure the integrity of our internal market–the basis of our national prosperity–and avoid subsidy races which might distort competition between the UK nations and be costly for the taxpayer'.[68]

The government's vision – at least as reflected in the document – is that the new subsidies policy will be designed to allow their use with minimum bureaucracy, and, when they are at low risk of distorting the UK's internal market, maximum flexibility in their use. The document stated: 'The Government wants … a subsidy control regime that meets its wider socio-economic objectives and international obligations without placing undue bureaucracy and cost on public authorities'.[69] The proposed regime would also incorporate a presumption of legality of public authorities' decisions to award subsidies, subject to relevant principles of judicial review of administrative decisions (e.g. material error of law or irrational actions).[70]

This is a highly political goal that is completely consistent with the rhetoric of the pro-Brexit 'taking back control' lobby and the ability to do things without the need of 'Brussels's approval'. The Consultation's suggestion of not requiring *ex ante* approval in the subsidy awards process[71] was to be later incorporated into the draft bill.

Under the proposed regime, public authorities can grant subsidies, without *ex ante* approval in most cases. Before so doing, the authority must assess their proposed programme against seven principles governing the granting of subsidies and must not grant a subsidy which is inconsistent with the principles (s 12). The principles set out in Schedule 1 to the Bill substantially mirror some of the EU's preconditions for permissible state aid.[72] Certain subsidies are prohibited or restricted (ss 14–29) – these prohibitions capture the restrictions agreed in the TCA. Other types of subsidies, termed 'Subsidy or Scheme of Interest' and 'Subsidy or Scheme of Particular Interest', must be granted *ex ante* approval before award. These are to

---

[68] Consultation, n. 66 Forword at 3.

[69] Ibid. para. 85.

[70] Ibid. para. 86.

[71] At para. 101, the Consultation dismisses the EU's *ex ante* approach in the following terms: 'The role the EU Commission plays in State aid rules, approving the award of certain subsidies before they are given and taking enforcement action against those illegally awarded, is unique. As such there is a broad spectrum of options for the role a regulator could play in the UK's domestic subsidy control regime and the possibilities are set out below.' The Consultation thus rejects the EU's unique feature as a global outlier, rather than examining what positive advantages *ex ante* approval provides for its regime, and whether these merit adopting.

[72] These speak about the need for subsidies to remedy a market failure or be based on equitable concerns, to be proportionate and necessary, to be designed to alter the recipient's behaviour, to not compensate for costs that would already be funded, to be the least distortive means of pursuing a policy objective, to not distort competition or investment within the UK and to have beneficial effects that outweigh negative effects. There are other requirements for energy and environmental subsidies. Cf. Commission, Common Principles, Chapter Three, text accompanying nn. 94 to 98.

be defined by Regulation (s. 11). The Explanatory Notes accompanying the Bill note that '[i]t is envisaged that regulations made under this clause will capture a relatively small number of subsidies and schemes that are more likely to be inconsistent with the subsidy control requirements or have distortive effects on competition and investment within the UK'.[73] A new Subsidy Advice Unit within the CMA would be responsible for this vetting (ss 52–55). The CMA is placed under a tight schedule (typically five working days) to examine the proposal (s 53). No referred subsidy could be implemented until after a cooling-off period (five working days but can be extended – s 54) has expired. The Bill includes provisions for voluntary referrals (ss 56–57) and post-award referrals (ss 60–62).

In addition to the CMA being tasked with vetting of some proposed subsidies, the CMA would also be required to monitor and report on the efficacy of the UK's subsidy and control scheme (ss 65–69). Additionally, the Bill appears to envisage private enforcement of the regime, with the CAT established as the competent Tribunal (ss 70–75).

The lack of a general *ex ante* approval process is likely the greatest mistake the government could make in establishing the new regime. While so-called bureaucracy may slow down an approvals process, it can serve as a check on the potentially wasteful spending of taxpayers' contributions to the Treasury. Further, *ex ante* approval provides an additional check on the use of subsidies by devolved and local governments. These governments are unlikely to use subsidies in the interest of the UK as a whole (contrary to the aspirations set out in the Forward to the Consultation).

There are further benefits to *ex ante* control. They can allow for a signalling function, with a check on wasteful expenditure. A politician can present themselves as willing to support a particular industry close to the hearts of their constituents; however, should the subsidy-scrutinising body regard the support as wasteful, it can annul the award decision, with the politician in turn pointing to the scrutinising body as the reason why the subsidy could not be granted.[74]

Blocking such expenditure *ex ante* not only saves the Treasury (or taxpayer) from wasteful expenditure but allows the politician to present themselves as an advocate for their community who is stymied by a 'bureaucratic agency'. This, of course, would set up the UK's new agency as the scapegoat. However, after years of using 'Brussels' as this scapegoat, substituting a UK agency for 'Brussels' may be counterproductive in conveying the advantages of Brexit to the public at large.

There is a final, more practical point as to why an *ex ante* approval regime is preferable. A body with such a mandate is best placed to undertake responsibility with the disclosure requirements established by Article 3.7(5) of the TCA. In the event of a request for information under that Article, it is the UK government's

---

[73] Subsidy Control Bill Explanatory Notes, para. 48.
[74] Dewatripont and Seabright, '"Wasteful" Public Spending and State Aid Control' at 520–521.

obligation to respond, not the obligation of a devolved or local government, and the failure to respond contrary to the provisions of the TCA would be attributed to the UK (and not the devolved or local government). This is a basic principle of international law[75] and would govern the attribution of responsibility under the TCA.

6.7 FREEPORTS IN POST-BREXIT POLICY

A further governmental hint about future industrial policy can be found in the 2021 budget, in which the chancellor of the exchequer announced that Freeports would be established in eight regions in England.[76] This confirmed the results of, and response to, a consultation of Freeports conducted in 2020.[77] Freeports is a project that has captured the chancellor's attention since he was a backbench MP.[78] A Freeport, as the chancellor describes, is:

> [A]n area that although inside the geographic boundary of a country, is considered outside the country for customs purposes. This means that goods can enter and re-exit the Zone without incurring usual import procedures or tariffs, which are only incurred when products enter the domestic economy. Typically, Free Trade Zones enjoy lower tax, trade tariff and duty environments than the rest of the domestic economy and are created with the explicit aim of attracting investment, promoting trade and boosting domestic manufacturing activity and local employment.[79]

Another discussion of Freeports focuses on the tax implications usually associated with such zones:

> Freeports are one type of 'special economic zones' (SEZs). SEZs are areas within a country where business activity is subject to different rules from those prevailing in the rest of the country. SEZs can include tax incentives for investment within the geographical area of the freeports, flexible regulation, and investment in infrastructure.[80]

The ability to establish a Freeport arises from a jurisdiction's ability to establish areas within their jurisdiction which are de jure outside of their customs zone. These are not competition or state aid concerns. State aid issues arise when subsidies, in the

---

[75] See in the context of International Economic Law, e.g. *Compañía de Aguas del Aconquija SA and Vivendi Universal v. Argentine Republic* (ICSID Case No. ARB/97/3), Decision on Annulment of 3 July 2002, fn. 17.
[76] Rt Hon Rishi Sunak MP, 'Budget Speech 2021'.
[77] HM Government, Freeports: Response to the Consultation.
[78] See Sunak, n. 4 supra.
[79] Ibid. at 6, reference to (US) Congressional Research Service Report, U.S. Foreign-Trade Zones: Background and Issues for Congress, 2013 at 2.
[80] UK in a Changing Europe, Freeports at 3.

form of lower taxes, are used in the development and operation of Freeports, described as a typical benefit of these facilities.

Brexit gave the UK greater opportunity to obtain control over its customs and tariff policy. It also gave a greater opportunity to use state aid to develop an industrial policy. But the key question is whether or not the policy will work, in the sense that it provides value for money for taxpayers.

The primary benefit of Freeports is that they allow manufacturers to take advantages of 'tariff inversion'. This is the situation when tariffs on components of goods are greater than the assembled good. In such a situation, a manufacturer can import the components into a Freeport, assemble the final good there and 'export' the final good at the lower tariff.[81] A Freeport can also be used as a form of bonded warehouse, into which goods can be brought and stored, in anticipation of later sales. This allows for a certain amount of duty deferral, e.g. during the Christmas period.[82] The non-tariff/customs-related benefits to Freeports is that they can be used as a means of regional development, through their location in lesser-developed regions.

Tariff inversion may be an overstated argument in support of Freeports. There are very few sectors where the tariff wedge (i.e. the difference between tariffs on intermediate and final product) is great. Serwicka and Holmes provide a list of only five items where the wedge exceeds 2.22 per cent.[83] They note that '[t]he above suggests that in some sectors tariff inversion savings could be made, but overall, there is limited scope for substantial savings in the UK context'.[84] In fact, the EU's tariff regime – on which the UK's is presently constructed – tends to escalate tariffs, and impose greater amounts on finished products than on their components.[85]

The utility of using Freeports to address tariff inversion in the Brexit context is suspect. As the TCA establishes DFQF trade between the UK and the EU there will be no gains for the UK in trade with its largest trading partner. Further, if tariff inversion is a significant problem, this would be better addressed by the UK through a recalibration of its applied tariff rates, for which Brexit provides an opportunity. This would extend the benefits of eliminating tariff inversion to manufactures more generally, i.e. throughout the UK. As the UK in a Changing Europe notes:

[81] Ibid. at 9.
[82] Ibid. at 8. However, savings from this duty deferral is minimal. Serwicka and Holmes calculate that storing £1,000,000 of goods dutiable at 3 per cent at a 5 per cent interest rate for three months yields only a £375 savings (assuming storage costs in the Freeport are equal to those outside the Freeport). See Serwicka and Holmes, 'What Is the Extra Mileage in the Reintroduction of "Free Zones" in the UK?' at 10.
[83] Ibid. at 9, these are: manufacture of starches and starch products (wedge of 27.18 per cent), manufacture of dairy products (7.52 per cent), manufacture of prepared animal feeds (6.92 per cent), manufacture of consumer electronics (2.81 per cent) and manufacture of furniture (2.22 per cent). This represented about 1.24 per cent of the UK's total imports in 2017.
[84] Ibid.
[85] Serwicka and Holmes, ibid., note that 'importers of automotive parts face lower tariffs (4.5%) than importers of final cars (10%)'.

If tariffs are too high or regulations too burdensome, they should be lowered for the whole country. If, on the other hand, the level of tariffs or regulation is justifiable, why would they be lowered for one part of the country? In practice, therefore, the real case for freeports is in developing countries where either the customs administration is chaotic or regulation is too high/dysfunctional, and there are political economy reasons why governments cannot change that for the whole country. That isn't the case for the UK.[86]

There is little reason for there to be differential tariffs or customs administration within a country like the UK, and denying the advantages of such adjustments to the majority of the country not located in a Freeport.

The job creation advantages of Freeports are also likely overtouted. One report, commissioned by the Tees Valley mayor in a successful attempt to secure such a facility, notes that:

> The free zone is expected to generate 32,000 jobs in the Tees Valley. Our model estimates that the zone will host 20,000 jobs with the combined indirect and induced effects adding around 12,000 new jobs to the region, as shown in ... . Applying a 50% deadweight and displacement factor to the overall effect, 16,000 of these would be additional.[87]

Even if this model is not optimistic, the Tees Valley mayor's concerns would focus solely on local employment and not the loss of 16,000 jobs elsewhere. Job creation in Freeports does not come without costs. The Tees model notes:

> Under the central investment scenario and enhanced free zone model, each additional job created comes with a cost of around £12,000 in forgone revenue. Deadweight and displacement effects directly affect these calculations.[88]

And:

> Although the policy could result more costly than similar regional development programmes, each additional job will produce an average of £53,000 in GVA [gross valued added] at a cost to the treasury of £12,000 per job in forgone revenue under the enhanced free zone.[89]

This cost of £12,000 per job may be optimistic. Other studies report that the cost is more likely in the range of £17,000 per job at 1997 prices.[90] The question remains as to whether or not this represents good value for the taxpayer.

This question is particularly salient if the gain for a given region comes at another region's cost (at least in part). Attracting businesses to a given region via a subsidised

---

[86] UK in a Changing Europe, n. 80 at 8.
[87] Tees Valley Mayor, A Proposal for a National Free Zone Policy, point 3.3.5.
[88] Ibid.
[89] Ibid. point 3.3.6.
[90] Serwicka and Holmes, n. 82 at 4, citing PA Cambridge Economic Consultants, Final Evaluation of Enterprise Zones.

Freeport has an identical economic effect as attracting business to the region via any other subsidy measure. When competition for jobs and investment is between an economically prosperous and a less developed region, the use of subsidies to drive investment to the latter can be efficient and may satisfy equity goals.[91] But otherwise, the use of subsidies as a means of attracting investment may be nothing more than an element of a 'beggar thy neighbour' strategy in a subsidies war.

Nevertheless, it is clear that Freeports will now become part the UK's post-Brexit industrial strategy. This was announced in the Response to Consultation[92] and the 2021 Budget Speech. Although the speech only announced the location of eight such facilities in England, the chancellor announced that this will be a UK-wide policy, suggesting that the government will work with the devolved governments in its implementation.[93]

However, the benefits to this policy appear to be limited. The employment gains seem to be inflated as a result of deadweight displacement of jobs. The cost of each job is significant (and models used in support appear to have optimistic assessments of this cost). If Freeports are needed as a result of difficulties with regulation (e.g. tariff inversion), the solution is to rectify the regulation – and grant the benefits of this to the entire UK.

It is important to note the effect of the post-Brexit regime on NI and the implications that this might have for the development of a subsidy-driven industrial policy within that nation. This is not an afterthought (as NI and its circumstances may have been for most English Brexiteers) but is to demonstrate that the Withdrawal Agreement's Protocol on NI significantly limits the so-called freedom of the UK to act in that devolved nation.

Key to understanding NI's situation in this regard is the relationship between the Protocol and the TCA. The Protocol keeps NI in the EU's internal market for goods. It has specific provisions for the application of the EU's state aid regime within NI. In particular, Article 10(1) of the Protocol provides:

> The provisions of Union law listed in Annex 5 to this Protocol shall apply to the United Kingdom, including with regard to measures supporting the production of and trade in agricultural products in Northern Ireland, in respect of measures which affect that trade between Northern Ireland and the Union which is subject to this Protocol.

Annex 5 explicitly enumerates the TFEU's provisions on state aid (Articles 107–109) along with what appears to be the entirety of the EU's Regulations and soft law on

---

[91] See e.g. Sleuwaegen, Pennings and De Voldere, 'Public Aid and Relocation within the European Community' and Friederiszick, Röller and Verouden, 'European State Aid Control' at 636.

[92] Freeports: Response to the Consultation, n. 77 at 6.

[93] This is confirmed in the Consultation Document: HM Government, Freeport Consultation at 11.

state aid. Pursuant to Article 12(4) of the Protocol, the ECJ still retains jurisdiction in interpretation of these areas of EU law in the context of NI.

The Commission, in a Notice to Stakeholders, succinctly states the legal status of state aid in NI as follows:

> This means that EU State aid rules will continue to apply to the EU Member States, as well as to the United Kingdom in respect of aid that has an effect on the trade between Northern Ireland and the European Union that is subject to the IE/NI Protocol. In this context, the Protocol foresees that these rules shall apply to trade in goods and to the wholesale electricity market. The European Commission, as well as the CJEU and the General Court ('the Union Courts'), will remain competent as regards such aid.[94]

The result of all of this is that NI is bound by the presently existing EU rules on state aid. Any aid granted to an undertaking in NI, which has an effect of trade between NI and the EU (which, as noted, is a low threshold), will be subject to the entire spectrum of the EU rules – including the procedural requirement of *ex ante* notification. Any hope of using Brexit to forward a new industrial policy in NI (which due to the historical legacy of the Troubles has only recently seen an influx of new investment) is fleeting. Similarly, the mantra of 'take back control' seems not to have been uttered in the NI context.[95] Although NI fishers might have obtained a very slight benefit,[96] there appears to be no benefit to NI from these new provisions.

Further, although the government's Freeport policy suggests that it will locate (at least) one of these facilities in NI, this may not be compatible with NI remaining in the EU's internal market and customs areas. It was Brexit's 'benefit' of leaving these that could allow the creation of such zones. If NI hasn't left, it can't reap this benefit of Brexit. Considered from another angle, if a Freeport or similar such zone is eventually established in NI, then the arrangements under which that zone operates would be identical to the arrangements that the UK could have adopted in the absence of Brexit.

It is clear that subsidies and Freeports will become a feature of the UK's post-Brexit industrial policy. Through these means, the UK may be able to pursue a more aggressive, state aid–based industrial policy. However, excessive use of these tools is likely unwise. In a report, commissioned by the government to assess the future of the UK's competition regime, John Penrose MP discusses the way forward. This way, Penrose suggests, is 'to reduce regulatory and political risks, by using stronger competition and consumer powers to cut the reach, costs, economic distortions and uncertainty of bureaucratic and political interventions so businesses and investors

---

[94] Commission, 'Notice to Stakeholders: Withdrawal of the United Kingdom and EU Rules in the Field of State Aid'.

[95] Arguably NI received the worst from the so-called freedom from EU law that the rest of the UK obtained.

[96] See n. 63 and accompanying text.

only have to deal with commercial problems instead'.[97] He sees the same principles as applying to state aid.

Cautioning against the use of subsidies as a means of promoting industrial policy due to their distortive effect, Penrose writes:

> They put all the benefits of politically-independent regulation into reverse, making Britain less attractive for investment in growth and jobs, and meaning investors need higher returns which raise costs and make our firms less productive as a result. Even worse, they create huge opportunities for deep-pocketed incumbent firms with good lawyers and lobbyists, or for political movements keen to flex their muscles, to get special deals for themselves at the expense of everyone else. And because the political pressures to intervene and prevent easily-identifiable and imminently-looming job losses are so much bigger than the ones created by people who fail to get as-yet-uncreated new jobs when investment goes abroad, it creates a 'losers paradox': that politicians are terrible at picking winners, but loser are brilliant at picking politicians.[98]

This report was commissioned by the government, and it author is a currently sitting MP. One can only hope that the government will listen to this. The government's proposed plan to exercise its new-found freedom in developing an industrial policy appears to be very different from our suggestions. This, we suggest, is likely a mistake and may cost the economy and UK taxpayers significantly.

6.8 CONCLUSION: ARE THERE ANY BREXIT BENEFITS?

The TCA, agreed to on Christmas Eve 2020, represents a Brexiteer's vision of independence. In this vision, Brexit would allow the UK to regain control of its fisheries (in spite of that industry's low contribution to the UK's economy as a whole) and laws. This would, in turn, enable the UK to develop its own competition rules and subsidy policy to act as a foundation for a new industrial policy suitable to its new place in the world.

But this vision appeared to be anchored in fantasy, rather than reality. The UK was able to claim some victory with regard to fisheries – if there was any victory it was Pyrrhic in the extreme. Although, from the supply side, UK fishers had greater apparent ability to catch fish, the TCA did not exempt their products from the EU's SPS measures. The EU, of course, was the UK fishers' largest market. The immediate impact was that trade in seafood from the UK to the EU ground to a halt,[99] leading to cries of betrayal.[100] The advantages of Brexit, as governed by the TCA, for fishers were small at best.

---

[97] Penrose, *Power to the People* at 68.
[98] Ibid. at 53.
[99] Kollewe, 'Fresh Seafood Exports from Scotland to EU Halted until 18 January'.
[100] See Parker and Dickie, n. 10 supra.

Taking back control of its laws was also chimeric. Upon further reflection, the UK's government has recognised that a wholesale 'slash and burn' of existing EU regulation is not an answer. Not only has the business community incorporated this regulation into their business models, but reducing standards (and thereby affecting the conditions of competition with the EU) may attract a retaliatory retaliation from the EU. More significantly, '[o]ne former Tory cabinet minister involved in previous attempts to root out red tape said: "You cast around and find virtually nothing anyone wants to repeal. Then you find there was a reason it was put there in the first place"'.[101]

State aid and competition rules have their purpose as well. As seen in Section 6.5, the TCA gives the UK greater independent regulatory space in these two areas. This, of course, raises the questions of how much space is gained, and whether – given the costs of the agreement – these costs were worth this new space.

The TCA changes little in the competition rules. The main difference in the post-Brexit competition regime will be in the international dimension. The UK is no longer a member of the ECN, and as such it no longer benefits from the ability to participate in the information-sharing aspects of this organisation. The TCA does provide for the establishment of something resembling this, and we suggest that both parties act on this as a matter of priority. As the past several decades of competition enforcement have shown, cartels and undertakings engaging in other anticompetitive practices do not respect international borders.

Also lamentable is the loss of the 'one-stop shop' of merger control. Now large mergers with a UK and EU dimension will need to be cleared by both authorities. This will add to the costs – both to the undertakings involved, who will be required to prepare an additional filing, and to taxpayers who fund the relevant agencies whose work is now to a large degree duplicated. These transaction costs are compounded by uncertainty. If the UK chooses to diverge from the EU's regime, either through a difference in standards by which mergers or evaluated or greater scope for political intervention in the merger control process, this will add uncertainty and hence risk to any proposed transaction. Increasing transactional risk will not aid the UK in boldly carving a new place in the post-Brexit world.

The TCA may be overtouted as a means of developing industrial policy. A post-Brexit Britain, where politicians attempt (and frequently fail) to pick winners, is unlikely to become the industrial or high-tech powerhouse that those on the leave side in the referendum promised. Indeed, such a strategy harks back to the past,[102] where the government supported the production of Morris Minors, British Leyland and Concorde among other failures. In terms of the three totemic issues of fish,

---

[101] Parker, '"Slash and Burn" of EU Rules Ruled Out post-Brexit'.
[102] Broadberry and Leunig, 'The Impact of Government Policies on UK Manufacturing since 1945'.

sovereignty and industrial policy, the TCA delivered little in the way of benefits. And with Brexit and its costs, any benefit was delivered at a significant price. In many respects the so-called advantages flowing from 'new' or different post-Brexit competition and state aid regimes make the same mistakes of the past, when these regimes were either suspended or subordinate to considerations of political expediency. Competition was weakened, for which consumers and taxpayers paid the price.

7

The Environment, Sustainability Goals and the Climate Crisis

7.1 INTRODUCTION

Although some media reporting of environmental problems may suggest otherwise, there is clear consensus in the scientific community that anthropogenic global warming is occurring.[1] The scientific consensus is clear: one 2013 study shows that 97.1 per cent of peer-reviewed papers taking a position on anthropogenic global warming accepted a human cause.[2] And if this is insufficient, the UN's Intergovernmental Panel on Climate Change's (IPCC) July 2021 Special Report remarked that with high confidence, anthropogenic emissions have and will continue to cause long-term change to the climate system, with corresponding 'risks to health, livelihoods, food security, water supply, human security, and economic growth'.[3] The draught, fires and flooding which the summer of 2021 brought appear to underscore the IPCC's conclusion.

The consequences of climate change will likely be profound. A 2005 study commissioned for the EC's director general of the environment noted that climate change will likely have impacts on: sea level rise, agriculture, energy use, human health and disease burdens, water resources (including supply, quality, flooding and draught), storm damage and alteration of sea and air circulation.[4] In addition to these, climate change may cause low-probability, high-impact events capable of provoking significant social and economic disruption on their own. Some have suggested that these events are the 'ticking time bombs' delivered by climate change.[5]

---

[1] See e.g. Cook et al., 'Quantifying the Consensus on Anthropogenic Global Warming in the Scientific Literature'.
[2] Ibid. at 6.
[3] IPCC, Global Warming of 1.5°C at 9.
[4] Watkiss et al., 'The Impacts and Costs of Climate Change' at 17.
[5] Nordhaus, 'Expert Opinion on Climatic Change' at 45.

Although there is consensus that climate change is occurring, there is disagreement – particularly in the economics[6] profession – about the costs of this change.[7] Arguably, there may be a few benefits to climate change – the growth and quality of English vineyards may be an example.[8] Some climatic change may displace some economic activities: lobster fisheries in the North American Atlantic are an example. As a result of warming water, stocks are migrating northward, hence Maine (and Canadian) lobster fishers are benefitting at the expense of the industry in Massachusetts. These so-called benefits are likely overstated.

Yet climate change is not the only environmental crisis that the earth presently faces. There is a significant amount of plastic pollution found in the world's oceans,[9] and this is entering the ecosystem and posing a threat to human health.[10]

As a result, concerns about pollution abatement, environmental remediation and sustainability are now part of mainstream social discourse. These concerns are also revealed in individual purchasing decisions and corporate social responsibility agendas. Sustainability and environmental concerns manifest themselves in the market and can have significance for the competitive conduct of firms acting on the market. These concerns show a need to examine how the competition rules can interact with sustainability concerns. The fear, of course, is that these rules will somehow hinder the promotion of these goals, whether through private measures or public means.

The purpose of this chapter is to examine the purported 'sustainability deficit'[11] in EU competition law. As the results of this chapter show, there is an element of truth to the claims that such a deficit exists. However, the size of the gap may be overstated. The real problem is likely not to be with competition law, and its effect on private and public sustainability initiatives, but rather with our expectations regarding what the competition regime may be able to accomplish on its own. Competition alone will neither solve nor substantially hinder solutions to environmental and sustainability concerns. This is not to say that the present competition

---

6   Carlyle had a reason for calling it 'the dismal science'.

7   Compare e.g. Nordhaus, 'Reflections on the Economics of Climate Change'; Tol, 'The Economic Impacts of Climate Change'; Stern, 'Imperfections in the Economics of Public Policy, Imperfections in Markets, and Climate Change'; and Hanemann, 'What Is the Economic Cost of Climate Change?'

8   'English Wine: Working on Sunshine – Weather Trends Are in Growers' Favour and Help to Explain the Surge in Vines Planted'. The statement of Agatha Christie's Hercule Poirot that 'the day the English create their own wines is the day I return home to Belgium' is now a very real threat (Agatha Christie, 'The Yellow Iris', ITV Adaptation).

9   Eriksen et al., 'Plastic Pollution in the World's Oceans'; see also Cózara, 'Plastic Debris in the Open Ocean'. This of course also indicates a need for revisions to thinking about the governance of oceans. See e.g. Marcus Haward, 'Plastic Pollution of the World's Seas and Oceans as a Contemporary Challenge in Ocean Governance'.

10   Waring, Harris and Mitchell, 'Plastic Contamination of the Food Chain' at 67.

11   See e.g. Gerbrandy, 'Solving a Sustainability-Deficit'.

regime is perfect and needs no refinement: it isn't and it does. But it cannot perform this function by itself.

The remainder of this chapter is organised as follows. Section 7.2 discusses the nature of the problem, and the market failures which gave rise to it. This provides a background to understanding possible responses to the problem, and how competition and state aid law could be viewed as blocking these. This is followed by an extended discussion of the framework of EU competition law in Section 7.3, to show how this framework is consistent with a measured response to sustainability issues. Yet the current regime is not perfect, and there is room for improvement. Section 7.4 concludes by addressing those areas in which the current regime could use some 'fine tuning' to better address longer-term sustainability concerns and not thwart legitimate public or private responses.

7.2 THE ENVIRONMENT AND MARKET FAILURE

The standard, market-based approach to the treatment of pollution is to regard it as a negative externality which arises from the production of another good or service. A producer of goods will consider only the costs that it must pay in the production process. If some costs – in this case, the social costs of negative externalities – are not internalised, the true costs of the good's production will not be incorporated into its price. Rather, the good will be underpriced, and thus the good and its externalities are overproduced. Failure to fully internalise the negative externalities associated with production is the relevant market failure.

One early approach to dealing with externalities was suggested by Pigou.[12] He reasoned that the imposition of a tax equal to the social costs of the externalities would correct the market failure of their overproduction (and subsidising the production of positive externalities would similarly correct their underproduction). The difficulty with this suggestion is its practical application. Too high or too low a tax results in under or overproduction, respectively. And the accuracy of the tax rate is thus dependent upon accuracy in pricing the externality. Further, in spite of the desire to use such a tax to internalise the social costs of a product or activity, there can be a tendency to set the tax too high to use it as a revenue-generating measure.

Coase gives us an insight into how such externalities can be accurately priced. In his 1962 paper, 'The Problem of Social Cost',[13] he shows that where property rights are well defined, and in the absence of transaction costs, property will flow to its most valued use, through private (contractual) arrangements. So, a manufacturer that produces pollution (thus creating some form of legally recognised nuisance) can bargain with those affected by the pollution for a 'right' to pollute. The outcome

---

[12] Pigou, *The Economics of Welfare* at 381.
[13] Coase, 'The Problem of Social Cost'.

of this bargaining process, a market solution based on an agreed price, represents an accurate costing of the social costs.

While Coasean bargaining may allow for the determination of an accurate, market-based price, it is limited. It contains strong assumptions that limit its use. It requires a clear, initial assignment of rights. Second, the transaction costs associated with the subsequent bargaining position must be sufficiently small, otherwise the wealth-maximising bargain will not occur. Third, all costs must be internalised (or privatised by the parties) in the bargaining process. Fourth, to accurately internalise these costs, all parties must have access to the relevant information, particularly about the effects of the externalities.[14] Fifth, all parties must have a seat at the bargaining table – hence when externalities (or their consequences) may not manifest themselves for years those affected by them may not be represented in the bargaining process. Sixth, those seated at the bargaining table must want to achieve a negotiated bargain (in other words, their relationship remains sufficiently intact so they can pursue a rational outcome). And finally, as the set of those sitting at the bargaining table expands, other forms of market failure emerge, particularly those associated with free riders and holdouts. Such failure will be fatal to achieving a negotiated outcome which establishes an accurate, market price for the externality.[15]

This discussion of the Pigouvian and Coasean solutions to the problems of externalities shows two things. First, both recognise the nature of the market failures that give rise to the production of externalities. But at the same time, both are incomplete as a resolution to the problem. Pigou's response requires a reasonably accurate determination of the true social costs (and benefits) of the activity in question. Coase's solution may work well in that set of limited situations where its strong assumptions hold. But in situations where multiple parties may suffer the costs of the externalities, or which are characterised by incomplete information, or where non-trivial transaction costs exist (to name a few), the Coasean ideal will not be realised. And cases that are marked by the last set of characteristics have typically led to the environmental problems and climate crisis we now face.[16]

Notwithstanding this, these two proposed solutions have shaped the EU's response to environmental and sustainability concerns. Internalising all the (social) costs of an activity is a keystone of the polluter pays principle, now entrenched as Article 191(2) TFEU (ex 174(2) TEU).[17] This principle is reflected in policies which

---

[14] This is highly significant in pollution cases, where health effects may not be known for years or generations.

[15] Some American judges seem to recognise this problem, and award damages when a nuisance affects a large set of parties. See e.g. *Boomer v. Atlantic Cement Company*, 294 NYS 2d 45 (NY CA 1968), 257 NE 2d 870 (NY SC 1970); and *Spur Industries v. Del E Webb Development Co.*, 494 P 2d 700 (Ariz SC 1972).

[16] Coase, n. 13 recognises this.

[17] This principle seems to have its EU genesis in the First Environmental Action Plan: Declaration of the Council of the European Communities and of the representatives of the

as waste disposal,[18] recycling[19] and freshwater conservation and management.[20] However, at the same time, this has seen as a barrier to the provision of subsidies (state aid) to firms to assist them in environmental remediation.[21]

A carbon tax, based on Pigouvian principles, was imposed in France in 2014, in an effort to promote a switch to more sustainable energy.[22] This measure imposed a tax per tonne of carbon dioxide produced, which increased on an annual basis. The tax was largely ineffective, as it came into effect when oil prices were falling. It had a regressive effect. It disproportionately affected those with less income and was seen as a revenue-producing measure. The government's (soon abandoned) 2018 proposal to raise the tax to €86.20 per tonne by 2022 was to fuel the violent Gilets Jaunes (Yellow Vests) movement. The EU's Emissions Trading System[23] uses a 'cap and trade' method, where (put simply) polluters are provided with a quota for emissions (which reduces on an annual basis). Underquota capacity can be traded (sold) on a market.[24] Assuming sufficient liquidity in the market, this sets a price on the emissions.

None of these measures are straightforward applications of competition law. This demonstrates the obvious point that competition measures on their own cannot be adequate responses to this problem. Indeed, the Commission's Directorate-General of Competition writes in its response to the EU's 'Green Deal':[25]

> Competition policy is not in the lead when it comes to fighting climate change and protecting the environment. There are better, much more effective ways, such as

---

Governments of the Member States meeting in the Council of 22 November 1973 on the programme of action of the European Communities on the environment [1973] OJ C-112/1, Title 2, point 5.

[18] E.g. Directive 2008/98/EC of the European Parliament and of the Council of 19 November 2008 on waste and repealing certain Directives [2008] OJ L-312/3, Articles 8 and 15.

[19] European Parliament and Council Directive 94/62/EC of 20 December 1994 on Packaging and Packaging Waste [1994] OJ L-365/10, Article 15.

[20] Directive 2000/60/EC of the European Parliament and of the Council of 23 October 2000 Establishing a Framework for Community Action in the Field of Water Policy [2000] OJ L-327/1, Article 9(1).

[21] See Communication from the Commission, Guidelines on State Aid for Environmental Protection and Energy 2014–2020 [2014] OJ C-200/1, points 156–157; and e.g. Commission Decision of 22 July 1993 concerning aid the Italian government intends to grant to *Cartiere del Garda* (93/564/EEC) [1993] OJ L-273/51.

[22] Ministère de la Transition écologique, 'Fiscalité carbone'.

[23] See Directive 2003/87/EC of the European Parliament and of the Council of 13 October 2003 Establishing a Scheme for Greenhouse Gas Emission Allowance Trading within the Community and Amending Council Directive 96/61/EC [2003] OJ L-275/32.

[24] See Holligan, 'Commodity or Propriety?'

[25] See Communication from the Commission to the European Parliament, the European Council, the Council, the European Economic and Social Committee and the Committee of the Regions, the European Green Deal (Brussels, 11.12.2019) (COM(2019) 640 final.

regulation and taxation. Competition policy, however, can complement regulation and the question is how it could do that most effectively.[26]

In addition to its complementary effect, competition (including state aid) policy can also hinder responses to environmental problems.

Effectively addressing these environmental concerns requires both public and private effort and action. In addition to the usual portfolio of regulatory responses, public effort can include the appropriate delivery of subsidies to encourage appropriate investment, in circumstances where market failure may preclude this. Further, private activity, in the form of collaboration among undertakings, may also prove to be a possible pathway to more environmentally friendly production of goods.

The IPCC Working Group recognises the merits of both public and private pathways to mitigation. It notes that innovation can lead to more energy-efficient products and processes. However, there are market failures associated with such progress. The group notes that '[b]arriers to implementing energy efficiency relate largely to the initial investment costs and lack of information. Information programmes are the most prevalent approach for promoting energy efficiency, followed by economic instruments, regulatory approaches, and voluntary actions.'[27] Market failures associated with informational asymmetries and uncertainties can lead to underinvestment. Additionally, they note that coordinated private action can also aid in this effort: 'Systemic approaches and collaboration within and across industrial sectors at different levels, e. g., sharing of infrastructure, information ... may provide further mitigation potential in certain regions or industry types.'[28] Yet both types of initiatives have the potential to breach the competition rules.

7.3 COMPETITION, ENVIRONMENT AND THE TREATIES

7.3.1 *Introduction*

The European Treaties establish a Union among its Member States, and in so doing they establish a legal order to govern this Union. These treaties set out the Union's goals and policies, which are linked to coordinate its activity. Competition, state aid control and the environment are only three such policies. The Treaty architecture is such that there is no hierarchy among these policies – one policy does supersede any other. Accordingly, the instruments use a polycentric approach to achieving these goals,[29] working in some form of symbiotic relationship.

---

[26] DG Competition, 'Competition Policy Supporting the Green Deal: Call for Contributions' at 1.

[27] IPCC, *Climate Change 2014* at 743.

[28] Ibid. at 743–744.

[29] The term is Lianos', 'Polycentric Competition Law'.

This symbiosis between competition and environmental policy has been recognised by the Commission since environmental goals were expressly incorporated into the Maastricht Treaty.[30] Yet, the Commission has continually maintained that incorporation of environmental considerations into fundamental EU law was not a one-way street, noting that the market has a role to play in achieving these goals. The PPP is then cited as such a market response.[31]

There are two prima facie responses for the competition regime when faced with an environmental challenge. It can serve to work to scrutinise a proposed course of action (whether public or private in origin), in an effort to determine the extent to which that action is consistent with or thwarts competition goals (e.g. to promote the efficient production of goods and services). Viewed this way, the regime incorporates and measures the environmental consequences (both beneficial and detrimental) in its assessment. Alternatively, the competition regime could be viewed as an instrument to promote an environmental (or other Treaty) goal. In this view, for instance, merger control may be used to block an otherwise welfare-enhancing transaction, solely on the grounds of environmental harm; or a welfare-reducing restrictive agreement would pass muster because of some (possibly limited) environmental benefits.

We suggest that this second approach is not just unwarranted, but is a potential rule of law threat. The general problems are, first, that certainty as to the meaning, interpretation and use of a particular rule is part of a legal system's rule of law norm; and second, that developed legal systems incorporate divisions of powers in their rule making and administrative processes. Particular bodies may be limited in their legislative competence, and even rules that may be created by an all-competent legislature are likely administered by specialised agencies or bodies.

In the context of European competition law, this has more general significance. As Nowag indicates, it is not for the Commission, on its own, to adopt environmental legislation:

> Furthermore, preventative integration in the context of competition law raises issues regarding the division of powers. Preventing undertakings from increasing pollution by means of Articles 101 and 102 TFEU where no 'competition problem' exists is a matter for environmental legislation. It is up to the legislative bodies, the Council, and the European Parliament to adopt environmental legislation. Doing so via competition law undermines the division of powers and might even be seen as a misuse of it.[32]

And, as Nowag also points out, this has greater significance in the decentralised enforcement of EU competition law under Regulation 1/2003 – where the use of

---

[30] *XXIIIrd Report on Competition Policy*, point 163.
[31] Ibid. points 164–165.
[32] Nowag, *Environmental Integration* at 142.

national competition law (albeit based on EU law) to pursue an environmental goal could conceivably result in criminal sanctions.[33]

Using competition law as a means to promote non-competition goals is prima facie illegitimate. Similarly, given the linking clauses in the Treaties, and the post-Maastricht position of the environment as part of the Union's aims, it would also be illegitimate to use competition law in a manner which failed to take into account these aims. 'Taking into account', however, does not imply a carte blanche exception for arrangements which purport to pursue an environmental aim. Rather, as the Commission explains, this is a process of determining whether the competitive constraints imposed by any agreement in fact achieve the environmental goals, in a manner consistent with the Treaties' goals.

In its 1993 *Report of Competition Policy*, the Commission describes its (pre-Regulation 1/2003) approach as follows:

> [T]he Commission will examine carefully all agreements between companies to see if they are indispensable to attain the environmental objectives. ... The Commission in its analysis of individual cases will have to weigh the restrictions of competition in the agreement against the environmental objectives that the agreement will help attain in order to determine whether, under this proportionality analysis it can approve the agreement.[34]

Post-Regulation 1/2003, the self-assessment would remain the same (albeit requiring more robust economic evidence); but the burden in assessing the agreement falls on the undertakings in question.

Greenwashing is a very real concern. In this context, competition law will analyse private environmental initiatives, and similarly state aid measures will be used to vet governmental subsidisation of industry. In the case of the former, it is well known that private enterprises will act to promote private gain. Advocate-General Jacobs warns us of this:

> It can be presumed that private economic actors normally act in their own and not in the public interest when they conclude agreements between themselves. Thus, the consequences of their agreements are not necessarily in the public interest. Competition authorities should therefore be able to scrutinise private actors' agreements even in special areas of the economy such as banking, insurance or even the social field.[35]

This work has provided many examples of private arrangements that, though presented as such, were not in the public interest. There is no reason to believe

---

[33] Ibid.

[34] *XXIIIrd Report on Competition Policy*, point 170.

[35] Cases C-115/97 to C-117/97, *Brentjens' Handelsonderneming BV v. Stichting Bedrijfspensioenfonds voor de Handel in Bouwmaterialen*, ECLI:EU:C:1999:434, para. 184.

that all private arrangements which purport to serve an environmental goal in fact do promote this goal and should be *a priori* exempt from competition scrutiny.

Similarly, state aid can also be misused. *Ferriere Nord*[36] provides an example of this. In that case, the Italian government subsidised some of the costs to upgrade a plant that produced steel mesh. This upgrade enhanced the plant's competitiveness, allowing for production in a more environmentally friendly manner.[37] However, as the Commission noted, 'simply claiming that environmental protection was the main aim of the investment is not enough to dispel the Commission's doubts'.[38] The genuine motivation behind the proposed subsidy was questionable, and thus merited further investigation.[39]

These two points suggest that the proper approach to the integration of competition and other Treaty goals is for competition enforcers to act as gatekeepers. That is, the competition regime should serve to vet proposed private measures and public subsidies for not just consistency with the purported environmental goal, but also with the competition (or state aid regime) as a whole. However, it is in this role that competition authorities deploying these economic principles are alleged to thwart environmental and other social goals, thereby creating a so-called sustainability gap. It is thus appropriate to examine these two regimes to determine the extent to which this is a fair criticism; and, if necessary, how to bridge this gap. This is the purpose of the remainder of this chapter.

7.3.2 *Undertaking as a Preliminary Threshold*

EU competition law applies to undertakings, which is a concept that 'encompasses every entity engaged in an economic activity, regardless of the legal status of the entity and the way in which it is financed'.[40] While some activities may be those that involve the production and administration of public goods, or require the coercive (sometimes police) power of the state, and are thus outside of market means of organisation. As such, entities engaged in these sorts of activities will not be considered 'undertakings', as we saw in Section 1.3.1.[41] There is case law which suggests that some environmental and conservation activities are provided for a social, hence non-economic benefit.[42] When an entity is engaged in these activities,

---

[36] Case C-49/05 P, *Ferriere Nord SpA v. Commission*, ECLI:EU:C:2008:259; T-176/01, Ferriere Nord v. Commission, ECLI:EU:T:2004:336; Commission Decision of 28 March 2001 on the state aid that Italy is planning to grant to *Ferriere Nord SpA* [2001] OJ L-310/22. On this case see Quigley, 'Review of Judgment in Case T-176/01'.

[37] Decision, ibid. Recitals 7–10 and 13–14.

[38] Ibid. Recitals 28–29.

[39] Commission, *XXIXth Report on Competition Policy*, point 254.

[40] Case C-41/90, *Klaus Höfner and Fritz Elser v. Macrotron*, ECLI:EU:C:1991:161, para. 21.

[41] See e.g. Case T-347/09, *Germany v. Commission* ECLI:EU:T:2013:418.

[42] Ibid. paras. 31–33.

it is not acting as an undertaking.[43] The case law, however, provides no guidance to assist in identifying what these non-economic activities are, and how they can be pursued by 'non-undertakings'.[44]

Nevertheless, most activities promoted in the name of sustainability are market-based, and therefore fall within the ambit of the competition rules' understanding of undertaking. This is particularly the case when private entities (which already have a market presence) enter into voluntary sustainability agreements or provide services that advance these goals. Characterising an organisation that promotes an environmental goal as something other than an undertaking removes that organisation from the scope of the competition provisions. But it is unlikely that many organisations can legitimately be so characterised. That an organisation has an 'environmental' or 'sustainability-focused' purpose will not, in itself, immunise that organisation from the competition regime. Similarly, it is also irrelevant if the state itself is conducting the activity, as when so engaged, the state acts as an undertaking.[45]

7.3.3 Article 101(1)

This provision deems agreements that have as their object or effect the restriction or distortion of competition in the internal market to be incompatible with the internal market. Unless Article 101(3) saves the agreement, it is void; and those entering into such arrangements are subject to sanction.

7.3.3.1 Ancillary Restrictions

However, it has been long known by competition authorities that any agreement between two or more parties, whether or not they are competitors, can restrict competition. Further, other agreements may have as their primary purpose a goal that is not restrictive of competition but may require some restrictions on competition to ensure that the agreement's primary activity is achieved.[46] A non-compete clause in a sale of a business is a common example.[47] Other examples can be found in franchising agreements,[48] social policy matters (pensions),[49] self-regulation[50] and

---

[43] Ibid.
[44] For this and other reasons, Nowag calls this case 'problematic', n. 32 at 64.
[45] See ibid. paras. 29–30, 48; Case 118/85, *Commission v. Italy*, ECLI:EU:C:1987:283.
[46] Case C-382/12P, *MasterCard v. Commission*, ECLI:EU:C:2014:2201, para. 89.
[47] Case 42/84 *Remia BV and Others v. Commission*, ECLI:EU:C:1985:327, paras. 19–20.
[48] Case C-161/84, *Pronuptia de Paris GmbH v. Pronuptia de Paris Irmgard Schillgallis*, ECLI:EU: C:1986:41, para. 27.
[49] Case C-67/96, *Albany International BV v. Stichting Bedrijfspensioenfonds Textielindustrie*, ECLI:EU:C:1999:430.
[50] Case C-309/99, *Wouters and Others v. Algemene Raad van de Nederlandse Orde van Advocaten*, ECLI:EU:C:2002:98.

sports regulation.[51] In the analysis of whether the secondary, competition-restricting element of the agreement is ancillary or not proceeds by counterfactual analysis: what would the state of competition be if the restrictive clause(s) did not exist?

This approach to the evaluation of environmental agreements may go some of the way to alleviating concerns of the incompatibility of competition and environmental goals. Subject to analysis of the proportionality of any restrictions they contain, environmental agreements may fall outside of Article 101's scope. As Kingston notes:

> [W]here a competitive restriction is objectively necessary to the achievement of an agreement's environmental objectives such that the agreement would not otherwise have been entered into (*Albany*), or is necessary to carry out an environmental regulatory task (*Wouters*), it is possible to interpret Article 101(1) TFEU in a way that favours environmental protection, and there is a potential conflict with the goals of competition policy, such that the proportionality principle applies to resolve this conflict.[52]

While this may be a means forward, at present it is rather unsatisfactory. Not only is there is no law, or even guidance, on environmental concerns as ancillary to other agreements, Regulation 1/2003's self-assessment regime places the onus on undertakings involved to evaluate their activities prior to their implementation. The threat of significant fines if the self-assessment is later proven to be incorrect (or at least the costs of a legal battle to justify the self-assessment) will act as a deterrent.

Nevertheless, Holmes remarks:

> [T]here is no reason why this approach should not be taken in the case of sustainability agreements such that proportionate restrictions inherent in a sustainability agreement, without which the Agreement would not have been concluded (cf *Albany*), and restrictions necessary to carry out an environmental regulatory task (cf *Wouters*) would fall outside Article 101(1) entirely.[53]

Rather than seeing the absence of existing law as a problem, Holmes more optimistically notes that this is an opportunity. Holmes further suggests that the ancillary restraint case law on non-environmental matters also reflects a policy choice made by the Court that was driven by its sympathies to the goal pursued by the agreement as a whole (e.g. collective bargaining and pensions in *Albany*, sports doping in *Mecca-Medina*). Environmental and sustainability considerations are likely to be treated sympathetically.[54] Arguably, the ancillary restrictions doctrine would open the door for arrangements that promote an environmental objective.

---

[51] Case C-519/04 P, *David Meca-Medina and Igor Majcen v. Commission*, ECLI:EU:C:2006:492.
[52] Kingston, *Greening* at 240.
[53] Holmes, 'Climate Change, Sustainability, and Competition Law' at 371.
[54] Ibid.

7.3.3.2 Restriction by Object or Effect

The vast majority of agreements which address environmental or sustainability concerns will fall within the ambit of Article 101. As a result of how EU competition law has evolved, there are three issues that parties to such agreements face. These concern, first, the assessment of such agreements. The post-Regulation 1/2003 regime places this burden on parties to agreements. The Commission has helped this process by promulgating some Regulations and Guidelines. However, Guidelines and Notices, as helpful as they may be in determining the Commission's viewpoint, are not binding on the Courts or the NCAs.

The second point relates to Article 101's focus on restrictions of competition by 'object or effect'. This distinction is of significance. The EU's case law is such that 'by object' restrictions will be inevitably be prohibited, unless they can be saved by the provisions of Article 101(3). In the post-MEA era there are no EU cases in which an agreement that contained a 'by object' restriction was saved by 101(3).[55] This is of course not to say that there were other agreements that the parties self-assessed as such, and the authorities implicitly agreed with this assessment by neither investigating nor sanctioning the arrangement.

The third point follows from this: the use of Article 101(3) to justify such agreements. The difficulty with 101(3), at least in the post-MEA era, is not what it in fact says, but rather with how the MEA approach may have forced a particular antitrust goal into this provision. As Holmes notes, 'much of the difficulty arises from an unnecessary focus on a (narrowly conceived) "consumer welfare" test which leads many writers to ask (with the best of intentions) unnecessary questions such as can "non-economic", "public interest", or "non-competition" issues be taken into account?'[56] Further, even to the extent that consumer welfare considerations may be rightly reflected in 101(3)'s test of compatibility, the current MEA approach to assessment may require some reinterpretation. This reinterpretation is necessary in order both to make 101(3)'s provisions more workable but also to bring its approach into better alignment with the Treaties' goals themselves.

7.3.3.3 Environmental Agreements and Guidance

Clarity of legal measures and certainty in their application are two hallmarks of a legal regime marked by the rule of law.[57] This is related to an understanding of a legal system as a guide for rational persons.[58] In addition to being a normative goal

---

[55] See the Luxembourgish Decision: 2018-FO-01 – *Webtaxi*, Decision of 7 June 2018.
[56] Holmes, n. 53 at 371.
[57] See e.g. Wardhaugh, *Competition, Effects and Predictability* at 16–40 and the works cited therein.
[58] See e.g. Rawls, *Theory of Justice* at 207.

for the EU's legal system,[59] rule of law considerations are manifested in legislative requirements, particularly those that affect a citizen's rights or obligations. The ECJ has been very clear about this. It has noted that '[t]he principle of legal certainty requires that rules imposing charges on the taxpayer must be clear and precise so that he may know without ambiguity what are his rights and obligations and may take steps accordingly'.[60] Although this was a tax matter, there is no reason to treat taxation legislation as a special case, or as irrelevant to completion concerns. The consequences of an administrative penalty under Regulation 1/2003 can be as dire as a tax fine.

In attempting to add clarity to the self-assessment process, and thereby collaterally fulfilling its rule of law obligations, the Commission has promulgated guidance that is of assistance in the evaluation of environmental agreements. The three key pieces of guidance are the 2001 Commission Guidance on Horizontal Cooperation Agreements,[61] the 2011 Guidance on Horizontal Cooperation Agreements[62] and the Guidelines on the Application of Article 101(3).[63] The last of these is covered in our discussion of Article 101(3) in Section 7.3.4.

In 2011, the Commission published a new set of Horizontal Cooperation Guidelines, and these Guidelines replace the earlier set[64] and subsuming environmental considerations within their relevant sections. The Commission footnotes:

> These guidelines do not contain a separate chapter on 'environmental agreements' as was the case in the previous guidelines. Standard-setting in the environment sector, which was the main focus of the former chapter on environmental agreements, is more appropriately dealt with in the standardisation chapter of these guidelines. In general, depending on the competition issues 'environmental agreements' give rise to, they are to be assessed under the relevant chapter of these guidelines.[65]

Nevertheless, the 2001 Guidelines still remain useful, as illustrative of Commission thinking.[66]

---

[59] See e.g. Case 294/83, '*Les Verts*', para. 23.

[60] Case 169/80, *Administration des Douanes v. Gondrand Freres*, ECLI:EU:C:1981:171, para. 17; Case C-143/93, *Gebroeders van Es Douane Agenten BV v. Inspecteur der Invoerrechten en Accijnzen*, ECLI:EU:C:1996:45, para. 27, and Case T-198/03, *Bank Austria Creditanstalt v. European Commission*, ECLI:EU:T:2006:136, paras. 57, 68–69 and 78.

[61] Commission Notice Guidelines on the Applicability of Article 81 of the EC Treaty to Horizontal Cooperation Agreements [2001] OJ C-3/2 (The 2001 Guidelines).

[62] Commission, Guidelines on the Applicability of Article 101 of the Treaty on the Functioning of the European Union to Horizontal Co-Operation Agreements [2011] C-11/1 (The 2011 Horizontal Guidelines).

[63] Commission, Guidelines on the Application of Article 81(3) of the Treaty [2004] OJ C-101/97.

[64] The 2011 Horizontal Guidelines, n. 62 point 18.

[65] Ibid.

[66] See Kingston, n. 52 at 243; Nowag n. 32 at 73–74.

In the 2001 Guidelines, after defining environmental agreements,[67] the Commission draws a threefold distinction among agreements: (1) those which are unlikely to come with in Article 101's scope; (2) those that may come within Article 101's scope; and (3) those that almost always come within Article 101's scope. The former class consists of loose arrangements that express voluntary commitments (analysis of these focuses on the parties' discretion), agreements which set out environmental performance that do not affect the range of products available on a given market (and do not involve the elimination of products from a market) and agreements that create new markets. The last of these is subject to the proviso that the parties cannot provide these goods/services individually (so genuine cooperation is needed) and that there are no competitors to the parties.[68]

The final class consists of disguised cartels, in the Commission's terms. Such agreements:

> [S]erve as a tool to engage in a disguised cartel, i.e. otherwise prohibited price fixing, output limitation or market allocation, or if the cooperation is used as a means amongst other parts of a broader restrictive agreement which aims at excluding actual or potential competitors.[69]

In more recent parlance, the final class consists of agreements which contains restrictions by object and are likely greenwashed to disguise this. These are required to be justified under 101(3). Both the *BIDS* and Dutch Chicken cases can be viewed as analogues to such environmental cases, insofar as the parties to both agreements entered into output restrictions. As the above also showed, neither case passed muster under 101(3).

The middle set – those which may come within the scope of 101(1) – are described by the Commission as those which restrict the parties' commercial behaviour or the commercial opportunities of others.[70] The Commission's examples of such agreements include those phasing out production of certain goods,[71] allocation of (pollution) quotas and appointment of an exclusive provider for environmental (e.g. collection and recycling) services.[72] These, for the most part, appear to imperfectly map on to restrictions of competition 'by effect'.

The 2001 Guidelines suggest the starting point for analysis is with the parties' market position – i.e. their share and the concentration of the relevant market as measured by HHI. They state that where market shares are low, 'a restrictive effect of the cooperation is unlikely and no further analysis normally is required'.[73] This is

---

[67] The 2001 Guidelines, n. 61 point 179.
[68] Ibid. points 184–187.
[69] Ibid. point 188.
[70] See The 2001 Guidelines, n. 61 point 189.
[71] Here the Commission may be implicitly referring to its Decision in *CECED*: Point 198 of the Guidelines is also an implicit reference.
[72] The 2001 Guidelines, n. 61 point 190–191.
[73] Ibid. point 28.

apparently inconsistent with subsequent developments in the case law,[74] While 'by object' restrictions of competition require no analysis – as the only means for their validation is via 101(3) – this is not what is implied by the 2004 Guidelines.

Further, these Guidelines give some initial – but somewhat superseded – thoughts about how 101(3) may apply to environmental agreements. Although the Commission notes its 'positive stance' towards such agreements to pursue the environmental goals in the Treaty, these agreements must be consistent with the competition rules.[75] Article 101(3)'s conditions are briefly discussed, noting that the key tests to consistency are benefits to consumers (either individually or in general[76]), the indispensability of the requirements and the non-elimination of competition. However, this discussion is superseded by the 2004 Guidelines on the Application of 101(3), discussed in Section 7.3.4.

The 2011 Guidelines on Horizontal Agreements supersede the 2001 Guidelines and provide no special status to or discussion of environmental agreements. These are now treated as particular instances of more general forms of commercial arrangements (e.g. research and development agreements, standardisation agreements, etc.). Standard setting will include the setting of quality marks, which can be used to address, *inter alia*, environmental and other similar concerns, thus the Commission sees this as an appropriate means to promote these goals. Indeed, the use of animal welfare standards in the Dutch supermarket industry subsequent to the Netherlands Authority for Consumers and Markets' intervention against the original CoT initiative shows the utility of such a standard-based approach.

The concern with standard setting centres on the ability of the standardisation to foreclose competition. Voluntary compliance with standards, and completion among standard-setting regimes, is seen as the appropriate way forward.[77] Further, there is a need for the standards and claims about their benefits to be scrutinised. Here standard-setting (or vetting) bodies have a role, as do consumer protection authorities.[78]

Additionally, as the Commission notes, analysis of such agreements under its (new) effects-based approach will consider the competitive effects that the standardisation regime will have on the markets concerned. Such analysis, in sustainability

---

[74] In particular, Case C-228/18, *Gazdasági Versenyhivatal v. Budapest Bank Nyrt and Others*, ECLI:EU:C:2020:265, paras. 34–36; and Case C-226/11, *Expedia Inc. v. Autorité de la concurrence and Others* ECLI:EU:C:2012:795.

[75] The 2001 Guidelines, n. 61 point 192.

[76] Ibid. point 194.

[77] The 2011 Guidelines, n. 62 point 280.

[78] In the Dutch Chicken case standards were set with the assistance of (and audited by) animal welfare bodies; the UK's CMA (in its consumer protection role) has announced a new Green Claims Code, and that it will scrutinise such claims and prosecute those who violate consumer law by making misleading claims. See CMA, 'Greenwashing'.

cases, would consider matters such as the possibility of alternative (competing) standards, access to the standard (ensuring openness and preventing discriminatory access) and market shares of participating entities.[79]

The 2011 Guidelines also considers how 101(3) can be applied in the analysis of standardisation agreements which infringe 101(1). The Commission pays lip service to environmental concerns by noting that '[s]tandards on, for instance, quality, safety and environmental aspects of a product may also facilitate consumer choice and can lead to increased product quality'.[80] Yet the remainder of the discussion is quite unsatisfactory from an environmental perspective, as its bulk considers the benefits to consumers of interoperability among technical platforms.

This Guidance applies to horizontal agreements. To the extent that a vertical relationship is in play, these fall within the jurisdiction of the relevant EU secondary legislation governing vertical relationships.[81] Economic reasoning suggests that vertical restraints are less of a threat to consumer welfare than horizontals. As a result, Regulation 330/2010 exempts such restraints from the scope of Article 101(1) TFEU, provided that the parties involved have small market shares and low turn-overs and that the agreements do not contain 'hardcore' restraints, i.e. by object restrictions.[82] While the Regulation will not exempt hardcore restrictions, these can theoretically fulfil the criteria of 101(3).[83]

The difficulty with the Regulation is the need for parties to such agreements to possess a low market share. It is unlikely that any non-trivial sustainability arrangement will fit within these market share requirements. Thus, such an agreement will require self-assessment under Article 101(1).

While some guidance is better than none, the guidance that has been provided by the Commission in this regard is thin at best. This serves to disincentivise undertakings from entering into such arrangements. The threat of large fines if the self-assessment is not accepted is a further deterrent. It is a very rational response to hold off from entering into these forms of agreements, when the rules governing them are uncertain and the consequences of an error are costly.

---

[79] Ibid. points 277–286 and 292–297.

[80] Ibid. point 308.

[81] Commission Regulation (EU) No. 330/2010 of 20 April 2010 on the Application of Article 101(3) of the Treaty on the Functioning of the European Union to Categories of Vertical Agreements and Concerted Practices [2010] OJ L-102/1 and Commission Guidelines on Vertical Restraints [2010] OJ C-130/1.

[82] Regulation No. 330/2010, ibid. Articles 3–5.

[83] Case C-209/07, *Competition Authority v. Beef Industry Development Society Ltd and Barry Brothers (Carrigmore) Meats Ltd*, ECLI:EU:C:2008:643, para. 21; Case T-17/93, *Matra Hachette SA v. Commission*, ECLI:EU:T:1994:89, para. 85; Case C-501/06 P etc., *GlaxoSmithKline Services Unlimited v. Commission*, ECLI:EU:C:2009:610, paras. 89–96 (affirming Case T-168/01, *GlaxoSmithKline Services Unlimited v. Commission*, ECLI:EU: T:2006:265, para. 233) and Guidelines, ibid. point 60.

7.3.3.4 Article 101(1)'s Object/Effect Distinction and Guidance

Restriction of competition by object or effect is a necessary condition for an agreement to be brought within Article 101's scope. Given that the Court of Justice has been interpreting this Article (and its identically worded predecessors) for nearly sixty years, one would expect that the distinction is not only clear, but also that the case law would have elaborated precise criteria for determining prohibited restrictions. This expectation has only been partially realised.

We have a relatively clear understanding of what a restriction by object consists of, which in turn allows us to demarcate the object/effect distinction. But the Court has yet to provide us with a clear account of the nature of prohibited restrictions by effect. Ibáñez Colomo rightly suggests that there are institutional reasons for this.[84] Competition enforcers will pursue the most obvious or harmful cases, which in turn will be litigated.[85] So-called 'by object' restrictions are these obvious and/or harmful cases. Witt confirms this, noting that between January 2005 and June 2017, 'around 88 percent of all prohibition decisions . . . have concerned hard-core cartels, which, as a matter of course, are not assessed as to their actual or likely effects'.[86] She continues, '[t]he 10 non-cartel cases prohibited since January 2005 also predominantly concerned object restrictions'.[87]

'By object' restrictions are those that have been shown by experience (which presumably includes experience gleaned from economic analysis,[88] perhaps supplementing, the casual empiricism of one's experiences in the marketplace) to be sufficiently likely to cause detrimental effects that further analysis is not needed. These are typically forms of horizontal collusion that lead to reductions of output, increases in prices and thus harm to consumer welfare.[89]

The Court's guidance regarding by effect restrictions is less clear. Ibáñez Colomo remarks that 'the aspects of the case law that shed light on the notion of anticompetitive effects tend to be available in a fragmentary (and sometimes embryonic) manner – and this, from a variety of disparate sources'.[90] In this regard, determining what restrictions by effects are, and the circumstances when these are prohibited, is a bit like divining the tenets of a Presocratic philosopher through an analysis of extant fragments. Fortunately, the state of the case law means we are looking more at a Heraclitus than a Thales or Anaximander.

---

[84] Ibáñez Colomo, 'Anticompetitive Effects in EU Competition Law'.

[85] Ibid. at 310–311.

[86] Witt, 'The Enforcement of Article 101 TFEU' at 427.

[87] Ibid.

[88] See Opinion of Advocate General Bobek in Case C-228/18, *Gazdasági Versenyhivatal v. Budapest Bank Nyrt.*, ECLI:EU:C:2019:678, point 42 citing Opinion of Advocate General Wahl in Case C-67/13P, *CB v. Commission*, ECLI:EU:C:2014:1958, point 79.

[89] *Budapest Bank*, ibid. paras. 35–36.

[90] Ibáñez Colomo, n. 84 at 311.

When an authority or court is required to analyse a 'by effects' restriction, this analysis is to take place in the light of the commercial context of the agreement, and evaluated against the counterfactual of what the state of competition would be in the absence of the agreement in question.[91] This applies to both inter- and intra-brand competition.[92] If the agreement is viewed as anticompetitive (or 'restrictive of competition'[93]) with a 'reasonable degree of probability'[94] after this evaluation, it would be considered as prohibited subject to justification under 101(3).

However, as stated earlier, the test is circular. There is a need to determine what is precisely meant by 'anticompetitive' or 'restrictive of competition'. Ibáñez Colomo identifies this criterion as follows:

> [I]t has long been clear that anticompetitive effects amount to more than a mere competitive disadvantage and/or a limitation of a firm's freedom of action. Something more, namely a reduction of competitive pressure resulting from a negative impact on equally efficient firms' ability and/or incentive to compete, is required.[95]

This test is consistent with the approaches taken by the Commission in Article 102 and merger cases.

This test is a substantively more difficult and resource-intensive test than that deployed in the case of by object restrictions. Competition authorities have limited resources and will seek to use them as efficiently as possible. The burden of proving an infringement of 101 rests on the competition authority (or other party challenging the legality of the agreement). The confluence of these factors has led to under-enforcement of the prohibition against restrictions of competition by effect.[96] A result of this (at best) underenforcement of this provision is that the Commission has provided no guidance as to how to appropriately evaluate the effects of agreements to assist undertakings in their self-assessment. The lack of guidance and the fragmentary nature of the discussions in the case law make *ex ante* planning difficult. Following the Presocratic metaphor – not only do we have to determine the philosopher's doctrines from the extant fragments, but we also have to live our lives by this posited doctrine. The former may be difficult, but the latter is even more so.

It would be irresponsible to suggest that this underenforcement entails that those contemplating developing private sustainability arrangements should structure them so that they contain no 'by object' restrictions and be indifferent of any other

---

[91] See Case 56–65, *Société Technique Minière v. Maschinenbau Ulm GmbH* ('STM'), ECLI:EU: C:1966:38 at 249–250 and *Budapest Bank*, n. 74 para. 55, citing Case C-382/12P, *MasterCard and Others v. Commission*, ECLI:EU:C:2014:2201, paras. 161 and 164.

[92] Jones, Sufrin and Dunne, *Jones and Sufrin's EU Competition Law* at 240.

[93] Ibid.

[94] Ibid. citing Article 101(3) Guidelines, n. 63 para. 24.

[95] Ibáñez Colomo, n. 84 at 361.

[96] See Witt, n. 86 at 435.

competitive effects. Rather, this underenforcement and lack of guidance for assessing proposed measures suggest that parties and competition authorities also consider the provisions of Article 101(3) to justify sustainability agreements which have a restrictive effect on competition.

7.3.4 *Justification under Article 101(3)*

There are reasons why the Commission adopted consumer surplus as its sole goal. A single goal prevents the need to balance or compare outcomes of multiple, and possibly incommensurable, standards.[97] Second, a single goal facilitates self-assessment. Previously, the Commission may have had sufficient 'institutional memory' to apply multiple objectives or goals in a consistent manner, but one cannot expect self-interested undertakings to do so. If anything, it would be appropriate to assume that these undertakings will overemphasise any non-economically verifiable benefits of a proposed arrangement (while discounting cost to consumers) in their effort to extract consumer surplus. Third, the use of the consumer welfare standard also allows for greater consistency with the antitrust law and policy of other jurisdictions. This not only facilitates transnational merger control but also permits international consistency in the evaluation of practices which may have global reach.

While this may serve as reasons why the Commission may desire to use a consumer welfare test, these reasons are valid only if promoting this goal is both consistent with the Treaties *and* if other understandings of competition policy's goals have not been ruled out (either by the wording of the Treaties or by their judicial interpretation). This latter point appears not to have been realised in other discussions.

The use of a single goal is apparently inconsistent with Treaty architecture and contents, particularly their linking clauses. Further, adopting consumer welfare appears inconsistent with the wording of Article 101 TFEU, and particularly the provisions of its third paragraph. Finally, while international consistency is a noble end, its pursuit is only legitimate to the extent that it is authorised by the legal regime.

A plain language approach to examining the Treaties' provisions is an appropriate means to consider how sustainability agreements can fit within 101(3)'s boundaries. Holmes takes this approach,[98] and I have made similar suggestions in earlier work.[99] When read in this light, the reader will note that there is no reference to consumer welfare in Article 101(3).

---

[97] Outcomes can only be 'balanced' or 'measured' against each other if a common metric is used. Hence, forcing the use of a consumer welfare metric to measure some goals may assist (albeit imperfectly) such comparison.

[98] See n. 53.

[99] See Wardhaugh, 'Crisis Cartels' at 327–336; and Wardhaugh, n. 57 passim.

The four conditions of 101(3) are cumulative. It is appropriate to analyse and evaluate each condition separately, in order to determine the Treaty's wording, how the provision is presently understood and the extent to which the provision can be rightly said to hinder the attainment of sustainability objectives.

7.3.4.1 Condition One: Technical or Economic Progress or Efficiencies

The wording of Article 101(3) requires that the arrangement in question 'contributes to improving the production or distribution of goods or to promoting technical or economic progress'. The Commission currently interprets this condition as defining (or, in fact, limiting) the sorts of efficiency gains that can be put forth to exempt the agreement under 101(3). If the gains fall within the set of permitted efficiencies, they are next tested by the second and third conditions of the paragraph.[100] Further, the Commission requires that these efficiencies be objectively justified, with paragraph 51 of the Guidelines providing a list of what needs to be established in any such justification. These requirements imply that these claims be broken down and presented using a common metric – a financial cost–benefit analysis.

This post-MEA attitude is a fundamental shift in the Commission's practice and is apparently inconsistent with the Article's wording. First, as has been noticed, the new interpretation is over-reliant on the need for – and thus proof of – particular sorts of efficiencies. Holmes, for instance, notes:

> 'Economic' progress is only one of four separate ways in which an agreement may meet the criteria of this condition (note the disjunctive 'or'). There is therefore no need to translate all improvements and progress into 'economic' terms – and still less reason to reduce them to narrow financial considerations.[101]

And the new requirement is also inconsistent with the Commission's, and other NCAs', previous practice.[102] In *CECED*, for instance, although the parties appear to have presented some 'economic' data to the Commission, from reading the Decision, it appears that by the standard now demanded by paragraph 51, either the data presented were thin or were not extensively used by the Commission to reach its conclusion.[103]

The Commission views efficiencies to be of two sorts: costs and qualitative efficiencies.[104] Cost efficiencies are self-explanatory. Qualitative efficiencies are those which relate to 'better' products or service in the consumer's eye. These efficiencies can extend not just to the product itself, but also the processes and

---

[100] Guidelines on the application of Article 81(3) of the Treaty, n. 63 para. 50.
[101] Homes, n. 53 at 372.
[102] See e.g. Kingston, n. 52 at 271.
[103] Commission Decision of 24 January 1999 (Case IV.F.1/36.718) (*CECED*) [2000] OJ L-187/47, paras. 47–51.
[104] Guidelines on the Application of Article 81(3) of the Treaty, n. 63, paras. 64–72.

production methods used in the product's manufacture. Hence, independent of the cost of an engine, one that produces less carbon emissions may be considered qualitatively better than a more polluting engine. Similarly, a chocolate bar made from Fair Trade cacao (where the farmers and labourers receive an appropriate, 'living wage') may also be viewed as 'better' in this sense.

These efficiencies are notoriously difficult to 'price'. We address this in Section 7.3.4.2, when we consider the distributive consequences of efficiencies – or how the benefits flow across markets. Suffice to say, some form of 'willingness to pay' measurement is used to assess this – as in the Dutch CoT initiative. However, there is no simple solution to the measurement of 'willingness to pay', particularly as different phrasings of the relevant question may yield differing responses.[105]

We make three final observations about this view of the first condition. The wording of the Treaty implies that progress and improvement, of the sort contemplated by this condition, can (pace the Commission's recent position) can be made without necessarily imputing a precise economic benefit to it. Second, even if some economic benefit must be shown, many 'progressive' products and process will fulfil this criterion so interpreted.[106] Finally, while a requirement to produce rigorous, objective evidence of efficiency gains may prevent parties from 'gaming' the system, by greenwashing otherwise anticompetitive agreements, this check can be and is carried out as part of the third and fourth of Article 101(3)'s conditions.

7.3.4.2 Condition Two: Consumers and Fair Share of the Benefits

The second condition requires that the agreement 'allow[s] consumers a fair share of the resulting benefit'. There are two concepts which call for clarification: the notions of 'consumers' and 'fair share'. The Commission defines 'consumers' as: all users of a product, whether as a final product or as input to another product.[107] This understanding works well regarding the types of markets with which traditional microeconomics has the greatest experience: the production of widgets for near immediate sale and consumption, with all costs of production internalised.

But where the costs, benefits and externalities of a product (or its production process) are geographically or temporally dispersed, and/or manifested in different markets, determining who the consumer is and how their shares of the benefits (and costs) can be assessed is not clear. The Commission further notes that as each and every gain is shared among consumers, a 'fair share' (discussed below) suffices.

'Consumers' is ambiguous between a narrow and wider meaning. The narrow meaning restricts that concept to those who are users, directly or indirectly, of the product in question. There is another meaning of the term, which extends to society

---

[105] See Gerbrandy, n. 11 at 541; and Holmes, n. 53 at 379 and 399.
[106] See Holmes, ibid. at 372.
[107] Guidelines on the Application of Article 81(3) of the Treaty, n. 63 para. 84.

at large.[108] The Commission's own guidance and past practice seems to give little concern to the difference between the two interpretations. But the difference has significance for meaningful assessment of agreements.

In *CECED*, the Commission recognised this difference, and noted that the agreement to phase out inefficient washing machines benefited consumers, interpreted both individually and collectively. Individual consumers, though they would pay more for the machine, would recoup this over time with the efficiency savings.[109] Similarly, more efficient machines reduce environmental damage (in the form of carbon emissions), providing a social benefit:

> [T]he benefits to society brought about by the CECED agreement appear to be more than seven times greater than the increased purchase costs of more energy-efficient washing machines. Such environmental results for society would adequately allow consumers a fair share of the benefits even if no benefits accrued to individual purchasers of machines.[110]

However, it is not certain whether this broader understanding of 'consumer' fully survived the switch to the MEA.

Paragraph 86 of the Guidelines reads:

> It is not required that consumers receive a share of each and every efficiency gain identified under the first condition. It suffices that sufficient benefits are passed on to compensate for the negative effects of the restrictive agreement. In that case consumers obtain a fair share of the overall benefits. If a restrictive agreement is likely to lead to higher prices, consumers must be fully compensated through increased quality or other benefits. If not, the second condition of Article 81(3) is not fulfilled.

The second sentence of this quote footnotes *Metro I*.[111] That case concerned an agreement which, *inter alia*, was directed to providing better service to customers via a selective distribution system. The qualitative improvement in *Metro* consisted in a wider range of products and a guarantee of continued supplies.[112]

It would appear that paragraph 86 suggests that qualitative gains need not be entirely passed on, presumably due to difficulty in their quantification. Yet if the agreement causes a price increase, those affected customers must be 'fully compensated'. The inclusion of the adverb 'fully' suggests that compensation must occur at the individual level.

This has implications for the understanding of the scope of 'consumer' and how 'fair share' is understood. But more significantly, paragraph 86 appears internally

---

[108] Kingston, n. 52 at 277.
[109] *CECED*, n. 103 at para. 52.
[110] Ibid. para. 56.
[111] Case 26–76, *Metro SB-Großmärkte GmbH & Co. KG v. Commission* ('Metro I'), ECLI:EU: C:1977:167.
[112] Ibid. para. 48.

inconsistent. This is particularly so in environmental and sustainability matters, where such improvements are correctly regarded as qualitative gains. As Kingston notes:

> A broader concept of consumer should be preferred when assessing environmental benefits, going beyond immediate users of the products and services in question. It is axiomatic that it would make no sense to include environmental benefits, which accrue to society at large, within the scope of the first condition only to read consumers in a narrow sense in this second condition.[113]

Kingston is certainly correct on this point. Until all externalities arising from the production of all goods can be fully internalised, the broader category of consumers will be affected by the environmental consequences of such production. In addition, sustainability concerns extend beyond the internalisation of negative externalities, but also incorporate issues of diminishing resources, and the obligations to conserve these resources for the future. The narrow focus on the immediate users of particular goods fails to grasp this fundamental point.

Further, cross-market comparisons are not unknown. *Star Alliance*[114] (the subject matter of which concerned the coordination of the transatlantic operations among three airlines) is an example. That proposed agreement had some positive effects for transatlantic passengers (in-market efficiencies), negative effects for premium passengers on the New York–Frankfurt route and benefits to passengers on other routes (out-of-market efficiencies).[115] The Commission was willing to accept there was 'significant commonality'[116] between the two groups (markets), and a flow of efficiencies between them existed. However, the agreement failed to generate sufficient out-of-market and in-market efficiencies to compensate the premium passengers. It is significant that the Commission relied upon the 'considerable commonality' in the two groups; hence, in their view, 'this assessment does not balance competitive harm to one customer group against benefits to another customer group'.[117]

In contrast to the Commission's reasoning, there is some CJEU case law which appears to take a broader conception of 'consumer'. The significance of these cases is that they arise in non-traditional markets, i.e. not the sorts of markets characterised by the mutual exchange of the microeconomics textbook. In *MasterCard*, where the competitive constraint concerned interchange fees in a two-sided market, the ECJ noted that 'under Article 81(3) EC, it is the beneficial nature of the effect on all

---

[113] Kingston, n. 52 at 277.
[114] Commission Decision of 23.5.2013 addressed to *Air Canada, United Airlines, Inc and Deutsche Lufthansa AG* relating to proceedings under Article 101 of the Treaty on the Functioning of the European Union in Case AT.39595, C(2013) 2836 final.
[115] Ibid. Recitals 70–79.
[116] Ibid. Recitals 60 and 76.
[117] Ibid. Recital 61.

consumers in the relevant markets that must be taken into consideration'.[118] Likewise (and involving a similar competitive concern), in *Cartes Bancaires* (*CB*), the ECJ notes that when coordination (i.e. the effects of the agreement) is of concern, market analysis may extend beyond a narrow conception of the relevant market.[119]

This points to the necessity of rethinking the scope of 'consumer', particularly in the contexts of environmental and sustainability arrangements. As Kingston rightly notes, a broader conception of 'consumer' is warranted in these contexts. This rethinking will necessarily be tied to distributional concerns attached to the second element of this condition: the 'fair share' that consumers are to receive. Given that consumers are to receive this benefit, any expansion of the class of who counts as a consumer has distributive implications.

There is an obvious preliminary point to any discussion of 'fair share'. That concept is not an economic concept. Although economists will talk of allocations being 'Pareto optimal' or 'Kaldor–Hicks efficient', these are merely descriptions of a distribution over a population. As such, they have no moral content, and certainly do not reference a 'fair' share. Rather, the concept of a 'fair share' is intrinsically normative, and a significant amount of material has been written about the relationship between normative conceptions of fairness and distributive justice.[120] Further, this normative work engages with questions of equity in intergenerational distribution and the obligations of the present generation to forego consumption for the benefit of future generations (a 'just savings principle').[121]

Further problems occur when gains manifest themselves over time, given the insistence that these must be discounted.[122] The methodology requires some form of monetising the benefits, and then applying an appropriate discount rate.[123] The discounting of future costs and benefits to compare the predicted outcomes of policy choices is not without precedent.[124]

Discount rates over the long term are arbitrary. By providing precision without accuracy, they give the illusion of scientific certainty. The results of any calculation in which they are used are also only as good as the calculation of the costs or benefits to which these rates are applied. Hence, any use of 'precise' discount rates is an attempt to determine an appropriate rate using present market signals.

Such precision is inappropriate in the case of environmental goods and the long-term nature of the 'market'. In his 2009 Presidential Address to the European

---

[118] Case C-382/12P, *MasterCard v. Commission*, ECLI:EU:C:2014:2201, para. 236, citing Case C-238/05, *Asnef-Equifax and Administración del Estado v. Asociación de Usuarios de Servicios Bancarios*, EU:C:2006:734, para. 70.

[119] C-67/13 P, *Groupement des cartes bancaires v. Commission* ECLI:EU:C:2014:2204, para. 78.

[120] The most significant is Rawls, n. 58, see e.g. at 11, 118–123.

[121] See ibid. at 251–267.

[122] Ibid. para. 88.

[123] Ibid.

[124] HM Treasury, *The Green Book*.

Economic Association, Nicholas Stern remarks, 'there are no markets with relevant interest rates or rates of return for collective decisions over a hundred or more years. Current markets for individuals and firms are generally for far shorter periods.'[125] Further, he notes, these numbers are everything. Stern remarks, 'we can make expected total discounted damages as small as we please by choosing sufficiently heavy pure-time discounting'. And, 'we can make (expected total discounted) damages as large as we please with a sufficiently severe set of damages'.[126]

Ultimately, this question is an ethical one; hence the Treaty is correct in using the term 'fair share' to capture this. The Treaty does not call for an 'appropriately discounted rate of return for future generations'.

One can envisage a contractarian ethical theory which holds that it is unjust for one set of individuals to gain from another set's (uncompensated sacrifices), and that, consequently, we have no obligation to sacrifice for those who will live generations from now. Most of us are unlikely to accept this view, at least in a strong version.

We have benefited from the activities and savings of previous generations, and it may not be unreasonable to expect us to make similar sacrifices for future generations. As Townley notes:

> We care about the conditions into which future generations will be born, think of the debates on nuclear power, or the preservation of wildlife ... . Through sympathy or commitment, or both, when acting as consumers, we share the spoils with future consumers, to some extent .... This seems right to me, as we, in turn, have benefited from the R&D and other efforts of past generations.[127]

An extended view of our obligations that takes into account the position of future generations in the analysis of sustainability agreements takes on additional, and explicit constitutional, significance, as the Treaties also demand a high degree of environmental protection. This is in addition to the Treaties' demands of intergenerational solidarity.[128]

The results of our discussion of the second condition of Article 101(3) show that there is a tension between how the condition is phrased and how it has been interpreted. Two points of tension have been identified: the range of people who count as 'consumers' for the purpose of the condition, and the very normative sense captured by the requirement that a 'fair share' of the benefit must be passed on. Environmental and sustainability initiatives and programmes, by nature, are long-term measures. A wide sense of 'consumers' seems to be the appropriate interpretation to catch those affected by both the benefits and burdens of the arrangements. Similarly, the normative call of 'fair share' suggests a rethinking of the distributive

---

[125] Stern, n. 7 at 276.
[126] Ibid. at 277; see also Watkiss, n. 4 at 33.
[127] Townley, 'Inter-generational Impacts in Competition Analysis' at 583.
[128] Article 3(3), second paragraph, TEU.

means of sharing benefits and burdens across generations. The use of an appropriate discounting method, while apparently useful for shorter-term time horizons, seems inapplicable in the (very) long run. At a minimum, this discussion shows the need for further thought and guidance regarding this condition and its application. To do otherwise risks the Commission's enforcement activity not fully reflecting the Treaties' words – a rule of law problem.

7.3.4.3 Condition Three: Indispensability of Restrictions

The Commission interprets this condition as requiring that both the agreement itself and the individual restrictions in the agreement are 'reasonably necessary in order to achieve the efficiencies'.[129] This serves as a check on the proposed agreement, to determine if the measures it proposes to implement can be done so in a manner that is less competitively restrictive. However, as Kingston observes, '[i]n numerous decisions to date, however, this condition has been the downfall of environmental agreements'.[130] It is of course true that this condition makes the design and implementation of sustainability agreements more difficult. However, we are of the opinion that this provides important protection against greenwashing anticompetitive agreements. The condition does not necessarily eliminate the ability of private actors to implement such arrangements; it merely requires that such implementation be done carefully, and proportionately to competition goals.

7.3.4.4 Condition Four: Non-elimination of Residual Competition

Like the third condition, this fourth condition provides an important check on greenwashing. Further, it ensures that the benefits of residual competition accrue in the markets that are affected by the agreement. Such residual competition can ensure that the 'door is not shut' on further innovation, thereby stunting new and innovative processes, which may be able to achieve the goal in a more efficient manner. The German scheme for recycling waste shows the advantages of competition. Prior to 2004, the scheme was inefficiently operated by a single undertaking, which required financial support from the state and its shareholders. The liberalisation of the waste-recycling sector admitted competition, which reduced costs, providing significant consumer welfare gains.[131] These benefits show the danger in eliminating residual competition.

This discussion of Article 101 TFEU shows that this provision does not *a priori* eliminate the possibility of private sustainability agreements. The Article will permit these, albeit under strict conditions, while some of the conditions – such as Article

---

[129] Guidelines on the Application of Article 81(3) of the Treaty, n. 63 para. 73.
[130] Kingston, n. 52 at 282, see also at 282–287.
[131] Rasek and Smuda, 'Ex-post Evaluation of Competition Law'.

101(3) conditions three and four – will ensure that such agreements do not eliminate any of the benefits of competition which might remain.

The greatest difficulty with 101 is uncertainty in it application. We know that the *Wouters* route allows for some agreements that advance a community goal, yet at the same time have a restriction on competition that is not caught by the provisions of 101(1). It would be helpful to those contemplating entering into innovative private sustainability arrangements if such guidance were provided. While the Commission is the obvious author of such a guide, it can only bind itself. The Courts are unlikely to provide this. If current practice is any indication, should such a case arise before them (which will be some years after the agreement has been implemented), the Court's reasons will be quite specifically focused on the practice in question, rather than directed towards producing a generic guide.

A similar problem can be found in the understanding of the first two conditions of Article 101(3). The Commission's Guidance on these points is simply inadequate to take into account the real operation of sustainability arrangements, given their wide effect both in present markets (e.g. beyond immediate consumers of the product) and as markets (or other social relationships) develop – intergenerational equity is a fundamental concern of many such arrangements. These are inherently normative issues, which cannot be entirely resolved through the approach of economics. This Guidance needs to be updated, if not completely rethought.

7.3.5 *Article 102*

Article 102 controls market failures that arise out of monopolistic conduct, and in particular the exploitative and exclusionary practices that monopolies (or near monopolies) find profitable to pursue. Under that Article, an 'abusive' practice committed by a dominant undertaking is prohibited.

But not all such behaviour is condemned. An undertaking involved can raise an efficiency defence or (more aptly put) propose an objective justification for their practice. Kingston has argued that '[t]here are strong theoretical arguments that, where a dominant undertaking engages in proportionate environmentally beneficial behaviour with prima facie exclusionary or exploitative effects, this behaviour should not be prohibited by Article 102 TFEU'.[132]

The argument would be analogous to Article 101's *Wouters* exclusion. Kingston is likely right on both points: there are such arguments (consistency of treatment between Articles 101 and 102 would demand this), and the argument is theoretical. Key to the success of any such argument is the proportionality of the restrictions – it is suggested that *ex post* analysis of such practices (particularly when engaged in by a dominant undertaking) can always show a less exclusionary (i.e. more proportionate) means of achieving the desired goal.

---

[132] Kingston, n. 52 at 307.

Although there have been Article 102 cases in the past that have involved environmental matters,[133] the environmental concern was not significant to the resolution of the matter, insofar as this feature did not enter into the Commission or Courts' reasoning. Typically, these cases concern access to a particular good or infrastructure network (in the cases of *Spa Monopole/GDB*, standardised recyclable bottles; and *DSD*, usage of and payment for recycling infrastructure[134]). It is submitted that these would have been identically resolved even if environmental issued played no role in the facts.

It would appear that Article 102 TFEU is also not in itself a barrier to the effective implementation of sustainability or environmentally friendly schemes. Nor, for that matter, does this Article require radical reinterpretation to address any lacunae or ambiguities in its content, which arise out of environmental or sustainability concerns.

7.3.6 Merger Control

The EU's merger control regime acts to prevent concentrations that have a European dimension and have a significant impact on effective competition.[135] There is no special place for environmental considerations. Although the environmental effects of a proposed concentration may be (imperfectly) measured and quantified, these impacts will be treated in the competitive assessment of the merger in the same manner that any other resulting (in)efficiency is treated. Any other interpretation would be contrary to the wording of the Merger Regulation.

If the merger significantly impacts effective competition, environmental considerations are irrelevant. But to use environmental considerations to prohibit a competitively acceptable merger would be not only to introduce environmental considerations into the merger control regime (contrary to the wording of the relevant Regulations), but would also place environmental considerations higher in a hierarchy of EU values – contrary to the wording of the Treaties. While the Treaties recognise a multiplicity of values, the Treaties do not rank these values in a hierarchy or anoint one as *primus inter pares*.[136]

Additionally, the rule of law considerations discussed in Section 7.3.1 would suggest that this approach could reduce legal certainty[137] and may require

---

[133] See e.g. Case C-385/07 P, *Der Grüne Punkt – Duales System Deutschland GmbH v. Commission*, ECLI:EU:C:2009:456 and *Spa Monopole/GDB* in Commission, XXIIIrd *Report on Competition Policy*, point 240; Kingston, ibid. at 307–326; and Nowag, n. 32 at 82–87 and 239–242 who cite others.

[134] See n. 133 supra.

[135] Council Regulation (EC) No. 139/2004 of 20 January 2004 on the Control of Concentrations between Undertakings (the EU Merger Regulation) [2004] L-24/1.

[136] This also applies to competition as an EU value or Treaty goal, see Wardhaugh, n. 99 at 327–331; see also Nowag, n. 32 at 262.

[137] See e.g. text accompanying n. 32.

specialised competition bodies to act outside their area of expertise. It is sufficient for the authorities to take regard of environmental considerations though their (admittedly imperfect) quantification and incorporate them into the assessments of the efficiencies which are generated (or thwarted) by the proposed merger. This is an acceptable means of integrating environmental concerns in the competition context.

The UK's introduction of the public interest test of 'financial stability' to its merger control regime provides a salutary lesson. Rather than addressing the problem for what it was – the undercapitalisation of a financial institution – the UK government attempted to solve the problem by weakening the merger control regime and added an additional element of market failure into the mix. The result was predictable – it did not help consumers and may have only briefly stabilised the financial system. This experience may be instructive for the environmental context to show why the addition of specific environmental considerations to merger control may be unwanted.

7.3.7 State Aid

The regime established by Articles 101 and 102 TFEU and the Merger Regulation is designed to address market failures arising from the monopoly problem. While this regime effectively addresses problems of collusion, abusive monopolistic practices and the market dangers that can arise through large concentrations, this regime does not *a priori* preclude undertakings from engaging in private sustainability and environmental agreements.

The state aid regime is designed to address other sorts of market failures, such as the failure associated with the underproduction of goods (as, e.g., they are public goods or their R&D expenditures may be incompletely captured). In these (and other) events, state aid can be used as a means to rectify such market failure, provided that it is not otherwise competition distorting. The fear with state aid is that it may be overinclusive; that is to say, governments may be encouraged (or lobbied) to provide subsidies for projects that ostensibly purport to be (in our case) promoting an environmental or sustainability goal, but in fact serve other purposes.

Given the post-Maastricht wording of the European Treaties, at minimum the EU and Member States have an obligation not to hinder the pursuit of environmental goals. Indeed, they have a positive obligation to work for aiming at 'a high level of protection and improvement of the quality of the environment'.[138] State aid can be a useful means for achieving these goals. The most obvious instruments include subsidies for private actors to compensate for what would otherwise be market failure–induced underinvestment, or through the taxation of unwanted

---

[138] Article 3(3) TEU.

(e.g. negative externality–producing) activity. Yet the concern is the compatibility of these instruments with the state aid provisions of the TFEU.

In considering the application of the state aid rules,[139] the jurisdictional requirements of Article 107 must be kept in mind. In brief, we note first that the aid must be imputable to the state, come from the state or be from state resources. Second, the Article prohibits 'favouring' certain undertaking or goods. This entails granting these an advantage not available to relevantly similar undertakings or goods (or, alternatively, not being disadvantaged to the extent that other goods may be). Subsidies and taxation[140] are the most common means of conferring an advantage or disadvantage. Similarly, undertakings or goods can be 'favoured' by how they are treated in the marketplace.

Underlying any favouring test is the Market Economy Operator (MEO) principle.[141] If the undertaking in question would have been able to obtain the advantage on the market on identical terms as it did from the state, then the state conferred no advantage.[142] Operating in this way applies to both public sector and private sector enterprises. This principle has two implications for investment in green initiatives. First, it may determine the type of initiative that can receive funding without falling within the jurisdiction of Article 107; and second, the principle may limit investment time frames, to accord with a private investor's expectations.

While considerations of corporate social responsibility, including sustainability concerns, have moved up the corporate agenda in recent years,[143] this does not entail that all investments of this sort are acceptable. Corporate law regulates the purpose for which a firm's financial assets can be used, and though the range is great, it is not unlimited.

Further, the MEO principle suggests that such an operator would expect a return on investment within a reasonable time frame. While a public operator's time frame may be slightly longer than that of a private sector investor, the ECJ has stated that a

---

[139] See Notice on the Notion of State Aid as Referred to in Article 107(1) of the Treaty on the Functioning of the European Union [2016] OJ C-262/1.

[140] However, by altering demand for a particular product (or set of products) a fiscal measure can be selective, notwithstanding its environmental objective. The measure may therefore fall under Article 107 (1) TFEU, but may be saved by 107 (2) or (3): see Case T-210/02 RENV, *British Aggregates Association v. Commission*, ECLI:EU:T:2012:110, Case C-279/08, *Commission v. Netherlands* (NOx), ECLI:EU:C:2011:551, and Lo Schiavo, 'The General Court Reassesses the British Aggregates Levy'.

[141] See Notice, n. 139 paras. 73–116.

[142] See Case C-124/10P, *Commission v. EDF*, EU:C:2012:318, paras. 77–93, Case C- 305/89, *Italy v. Commission* (Alfa Romeo No. 1) ECLI:EU:C:1991:142, paras. 18–23, Jones and Sufrin, 'State Aid' Supplementary Chapter to *EU Competition Law* at 31–53; and Kreuschitz and Nehl, 'The Notion of State Aid'.

[143] See Kingston's discussion, n. 52 at 381–382.

return is necessary.[144] Ordinary investors are not motivated by charitable motives, and will require at least a medium- to long-term return. The benchmark for the latter time horizon may be the sort of return expected by a pension fund when it buys and holds assets for the long term.

7.3.7.1 Public Service Obligations

Where an undertaking is compensated for a public service obligation, this compensation can be deemed not to be state aid in some circumstances. These circumstances were set down in the *Altmark* case[145] and require the recipient provider of public services not to gain an advantage over their competitors by being placed in an advantageous competitive position.[146] In particular, the regime must satisfy four conditions:

1. The recipient must have a real, clearly defined public service obligation.
2. Compensation for the obligation must be calculated *ex ante* to avoid conferring an economic advantage that may favour the recipient undertaking.
3. The compensation may not exceed the costs of providing the service (including profit).
4. When competitive tender is not used, remuneration must be determined by using the cost-base costs of a typical, well-run undertaking, able to meet the necessary public service requirements.[147]

Environmental services can be public service obligations, and may well intertwine with the understanding of 'undertaking' discussed earlier.[148] There is a compelling argument that an organisation which provides, or facilitates the provision of, public goods may not necessarily be regarded as an undertaking for the purposes of competition law, as it may not be operating in a market context. (*Calì & Figli*[149] comes to mind.) However, to the extent (or when) that organisation 'crosses the line' and operates on the market, then its activities could be saved by the exercise of a public service obligation, assuming that the *Altmark* criteria are fulfilled. To its credit, the Commission has incorporated guidance on its understanding of these

---

[144] Case C-42/93, *Spain v. Commission*, ECLI:EU:C:1994:326, para. 14, mentioning Case C-305/89, *Italy v. Commission*, ECLI:EU:C:1991:142.

[145] Case C-280/00, *Altmark Trans GmbH und Regierungspräsidium Magdeburg v. Nahverkehrsgesellschaft Altmark GmbH*, ECLI:EU:C:2003:415.

[146] Ibid. para. 87.

[147] Ibid. paras. 89–93.

[148] See Section 1.3.1, 'Undertakings as the Subjects of EU Competition Law'.

[149] Case C-343/95, *Calì & Figli*; see our discussion ibid. Further, Article 106(2) TFEU could possibly justify such activities; see Kingston, n. 52 at 405.

criteria in its guidance on state aid,[150] and from time to time issued guidance on state aid in environmental matters.

7.3.7.2 Article 107(3) TFEU

Article 107(3) TFEU provides for some exceptions for the Treaty's otherwise general prohibition on state aid. Funding for 'important projects of common European interest' may in appropriate circumstances be an exception to this prohibition; and environmental concerns – particularly when explicitly linked to a Union pro-gramme – count as such projects. To aid in assessing whether a sustainability project fulfils the criteria for exemption, the Commission has promulgated a Block Exemption[151] and Guidelines on State Aid for Environmental Protection.[152]

7.3.7.3 Environmental Provisions in the Block Exemption

Regulation 651/2014 exempts aid for some projects that are aimed at environmental protection, defined as:

> [A]ny action designed to remedy or prevent damage to physical surroundings or natural resources by a beneficiary's own activities, to reduce risk of such damage or to lead to a more efficient use of natural resources, including energy-saving measures and the use of renewable sources of energy.[153]

Section 7 of the Regulation applies to investment aid for fourteen different types of projects, which include exceeding or early adaptation of EU environmental standards, development, aid for energy efficiency measures, the production and promotion of sustainably generated energy, energy infrastructure and waste recycling. Such aid can be granted (and exempted from the notification process that Article 108(3) TFEU would otherwise require), should the aid meet the criteria specified under the relevant Article. Among these criteria is the aid intensity of the proposed

---

[150] See, in particular, Communication from the Commission on the application of the European Union State Aid Rules to Compensation Granted for the Provision of Services of General Economic Interest [2012] OJ C-8/4.

[151] Commission Regulation No. 651/2014 of 17 June 2014 Declaring Certain Categories of Aid Compatible with the Internal Market in Application of Articles 107 and 108 of the Treaty [2014] OJ L-187/1; this was due to expire on 31 December 2020 (point 246) but was extended until December 2023 due to Covid-19.

[152] The most recent of which is Guidelines on State Aid for Environmental Protection and Energy 2014–2020 [2014] OJ C-200/1, this was also extended until December 2021. There are other Guidelines, e.g. Guidelines on Certain State Aid Measures in the Context of the Greenhouse Gas Emission Allowance Trading Scheme Post-2012 (SWD(2012) 130 final) (SWD(2012) 131 final) [2012] OJ C-158/4.

[153] Regulation 651/2014, n. 151 Article 2(101).

measure, limiting the aid to a percentage of the aid intensity[154] that acts as a ceiling for block exempted aid – though aid that exceeds the ceiling can be approved through the normal process.

This Block Exemption serves as a means by which Member States can grant proportionate aid to assist in achieving certain environmental and sustainability goals, as matters of pressing EU concern. There will inevitably be projects aimed at this goal, which due to market failure of one sort or another will require some form of aid to ensure their effective development and/or deployment. The Block Exemption does not prevent the granting of aid in these circumstances. Rather, the measures will need to be assessed using the regular notification procedure,[155] albeit with the assistance of a set of Guidelines.

7.3.7.4 The 2014–2020 Environmental Protection and Energy Guidelines

These Guidelines recognise the environmental and sustainability goals announced by the Union reflected in several initiatives,[156] and the goals of the 2012 State Aid Modernisation programme. The Guidelines are not novel in their analytic methodology, focusing on the standard concerns which flow from considering the utility of state aid as a means of correcting market failure: e.g. its appropriateness as an instrument, proportionality, market distortion and incentive effects. To this end, its discussion contains little that is new.

The Guidelines' utility consists in its analysis of specific programmes (e.g. renewable energy, carbon capture schemes, waste management, environmental taxation relief schemes) – given the importance of these sorts of programmes in addressing sustainability concerns and the market failures that may be associated with their implementation, there will be a need for them to be designed in a manner that ensures their compatibility with the Treaty's provisions. The Guidelines will aid in this. But more significantly, the promulgation (and ongoing revision) of these guidelines serves a signalling function, namely that the Commission recognises that market failure can hinder the implementation of these EU projects, which would result in a delay in the realisation of their goals. These Guidelines signal the Commission's awareness of the need to facilitate Member States' appropriate and proportionate contributions to these Union goals.

7.3.7.5 The State Aid Regime: Some Final Remarks

State aid is generally one of the most distorting economic activities, having deleterious consequence for competition within markets, and – in the case of the EU – disturbing the 'level playing field' of the internal market. Yet this general observation

---

[154] This is the amount of aid, divided by the extra costs for which the aid is to compensate, expressed as a percentage: see ibid. Article 2(26).

[155] Regulation 651/2014, n. 151 Recital 7.

[156] Guidelines on State Aid for Environmental Protection, n. 152 paras. 3–9.

does not support a universal conclusion that condemns all state aid. State aid can be used to pursue environmental objectives; subject – of course – to the standard controls, e.g. proportionality, distortion competition and incentive effects. In this regard, the Commission has developed a Block Exemption and prepared Guidance to indicate which projects may be deemed to be compatible with the Treaty, and to allow the assessment of other projects that may fall outside the Regulation. It is possible to claim that the Block Exemption Regulation does not 'go far enough', and as such precludes wider use of state aid. This argument fails, as it does not recognise the possibility of a wider exemption, even when the measures may be competitively distorting, through the 'normal' regime review, approval and monitoring regime of Article 108, as has been done effectively in the past.[157] It cannot be said that the EU's state regime is per se incompatible with environmental goals; rather, it ensures that the pursuit of these goals is done in a manner consistent with other Treaty goals.

7.4 CONCLUSION: THE COMPETITION REGIME AND THE ENVIRONMENTAL CRISIS

The EU's competition regime acts to prevent the sorts of market failures which arise from the monopoly problem, and Article 101 TFEU is designed to prohibit, *inter alia*, those sorts of collusive activities which result in a loss of consumer welfare. This is not to say that there are no other goals which underlie that Article or that the Article should not be interpreted without reference to other Treaty goals. Article 101 has other underlying considerations, which include the goal of completing the internal market. The linking clauses of the Treaties indicate the need to view the competition provisions in their relation to other European goals. Article 102 of the TFEU and the merger control regime are also designed to prevent monopolistic exploitation – the former in regard to actual exercise of (quasi-)monopolistic power, the latter to prevent the acquisition of such power. The state aid regime is directed differently: to avoid tilting a level playing field.

It would be overstating it to say that these regimes preclude the adequate development of environmental and sustainability measures. Nevertheless, it is true that, at least with the present understanding of the regime, there is some uncertainty that may prevent more extensive development of environmental and sustainability measures. In particular, we have seen that there is uncertainty surrounding the application of Article 101(3) TFEU. This uncertainty arises out of the Commission's more economic approach, and the demands that 101(3) justifications be expressed in consumer welfare terms. This is almost certainly contrary to the wording of the Treaty. As such, this is a rule of law issue. Our conclusion suggests that this approach, at minimum, be rethought, and that the Commission (and other authorities) provide more extensive Guidance (and greater use of comfort letters).

---

[157] On this point, see e.g. NOx, n. 140.

The state aid regime is consistent with the proportionate funding of environmental projects. The post-Maastricht recognition of the importance of the environment as an EU policy gives wide scope for the approval of such aid. TFEU Article 102 can be, and has been, used as a sword, in the event that a dominant undertaking exploits its position in environmental matters. Here the environmental nature of the problem is almost secondary. The merger regime is neutral, as it should be. It is designed to look at the state of competition in the market before and after the merger, and to determine if that particular concentration would significantly impede competition on the market. Environmental considerations are not directly part of the assessment. This does not preclude a Member State from independently adopting a public policy criterion requiring environmental assessment. But this may not be a solution – one can look to the consequences of the UK's ad hoc incorporation of 'financial stability' in its merger regime during the financial crisis.

The current climate crisis calls out for action, and to this end coordination among actors can aid in meeting some of the challenges. Article 101 TFEU does not prohibit coordinated efforts – it prohibits such efforts that are harmful to competition. There is room within the Article for coordinated activity that promotes this end. Standardisation is one very effective means forward.

The Dutch CoT initiative suggests the general suitability of standards as a means of achieving such goals. In addition to animal welfare labelling, as in the Dutch case, a coordinated approach could permit the development of, for instance, recyclability and carbon footprint standards. However, this requires consistency – presupposing agreement – among the metrics used in expressing these standards. There is no point in developing standards if they cannot be clearly expressed, readily understood or easily compared by consumers of the relevant products. A recent article notes:

> Marc Engel, chief supply chain officer at Unilever, says carbon labelling will help businesses prepare for an era of carbon taxes, and a world in which consumers will want to calculate their own personal environmental impact.
>
> But it will require coordination among companies. 'You need to have alignment ... on the methodology you use, otherwise it's going to be a jungle of all kinds of labels,' he says. Aude Gandon, global chief marketing officer at Nestlé, agrees, adding that the group supports 'an EU-wide harmonised approach'.[158]

Industry-wide coordination that allows for meaningful comparisons of, say, the carbon footprint of comparable goods will provide information to consumers to inform their consumption.[159]

The main barrier to such effective implementation is lack of guidance. Some guidance has been provided for elements of the state aid regime, and for

---

[158] Evans, 'Could Carbon Labelling Soon Become Routine?'
[159] See also Holmes, n. 53 at 382–383.

standardisation under Article 101,[160] the Commission and NCAs can assist further. In this regard the ACM approach is commendable.

In a 2020 submission to the OECD, the ACM notes:

> With respect to competitors starting collaborations related to sustainability initiatives, there are at least four avenues to explore by competition authorities, without the need to adapt competition laws.
>
> In the first place, to prevent a potential stalemate in sustainable initiatives, for example, because market participants refer to competition rules as a barrier to sustainable production, competition authorities could provide more clarity. ... For example, authorities can indicate what types of agreements are, in general, not anticompetitive, such as agreements that incentivize undertakings to make a positive contribution to a sustainability objective without being binding on the individual undertakings. Another category concerns covenants by which companies bind themselves and their suppliers to comply with laws abroad in areas such as labor rights or the protection of the environment, and for which the companies, for example, jointly organize oversight by an independent body. Also, agreed codes of conduct, joint trademarks or logos promoting environmentally-conscious or climate-conscious practices are, in general, not anticompetitive if the participation criteria are transparent, and access will be based on the basis of reasonable and non-discriminatory criteria.[161]

The need for guidance is important, and the more specific the guidance the better.

This view is consistent with other research on corporate attitudes towards sustainability initiatives. A recent study for Linklaters showed that '[a]n overwhelming number of businesses want to work closely with peers when pursuing sustainability goals, with nine in ten saying that collaboration is key to achieve progress on ESG [environmental, social and governance] issues'. And:

> 57% of sustainability leaders say that there are concrete examples of sustainability projects that they have not pursued because the legal risk was too high. As advisors we see examples of companies walking away from genuinely beneficial projects because of competition law risk.

They add:

> 32% want to see explicit guidance from competition authorities on what counts as lawful and unlawful cooperation. This guidance would offer much-needed reassurance on the rules of engagement for companies wanting to work together on sustainability initiatives and substantially lower the legal risk.[162]

---

[160] The 2011 Horizontal Cooperation Guidelines, n. 62 paras. 257–335.

[161] OECD 'Sustainability and Competition – Note by the Netherlands', paras. 8–9, see also para. 2.

[162] Linklaters, 'Competition Law Needs to Cooperate: Companies Want Clarity to Enable Climate Change Initiatives to Be Pursued'.

Guidance adds certainty, reducing risk and encouraging investment.

Indeed, for novel or unusual arrangements, specific guidance might be appropriate. The ACM recognises this.[163] It is unfortunate that other NCAs have yet to share this recognition. Although it is true that the post-Regulation 1/2003 regime imposes a duty on undertakings to self-assess proposed arrangements, in novel cases, such self-assessment is difficult. Given the costs of running afoul of the competition regime, the prudential risk adverse to risk neutral response would be that if there were doubt, to forego entering into such measures. This approach may therefore hinder, if not thwart, the development and implementation of measures to advance otherwise beneficial aims.

Providing guidance for novel situations or arrangements is not inconsistent with a general duty for undertakings to self-assess. The Commission recognises this and suggests that in novel or uncertain cases, undertakings approach it to seek informal guidance. This, the Commission suggests, adds certainty and promotes investment.

Although the interests of certainty would suggest more than infrequent use of guidance, the Commission's practice has not even approached that threshold. Until the 2020 Covid-19 crisis, the Commission had not provided any informal guidance. There is no point in suggesting that undertakings may be able to obtain guidance, if its availability is a chimera. Additionally, the same concerns can also be raised with the practice of NCAs, given their analogous role. Our discussion of Irish Beef suggested that the Irish Competition Authority could have acted to guide the parties towards an appropriate resolution of the problem. At minimum, this would have imposed less cost on all parties – including the NCA itself.

Here, again, the Dutch ACM's approach in the CoT matter is commended – the close work with the parties enabled a solution to the issue. While the parties' first choice of solutions proved to be anticompetitive, this did not entail that no solution could be found. Indeed, through dialogue involving multiple stakeholders, including the ACM and the government, the parties found a solution, which – it must be added – went further to achieving the stated goal, with fewer anticompetitive effects, than was the case with the parties' first choice of a collusive 'solution'.

Yet collaboration is not the only solution, as the CoT case instructs us. The use of standards to frame an issue (there, animal welfare; here, sustainability and environmental matters) can drive competition around that parameter. In the CoT case, the goal was identified, and competing standards advancing that goal were developed and consumers were offered a choice. The result was that through standardisation, and competition among products reflecting varying standards, the desired goal was achieved in a relatively rapid manner, with less detriment to consumer welfare than their collaborative alternative.

However, when one considers the climate crisis and competition policy's role in resolving it, it is important to keep in mind that this is a multifaceted problem.

---

[163] Ibid. paras. 11–13.

Competition and state aid law and policy will not resolve the problem by themselves, nor should they be expected to. It is a problem that will require the coordination of numerous national and international policy measures, as well as personal efforts to alter consumption patterns. The Commission is likely right, in its Autumn 2020 suggestions raised in the Green Deal, that an economy-wide approach is needed to address these concerns.[164] Given the economic significance of the competition regime, it is right that it does not unduly hinder these efforts; yet at the same time it will act as a useful means of oversight – to ensure the efficient implementation of these goals in a consumer-friendly manner. This may well be the two-way process envisaged by DG Comp in the post-Maastricht era.[165] But in any event, it is clear that the competition regime is neither the solution to the problem by itself, nor entirely responsible for erecting barriers to environmental progress.

---

[164] Communication from the Commission to the European Parliament, the European Council, the Council, the European Economic and Social Committee and the Committee of the Regions, the European Green Deal Brussels, 11.12.2019 COM(2019) 640 final, point 2.1.

[165] *XXIIIrd Report on Competition Policy*, n. 133 point 95.

Conclusion

This work has considered a number of economic crises, some recent, others more historical. Each of these crises imposed (or, in the case of one of them – the climate crisis – has the potential to impose) a significant economic shock. The effects of these shocks varied. In some cases – those effecting particular industries – the shock was restricted to particular regions or sectors of the economy. In other cases – the financial crisis of 2008 and the economic fallout of the Covid-19 pandemic – the shock was more widespread, having transnational consequences. The full force of the economic consequences of Brexit have yet to be felt, with delays in implementing some of the more costly elements of the agreements between the UK and EU, and many of its other economic consequences have been masked by the effect of the Covid-19 pandemic. The effects of the environmental crisis may be broader still, affecting the world's population for generations to come.

Each crisis we considered was different from the others, and although they had differing causes, a drop in demand was seen in the majority of the crises. Here there are certain symmetries in the industrial crises (e.g. *Synthetic Fibres*, the *Dutch Brick* and *Irish Beef*). The Covid-19 crisis was marked by a significant decline in demand in some sectors of the economy, and the financial crisis of 2008 was marked by a mismatch of supply and demand, in particular to and of wholesale financing. The cause of the financial crisis can likely be traced to regulatory failure; however, its solution – in part – was to provide additional supply (of funding and capital) via governmental intervention. The environmental crisis is marked by market failure. This failure is characterised by externalities and inadequate incentives for investment in the means that may abate the problem due to their nature as quasi-public goods. Brexit is a unique problem – it arose from political failure and illusory opportunities for a unique regulatory regime.

As this point, Brexit has clear economic consequences. The more apparent of these include shortages of food and trade. Any opportunity to use the so-called new freedom to develop a 'made in the UK' subsidies programme to fuel trade in a post-Brexit 'Global Britain' has been squandered. Rather, the door has been opened for politicians at all levels to make politically motivated choices to support favoured firms and industries.

One commonly proffered response to addressing these crises has been a suggestion that the competition regime hinders effective solutions to these crises, and consequently that this regime needs to be disapplied to some degree or another in order to permit effective mitigation of any shock and to allow for a rapid resolution of the underlying economic conditions that have given rise to the problem. Indeed, the UK government's post-Brexit response exemplifies this line of thinking. This work has shown that this response is at best flawed or false, and at its deeply cynical worst is nothing more than an attempt to justify obtaining a legal cartel (and thus appropriate consumer welfare) under the guise of a crisis of one form or another.

However, as we have stressed throughout, the competition regime addresses market failures posed by the monopoly problem. The clearest examples of this are when a monopoly, or a group of firms acting as a monopoly (i.e. a cartel), acts to reduce supply, share markets, fix prices or engage in other activities with similar effect. The consequences for this, to consumers, is higher prices and/or a reduction in the quality of the goods supplied. Yet, as we have seen, not all forms of cooperation among competitors have this negative consequence for consumer welfare, as not all cooperation is necessarily collusive. Indeed, just as sports leagues need to collaborate on matters such as rules and schedules to compete,[1] some collaboration among competitors may fuel more effective competition. Under some conditions the development and production of goods and services under industry standards will promote competition. Yet cooperation is no panacea. Competition with the desired quality as its parameter can be equally – or more – effective in achieving the intended goal.

A well-formulated state aid regime is also aimed at addressing certain market failures, in particular those that arise from the provision of common goods, involve the reduction of externalities and mitigate uncertainty surrounding the investment of benefits that may not be entirely privatised. This regime also performs an important redistributive (or equitable) function, allowing society to share its wealth with less well-off regions. However, as we have seen, state aid may not always be the best instrument to resolve a given problem in the market.

State aid can be distortive of competition, creating an uneven playing field, not just among Member States but also within a given Member State. State aid can be used for political objectives – R&R aid is perhaps the most 'political' of these uses. As such, unless properly controlled, this regime is open to manipulation by rent-seeking interests. Here, the EU regime, anchored by the TFEU's presupposition against (most) aid and the Commission's monitoring of proposed and granted aid, provides a

---

[1] See e.g. *National Collegiate Athletic Association v. Board of Regents of the University of Oklahoma* 468 US 85, 101 (1984) referring to Bork, *Antitrust Paradox* at 278.

somewhat effective check on such market distortions. Unfortunately, this important 'check' was deliberately removed in the UK's post-Brexit regime.

Our preceding discussion has shown two significant points. The first is that while the causes of each of these crises have been varied in their nature, there was no need for a monopoly or cartel (and hence no consequent need for the disapplication of competition law) to mitigate the crises or their shocks. But there is a second, more significant point: the use of cartel and cartel-like behaviour has tended to aggravate (or at least fail to mitigate) those conditions that gave rise to the problem.

Chapter 2 of this work began by considering the use and disapplication of competition law during before World War II. The disapplication of competition law provides a significant lesson for our study, and this lesson should shape any future response to economic crises, particularly those that occur when there is a drop in demand for goods. Recessions and the Great Depression of the 1930s are these sorts of crises, as are the industrial crises that occur when there is a drop in demand for a particular set of goods or services. The latter, of course, are of a smaller scale than the former.

Our discussion of the response to the Great Depression showed that on both sides of the Atlantic, collusive strategies of one form or another were implemented. In the UK, in an effort to alleviate the coal industry's poor economic situation, the UK government passed the Coal Mines Act of 1930, which would provide a statutory basis to cartelise that industry. There was no doubt that the coal industry was in trouble during that time.

During the late 1920s there was significant drop in demand for coal, as a result of an economy-wide decline in consumption; this was combined with the haphazard growth of smaller enterprises. There were two competing political goals behind this Act – one was to stabilise the industry (and increase the prices paid for coal and miners' wages), the other to 'rationalise' the industry. These two goals were incompatible: cartelisation would increase prices and increase wages (and to a limited extent it was successful on both regards). However, cartelisation freezes the status quo of a declining industry. Rationalisation of the industry requires moving away from this status quo.

But more significantly, the industry was cartelised, and members of the coal industry behaved as members of a cartel do: they cheated on the cartel agreement. Not only did this result in the loss of any advantages (to the industry) of the collusive arrangement, but this cheating was entirely predictable from the point of modern reasoning regarding cartel stability. The collusive strategy was poorly implemented and appeared to have few – if any – beneficial consequences for either the industry or the economy as a whole. It would take until after World War II for the industry to be rationalised. Indeed, the UK government's handling of the coal industry would be an important constituent of its industrial and labour relations policies until the mid-1990s.

As part of the New Deal, the US government implemented the NIRA in an effort to mitigate the Great Depression. This permitted the wholesale cartelisation of many industries, provided that the members of these industries could agree upon industry-wide trade practices. These practices governed investment in plants, the terms of the workweek and agreements on resale price maintenance and minimum prices. Although over 550 codes were approved in the first two years of the legislation, not all industries could agree on such codes.

The consequences of the NIRA were significant, and not what was intended. Workers in industries that were covered by codes made more than those doing comparable work in non-covered industries. Not only did this create an 'in' versus 'out' social friction, it also artificially propped up wages in covered industries (thereby preventing an employment-generating decrease in wages) and allowed for the acquisition of other rents by those involved in the industries. These neither lessened nor ended the impact of the Depression. That required the inflow of capital and a second world war. Indeed, the cartelisation policy pursued by this Act likely prolonged the consequences of the Depression.

Cartelisation did not work then. The cause of the Depression was not a form of market failure which could be redressed by the activities of monopolists. The proximate cause of the Depression was a drop in demand (of course, there were other links in that chain of causation which would explain this drop). To attempt to cure such a drop in demand through a monopoly is the wrong medicine. Simple microeconomics tells us that, if anything, the presence of monopolies in a market cause prices to rise, which will cause a further drop in demand. Cartels are the wrong medicine in these circumstances.

Our scepticism of cartels and cartel-like solutions to resolving these problems is given further support when we considered how failing industries have been treated under the EU's competition regime – both before and after the development of the MEA. We considered the restructuring of the European Synthetic Fibres, Dutch Brick and Irish Beef industries. The first two began prior to the MEA, the last with the development of that approach. Prior to the MEA, the Commission gave wide scope to private initiatives, which 'rationalised' a failing industry.

The Dutch case was the purist expression of this. There the industry was permitted to organise its own restructuring, including determining how capacity could be reduced. In non-crisis times, this would be regarded as an illegal cartel and prosecuted. In crisis times it is still a cartel yet was accepted. That cartel was accepted simply because the Commission took an imprecisely 'quantified' account of the benefits which the restructuring arrangement provided.

A similar expression can be found in *Synthetic Fibres*. This too involved industry-coordinated restructuring. However, in addition to such an agreement, the restructuring of this industry also involved the participation of Member States, through the grant of aid to mitigate the economic costs of plant closure. In addition, Commission-approved codes of practice for that industry were also developed and implemented. In assessing the benefits of the restructuring agreement, the Commission used an imprecisely quantified picture of these (indeed, the methodology here was likely influential in for *Dutch Brick*).

Further, and of significance to *Synthetic Fibres*, was the use of state aid to facilitate this reorganisation of the industry. It may be cynical to suggest that in *Synthetic Fibres* – given the costs that large undertakings had sunk into the development of plants which produced these fibres, and the local economies dependent on employment therein – Member State governments may have been amenable to lobbying efforts. Nevertheless, this use of state aid in industrial R&R gave us an opportunity to reflect on such use generally.

State aid is by its very nature distortive of competition. And of the forms which state aid can take, rescue aid is probably the most competition distorting. Rescue aid interferes with the normal process of competition, by which an inefficient firm exits the market, so that resources can be more productively deployed elsewhere. In addition to preventing this exit process from occurring, rescue aid can also contribute to moral hazard. The existence of such a lifeline may encourage risk taking at the margin. Rescue aid does not address a market failure; rather, it obstructs the proper functioning of the market.

However, granting rescue aid is often an expedient alternative to witnessing the failure of an undertaking. No politician wishes to see plant closures and consequent unemployment in their country or constituency, and will be acutely aware that if she is seen to be doing nothing, she will face the wrath of the voters at the next election.

The state aid regime permits the use of rescue aid in limited circumstances. This is almost certainly a political concession, as such grants of aid do not easily fit into any conception of smarter, better-targeted aid – as is the Commission's new strategy. But expediency does not necessarily entail appropriateness. We have seen that rather than aiding in the rescue process and keeping firms from failure, the grant of rescue aid is often incommensurate with the resulting effects. The political justification for such aid is retention of employment; however, rather than promoting this goal, this aid disproportionately supports capital, rather than employees. A smarter rescue aid regime would direct such funding towards those who may have lost employment, via schemes which promote retraining, early retirement, relocation, etc., rather than directing funds to those who justify receiving a return on their capital by (in part) the risks they took with that capital. In this regard, it may be time for a rethink of the current rescue aid regime.

Yet this argument is not to universally condemn rescue aid. Chapter 4's discussion of the financial crisis showed that it might be necessary to deploy such a support instrument in particularly severe circumstances. The financial crisis of 2008 was such a circumstance. As a result of collective realisation that the assets used for collateral in the wholesale markets for funding were less valuable than thought, not only did the wholesale market freeze up, but many financial institutions were left undercapitalised. If this undercapitalisation did not force the institution into insolvency, it would impair its ability to fulfil its function in the economy and assist in financing of other undertakings' commercial activities. This would fuel a public perception of instability and lack of confidence in the financial system. In the UK, similar (albeit not at the magnitude found in 2008) events led to a bank run in 2007.

Member states opted for two policy instruments to address this crisis: state aid and merger. The sums of money required to effectively recapitalise these institutions were significant, hence governmental resources would be the only source for rescue funds. To assist in directing this aid, the Commission not only produced a set of guidance, but was also responsive in developing a process for the expedited approval of such aid. This recapitalisation appeared to work; indeed, balanced against the dystopian counterfactual of a collapse of the financial system, it was a success. It may have been the case that in some Member States (such as the UK) the government put more 'in' in the form of aid than it later took 'out' as a result of the sale of their ownership of these institutions. However, sale at a given time may have been a political choice,[2] while at the same time, the costs to the economy of not providing this support would have been more significant.

In addition to state aid, Member States also used merger as a means of mitigating the financial crisis. Mergers have the same effect as collusive activity. In using merger as a means of crisis mitigation, governments chose to permit (or perhaps compel) the merger of a failing financial institution with institutions whose circumstances were more robust. These mergers were between an institution that would immediately exit the market and another that was stable. In those cases, the transaction entailed few, if any, anticompetitive consequences. However, we saw two mergers where this was not the case – it would be reasonable to suggest that there were others throughout the EU.

In the Dutch case involving the merger of Fortis and ABN AMRO, we saw that the consolidation of two large players led to a weakening of competition in that market. The effect of weakened competition had the greatest impact on savers, and particularly those who had fewer savings, i.e. the less well off. We also examined the UK case involving Lloyds and HBOS. This was particularly noteworthy, as upon referral to the OFT, this (proposed, as it then was) merger was viewed to be anticompetitive. Not only would it remove one of the large 'challenger' banks, it was also above the thresholds of a previous proposed merger involving Lloyds and Abby National that the Competition Commission had blocked seven years previously. To effect this merger, the government amended the statutory basis of the merger regime, by expressly adding 'the interest of maintaining the stability of the UK financial system' as grounds for merger assessment. Once the new criterion was added, the government approved the merger (in spite of its strong likelihood for an

---

[2]   Cynically, such a sale would be designed to take a loss and blame the previous government for putting the present government and taxpayers in this position.

anticompetitive outcome). The merger almost certainly had adverse effects for the banks' customers – particularly in Scotland.

Additionally, the need not to use public funds was part of the touted advantages of using merger as a rescue instrument. However, that representation proved to be incorrect, as the merged entity required some £37 billion in recapitalisation aid from the UK government within weeks of the merger. The use of merger in this case, where neither of the parties to the merger was likely to exit the market,[3] was inappropriate. The efficiencies generated by mergers of this sort are those which are consequent on consolidation – economies of scale, for instance. The inefficiencies generated by this merger included a loss of a competitive force in the market (particularly in a significant geographical market). The problem which necessitated action was undercapitalisation – which could not be solved (as later events clearly demonstrated) via consolidation, and any efficiencies gained thereby. Merger, in this case, was an inappropriate policy instrument to attempt to achieve the ostensible goal of financial stability. Direct intervention through a state aid-based recapitalisation programme would not only have been more effective, it would have also preserved a more competitive environment.

Our discussion of the economic crisis resulting from the Covid-19 pandemic established a number of significant points. First, at the initial stages of the crisis, there was the expected cry from those involved in the production of some goods for the suspension of some competition provisions to allow for collaborative supply efforts. These calls were heeded in the UK. However, the extent to which such collaboration was effective in mitigating shortages was not clear. In fact, as there is a deafening absence of shouts of 'we did it through our collective efforts', the extent to which collaboration mitigated any supply problems is far from clear.

Additionally, it is likely that any benefit (assuming there was some) from the collaborative process may be outweighed by a collusive culture which persists after the bulk of the pandemic's consequences have subsided. The most noticeable change in the competition regime due to the pandemic was that the Commission issued its first 'comfort letter'. It is to be hoped that the Commission will continue this manner of providing guidance in the future.

The bulk of governmental support during the Covid-19 pandemic came through state aid and/or direct support to individuals. Although state aid to business, particularly in downturns, is distortive of the market, in a downturn such as that caused by Covid-19, in effect governments had little choice. The real problem in the design of support programmes rested in the ability to determine *ex ante* which businesses (or perhaps industries) would remain viable post-Covid-19, and support only these. Even well-intended politicians and bureaucrats do not have this degree of omniscience. It is inevitable that some of these funds were ill-spent.

---

[3] Indeed, the OFT specifically rejected a FFD, as it was evident that it was inconceivable that the UK government would allow the failure of HBOS.

But a key point that the Covid-19 crisis has taught us is that, even in a crisis, competition works. The 'vaccine race' could be taken as an example. The well-known, Western-produced vaccines were each developed through the cooperation of several firms, in a competitive environment. As a result, a portfolio of these vaccines were developed, giving a degree of therapeutic choice, and mitigating some of the problems associated with the pandemic. This was all done without any disapplication or relaxation of the competition rules.

Chapter 6 discussed the problems associated with Brexit. Brexit was defined by three shibboleths – sovereignty, fisheries and the ability for the UK to pursue its own industrial policy in its new form as 'Global Britain'. Of course, Brexit has a cost (not admitted by those in favour). While the costs of Brexit have been hidden to a significant degree under the cloud of Covid-19, the chapter has shown that any opportunities to use Brexit as a means of developing a subsidies regime fit for a twenty-first century industrial policy have been squandered. Rather than developing a regime that can aid in making the UK's markets more competitive, those designing the regime have deliberately chosen to craft a system where politicians at all levels can squander taxpayers' money on favoured firms and industries, with little *ex ante* supervision. This new regime is hardly a benefit of Brexit and may well exacerbate the economic problems resulting from that decision.

Chapter 7's discussion of the environmental crisis demonstrated, *inter alia*, that the competition regime does not per se act as an impediment to the achievement of sustainability goals. Article 102 TFEU can aid in the achievement of these sorts of initiatives – by preventing abusive refusals to access important infrastructure, networks and material.

The merger regime is neutral to environmental concerns. Merger considers the competitive effects of a concentration among undertakings. While it may be feasible that some of these effects can be quantified and incorporated into the assessment of the efficiency gains and losses from a merger, environmental considerations are not a separate item in the assessment of whether a merger should take place. Although Member States may be entitled to adopt a public interest/environmental criterion for merger approval, this would not affect those mergers with a Community dimension over which the Commission has jurisdiction. Further, it may well be a mistake to add such criteria to any merger control regime. Merger control authorities have expertise in assessing the welfare consequences of concentrations; they don't necessarily have the expertise of evaluating the environmental consequences of business activity. Further, as the UK experience with the incorporation of non-welfare considerations in merger control has demonstrated, reliance on these sorts of criteria will ultimately harm the consumer and may be unlikely to achieve the desired goal.

But this is not to say that the European regime – at least as presently understood – does not present an obstacle to the attainment of such objectives. It does. The main difficulty that the current regime presents is not one that results from the wording of the Treaties but is one the Commission has imposed as a result of adopting a consumer welfare–focused methodology.

As we have argued throughout this work, the goal of competition law is to reduce market failure associated with the monopoly problem. By so doing it allows for a market-based society to generate wealth (expressed as consumer or total welfare, though we have preferences for the primacy of the latter). A second set of legal and policy instruments (which include taxation and state aid) have the redistribution of this wealth as its goal.

The traditional toolkit of the competition policymaker is useful to evaluate proposed (or existing) arrangements in an effort to determine their effects, and when appropriate suggest that the proposed agreement be prohibited. This toolkit is useful to determine the real effects of mooted agreement, particularly when – in times of crisis – an otherwise consumer-unfriendly cartel is being 'crisis-washed' to disguise rent-seeking activity. In this regard the Commission's MEA is a useful step forward.

However, the European Treaties do not put competition in a silo. The linking clauses require that other, non-competition values be taken into account in Union action, but similarly these clauses do not exclude competition (and other market concerns) from other areas of Union activity (such as, e.g., the market and animal welfare).

As a result, an exclusive focus on economic effects (as may be found with some interpretations of the MEA) may be inconsistent with the linking clauses (and hence wording) of the Treaties. And, by the same token, ignoring market consequences when acting in other policy areas may also suffer from the same inconsistency. The implication of this is a rule of law problem, when actors ignore the law as written

Nevertheless, we have also shown that the competition rules do not preclude all private and collaborative actions which may facilitate the mitigation of crises. In the case of environmental matters, standardisation agreements are an ideal way forward, as we saw. We can take a lesson from the Dutch CoT initiative. There, a proposed, and highly popular, agreement on animal welfare was determined to be anticompetitive. Yet the various stakeholders and the ACM were able to put together an alternative regime, based on voluntary standards. This alternative regime exceeded the original regime's goals and did so in a manner that was compatible with the Dutch (and thus EU) competition regime. This latter point is significant: it demonstrates that the goals could be better realised in a manner that was friendlier to consumers' pocketbooks. Key to the success of the revised welfare regime was the willingness of the parties and the NCA to work together to craft such an outcome. This required that authority to provide guidance on a novel situation.

The environmental crisis is a multifaceted problem. The competition regime cannot be expected to solve this problem by itself, but competition policy can be linked with other policy instruments to aid in addressing this crisis. However, this linkage should be a two-way street, at least as proposed by the Commission. Competition policy and its analytic method can be used as a means (or at least as part of an larger strategy) of identifying effective market-based solutions to a given problem. However, this must be a real two-way street: competition policy must also yield to non-economic considerations in appropriate circumstances, which always includes those cases described by the words of the linking clauses contained within a Treaty.

Our analysis of the environmental crisis can be generalised. The crises this book has considered are all different from one another, and although they share some features, they have different causes. As such, their resolution (and/or the mitigation of their effects) will almost certainly require different policy instruments. The competition and state aid regimes are put into place in the European economy to address two types of market failure: the monopoly problem and the market failures that arise from externalities and/or the provision of public goods. However, both regimes are susceptible to exploitation by rent-seeking interests.

State aid is the obvious example. Undertakings can be quite effective in lobbying governments into providing subsidies and other forms of assistance in an effort to promote a national champion, regional development, local employment or even innovative and 'green' products and processes. But such subsidies can distort competition within the internal market. For this reason, such aid is carefully controlled, notwithstanding the alleged benefits of any other ostensible goal promised by those seeking the aid.

Crises also present opportunities for similar lobbying, in this case to suspend competition law. A crisis provides an opportunity for private actors to crisis-wash their agreement, and to allow them to appropriate consumer surplus under the guise of crisis resolution. This work has shown numerous instances of this sort of behaviour. Calls for the suspension of the competition rules should therefore be answered with scepticism. In this regard, the competition regime's utility rests in its ability to detect such crisis-washing. Here a strong economic focus on the consequences of the arrangement is appropriate, and in this regard the MEA is an improvement over previous regimes.

Yet one theme emerges from a number of the crises this work has considered: the need for, and utility of, guidance promulgated by competition authorities, and a correlative need to work with stakeholders (a concept that extends beyond the undertakings involved in a proposed arrangement) in ensuring that any proposals are compliant with competition law. During the financial crisis, the rapid response of the Commission to inquiries, and the series of guidance that it produced, went a long way to aiding Member States in their efforts to mitigate this crisis. Our discussion suggests that a revision of the guidance surrounding private arrangements would be appropriate, particularly in the context of horizontal cooperation agreements and the environment. Although such a discussion was contained in the 2001 version of the Guidelines, they were removed from the most recent (2011) edition. Similarly, guidance can be case specific – as in the Dutch CoT case. Here the Dutch authorities should be commended for the guidance they provided to the parties. This contrasts with the Irish authority's approach in the *BIDS* matter. Similarly, one can only hope that the Commission's actions in issuing a comfort letter should be viewed, not as a one-off, but as a precedent for future guidance.

The lessons from this study have shown the flexibility of the current competition regime in not hindering a response to varying crises. The real problem lies in an unrealistic expectation regarding what competition law can accomplish and how it can deal with those tasks that are appropriately assigned to it. Competition law is not a panacea for all social and environmental ills. As a policy mechanism it is designed to remedy market failure associated with the monopoly problem, and it can do little beyond this. Few crises are caused by monopolistic behaviour; indeed, none we have considered were so caused. These crises had other causes. Industrial crises are caused by the shock of a perhaps sudden drop in demand. Other crises are caused by other forms of market failure – externalities are one of the underlying causes of the environmental crisis. Competition law, on its own, cannot address these latter sorts of failure.

Similarly, suspending competition law in the face of a crisis is no solution to either solving or mitigating the problem. A competition regime is that jurisdiction's means of addressing market failures associated with the monopoly problem. An effective competition regime will ensure that monopolists (and firms acting as cartels) will not appropriate wealth at the expense of consumers or the economy as a whole. In a crisis, suspending competition law only adds additional market failure to the problem. And this point is well illustrated by this work's analysis. In fact, as we have also shown, this suspension of the competition regime may exacerbate and prolong crises, leaving a lasting anticompetitive legacy that continues to harm, even after the original crisis has been resolved.

Bibliography

'Business Borrowing from Banks "Up Fivefold" amid Coronavirus' *BBC News*, 2 November 2020.

'Covid: UK Seeing Second Wave, Says Boris Johnson' *BBC News*, 18 September 2020.

'Dairy Farmers Rally in London' *BBC News*, 15 March 2000.

'English Wine: Working on Sunshine – Weather Trends Are in Growers' Favour and Help to Explain the Surge in Vines Planted' *Financial Times*, 11 August 2018.

'Food Supply Problems in NI Clearly a Brexit Issue – Coveney' *BBC News*, 21 January 2021.

'Milk Protests Continue across Wales' *BBC News*, 9 March 2000.

'Northern Ireland Secretary Admits New Bill Will "Break International Law"' *BBC News*, 8 September 2020.

'Timeline: The Northern Rock Crisis' *The Guardian*, 26 March 2008.

Ahlborn, Christian and Daniel Piccinin, 'The Great Recession and Other Mishaps: The Commission's Policy of Restructuring Aid in a Time of Crisis' in Erika Szyszczak (ed.) *Research Handbook on European State Aid Law* (Cheltenham: Edward Elgar, 2012) pp. 124–175.

Allam, Zaheer, 'The First 50 Days of COVID-19: A Detailed Chronological Timeline and Extensive Review of Literature Documenting the Pandemic' in Zaheer Allem, *Surveying the Covid-19 Pandemic and Its Implications: Urban Health, Data Technology and Political Economy* (Amsterdam: Elsevier, 2020) pp. 1–7.

Alter, Karen J. and David Steinberg, 'The Theory and Reality of the European Coal and Steel Community' in Sophie Meunier and Kathleen R. McNamara (eds.) *Making History: European Integration and Institutional Change at Fifty* (Oxford: Oxford University Press, 2007) pp. 89–104.

Ambrose, Jillian, 'One of England's Last Coalmines to Close near Durham' *The Guardian*, 16 August 2020.

Ashcraft, Adam B. and Til Schuermann, 'Understanding the Securitization of Subprime Mortgage Credit' Federal Reserve Bank of New York Staff Reports, no. 318 (March 2008).

Autoriteit Consument en Markt, 'ACM's Analysis of the Sustainability Arrangements concerning the "Chicken of Tomorrow"' ACM/DM/2014/206028 (January 2015).

Barriers to Entry into the Dutch Retail Banking Sector (The Hague: Autoriteit Consument En Markt, 2014).

Bailey, David and Laura Elizabeth John (eds.), *Bellamy and Child: European Union Law of Competition*, 8th edition (Oxford: Oxford University Press, 2018).

Bailey, Elizabeth E. and William J. Baumol, 'Deregulation and the Theory of Contestable Markets' (1983) 1 *Yale Journal on Regulation* 111.

Ball, John A., *Canadian Anti-trust Legislation* (Baltimore: Williams & Wilkins, 1934).

Bank of England, *Financial Stability Report: June 2009* (London: Bank of England, 2009).

Barrell, Ray and E. Philip Davis, 'The Evolution of the Financial Crisis of 2007–8' (2008) 208 *National Institute Economic Review* 5.

Baumol, William J., John C. Panzar and Robert D. Willig, *Contestable Markets: The Theory of Industry Structure* (New York: Harcourt Brace Jovanovich, 1982).

Bernanke, Ben, 'Nonmonetary Effects of the Financial Crisis in the Propagation of the Great Depression (1983) 73 *American Economic Review* 257.

Black, John, Nigar Hashimzade and Gareth Myles (eds.), '*Shock*': A *Dictionary of Economics*, 3rd edition (Oxford: Oxford University Press, 2009).

Black, William K., 'When Liar's Loans Flourish' *New York Times* (30 January 2011).

Blair, Roger D. and D. Daniel Sokol, 'The Rule of Reason and the Goals of Antitrust: An Economic Approach' (2012) 78 *Antitrust Law Journal* 471.

BNP Paribas, 'BNP Paribas Investment Partners Temporarily Suspends the Calculation of the Net Asset Value of the Following Funds: Parvest Dynamic ABS, BNP Paribas ABS EURIBOR and BNP Paribas ABS EONIA' Press Release, 9 August 2007.

Bork, Robert, *The Antitrust Paradox: A Policy at War with Itself* (New York: Basic Books; revised edition, 1993).

Bos, Jacqueline M., Henk van den Belt and Peter H. Feindt, 'Animal Welfare, Consumer Welfare, and Competition Law: The Dutch Debate on the Chicken of Tomorrow' (2018) 8 *Animal Frontiers* 20.

Boshoff, Willem H., 'The Competition Economics of Excessive Pricing and Its Relation to the Covid-19 Disaster Period' SSRN=3593292.

Broadberry, Stephen and Tim Leunig, *The Impact of Government Policies on UK Manufacturing since 1945* (London: UK Government Office for Science, 2013).

Brock, William A., 'Contestable Markets and the Theory of Industry Structure: A Review Article' (1983) 91 *Journal of Political Economy* 1055.

Brook, Or, 'Struggling with Article 101(3) TFEU: Diverging Approaches of the Commission, EU Courts, and Five Competition Authorities' (2019) 56 *Common Market Law Review* 121.

Bryner, Jenna, '1st Known Case of Coronavirus Traced Back to November in China' (2020); www.livescience.com/first-case-coronavirus-found.html.

Buccirossi, Paolo (ed.) *Handbook of Antitrust Economics* (Cambridge MA: Massachusetts Institute of Technology Press, 2008).

Buelens, Christian et al., 'The Economic Analysis of State Aid: Some Open Questions' European Commission Directorate-General for Economic and Financial Affairs, Economic Paper No. 286 (September 2007).

Buhart, Jacques and David Henry, 'COVID-20: The Comfort Letter Is Dead – Long Live the Comfort Letter?' (2020) 43 *World Competition* 305.

Bundeskartellamt, 'Crisis Management Measures in the Automotive Industry – Bundeskartellamt Supports the German Association of the Automotive Industry (VDA) in Developing Framework Conditions under Competition Law Aspects' 9 June 2020.

Burgess, Kate, 'BNP Reopens Funds that Sparked Crisis' *Financial Times*, 23 August 2007.

Butler, Sarah, 'JD Sports Says Blocking Footasylum Merger Is "Absurd" amid Covid 19 Crisis' *The Guardian*, 7 May 2020.

Christie, Agatha, 'The Yellow Iris' ITV Adaptation (first broadcast 31 January 1993).

Cini, Michelle, 'From Soft Law to Hard Law? Discretion and Rule Making in the State Aid Rule Regime' European University Working Papers, RSC No. 2000/35 (Badia Fiesolana: Italy, 2000).

Clark, Nicola, 'German State-Run Bank, Caught in Subprime Mess, Is Sold' *New York Times* (26 August 2007).

Coal Industry Commission, *Coal Industry Commission Act 1919. Second Stage. Reports Cmd 210* (HMSO: London, June 1919).

  Reports and Minutes of Evidence on the First Stage of the Inquiry, v 1, Cmd 359 (HMSO: London, March 1919).

Coase, Ronald, 'The Problem of Social Cost' (1962) 3 *Journal of Law and Economics* 1.

Coffee, John C Jr., 'What Went Wrong? An Initial Inquiry into the Causes of the 2008 Financial Crisis' (2009) 9 *Journal of Corporate Law Studies* 1.

Cole, Harold L. and Lee E. Ohanian, 'New Deal Policies and the Persistence of the Great Depression: A General Equilibrium Analysis' (2004) 112 *Journal of Political Economy* 779.

Collinson, Patrick, 'Government Guarantees Northern Rock Deposits' *The Guardian*, 17 September 2007.

Comite Intergouvernemental, Rapport des Chefs de Delegation aux Ministres des Affaires Etrangeres (Bruxelles, 21 avril 1956); https://web.archive.org/web/20080227172535/www.unizar.es/euroconstitucion/library/historic%20documents/Rome/preparation/Spaak%20report%20fr.pdf.

Competition and Markets Authority, Anticipated Acquisition by Amazon of a Minority Shareholding and Certain Rights in Deliveroo Final Report (4 August 2020).

  Anticipated Acquisition by Amazon of a Minority Shareholding and Certain Rights in Deliveroo Provisional Findings Report (16 April 2020).

  Completed Acquisition by JD Sports Fashion plc of Footasylum plc Provisional Report on the Case Remitted to the Competition and Markets Authority by the Competition Appeal Tribunal (3 September 2021).

  'Hand Sanitiser Products: Suspected Excessive and Unfair Pricing' Case Page; www.gov.uk/Competition and Markets Authority-cases/hand-sanitiser-products-suspected-excessive-and-unfair-pricing.

  'Greenwashing: CMA Puts Businesses on Notice' Press Release (20 September 2021).

  Lloyds TSB Group plc and Abbey National plc: A Report on the Proposed Merger (July 2001).

  'Summary of CMA's Position on Mergers Involving "Failing Firms"' Annex to *Guidance on Merger Assessments During the Coronavirus (COVID-19) Pandemic* (22 April 2020).

Competition Commission, Arla Foods amba and Express Dairies plc, A Report on the Proposed Merger, Cmd 5983 (October 2003).

Congressional Research Service Report, U.S. Foreign-Trade Zones: Background and Issues for Congress, 2013.

Conner, Ian, 'On 'Failing' Firms – and Miraculous Recoveries' FTC Blog: Competition Matters (27 May 2020).

Constable, Simon, 'What Is "Economic Shock"? to Qualify As an Economic Shock, an Event Needs to Have a Major Economic Impact – and Be a Surprise' *The Wall Street Journal*, 6 October 2019.

Cook, John et al., 'Quantifying the Consensus on Anthropogenic Global Warming in the Scientific Literature' (2013) 8 *Environmental Research Letters* 8024024.

Coppi, Lorenzo, 'The Role of Economics in State Aid Analysis and the Balancing Test' in Erika Szyszczak (ed.) *Research Handbook on European State Aid Law* (Cheltenham: Edward Elgar, 2012) pp. 64–89.

Corbyn, Jeremy, 'Britain after Brexit' 26 February 2018; https://labour.org.uk/press/jeremy-corbyn-full-speech-britain-brexit/.

Costa-Cabral, Francisco et al., 'EU Competition Law and Covid-19' TILEC Discussion Paper, No. DP2020–007 (22 March 2020), University of Tilburg, Tilburg; (SSRN = 3561438).

Court, W. H. B., 'Problems of the British Coal Industry between the Wars' (1945) 15 *Economic History Review* 1.

Cózara, Andrés, 'Plastic Debris in the Open Ocean' (2014) 111 *Proceedings of the National Academy of Sciences of the United States of America (PNAS)* 10239.

Crick, James M. and Dave Crick, 'Cooperation and COVID-19: Collaborative Business-to-Business Marketing Strategies in a Pandemic Crisis' (2020) 88 *Industrial Marketing Management* 206.

Croft, Jane, 'Lloyds Not "Compelled" by Government to Acquire HBOS' *Financial Times*, 25 October 2017.

Cruickshank, Don, *Competition in UK Banking: A Report to the Chancellor of the Exchequer* (HMSO, March 2000).

Cseres, K. J. and A. Reyna, 'EU State Aid Law and Consumer Protection: An Unsettled Relationship in Times of Crisis' (2020) Amsterdam Law School Legal Studies Research Paper No. 2020–2032 (SSRN = 3624798).

Culpepper, Dreda and Walter Block, 'Price Gouging in the Katrina Aftermath: Free Markets at Work' (2008) 35 *International Journal of Social Economics* 512.

Davydenko, Sergei A. and Julian R. Franks, 'Do Bankruptcy Codes Matter? A Study of Defaults in France, Germany, and the U.K.' (2008) 68 *Journal of Finance* 565.

De Stefano, Gianni, 'Covid-19 and EU Competition Law: Bring the Informal Guidance On' (2020) 11 *Journal of European Competition Law and Practice* 121.

Department for Business, Energy and Industrial Strategy, Subsidy Control: Designing a New Approach for the UK (February 2021).

Dewatripont, Mathias and Paul Seabright, 'Wasteful Public Spending and State Aid Control' (2006) 4 *Journal of the European Economic Association* 513.

Dickie, Mure, Peter Foster and Jim Brunsden, 'Fishermen Feel Waves of Betrayal over Boris Johnson's Brexit Deal' *Financial Times*, 22 January 2021.

Dickson, Annabelle, 'Boris Johnson: "Goodwill" and "Imagination" Can Fix post-Brexit Border Problems' *Politico*, 8 March 2021.

Djelic, Marie-Laurie, 'Does Europe Mean Americanization? The Case of Competition' (2002) 6 *Competition and Change* 233.

Doggett, Lloyd (D-TX 35 District), 'Timeline of Trump's Coronavirus Responses'; https://doggett.house.gov/media-center/blog-posts/timeline-trump-s-coronavirus-responses.

Doleys, Thomas J., 'Fifty Years of Molding Article 87: The European Commission and the Development of EU State Aid Policy (1958–2008)' Paper prepared for presentation at the 11th Biennial International Conference of the European Union Studies Association, 23–25 April 2009 in Marina Del Ray, California.

Douglas, W. Diamond and Philip H. Dybvig, 'Bank Runs, Deposit Insurance, and Liquidity' (1983) 91 *Journal of Political Economy* 401.

Doumanis, Nicholas (ed.) *The Oxford Handbook of European History, 1914–1945* (Oxford: Oxford University Press, 2016).

Doylem, John and Eileen Connolly, 'Brexit and the Northern Ireland Question' in Federico Fabbrini (ed.) *The Law and Politics of Brexit* (Oxford: Oxford University Press, 2017) pp. 139–159.

Duhamel, Marc, 'On the Social Welfare Objectives of Canada's Antitrust Statute' (2003) *Canadian Public Policy/Analyse de Politiques* 301.

Eaglesham, Jean et al., 'UK to Guarantee Northern Rock Deposits' *Financial Times*, 17 September 2007.

Eastman, Mack, 'International Aspects of the European Coal Crisis in 1926' (1928) 36 *Journal of Political Economy* 229.

Economic Advisory Group on Competition Policy (EAGCP), Commentary on European Community Rescue and Restructuring Aid Guidelines (6 February 2008).

Eddy, Arthur Jerome, *The New Competition: An Examination of the Conditions Underlying the Radical Change That Is Taking Place in the Commercial and Industrial World* (New York: D. Appleton, 1912; 7th edition, 1920).

Edwards, Corwin D., *Control of Cartels and Monopolies: An International Perspective* (Dobbs Ferry, NY: Oceana Publications, 1967).

Ehlermann, Claus-Dieter, 'State Aids under European Community Competition Law' (1994) 18 *Fordham International Law Journal* 410.

Eichengreen, Barry, 'Viewpoint: Understanding the Great Depression' (2004) 37 *Canadian Journal of Economics/Revue canadienne d'Economique* 1.

Eley, Jonathan, 'Supermarkets Take Measures to Control Panic Buying' *Financial Times*, 18 March 2020.

Eley, Jonathan, and Judith Evans, 'Supermarkets Raid Restaurants to Restock Shelves' *Financial Times*, 20 March 2020.

Eriksen, Marcus et al., 'Plastic Pollution in the World's Oceans: More than 5 Trillion Plastic Pieces Weighing over 250,000 Tons Afloat at Sea' (2014) 9 *PLoS ONE*: e111913.

Ernst and Young LLP, 'Bank Lending to Firms Surges to a 13-Year High as COVID-19 Leads to UK Businesses Borrowing More' Press Release, 10 August 2020.

European Centre for Disease Prevention and Control, 'Cluster of Pneumonia Cases Caused by a Novel Coronavirus, Wuhan, China' (17 January 2020) (ECDC: Stockholm, 2020); www.ecdc.europa.eu/sites/default/files/documents/Risk%20assessment%20-%20pneumo nia%20Wuhan%20China%2017%20Jan%202020.pdf

European Commission, *Ist Report on Competition Policy* (Brussels and Luxembourg, 1971).
IIIrd Report on Competition Policy (Brussels and Luxembourg, 1973).
IVth Report on Competition Policy (Brussels and Luxembourg, 1974).
Vth Report on Competition Policy (Brussels and Luxembourg, 1975).
VIIth Report on Competition Policy (Brussels and Luxembourg, 1977).
VIIIth Report on Competition Policy (Brussels and Luxembourg, 1978).
IXth Report on Competition Policy (Brussels and Luxembourg, 1979).
Xth Report on Competition Policy (Brussels and Luxembourg, 1980).
XIth Report on Competition Policy (Brussels and Luxembourg, 1981).
XIIth Report on Competition Policy (Brussels and Luxembourg, 1982).
XIIIth Report on Competition Policy (Brussels and Luxembourg, 1983).
XIVth Report on Competition Policy (Brussels and Luxembourg, 1984).
XIXth Report on Competition Policy (Brussels and Luxembourg, 1989).
XXth Report on Competition Policy (Brussels and Luxembourg, 1990).
XXIInd Report on Competition Policy (Brussels and Luxembourg, 1992).
XXIIIrd Report on Competition Policy (Brussels and Luxembourg, 1993).
XXIVth Report on Competition Policy (Brussels and Luxembourg, 1994).
XXVIIth Report on Competition Policy (Brussels and Luxembourg, 1997).
XXVIIIth Report on Competition Policy (Brussels and Luxembourg, 1998).
XXIXth Report on Competition Policy (Brussels and Luxembourg, 1999).

XXXth Report on Competition Policy (Brussels and Luxembourg, 2000).

XXXIInd Report on Competition Policy (Brussels and Luxembourg, 2002).

XXXIIIrd Report on Competition Policy (Brussels and Luxembourg, 2003).

XXXIVth Report on Competition Policy (Brussels and Luxembourg, 2004).

Bulletin of the European Communities 1977(7-8) (July/August 1977).

Bulletin of the European Communities 1977(11) (November 1977).

'Commission Welcomes Political Agreement on Recovery and Resilience Facility' Press Release, 18 December 2020.

'Competition Policy Supporting the Green Deal: Call for Contributions'.

'The Effects of Temporary State Aid Rules Adopted in the Context of the Financial and Economic Crisis' Commission Staff Working Paper (October 2011).

'Recovery and Resilience Facility'; https://ec.europa.eu/info/business-economy-euro/recovery-coronavirus/recovery-and-resilience-facility_en.

'State Aid: Overview of Decisions and On-going In-Depth Investigations of Financial Institutions in Difficulty' Memo (31 December 2017).

'Tackling the Financial Crisis' (12 August 2011).

'Withdrawal Agreement: Commission Sends Letter of Formal Notice to the United Kingdom for Breach of Its Obligations under the Protocol on Ireland and Northern Ireland' Press Release (Brussels, 15 March 2021); https://ec.europa.eu/commission/press corner/detail/en/ip_21_1132.

European Competition Network, 'Antitrust: Joint Statement by the European Competition Network (ECN) on Application of Competition Law during the Corona Crisis' (23 March 2020).

European Union, Contribution OECD, *Policy Roundtable: Crisis Cartels* (DAF/COMP/GF (2011)11) (Paris: OECD, 2011).

Evans, Judith, 'Could Carbon Labelling Soon Become Routine?' *Financial Times*, 19 November 2020.

Fabbrini, Federico (ed.) *The Law and Politics of Brexit* (Oxford: Oxford University Press, 2017).

Federal Reserve Bank of St. Louis, 'Interest Rates, Discount Rate for United States'; https://fred.stlouisfed.org/series/INTDSRUSM193N.

Feldenkirchen, Wilfried, 'Big Business in Interwar Germany: Organizational Innovation at Vereinigte Stahlwerke, IG Farben, and Siemens' (1987) 61 *The Business History Review* 417.

'Competition Policy in Germany' (1992) 21 (2nd series) *Business and Economic History* 257.

Ferguson, Amanda, 'Food Shortages as Northern Ireland Nears New Brexit Deadline' *The Times* (London), 16 January 2021.

Ferruz, Miguel Ángel Bolsa and Phedon Nicolaides, 'An Economic Assessment of State Aid for Restructuring Firms in Difficulty: Theoretical Considerations, Empirical Analysis and Proposals for Reform' (2014) 37 *World Competition* 207.

Fetzer, Thiemo, 'Subsidizing the Spread of COVID19: Evidence from the UK's Eat-out-to-Help-out Scheme' CAGE working paper No. 517/Warwick Economics Research Papers (29 October 2020).

Fiebig, Andre, 'Crisis Cartels and the Triumph of Industrial Policy over Competition Law in Europe' (1999) 25 *Brooklyn Journal of International Law* 607.

Financial Conduct Authority (Bank of England) and Prudential Regulation Authority, *The Failure of HBOS plc (HBOS): A Report by the Financial Conduct Authority (FCA) and the Prudential Regulation Authority (PRA)* (November 2015).

Financial Crisis Inquiry Commission, *Final Report of the National Commission on the Causes of the Financial and Economic Crisis* (January 2011).

Financial Times, Editorial Board, 'EU Should Resist Blackmail over Recovery Fund' *Financial Times*, 18 November 2020.

Finch, Vanessa and David Milman, *Corporate Insolvency Law: Perspectives and Principles* (Cambridge: Cambridge University Press; third edition, 2017).

Fine, Ben, 'Economies of Scale and a Featherbedding Cartel?: A Reconsideration of the Interwar British Coal Industry' (1990) 44 (2nd series) *Economic History Review* 438.

First, Harry, 'Robbin' Hood' *CPI Antitrust Chronicle* (September 2020) 26.

Foster, Peter, Sebastian Payne and Arthur Beesle, 'Northern Ireland Ports to Resume Checks after Security Fears' *Financial Times*, 10 February 2021.

Friederiszick, Hans W., Lars-Hendrik Röller and Vincent Verouden, 'European State Aid Control: An Economic Framework' in Paolo Buccirossi (ed.) *Handbook of Antitrust Economics* (Cambridge, MA: Massachusetts Institute of Technology Press, 2008) pp. 625–669.

Friedman, Milton and Anna Schwartz, *Monetary History of the United States 1867–1960* (Princeton: Princeton University Press, 1963).

Fumagalli, Chiara, Massimo Motta and Martin Peitz, 'Which Role for State Aid and Merger Control during and after the Covid Crisis?' (2020) 11 *Journal of European Competition Law and Practice* 294.

Garber, Peter, 'Famous First Bubbles' (1990) 4 *Journal of Economic Perspectives* 34.

Gerber, David J., *Law and Competition in Twentieth Century Europe: Protecting Prometheus* (Oxford: Oxford University Press, 1998).

Gerbrandy, Anna, 'Rethinking Competition Law within the European Economic Constitution' (2019) *Journal of Common Market Studies* 127.

'Solving a Sustainability-Deficit in European Competition Law' (2017) 40 *World Competition* 539.

Giles, Chris, 'May's Brexit Dividend and Other Myths Worth Exploding: Poor Policymaking Results from a Misguided Understanding of the Economy' *Financial Times*, 21 June 2018.

Peter Foster and Valentina Romei, 'UK Exports to EU Slump as Brexit Hits Trade' *Financial Times*, 12 March 2021.

Giosa, Penelope, 'Exploitative Pricing in the Time of Coronavirus – The Response of EU Competition Law and the Prospect of Price Regulation' (2020) 11 *Journal of European Competition Law and Practice* 499.

Glaeser, Edward L., 'The Economics of Location-Based Tax Incentives' Discussion Paper No. 1932 (Cambridge, MA: Harvard Institute of Economic Research, 2001).

and Erzo F. P. Luttmer, 'The Misallocation of Housing under Rent Control' National Bureau of Economic Research Working Paper No. 6220 (Cambridge, MA, October 1997).

Goodhart, C. A. E., 'The Background to the 2007 Financial Crisis' (2008) 4 *International Economics and Economic Policy* 331.

Gove, Rt Hon. Michael, PC, MP, 'A Brighter Future for Farming' Speech at the National Union of Farmers Farming Conference 2018 (20 February 2018).

in response to Sir Iain Duncan Smith MP, *Hansard*, 2 February 2021, Volume 688, Column 837.

Greasley, David, 'Fifty Years of Coal-Mining Productivity: The Record of the British Coal Industry before 1939' (1990) 50 *Journal of Economic History* 877.

Greenstone, Michael and Enrico Moretti, 'Bidding for Industrial Plants: Does Winning a "Million Dollar Plant" Increase Welfare?' National Bureau of Economic Research Working Paper 9844 (July 2003).

Hanemann, W. Michael, 'What Is the Economic Cost of Climate Change?' CUDARE Working Papers 46999 (University of California, Berkeley, Department of Agricultural and Resource Economics, 2008).

Hardie, Iain and David Howarth, '*Die Krise but not La Crise?* The Financial Crisis and the Transformation of German and French Banking Systems' (2009) 47 *JCMS: Journal of Common Market Studies* 1017.

Harding, Christopher and Julian Joshua *Regulating Cartels in Europe*, 2nd edition (Oxford: Oxford University Press, 2010).

Harra, Jim (chief executive and first permanent secretary HM Treasury) Letter to Rt Hon. Rishi Sunak MP (chancellor of the exchequer) dated 7 July 2020; https://assets .publishing.service.gov.uk/government/uploads/system/uploads/attachment_data/file/ 899017/Direction_letter_-_Jim_Harra_to_Chancellor_-_Eat_Out_to_Help_Out_ Scheme.pdf

Haughwout, Andrew et al., 'The Supply Side of the Housing Boom and Bust of the 2000s' Federal Reserve Bank of New York Staff Reports, Staff Report No. 556 (March 2012; revised October 2012).

Haward, Marcus, 'Plastic Pollution of the World's Seas and Oceans as a Contemporary Challenge in Ocean Governance' (2018) 9 *Nature Communications* 1.

Hawk, Barry E., 'System Failure: Vertical Restraints and EC Competition Law' (1995) 32 *Common Market Law Review* 973.

Health and Safety Executive (UK), 'Manufacture and Supply of Biocidal Hand Sanitiser Products during the Coronavirus Pandemic'; www.hse.gov.uk/coronavirus/hand-sani tiser/hand-sanitiser-manufacture-supply.htm.

Hegarty, Stephanie, 'Coronavirus: Where Has All the Hand Sanitiser Gone?' *BBC News*, 2 April 2020.

Heide-Jorgensen, Caroline (ed.) *Aims and Values in Competition Law* (Copenhagen: Djoef Publishing, 2013).

Heim, Seven et al., 'The Impact of State Aid on the Survival and Financial Viability of Aided Firms' (2016) ZEW Discussion Papers, No. 16–035, *Zentrum für Europäische Wirtschaftsforschung* (Mannheim, 2016).

Hellwig, Martin, 'Germany and the Financial Crises 2007–2017' Annual Macroprudential Conference (Sveriges Riksbank, Stockholm 2018).

and Falk Hendrik Laser, 'Bank Mergers in the Financial Crisis: A Competition Policy Perspective' ZEW Discussion Papers, No. 19-047, ZEW – Leibniz-Zentrum für Europäische Wirtschaftsforschung (Manheim, 2019).

Henley, Andrew, 'Price Formation and Market Structure: The Case of The Inter-War Coal Industry' (1980) 50 *Oxford Bulletin of Economics and Statistics* 263.

Heyer, Ken, 'Failing Firm Analysis and the Current Economic Downturn' *CPI Antitrust Chronicle*, September 2020, 15.

Himmelberg, Robert F., *The Origins of the National Recovery Administration: Business, Government, and the Trade Association Issue, 1921–1933* (New York: Fordham University Press, 1993).

HM Government, Freeport Consultation: Boosting Trade, Jobs and Investment across the UK (CP 222, February 2020).

Freeports: Response to the Consultation (CP 302, October 2020).

HM Treasury, *The Green Book: Appraisal and Evaluation in Central Government* (London: The Stationary Office, 2018).

The Nationalisation of Northern Rock (Report by the comptroller and auditor general, HC 298 Session 2008–2009, 20 March 2009).

Hodge, Tom C., 'Compatible or Conflicting: The Promotion of a High Level of Employment and the Consumer Welfare Standard under Article 101' (2012) 3 *William and Mary Business Law Review* 59.

Hodson, Dermot and Lucia Quaglia, 'European Perspectives on the Global Financial Crisis: Introduction' (2009) 47 *JCMS: Journal of Common Market Studies* 939.

Holligan, Bonnie, 'Commodity or Propriety? Unauthorised Transfer of Intangible Entitlements in the EU Emissions Trading System' (2020) 83 *Modern Law Review* 979.

Holmes, Simon, 'Climate Change, Sustainability, and Competition Law' (2020) 8 *Journal of Antitrust Enforcement* 354.

House of Commons, *Banking Crisis: Dealing with the Failure of the UK Banks* (Seventh Report of Session 2008–2009, 21 April 2009).

Early Day Motion 1764 of 2001–2002, tabled 16 October 2002.

Environment, Food and Rural Affairs Committee, Milk Pricing in the United Kingdom Ninth Report of Session 2003–2004 (26 May 2004, HC 335).

Library, 'Eat out to Help out Scheme' Briefing Paper Number CBP 8978 (22 December 2020).

Northern Ireland Affairs Committee, Brexit and Northern Ireland: Fisheries (Fourth Report of Session 2017–2019, HC 878, 15 September 2018).

Public Accounts Committee, *The Nationalisation of Northern Rock*, Thirty-first Report of Session 2008–2009 (1 June 2009).

The UK-EU Trade and Cooperation Agreement: Governance and Dispute Settlement Briefing Paper 09139 (19 February 2021).

Treasury Committee, *The Run on the Rock*, Fifth Report of Session 2007–2008, Volume 1, Report, together with formal minutes HC 56–I, Incorporating HC 999 i–iv, Session 2006–2007 (26 January 2008).

House of Lords, Select Committee on the Constitution, The Legislative Process: Preparing Legislation for Parliament, 4th Report of Session 2017–2019, published 25 October 2017, HL Paper 27.

Hutcheson, Francis, *Inquiry Concerning Moral Good and Evil* (1725).

Ibáñez Colomo, Pablo, 'Anticompetitive Effects in EU Competition Law' (2021) 17 *Journal of Competition Law and Economics* 309.

'Article 101 TFEU and Market Integration' (2016) 12 *Journal of Competition Law and Economics* 749.

Independent Commission on Banking, Final Report: Recommendations (September 2011).

Intergovernmental Panel on Climate Change, *Climate Change 2014: Mitigation of Climate Change. Contribution of Working Group III to the Fifth Assessment Report of the Intergovernmental Panel on Climate Change*, O. Edenhofer et al. (eds.) (Cambridge: Cambridge University Press, 2014).

Global Warming of 1.5°C: An IPCC Special Report on the Impacts of Global Warming of 1.5°C above pre-Industrial Levels (2021).

International Monetary Fund, *Global Financial Stability Report: October 2007* (Washington, DC: International Monetary Fund, 2007).

Italian Competition Authority, 'ICA: Coronavirus, the Authority Intervenes in the Sale of Sanitizing Products and Masks'; https://en.agcm.it/en/media/press-releases/2020/3/ICA-Coronavirus-the-Authority-intervenes-in-the-sale-of-sanitizing-products-and-masks.

Johnson, Rt Hon. Boris MP, PM, in response to Sir Jeffrey M. Donaldson, *Hansard*, Volume 687, Column 290, 13 January 2021.

Joliet, René, 'Cartelisation, Dirigism and Crisis in the European Community' (1981) 3 *The World Economy* 403.

Jones, Alison and Niamh Dunne, *Jones and Sufrin's EU Competition Law: Text, Cases, Materials*, 7th edition (Oxford: Oxford University Press, 2019).

and Brenda Sufrin, 'State Aid' Supplementary Chapter to EU Competition Law: Text, Cases, and Materials, 6th edition (Oxford: Oxford University Press, 2016); https://global.oup.com/uk/orc/law/competition/jones_sufrin6e/.

Kaplow, Louis, 'On the Choice of Welfare Standards in Competition Law' in Daniel Zimmer (ed.) The Goals of Competition Law (Cheltenham: Edward Elgar, 2012) pp. 3–26.

Kaupa, Clemens, 'The More Economic Approach – A Reform Based on Ideology' (2009) European State Aid Law Quarterly 311.

Kerber, Wolfgang, 'Should Competition Law Promote Efficiency? Some Reflections of an Economist on the Normative Foundations of Competition Law' in Josef Drexl, Laurence Idot and Joël Monéger (eds.) Economic Theory and Competition Law (Cheltenham: Edward Elgar, 2009) pp. 93–120.

Kilduff, P. D. F. and K. C. Jackson, 'The Competitive Characteristics of the Man-Made-Fibre Industry in Western Europe' (1989) 80 Journal of the Textile Institute 185.

Kingston, Suzanne, 'Competition Law in an Environmental Crisis' (2019) 10 Journal of European Competition Law and Practice 517.

Greening EU Competition Law and Policy (Cambridge: Cambridge University Press, 2011).

'Integrating Environmental Protection and EU Competition Law: Why Competition Isn't Special' (2010) 16 European Law Journal 780.

Kirby M. W., 'The Control of Competition in the British Coal-Mining Industry in the Thirties' (1973) 26 Economic History Review 273.

'Government Intervention in Industrial Organization: Coal Mining in the Nineteen Thirties' (1973) 15 Business History 160.

Kleiner, Thibaut, 'Modernization of State Aid Policy' in Erika Szyszczak (ed.) Research Handbook on European State Aid Law (Cheltenham: Edward Elgar, 2011) pp. 1–27.

Kokkoris, Ioannis and Rodrigo Olivares-Caminal, Antitrust Law amidst Financial Crises (Cambridge: Cambridge University Press, 2010).

Kolasky, William, 'Conglomerate Mergers and Range Effects: It's a Long Way from Chicago to Brussels' (2002) 10 George Mason Law Review 533.

Kollewe, Julia, 'Brexit Problems Halt Some Scottish Seafood Exports to EU' The Guardian, 14 January 2021.

'Fresh Seafood Exports from Scotland to EU Halted until 18 January' The Guardian, 13 January 2021.

Konkurrensverket, The Pros and Cons of High Prices (Kalmar: Konkurrensverket, 2007).

Kovacic, William E., 'Transatlantic Turbulence: The Boeing-McDonnell Douglas Merger and International Competition Policy' (2001) 68 Antitrust Law Journal 805.

Kreuschitz, Viktor and Hanns Peter Nehl, 'The Notion of State Aid, Criterion of Advantage' in Herwig C. H. Hofmann and Claire Micheau (eds.) State Aid Law of the European Union (Oxford: Oxford University Press, 2016) pp. 84–129.

Kroes, Neelie, 'The Law and Economics of State Aid Control – A Commission Perspective' Joint EStALI/ESMT Conference, Berlin, 8 October 2007; https://ec.europa.eu/commission/presscorner/detail/en/SPEECH_07_601.

'The State Aid Action Plan – Delivering less and Better Targeted Aid' UK Presidency Seminar on State Aid London (14 July 2005).

Krugman, Paul, 'Very Scary Things' New York Times, 10 August 2007.

La Porta, Rafael et al., 'Law and Finance' (1998) 106 Journal of Political Economy 1113.

Labaton, Stephen, 'Agency's '04 Rule Let Banks Pile up New Debt' New York Times, 2 October 2008.

Labonte, Marc and Gail E. Makinen, 'Federal Reserve Interest Rate Changes: 2000–2008' Congressional Research Services/Library of Congress, CRS Report for Congress (19 March 2008).

Leahy, Pat, Denis Staunton and Freya McClements, 'Government Brands UK Move to Delay Checks on Goods Entering North from Britain "Deeply Unhelpful"' *Irish Times* (Dublin), 3 March 2021.

Lessing, R., 'Report of the Royal Commission on the Coal Industry (1925)' (1926) *Chemistry and Industry* 196.

Levenstein, Margaret C. and Valerie Y. Suslow, 'What Determines Cartel Success?' (2006) 44 *Journal of Economic Literature* 43.

Levitin, Adam J. and Susan M. Wachter, 'Explaining the Housing Bubble' (2012) 100 *Georgetown Law Journal* 1177.

Li, Qun et al., 'Early Transmission Dynamics in Wuhan, China, of Novel Coronavirus–Infected Pneumonia' (2020) 382 *New England Journal of Medicine* 1199.

Lianos, Ioannis, 'Polycentric Competition Law' (2018) 70 *Current Legal Problems* 161.

   Valentine Korah and Paolo Siciliani *Competition Law Analysis, Cases, and Materials* (Oxford: Oxford University Press, 2019).

Linklaters, 'Competition Law Needs to Cooperate: Companies Want Clarity to Enable Climate Change Initiatives to Be Pursued' (29 April 2020); https://lpscdn.linklaters .com/-/media/files/document-store/pdf/uk/2020/april/linklaters_competition-law-needs-to-cooperate_april-2020.ashx?rev=2c2c8c7d-91a8-496f-99fb-92a799c55cb2&extension=pdf&hash=6641BEDB36EC877CA43C7D995BD6EEDA.

Lo Schiavo, Gianni, 'The General Court Reassesses the British Aggregates Levy: Selective Advantages "Permeated" by an Exercise on the Actual Effects of Competition?' (2013) *European State Aid Law Quarterly* 384.

London Economics, 'Ex-post Evaluation of the Impact of Rescue and Restructuring Aid on the International Competitiveness of the Sector(s) affected by such Aid' Report prepared for the European Commission, Directorate General Enterprise (2004).

Lucas Arthur F., 'A British Experiment in the Control of Competition: The Coal Mines Act of 1930' (1934) 48 *Quarterly Journal of Economics* 418.

Mayer, Christopher, Karen Pence and Shane M. Sherlund, 'The Rise in Mortgage Defaults' (2009) 23 *Journal of Economic Perspectives* 27.

Maziarz, Aleksander, 'Do Non-economic Goals Count in Interpreting Article 101(3) TFEU?' (2014) 10 *European Competition Journal* 341.

McCormick, Myles, 'Investors Hoard Cash to Ward off Worst Effects of Coronavirus Crisis' *Financial Times*, 14 April 2020.

Meese, Alan J., 'Competition Policy and the Great Depression: Lessons Learned and a New Way Forward' (2013) 23 *Cornell Journal of Law and Public Policy* 255.

Merrick, Rob, 'Brexit: Peers Inflict Heaviest Defeat for More than 20 Years over Bill that Will Break International Law' *The Independent*, 20 October 2020.

Mestmäcker, Ernst-Joachim, 'The Applicability of the ECSC-Cartel Prohibition (Article 65) during a "Manifest Crisis"' (1984) 82 *Michigan Law Review* 1399.

Meunier Sophie and Kathleen R. McNamara (eds), *In Making History: European Integration and Institutional Change at Fifty* (Oxford: Oxford University Press, 2007).

Mian, Atif R. and Amir Sufi, 'The Consequences of Mortgage Credit Expansion: Evidence from the U.S. Mortgage Default Crisis' (12 December 2008) (SSRN = 1072304).

Middleton, Roger, 'The Great Depression in Europe' in Nicholas Doumanis (ed.) *The Oxford Handbook of European History, 1914–1945* (Oxford: Oxford University Press, 2016) pp. 179–206.

Ministère de la Transition écologique, 'Fiscalité carbone'; www.ecologie.gouv.fr/fiscalite-carbone.

Ministry of Justice, *Government Response to Consultation: Response to the Consultation on the Departure from Retained EU Case Law by UK Courts and Tribunals* (CP 303, 15 October 2020).

Montgomerie, Johnna, 'Austerity and the Household: The Politics of Economic Storytelling' (2016) 11 *British Politics* 418.

Monti, Giorgio and Jotte Mulder, 'Escaping the Clutches of EU Competition: Law Pathways to Assess Private Sustainability Initiatives' (2017) 42 *European Law Review* 635.

Morrison, Alan D., 'Systemic Risks and the "Too-Big-to-Fail" Problem' (2011) 27 *Oxford Review of Economic Policy* 498.

Motta, Mario, 'Price Regulation in Times of Crisis Can Be Tricky' *Daily Maverick*, 22 April 2020.

Motta, Massimo and Alexandre de Streel, 'Excessive Pricing in Competition Law: Never Say Never?' in Konkurrensverket, *The Pros and Cons of High Prices* (Kalmar: Konkurrensverket, 2007) pp. 14–46.

Mulder, Machiel and Sigourney Zomer, 'Dutch Consumers' Willingness to Pay for Broiler Welfare' (2017) 20 *Journal of Applied Animal Welfare Science* 137.

Mulder, Machiel et al., 'Economische effecten van "Kip van Morgen" Kosten en baten voor consumenten van een collectieve afspraak in de pluimveehouderij' (Office of the Chief Economist ACM, October 2014).

Nederlandsche Bank De, *Perspective on the Structure of the Dutch Banking Sector* (Amsterdam: De Nederlandsche Bank, 2015).

New Century Financial Corporation, 'New Century Financial Corporation Files for Chapter 11; Announces Agreement to Sell Servicing Operations' News Release, 2 April 2007.

Newey, Sarah et al., 'Coronavirus: Chance to Contain Outbreak is "Narrowing" says WHO' *Telegraph*, 21 February 2020.

Nicolaides, Phedon, 'Application of Article 107(2)(b) TFEU to Covid-19 Measures: State Aid to Make Good the Damage Caused by an Exceptional Occurrence' (2020) 11 *Journal of European Competition Law and Practice* 238.

Nordhaus, William D., 'Expert Opinion on Climatic Change' (1994) 82 *American Scientist* 45.

'Reflections on the Economics of Climate Change' (1993) 7 *Journal of Economic Perspectives* 11.

Nowag, Julian, *Environmental Integration in Competition and Free-Movement Laws* (Oxford: Oxford University Press, 2016).

Nulsch, Nicole, 'Is Subsidizing Companies in Difficulties an Optimal Policy? An Empirical Study on the Effectiveness of State Aid in the European Union' IWH Discussion Papers, No. 9/2014, Leibniz-Institut für Wirtschaftsforschung Halle (IWH) (Halle (Saale), 2014).

O'Donoghue, Robert and Jorge Padilla, *The Law and Economics of Article 102 TFEU*, 3rd edition (Oxford: Hart, 2020).

O'Carroll, Lisa, 'Cheshire Cheesemaker Says Business Left with £250,000 "Brexit Hole"' *The Guardian*, 23 January 2021.

'Crisps Lorry Held up for Two Days by Northern Irish Brexit Checks, MPs Told' *The Guardian*, 21 January 2021.

'Eight Days for Carrots to Get to Belfast with Complex Brexit Checks' *The Guardian*, 31 January 2021.

O'Connell, Martin, Áureo de Paula and Kate Smith, 'Preparing for a Pandemic: Spending Dynamics and Panic Buying during the COVID-19 First Wave' Working Paper 20-34 (London, Institute for Fiscal Studies, 2020).

O'Donnell, Kathy, 'Pit Closures in the British Coal Industry: A Comparison of the 1960s and 1980s' (1988) 2 *International Review of Applied Economics* 62.

Odudu, Okeoghene, *The Boundaries of EC Competition Law: The Scope of Article 81* (Oxford: Oxford University Press, 2006).

'Feeding the Nation in Times of Crisis: The Relaxation of Competition Law in the United Kingdom' (2020) 19 *Competition Law Journal* 68.

'Restrictions of Competition by Object – What's the Beef?' (2009) 8 *Competition Law Journal* 11.

Office of Fair Trading, Anticipated Acquisition by Lloyds TSB plc: Report to the Secretary of State for Business Enterprise and Regulatory Reform (24 October 2008).

Office of National Statistics, UK Trade: January 2021 (12 March 2021).

Office of the Special Inspector General for the Troubled Asset Relief Program, Quarterly Report to Congress (26 January 2011).

Olsen, Edgar O., 'An Econometric Analysis of Rent Control' (1972) 80 *Journal of Political Economy* 1081.

Organisation for Economic Co-operation and Development, 'Background Note' OECD Policy Round Table, Failing Firm Defence (2009) (DAF/COMP(2009)38) (Paris: OECD, 2010).

'Exploitative pricing in the time of COVID-19' (26 May 2020).

'Sustainability and Competition – Note by the Netherlands' Contribution for 134th OECD Competition Committee Meeting on 1–3 December 2020 DAF/COMP/WD(2020)66 (Paris, OECD, 2020).

Ormosi, Peter and Andreas Stephan, 'The Dangers of Allowing Greater Coordination between Competitors during the COVID-19 Crisis' (2020) 8 *Journal of Antitrust Enforcement* 299.

Oxera, *Should Aid Be Granted to Firms in Difficulty? A Study on Counterfactual Scenarios to Restructuring State Aid* (prepared for the European Commission) (Luxembourg, Publications Office of the European Union, 2009).

PA Cambridge Economic Consultants, *Final Evaluation of Enterprise Zones* (London: Department of the Environment, 1995).

Parker, George, '"Slash and Burn" of EU Rules Ruled out post-Brexit' *Financial Times*, 17 February 2021.

and Mure Dickie, 'Boris Johnson Accused of Betraying Fishing Industry over Brexit Disruption' *Financial Times*, 14 January 2021.

and Peter Foster, 'UK Postpones Imposing Checks on EU Goods until 2022' *Financial Times*, 14 September 2021.

and Sylvia Pfeifer, 'UK Rejects Industry Plea for Visas for EU Truck Drivers' *Financial Times*, 22 August 2021.

et al., 'Gove Urges Brussels to Take Action as Northern Ireland Tensions Rise' *Financial Times*, 2 February 2021.

Partington, Richard, 'Business Leaders Call for Relaxation of post-Brexit Visa Rules' *Guardian*, 25 August 2021.

Pastor-Merchante, Fernando, *The Role of Competitors in the Enforcement of State Aid Law* (Oxford: Hart, 2017).

Pavlov, Andrey and Susan Wachter, 'Subprime Lending and Real Estate Prices' (2011) 39 *Real Estate Economics* 1.

Penrose, John MP, *Power to the People: Independent Report on Competition Policy* (16 February 2021).

Peretz, George, 'Corbyn on State Aid: Fact-Checked' *Politics Today*, 27 February 2018.

'State Aid and Brexit: Slowly Dawns' (2018) 17 *European State Aid Law Quarterly* 80.

Pflanz, Matthias and Cristina Caffarra, 'The Economics of GE Honeywell' (2002) 23 *European Competition Law Review* 115.

Pigou, Arthur C., *The Economics of Welfare*, 4th edition (London: Macmillan, 1932).

Pisani-Ferry, Jean and André Sapir, 'Banking Crisis Management in the EU: An Early Assessment' (2010) 35 *Economic Policy* 341.

Plummer, Robert and Simon Read, 'Eat out to Help out Will Definitely Affect the Weekend' *BBC News*, 3 August 2020.

Posner, Richard A., *Antitrust Law: Cases, Economic Notes and Other Materials*, 2nd edition (Minneapolis: West Publishing, 1981).

'A Statistical Study of Antitrust Enforcement' (1970) 13 *Journal of Law and Economics* 365.

Pozdnakova, Alla, 'Excessive Pricing and the Prohibition of the Abuse of a Dominant Position under Article 82 EC' (2010) 33 *World Competition: Law and Economics Review* 120.

Quigley, Conor, 'Review of Judgment in Case T-176/01 – *Ferriere Nord SpA v. European Commission*' (2005) *European State Aid Quarterly* 57.

Rasek, Arno and Florian Smuda, 'Ex-post Evaluation of Competition Law Enforcement Effects in the German Packaging Waste Compliance Scheme Market' (2018) 116 *De Economist* 89.

Ratshisusu, Hardin and Liberty Mncube, 'Addressing Excessive Pricing Concerns in Time of the COVID-19 Pandemic – A View from South Africa' (2020) 8 *Journal of Antitrust Enforcement* 256.

Rawls, John, *A Theory of Justice*, revised edition (Cambridge, MA: Harvard University Press, 1999).

Reynolds, Robert and Janusz Ordover, 'Archimedean Leveraging and the GE/Honeywell Transaction' (2002) 70 *Antitrust Law Journal* 171.

Roosevelt, Franklin D., First Inaugural Address of Franklin D. Roosevelt, 4 March 1933; https://avalon.law.yale.edu/20th_century/froos1.asp

Royal Commission on the Coal Industry (1925), *Report of the Royal Commission on the Coal Industry (1925) with Minutes of Evidence and Appendices*, Volume 1, *Report*. Cmd 2600 (London: HMSO, 1926).

Rubini, Luca, *The Definition of Subsidy and State Aid: WTO and EC Law in Comparative Perspective* (Oxford: Oxford University Press, 2009).

Safi, Michael, 'Coronavirus from Unknown Virus to Global Crisis – Timeline' *The Guardian*, 14 December 2020.

Salinger, Michael A., 'Price Gouging and the Covid-19 Crisis – This Time Is (a Little) Different' *CPI Antitrust Chronicle* (September 2020).

Sawer, Patrick, 'Supermarkets Could Join Forces at Peak of Crisis' *Telegraph*, 14 March 2020.

Schinkel, Maarten Pieter, 'On Distributive Justice by Antitrust: The Robin Hood Cartel' Amsterdam Law School Research Paper No. 2021-2016/Amsterdam Center for Law and Economics Working Paper No. 2021-2006 (18 June 2021) (SSRN = 3869561).

and Abel d'Ailly, 'Corona Crisis Cartels: Sense and Sensibility' Amsterdam Law School Legal Studies Research Paper No. 2020-2031/Amsterdam Center for Law and Economics Working Paper No. 2020-2003 (11 June 2020) (SSRN = 3623154).

and Lukas Toth, 'Compensatory Public Good Provision by a Private Cartel' TI 2019–2086/VII Tinbergen Institute Discussion Paper (March 2020).

Schmitt, Hans A., 'The European Coal and Steel Community: Operations of the First European Antitrust Law, 1952–1958' (1944) 38 *Business History Review* 102.

Scholtes, Saskia and Richard Beales, 'New Century Files for Chapter 11' *Financial Times*, 3 April 2007.

Schröter, Harm G., 'Cartelization and Decartelization in Europe, 1870–1995: Rise and Decline of an Economic Institution' (1996) 25 *Journal of European Economic History* 129.

Schweiger, Helena, 'The Impact of State Aid for Restructuring on the Allocation of Resources' European Bank for Reconstruction and Development Working Paper No. 127 (May 2011).

Scott Morton, Fiona M., 'Innovation Incentives in a Pandemic' (2020) 8 *Journal of Antitrust Enforcement* 309.

Serwicka, Ilona and Peter Holmes, 'What Is the Extra Mileage in the Reintroduction of "Free Zones" in the UK?' UK Trade Policy Observatory Briefing Paper 28 (February 2019).

Shaw, R. W. and S. A. Shaw, 'Excess Capacity and Rationalisation in the West European Synthetic Fibre Industry' (1984) 32 *Journal of Industrial Economics* 149.

Sheehy, Seamus J., 'The Impact of EEC Membership on Irish Agriculture' (1980) 31 *Journal of Agricultural Economics* 297.

Shepherd, William G., '"Contestability" vs. Competition' (1984) 74 *American Economic Review* 572.

Shin, Hyun Song, 'Reflections on Northern Rock: The Bank Run That Heralded the Global Financial Crisis' (2009) 23 *Journal of Economic Perspectives* 101.

Simensen Ivar, 'Sachsen Falls Victim to Credit Crisis' *Financial Times*, 17 August 2007.

Sleuwaegen, Leo, Enrico Pennings and Isabelle De Voldere, 'Public Aid and Relocation within the European Community' Report to the European Commission, Directorate General III (Brussels, 2000).

Stephan, Andreas, 'Did Lloyds/HBOS Mark the Failure of an Enduring Economics-Based System of Merger Regulation?' (2011) 62 *Northern Ireland Legal Quarterly* 539.

Stern, Nicholas, 'Imperfections in the Economics of Public Policy, Imperfections in Markets, and Climate Change' (2010) 8 *Journal of the European Economic Association* 253.

Stewart, Heather and Rowena Mason, 'Nigel Farage's Anti-migrant Poster Reported to Police' *The Guardian*, 16 June 2016.

Sullivan, Lawrence A. and Warren S Grimes, *Law of Antitrust: An Integrated Handbook*, 2nd edition (St. Paul, MN: West, 2006).

Sunak, Rishi MP, 'Budget Speech 2021' (3 March 2021); www.gov.uk/government/speeches/budget-speech-2021.

'The Free Ports Opportunity: How Brexit Could Boost Trade, Manufacturing and the North' (London: Centre for Policy Studies, November 2016).

Supple, Barry, 'The British Coal Industry between the Wars' (1989) 9 *ReFresh* 5.

The History of the British Coal Industry 1914–1946, Volume 4, *The Political Economy of Decline* (Oxford: Oxford University Press, 1987).

Swormink, Berrie Klein, 'Chicken of Tomorrow Is Here Today' *Poultry World*, 13 March 2017.

Talbot, Conor, 'Finding a Baseline for Competition Law Enforcement during Crises: Case Study of the Irish Beef Proceedings' (2015) 18 *Irish Journal of European Law* 55.

Tannam, Etain, 'Intergovernmental and Cross-Border Civil Service Cooperation: The Good Friday Agreement and Brexit' (2018) 17 *Ethnopolitics* 243.

Tarrant, Andy and Andrea Biondi, 'Labour's Programme and EU Law' (2017) 25 *Renewal* 66.

Taylor, Jason E., 'Cartel Code Attributes and Cartel Performance: An Industry-Level Analysis of the National Industrial Recovery Act' (2007) 50 *Journal of Law and Economics* 597.

'The Output Effects of Government Sponsored Cartels during the New Deal' (2002) 50 *Journal of Industrial Economics* 1.

Tees Valley Mayor, A Proposal for a National Free Zone Policy (London: Vivid Economics, ND); www.vivideconomics.com/wp-content/uploads/2019/08/A-Free-Zone-Policy-fit-for-the-UK-Main-Report.pdf.

Temin, Peter, 'The Great Depression' in Stanley L. Engerman and Robert E. Gallman (eds) *The Cambridge Economic History of the United States*, Volume 3, *The Twentieth Century* (Cambridge: Cambridge University Press, 2000).

Thomas, Daniel and Jim Pickard, 'Northern Ireland Firms Hit by EU State Aid Restrictions on UK Covid Loans' *Financial Times*, 24 March 2021.

Tol, Richard S. J., 'The Economic Impacts of Climate Change' (2018) 12 *Review of Environmental Economics and Policy* 4.

Townley, Christopher, *Article 81 EC and Public Policy* (Oxford: Hart, 2009).
  'Inter-generational Impacts in Competition Analysis: Remembering Those Not Yet Born' (2011) 32 *European Competition Law Review* 580.
  'Is There (Still) Room for Non-economic Arguments in Article 101 TFEU Cases?' in Caroline Heide-Jorgensen (ed.) *Aims and Values in Competition Law* (Copenhagen: Djoef Publishing, 2013) pp. 115–182.

Treanor, Jill, 'Lloyds TSB Chairman Struck HBOS Deal with Brown at City Drinks Party' *The Guardian*, 18 September 2008.

Trustee Savings Bank, *Annual Report 2014* (London: TSB, 2015); www.tsb.co.uk/investors/results-reports/TSB-Annual-Reports-Accounts-2014.pdf.

Tyrie, Andrew, *How Should Competition Policy React to Coronavirus?* (London: Institute for Public Policy Research, 2020).

Uberoi, Elise et al., 'UK Fishery Statistics' House of Commons Library Briefing Paper Number 2788, 23 November 2020.

UK in a Changing Europe, Freeports (2 March 2021).

UK Marine Management Organisation, 'Fishing Industry in 2019 Statistics Published' Press Release, 24 September 2020.

UK Parliament, *Hansard*, Business of the House, Volume 687, 14 January 2021.

United States Securities and Exchange Commission Office of the Inspector General (Office of Audits), *SEC's Oversight of Bear Stearns and Related Entities: The Consolidated Supervised Entity Program*, Report No. 446-A (25 September 2008).

Vaughan, David CBE QC and Aidan Robertson QC (eds.) *Law of the European Union* (Oxford: Oxford University Press, loose leaf).

Vickers, John, 'The Financial Crisis and Competition Policy: Some Economics' (2008) 1 *Global Competition Policy* 9.

Vickers, Noah, 'Spokesman Indicates Boris Johnson Has Not Read Brexit Trade Deal Text' *The New European*, 14 January 2021.

Vives, Xavier, *Competition and Stability in Banking: The Role of Regulation and Competition Policy* (Princeton, NJ: Princeton University Press, 2016).

Wang, Chen et al., 'A Novel Coronavirus Outbreak of Global Health Concern' (2020) 395 *The Lancet* 470.

Wardhaugh, Bruce, *Cartels Markets and Crime: A Normative Justification for the Criminalisation of Economic Collusion* (Cambridge: Cambridge University Press, 2014).
  'Chapter 23: Economic and Monetary Union' in David Vaughan CBE QC and Aidan Robertson QC (eds.) *Law of the European Union* (Oxford: Oxford University Press, loose leaf).
  Competition, Effects and Predictability: Rule of Law and the Economic Approach to Competition (Oxford: Hart, 2020).

'Crisis Cartels: Non-economic Values, the Public Interest, and Institutional Considerations' (2014) 10 *European Competition Journal* 311.

Waring, R. H., R. M. Harris and S. C. Mitchell, 'Plastic Contamination of the Food Chain: A Threat to Human Health?' (2018) 115 *Maturitas* 64.

Watkiss, Paul et al., 'The Impacts and Costs of Climate Change' Final Report for the European Commission DG Environment (September 2005).

Weale, Martin, 'Northern Rock: Expert Views' *BBC News*, 17 September 2007.

Wentworth, Jonathan, 'Rapid Response: Effects of COVID-19 on the Food Supply System' *UK Parliament Post*, 13 July 2020.

Wesseling, Rein, *The Modernisation of EC Antitrust Law* (London: Hart, 2000).

Wheelock, David C., 'Comparing the COVID-19 Recession with the Great Depression' Economic Synopses 2020 No. 39, St. Louis Federal Reserve Bank (12 August 2020).

Whish, Richard and David Bailey, *Competition Law*, 9th edition (Oxford: Oxford University Press, 2018).

White and Case, 'A Re-awakening of the Failing Firm Defence in the EU in the Aftermath of COVID-19?' (16 April 2020); www.whitecase.com/publications/alert/re-awakening-failing-firm-defence-eu-aftermath-covid-19.

Williamson, Oliver E., 'Economies as an Antitrust Defense: The Welfare Tradeoffs' (1968) 58 *American Economic Review* 18.

Witt, Anne C., *The Economic Approach to EU Antitrust Law* (Oxford: Hart, 2016).

'The Enforcement of Article 101 TFEU: What Has Happened to the Effects Analysis?' (2018) 55 *Common Market Law Review* 417.

'The European Court of Justice and the More Economic Approach to EU Competition Law – Is the Tide Turning?' (2019) 64 *The Antitrust Bulletin* 172.

'Public Policy Goals under EU Competition Law – Now Is the Time to Set the House in Order' (2012) 8 *European Competition Journal* 443.

Wolf, Nikolaus, 'Europe's Great Depression: Coordination Failure after the First World War' (2010) 26 *Oxford Review of Economic Policy* 339.

Wolf, Martin, 'The Brexit Delusion of Taking Back Control' *Financial Times*, 26 March 2019.

Wollenschläger, Ferdinand, Wolfgang Wurmnest and Thomas M. J. Möllers (eds.), *Private Enforcement of European Competition and State Aid Law: Current Challenges and the Way Forward* (Alphen aan den Rijn: Wolters Kluwer, 2020).

Woodmansey, David, 'A Dog Is for Life, Not Just for Lockdown' *Vet Times*, 4 May 2020.

World Health Organization, 'Pneumonia of Unknown Cause – China' *Disease Outbreak News* (5 January 2020).

'Weekly Epidemiological Update – 29 December 2019'.

Young, Sarah, 'Third of Shoppers Stung by Price-Gouging on Essential Hygiene and Medical Products during Lockdown, Investigation Finds' *The Independent*, 3 July 2020.

Zand, Bernhard and Veronika Hackenbroch, 'A Failed Deception: The Early Days of the Coronavirus Outbreak in Wuhan' *Der Spiegel* (International Edition) (5 May 2020).

Zimmer, Daniel (ed.), *The Goals of Competition Law* (Cheltenham: Edward Elgar, 2012).

Index

CPSIA information can be obtained
at www.ICGtesting.com
Printed in the USA
LVHW040449270922
729373LV00009B/529